Corporate Finance and Governance

Herausgegeben von Dirk Schiereck

Band 4

PETER LANG
Frankfurt am Main · Berlin · Bern · Bruxelles · New York · Oxford · Wien

Underpricing, Long-Run Performance, and Valuation of Initial Public Offerings

Fabian Braemisch

Underpricing, Long-Run Performance, and Valuation of Initial Public Offerings

PETER LANG
Internationaler Verlag der Wissenschaften

Bibliographic Information published by the Deutsche Nationalbibliothek
The Deutsche Nationalbibliothek lists this publication in the Deutsche Nationalbibliografie; detailed bibliographic data is available in the internet at http://dnb.d-nb.de.

Zugl.: European Business School, Univ., Diss., 2009

Cover Design:
Olaf Glöckler, Atelier Platen, Friedberg

D 1540
ISSN 1869-537X
ISBN 978-3-631-60405-2

www.peterlang.de

Meinen Eltern

PREFACE

Nachdem in den letzten Jahren vor der Finanzkrise die Zahl der Börseneinführungen in Europa und hier insbesondere in Großbritannien insgesamt wieder stark zugenommen hatte und dabei ein nicht unerheblicher Anteil der Börsenneulinge jeweils von Emittenten aus dem Immobiliensektor gestellt wurde, sind zahlreiche jüngere Versuche der Börseneinführung von Immobilienaktien meist gescheitert. Die dabei unter dem Begriff ‚Immobilienaktien' zusammengefassten Gesellschaften weisen zum Teil sehr unterschiedliche Geschäftsmodelle auf – von Wohnungsbestandshaltern in etablierten Märkten bis hin zu Projektentwicklern in den jüngsten Beitrittsländern der EU.

Aus Anleger- wie auch aus Börsensicht fällt eine Bewertung des in den letzten Jahren vor der Finanzkrise so belebten Aktienemissionsgeschäfts in Verbindung gerade mit Blick auf Börsenneulinge aus dem Immobilienbereich auch deshalb schwer, weil die nachhaltige Entwicklung dieser Aktiengruppe bislang wissenschaftlich nur unzureichend aufgearbeitet wurde. Die längerfristige Performance und Aktienkursentwicklung von Immobilienaktien an europäischen Wertpapierbörsen war bis dato eher Vermutung als gesicherte Erkenntnis. Hier setzt nun die Analyse von Herrn Brämisch an. Seine Ausführungen dokumentieren u.a., dass die Einbeziehung von Immobilienaktien in die Wertpapierdepots von Privatanleger für die Vergangenheit insgesamt nur bedingt positiv zu bewerten ist. Diese Aktien zeichnen sich durch ein vom Unsicherheitsgrad abhängiges kurzfristiges Underpricing und eine unbefriedigende langfristige Underperformance im Vergleich zur Gesamtmarktentwicklung aus. Auch diese Erkenntnis mag zukünftig zu einer Verbesserung von Effizienz und Rentabilität bei der Strukturierung insbesondere von Privatanlegerportfolios beitragen und damit auch die langfristige Vermögensposition dieser Anleger verbessern.

Herr Brämisch verzichtet in seiner Arbeit auf jede politische Wertung ihrer Ergebnisse. Diese Zurückhaltung mag für eine betriebswirtschaftliche Dissertationsschrift angemessen sein. Nichtsdestotrotz sollten gerade auch die wirtschaftspolitischen Entscheidungsträger in unserem Land diese Arbeit mit großer Aufmerksamkeit lesen. Sie enthält eine Fülle hoch interessanter Resultate zum Beitrag von Immobilienaktien auf europäischen Börsenkurszetteln und ist so geschrieben, dass es dem Leser sicherlich Freude machen wird, sie bis zum Ende zu lesen. Ich wünsche der Arbeit und ihren Erkenntnissen eine weite Verbreitung.

Professor Dr. Dirk Schiereck

SUMMARY OF CONTENTS

CONTENTS

LIST OF FIGURES

LIST OF TABLES

LIST OF ABBREVIATIONS

AIM	Alternative investment market
BHAR	Buy-and-hold abnormal returns
CAR	Cumulative abnormal returns
CEE	Central and Eastern Europe
EPC	European property company
EPRA	European public real estate association
IPO	Initial public offering
IV	Instrumental variable
OLS	Ordinary least square
REIT	Real estate investment trust
US	United States
VIF	Variance inflation factor

1 INTRODUCTION

The present study – underpricing, long-run performance and valuation of initial public offerings – contains three empirical research papers which examine three uniquely identified research gaps in the field of initial public offering (IPO) research. The empirical analyses are based on a sample of European property company IPOs taking place between 1997 and 2007. The aim of this first chapter is to give a brief introduction to the complex topic of IPOs and to provide a rationalisation for the focus on European property companies. A short description of the structure of all three research paper is included too.

An initial public offering is a major milestone in the life cycle of a company. It helps firms to raise new equity capital in the so called primary market by selling newly created shares to investors outside of the firm. The proceeds from selling these shares accrue to the company. As long as the capital raising function is cost efficient and easy to accomplish, it will increase the availability and lower the cost of equity finance. An IPO also enables firms to trade its shares in the so called secondary market. As long as the market is liquid and transparent, it will encourage investors to participate in the stock market, which in turn, increases the availability of overall equity financing. Consequently, the efficient functioning of both markets is an important prerequisite for the functioning of financial markets and the economy as a whole.

But why do only some firms decide to go public and others decide to stay private? The answer to this question is a typical trade-off decision between the costs and benefits of both choices. Whereas the benefits of being publicly listed include the advantages of an easier access to equity capital and an easier exchange of ownership and control rights, the costs incurred by conducting an IPO are substantial and have to be thoroughly assessed when considering an IPO decision.

These costs can typically be divided into two broad groups. There are costs borne by the company in preparing the IPO and there are costs that occur after the IPO took place and the company is publicly listed. Costs for preparing an IPO comprise the costs of conducting IPO prospectuses and marketing road shows, the opportunity cost of management time, fees paid to legal and auditing companies, and selling commissions and underwriting fees paid for investment banks' services. Next to these directly measurable costs, there are also indirect costs that can develop once the company's shares are trading on the stock exchange. The probably most well-known indirect cost is the initial underpricing of IPO shares. This is, "the shares of companies that go public are offered to investors at prices considerably below the prices at which they subsequently trade on the stock market" (Jenkinson and Ljungqvist (2001), p. 4). The actual cost component stems from the fact that initial owners of an underpriced IPO 'leave money on the table'. This is because (i), in the case initial owners wanted to exit their investment, they could have sold their shares at higher prices if they had retained their shares and sold them in the aftermarket, or (ii), in the case initial owners wanted to raise capital, they could have raised the same amount of money by selling fewer shares for a higher offer price and thus would have been diluted to a lesser extent.

The underpricing phenomenon is confirmed by an overwhelming amount of empirical studies. Its persistent existence puzzles economists to present as it violates the fundamental tenet of 'no arbitrage'. Simple trading rules such as selling the IPO stock immediately on the first trading day, commonly known as flipping, would not only be highly profitable for investors but would also cause the underpricing levels to decrease and thus the anomaly to disappear. However, empirical evidence does not support this argument.

Moreover, researchers have detected a further anomaly: Companies that go public appear to suffer from long-run underperformance. That is, "relative to other quoted companies, investors appear to lose out by continuing to hold the shares of companies that have recently gone public" (Jenkinson and Ljungqvist (2001), p. 6). This anomaly even supports the benefit of a flipping strategy as holding on to an IPO investment is very likely to generate negative benchmarked returns.

The existence of these stylized facts rationalises the vast amount of theoretical and empirical research conducted in the field of IPOs. Most of these studies thereby draw on samples of US firms to take advantage of the country's mature capital markets which provide transparent data and long time-series. Loughran et al. (1994) review empirical research documenting the returns earned by investors on IPOs in countries outside the US and report that the degree of underpricing varies enormously across countries. Jenkinson and Ljungqvist (2001) explain that many predictions of the theoretical literature rely upon US stock market specific institutional and regulatory characteristics which are, in parts, grossly deviating from the stock market characteristics of countries outside the USA.

Further, many studies draw on inter-industry samples, mainly in order to assess the validity of theoretical models for IPO firms in general. However, Ritter (1984) shows in his pioneering study that IPO returns vary dramatically across industries, too. For example, IPO analyses with sample firms solely comprising US real estate investment trusts (REITs) find underpricing levels to be significantly lower than the levels found for inter-industry samples (Ling and Ryngaert (1997)). Wang et al (1992) even find US REIT offer prices to be overpriced and Buttimer et al. (2005) does not detect the common phenomenon of long-run underperformance. However, these studies focus mainly on US REITs. Only scarce literature exists on real estate firms without REIT structures from outside the US. The boom in listings of European property companies between

1997 and 2007 therefore provide a unique opportunity to add to existing IPO literature. The present thesis thus comprises three individual research papers that formulate three individual research questions designed to answer uniquely identified research gaps within the context of the European property IPO market:

The goal of paper 1 (chapter 2) is to analyse whether IPO signals reveal proprietary information about the prospects of an issuing firms' underlying industry. The study's motivation stems from the ambiguous results of previous empirical studies that let one infer that company specific performance characteristics might be a weak dependent variable to use when analysing the signalling hypotheses proposed by Allen and Faulhaber (1989), Grinblatt and Hwang (1989), and Welch (1989). Further, Jain and Kini (2006) note that IPOs from one industry tend to cluster in time which implies that pioneering IPOs must signal some information that let follower IPOs either accelerate or rethink their issuing decision. As the latter strand of research proposes some relation between IPO signals and industry, no study so far has measured the relationship of IPO signals and industry quality.

The motivation of paper 2 (chapter 3) is to rationalise why previous real estate IPO studies document no long-run underperformance, a phenomenon that is rather common among industrial IPOs. The paper introduces market transparency as one possible explanation approach. Most prior studies base their empirical analyses on data of property companies operating in mature and transparent real estate markets, i.e., the US, Australia and the UK, where decision making is expected to be facilitated when compared to less transparent real estate markets. Thus far, no study has analysed the influence of market transparency. It is hypothesised that real estate market transparency leads to over-optimism either on the investor or the manager side. Since over-optimism also provides an opportunity for poor quality companies to issue equity, it is hypothesised that a lower degree of market transparency reduces rational decision making, helping poor quality issuings to time the market. In the end, these poor quality issuings perform worse than the market and pull down the sample performance.

Paper 3 (chapter 4) is motivated to shed further light on the contradicting evidence found for the impact of corporate governance on valuation. By focusing on an IPO setting, we can examine how insiders install corporate governance to maximise IPO valuation. It is assumed that insiders use corporate governance mechanisms in such a way so as to maximise valuation and thus IPO proceeds, as they are the ones who suffer the most from any negative valuation effects. By analysing a set of European property companies that are more likely to suffer from negative consequence of managerial opportunism, we expect to find different results as previous studies.

All three papers are structured as follows: Brief introductions isolate research question and research gap, followed by a literature review from which testable hypotheses are derived. Next, the research design to test the hypotheses is described, including a brief overview of the identification of the sample, a justification and description of the empirical methodology and of the measures of variables used. The description of the results includes a summary of the descriptive statistics as well as an economic interpretation of the univariate and multivariate analyses. Each paper includes robustness checks which test for the sensitivity of the results and concludes by summarizing its major findings.

The thesis concludes with chapter 5 where the papers one to three are briefly reviewed in order to derive some overall conclusions of thesis. Lastly, some hints for future research are presented.

2 IPO UNDERPRICING, SIGNALLING, AND PROPERTY RETURNS

2.1 INTRODUCTION

One of the most researched stock price patterns in capital markets is that initial public offerings (IPOs) provide significant abnormal returns in the initial days of trading, commonly referred to as the underpricing phenomenon. One major strand of research models IPO underpricing as a mechanism for signalling firm quality (Allen and Faulhaber (1989), Grinblatt and Hwang (1989) and Welch (1989)). Proponents of this line of research argue that firms have information about their future prospects that is only partially disclosed in the public market. This information asymmetry, according to Akerlof (1970), creates an adverse selection problem which causes the market to fail in the sense that only low quality companies offer their IPO for sale. In order to avoid this dilemma, high quality companies use underpricing as a signalling mechanism to convince shareholders to invest in the IPO.

Although the signalling argument is intuitively appealing, empirical evidence is mixed. Michaely and Shaw (1994) provide results that are generally inconsistent with implications of the signalling effect of underpricing. In contrast, Zheng and Stangeland (2007) show that IPO underpricing is positively related to post-IPO growth in company specific performance measures such as sales and EBITDA and thereby provide evidence in favour of the signalling prediction. Thus, one is bound to argue that underpricing as a signalling mechanism has low explanatory power in general or previous studies have too narrowly focused on one dependent variable only. The latter interpretation thereby provides the decisive departure point for our analysis. So far, empirical studies mainly concentrated on firm specific performance measures as dependent variables, thereby indirectly implying that firm's internal environment is the primary determinant of firm performance. However, focusing on research that deals with explaining the sources of performance differences among firms (Schmalensee (1985), Rumelt (1991)), two major strands of theoretical research exist. On the one hand, there is the resource based view arguing that *firm's internal environment* is the primary determinant of firm performance, on the other, the industrial organisation view arguing that *industry factors* drive competitive advantage. A closer look at extant IPO signalling studies however reveals that these analyses mainly rest on the resource based view. Given that IPO firms are normally young companies and are often too small to achieve considerable advantages from strategic management we suspect to find a positive relation of signalling effects and future industry performance.

Thus, the aim of the paper is to analyse if signalling mechanisms of IPO firms do reveal any information about the quality of the industry the company is operating in. Remarkably, this question has not been addressed so far in the context of property IPOs. Usually, the performance of the IPO firm's underlying industry is often difficult to measure. However, this is not the case in the field of real estate. In fact, Hartzell et al. (2005) took advantage of the data availability of the underlying real asset market of real estate investment trusts (REITs) and analysed the relation between the state of US real estate market and the performance of US REITs. Yet, this is only an ex post analysis as it examines if the heat of the IPO market is a function of the underlying real estate market. So far, no study explored if the causality also runs from IPO behaviour to future real estate market performance, i.e. an ex ante analysis. Findings derived by such an analysis might assist un-informed real estate investors in deriving some ideas from the transparent IPO behaviour for the future performance of real estate markets.

In order to address this apparent research gap, we use a hand-collected sample of European property companies (EPCs). Since Europe is characterised by in parts large variations concerning the maturity and state of its real estate markets, EPCs should provide a powerful setup to analyse the relation of underpricing and future property returns.

Multiple OLS regressions are performed to analyse the influence of common signalling variables on real estate market performance measures. Further, initial IPO returns are regressed on ex ante uncertainty variables in order to verify the preconditioned assumption of information asymmetry as otherwise there is no need for signalling (Grinblatt and Hwang (1989) and Welch (1989)). The explicit testing is necessary because previous studies of real estate IPOs show particularly low underpricing levels which have been interpreted as the result of lower information asymmetry because of the special risk return characteristics of real estate.

Overall, results conformingly show that European property companies underprice their IPOs in order to signal inside information about the prospects of their target real estate markets. In contrast, the degree of insider dilution and investment bank reputation, two common IPO signals, are found to have no signalling function with regard to industry prospects. Total return specifications are, in contrast to yield specifications, particularly poor, lending support to the notion that appraisal based real estate performance measures might suffer from measurement errors. Lastly, tests for general information asymmetry reveal that European property companies significantly increase underpricing when firm specific risk is present but abstain from underpricing when real estate market specific risk is present.

The rest of the paper is organised as follows. Section 2.2 starts with a discussion on the relevance of asymmetric information within an IPO context and its consequences for issuing firms and outside investors. Thereby, we lay particular attention on the theoretical models' different assumptions regarding the involved parties' informational advantage and how underpricing is hypothesised to close informational gaps. Based on the insights gained from this literature review, a new reasoning is proposed which rationalises a relationship between IPO signals and industry prospects and for which testable hypotheses are developed. Section 2.3 covers the research design, which includes a justification of the sample selection, an explanation of the chosen methodology and a definition of the measurement of the chosen variables. Empirical results are then presented in section 2.4, which includes descriptive statistics, multiple OLS regressions, and various robustness checks. Section 2.5 concludes.

2.2 LITERATURE REVIEW AND HYPOTHESIS DEVELOPMENT

2.2.1 Asymmetric information and underpricing in property IPOs

Like most investment markets, an IPO market is characterised by informational differences between inside and outside investors. These informational differences, commonly referred to as information asymmetries, represent the difference between the level of information held by firm insiders about the true value of the firm and the level of information held by firm outsiders. One widely observed outcome of this information asymmetry is that issuing firms experience high abnormal stock returns on the first trading day, leaving the impression that the IPO price is persistently lower than the true value of the firm. The phenomenon of new issues being 'underpriced' is observed among large samples of firms operating in a broad range of industries in various countries (Loughran et al. (1994)). In attempting to explain this peculiarity, research has come up with many different explanations. Rock's (1986) adverse selection model is the most prominent work that rationalises underpricing as the result of asymmetric information. The model is based on the underlying assumption that some investors are better informed about the true value of the offered shares than are either the owner of the firm or another group of uninformed investors. This imposes a winner's curse on uninformed investors. Since there is too much supply of correctly priced IPOs than there is demand by informed investors, Rock argues that shares must be underpriced on average in order to get less informed investors subscribing to new issues.

Numerous studies tested the winner's curse model, both for industrial and real estate companies, and overall find empirical evidence supporting the theoretical predictions. Using institutional investors as a proxy for informed investors, Ling and Ryngaert (1997) analyse a set of US REIT IPOs between 1991 and 1994 and report a positive relation between institutional investors' involvement in IPOs and underpricing. In contrast, Wang et al. (1992) and Buttimer et al. (2005) find no underpricing for a sample of US REIT IPOs between 1971 and 1988. They explain their deviating results with a general lack of institutional involvement for pre-1990 REIT IPOs. In fact, whilst in this early period institutional investors' hold on average 8% at the offering, Ling and Ryngaert (1997) document a significantly higher average of 42%. The increased involvement of institutional investors in REIT IPOs has been attributed to the growing acceptance of listed real estate companies as viable alternatives to direct investments in real estate (Gyourko (1994)) and the prospects of greater liquidity in the REIT market (Chadwick (1993)).

Another key empirical implication of Rock's model, formalised by Beatty and Ritter (1986), is the relationship between the issuing company's fundamental risk and its level of underpricing. Beatty and Ritter argue that an investor who decides to engage in information gathering about an issuing company implicitly invests in a call option on the IPO, which will be exercised if the 'true' price exceeds the offer price. Since option valuation theory states that the value of options increases with volatility, i.e. ex ante uncertainty, more investors are willing to invest in information about the company the greater the valuation uncertainty. As a result, IPOs of companies with high ex ante uncertainty must be more underpriced as informed investors expect to be compensated for the cost of information acquisition by higher initial day returns. First evidence for a positive relation of ex ante uncertainty and underpricing among property companies is provided by Brounen and Eichholtz (2002) who show that issue size and aftermarket return standard deviation is positively related with underpricing whilst the opposite is the case for the debt ratio. Brounen and Eichholtz (2002) also find a relation between property type and specialisation levels with underpricing. Diversified companies generate lower first day returns than their specialised peers which might be attributable to the companies' investment strategy which attempts to reduce systematic risk. Even among specialised companies, underpricing levels differ significantly, depending on property type. Ling and Ryngaert (1997) confirm these findings by showing that apartment and shopping centre REITs have lowest underpricing levels. Overall, there is a vast array of empirical evidence supporting Rock's (1986) winner's curse model, independent of samples covering industrial or real estate companies.

Nevertheless, the model's simplistic intuition that uninformed investors are discriminated via rationing in attractively priced issues provides some grounds for scepticism of the model's applicability in practice: Hanley and Wilhelm (1995) address this issue and test whether better informed institutional investors are able to selectively invest in better performing IPOs. In line with Rock's (1986) analyses, they find that institutional investors are indeed the recipients of a large fraction of the short-run profits associated with IPOs. However, institutional investors, being favoured in the allocation of underpriced IPOs, carry a quid pro quo expectation that they will participate in less-attractive issues, too. In other words, if institutional investors are well-informed relative to poorly informed retail investors, they are unable to use their information advantage to avoid investments in overpriced offerings.

Further criticism is stated by Jenkinson and Ljungqvist (2001) who question the assumption that issuers must pay for the uninformed investors' participation in the offering. If informed investors have insufficient resources, uninformed investors could simply invest, in exchange for a fee, through the informed investors to avoid subscribing to overpriced issues. In fact, the existence of investment funds, which provide this kind of service, supports Jenkinson and Ljungqvist's scepticism and demonstrates that becoming informed on a large scale basis inherits the possibility of taking advantage of economies of scale.

Rock's model also predicts that uninformed investors yield zero initial returns and informed investors earn initial returns that just cover the costs of becoming informed. Koh and Walter (1989) examine this prediction and conformingly show that, when adjusted for rationing, average initial returns for uninformed investors fall substantially from 27% to 1%. In contrast, Levis (1990) and Amihud et al. (2003) report for UK and Israel IPOs that rationing-adjusted first day returns are different from zero, findings that do not conform the model's prediction.

Collectively, Rock's (1986) adverse selection model finds wide acceptance among researchers in capital markets and the vast amount of empirical studies with results that are in line with the author's propositions further strengthen the validity of this theoretical approach. However, there is also an array of empirical findings that challenge the model's presumed assumption that a group of outside investors has better information than a group of uninformed investors and firm insiders. In fact, signalling models as proposed by Allen and Faulhaber (1989), Grinblatt and Hwang (1989), and Welch (1989) specifically address this issue and reverse Rock's assumption by arguing that it is more likely that there is an informational advantage of issuers towards investors.

Signalling models are expected to be of particular importance in the analysis of real estate IPO studies for two reasons: First, valuing real estate companies is asset based and therefore straight forward (Buttimer et al. (2005), Hartzell et al. (2005), Eichholtz et al. 2008). So the discrepancy between informed and uninformed investors is expected to be smaller among real estate companies compared to industrial companies. Second, Sirmans (1999) and Ooi (2000) argue that managerial opportunism is more likely to be present among real estate companies, a characteristic that fosters the signalling models' presumed assumption of IPO management's informational advantage over outside investors. As a consequence, the following sections will discuss the role of signalling models in general and will point to a new testable implication for a empirical analysis of property companies.

2.2.2 Signalling as a means to overcome information asymmetry

Allen and Faulhaber (1989), Grinblatt and Hwang (1989), and Welch (1989) propose models where IPO underpricing is assumed to be a mechanism for signalling firm quality. The common idea behind these models is that firms have private information about their future prospects that will be at least partially revealed at some future date. As a consequence of the investors' informational disadvantage, adverse selection will cause the market to fail in the sense that only low quality firms issue equity. Investors will never pay a fair value for a high quality company given the chance that it might in fact be of low quality (Akerlof (1970)). In order to solve this dilemma, the informed inside party has to create a signal that is designed to communicate the uninformed party, the outside investor, the quality of the firm. In order to prevent low quality companies from imitating the signal, the signal has to be costly. Given the overall maxim of an issuing firm is to maximise its proceeds from the offering, underpricing represents a costly and therefore strong signal for firm quality.

High quality firms are only willing to bear signalling costs if later benefits outweigh these initial costs. The models imply that it is, in fact, beneficial for high quality companies to ignore their proceeds maximising requisite and to set the offer price below the firm's true value. Firms of high quality can then recoup these costs by setting a higher offer price in a secondary stage sale, either in form of an seasoned equity offering (SEO) or an open-market sale. This line of argumentation is the common idea of how signalling works in an IPO context and at the same time marks the basis of the theoretical models developed by Allen and Faulhaber (1989), Grinblatt and Hwang (1989) and Welch (1989). However, the models differ in terms of their assumptions about the market's perception of the signal and are thus discussed in more detail in the following paragraphs.

Welch (1989) assumes a link between underpricing and the amount of subsequent seasoned equity or debt offerings. Similar to Ibbotson (1975), he argues that the firm's main intention to underprice is to "'leave a good taste in investors' mouths so that future underwritings from the same issuer could be sold at attractive prices" (Ibbotson (1975, p.264)). By self incurring forgone IPO proceeds, issuing firms are expected to be rewarded at the time of subsequent equity offerings by a higher price for the shares. Low quality firms, mimicking the signals from high quality firms, will, with a certain probability, be detected before they can place an SEO which in turn would prevent them from recouping the costly signal.

Empirical evidence supporting Welch's (1989) argument is mixed. Garfinkel (1993) finds results that are generally inconsistent with the implications of the signalling models. Underpricing is found to have neither an effect on the likelihood of future secondary offerings nor on the probability that insiders will sell shares in the open market. Moreover, Michaely and Shaw (1994) propose that the decision about the amount offered in the seasoned equity offering is made simultaneously with the decision of the degree of underpricing to send as a signal to the market during the IPO. Applying a simultaneous equations model in order to account for the proposed endogenity problem they find, contrary to the signalling hypothesis prediction, that firms that underprice more enter the reissue market less frequently and for smaller amounts than firms that underprice less. In contrast, McGuinness (1992) documents that the incidence of secondary issues of stock, following shortly after an IPO, is positively and significantly related to initial IPO returns and hence in line with the signalling hypothesis.

The signalling model proposed by Allen and Faulhaber (1989) argues that investors update their pre-IPO beliefs about the value of the firm through the company's dividend and earnings policy. Firms, that underprice more, are expected to be more favourably valued by the market. This is because the market expects these firms to more likely have higher earnings, i.e. to be of higher quality. Only firms with high earnings are expected to be able to recoup the foregone proceeds caused by the underpricing. Hence, good firms benefit more from underpricing which makes signalling worthwhile.

In line with this argumentation, Zheng and Stangeland (2007) analyse whether growth rates of accounting performance variables are good measures of firm quality. In fact, they show that the relation between IPO underpricing and post-IPO growth rates of accounting performance variables is positive and statistically significant. In contrast, Michaely and Shaw (1994) find a negative relation between underpricing and future earnings performance and dividend levels, suggesting that underpricing might not be a suitable signalling device.

Lastly, the model of Grinblatt and Hwang (1989) builds on the assumption that the issuer has better information about its firm's future cash flows than outside investors have. In order to signal mean and expected variance of future cash flow streams, Grinblatt and Hwang (1989) argue that firms employ underpricing and the fraction of shares held by insiders as signalling mechanisms. However, empirical evidence by Michaely and Shaw (1994) shows that initial day returns do not explain the value of the firm two years after the IPO.

In sum, empirical evidence on the suitability of underpricing as signal of firm quality is mixed. Further, it can be inferred from previous literature that studies analysing IPO signalling effects primarily focus on the signal an IPO sends with regard to the performance of the individual IPO firm. Surprisingly, only a small amount of literature assesses whether an IPO also sends a signal with regard to the issuing firms' general industry. Theoretical models that rationalise an interlinkage between the IPO behaviour of an individual firm and that of this firm's industry are provided by Benveniste et al. (2002), Lowry and Schwert (2002), and Benninga et al. (2005). More specific research that analyses the signalling effect of IPOs on price reactions of other firms that are trading at the time of the IPO issuance is provided by Akhigbe et al. (2004, 2006). However, hardly any research has been done on the signalling effect of IPOs on the performance of the issuing firm's underlying assets. The latter is the main research question addressed in this study. Thus, the next section is designed to explain the link between IPO signals and industry performance in order to derive new testable hypotheses that will be empirically analysed in section 2.4.

2.2.3 Industry clusters and IPO signals for industry prospects

We can conclude from the section above that IPO firms use signals to demonstrate firm quality in order to convince capital market participants to invest in the company. An extension of these arguments is the notion that signals may also reveal some useful information for yet privately-held rival firms which can monitor the IPO effort of pioneering companies and thereby determine whether they are properly positioned for an IPO, too. In line with this argument, Jain and Kini (2006) argue that IPOs of pioneering firms in emerging industries reveal industry-specific proprietary information which might spill over to follower firms who use this information to revaluate their investment decisions and financing options. For example, a favourable market reaction to an early IPO might signal private companies considering an IPO to accelerate their intention to go public whereas a negative reaction rather deters companies from seeking access to the primary markets.

Benninga et al. (2005) develop a formal model to demonstrate that firms go public when their cash flows are high, which indicates that if one firm considers it optimal to issue stock, so do other firms. Since the correlation between the cash flows of firms within the same industry is likely to be greater than the cross-sectional correlation among industries, the model of Benninga et al. (2005) predicts that IPOs will cluster in industry waves. Similarly, Lowry and Schwert (2002) contend that IPO volume is predominantly driven by information learned during the registrations period and positive information results in higher initial returns at IPO which lead more companies to file IPOs soon thereafter. Benveniste et al. (2002) argue that firms that go public produce information that influences the issuance decisions of their rivals. If follower IPOs free ride on the information production borne by pioneering firms, market failures can occur resulting in a potential stop of general issuing activity. To alleviate this problem, investment banks bundle IPOs and thereby force follower firms to also engage in the costly information producing process.

These models' empirical evidence shows that industry clustering can be the rational outcome of signals associated with IPOs of firms within one industry. Although these models do establish a link between a firm that goes public and its corresponding *privately-held* rivals, they do not measure if and how an IPO by one firm affects a firm's corresponding *listed* rivals. This question is analysed by Akhigbe et al. (2004, 2006) who contend that an IPO may signal an abrupt increase in the supply of shares available to investors which, in turn, might trigger a substitution effect among already listed industry rivals. As a result, rival firms are expected to suffer from negative price pressures as more substituting companies are then fighting for the same pool of funds. Further, an IPO might signal that the prices of already listed firms within the same industry are at its peak and any marginal IPO is a means by which existing owners want to use favourable market valuations to cash out. Alternatively, in the case of real estate firms, an IPO might signal favourable prospects for the overall real estate market and the availability of additional real estate investment opportunities. Empirical results by Akhigbe et al. (2004) reveal that the date of issuance has a significant and negative effect on the stock prices of a portfolio of rival firms. The authors attribute this effect either to the dilutive effect of the increased number of REIT shares or to a negative signal associated with market timing. However, it is not tested the link between IPO signals and underlying real estate market prospects explicitly.

In sum, existing evidence proposes some relation between IPO signals and industry conditions. However, the cited studies do not analyse whether the signals are intended mainly to reveal inside information about firm quality or about overall industry quality. As the 'firm quality' relationship implicitly assumes that a firm's individual resources, management power, and other firm attributes separate the firm from its rivals, the 'industry quality' relationship assumes that firm quality is mainly determined by the performance of its underlying industry. Considering this lack of differentiation and drawing on the fact that previous research provides mixed results when focusing on firm performance as measure of firm quality, one may suspect that firms might use signalling to reveal proprietary information about their expectation of industry prospects rather than to signal individual firm prospects.

The question whether firm quality and performance is mainly a result of superior managerial skills or the result of a booming industry is still subject to continuing debate. In general, two opposing strands in strategic management literature exist, as introduced in section 2.1: The resource based view and the industrial organisation view: The resource based view argues that rent-producing resources determine the profit level of firms. In order to sustain competitive advantage, the resources have to be difficult to copy and to substitute and have to be difficult to trade in factor markets (Wernerfelt (1984)). The resource based view assumes that a company's individual resources are the main determinant of the firm's (operating and/or stock price) performance. By analysing the impact of underpricing on firm specific performance measures, such as return on assets (Jain and Kini (1994)) and EBITDA (Zheng and Stangeland (2007)), it is implicitly assumed that company performance stems from the usage of the resources of each individual firm.

The industrial organisation view argues that the structural characteristics of industries are the primary determinants of performance (Porter (1980)). The structure-conduct-performance framework is based on a deterministic relationship between market structure and corporate profitability. This idea goes back to Mason (1939) who argues that the structural characteristics of an industry constrain the conduct or strategies of its component firms which in turn determine the inter-industrial performance differences. Thus, firm performance is to a large extend dependent on the performance of the firm's underlying industry. In this context, Schmalensee (1985) empirically analyses how industry and firm factors respectively contribute to overall profitability. The study concludes that industry effects play a major role in determining firm performance whereas firm specific factors play only a minor role. Thus, in line with the industrial organisation view, it is reasonable to argue that firm performance is determined by the performance of the firm's underlying assets.

As stated above, so far, there exists no study that has addressed this issue for any specific industry. A potential explanation for this apparent research gap might be a general difficulty associated with identifying the actual underlying industry of diversified industrial companies and /or tracking the underlying industry's performance. The analysis of European property companies alleviates these problems. Adams and Venmore-Roland (1990) argue that the performance of property companies should be linked to the performance of the properties owned by the property company. They argue that property company shares are valued on a net asset value basis. Hence, rises and falls in the value of the properties are expected to be reflected in stock price variability. Supporting evidence is provided by Liow (1996) who reports significant co-movement between property direct property returns and listed property companies' stock returns. Hartzell et al. (2005) is the only study that analyses the relation between the state of US real estate market and the performance of US REITs. They present evidence that REIT IPO activity is linked to the conditions of the underlying real estate markets. Yet, this is only an ex post analysis as it examines if the heat of the IPO market is a function of the underlying real estate market. So far, no study explored if the causality also runs from IPO behaviour to future real estate market performance, i.e. an ex ante analysis.

As discussed in section 2.2.2, underpricing is theoretically assumed and empirically tested to have signalling power in an IPO context. Higher underpricing represents a costly signal that can only be sustained by high quality companies. Assuming, in line with the industrial organisation view, that firm quality is mainly determined by the underlying industry quality (Mason (1939), Porter (1980)), which is in the case of property companies the demand for real estate, we expect underpricing to be positively related to future property performance. This is the first hypothesis tested in this paper.

H1a: Underpricing is positively related to property performance

Next to underpricing, other IPO characteristics have been proposed to be valid signals, too. Trueman (1986) argues that management has better information about the performance of the firm's future projects. If management raises capital in order to finance a new project and thereby deliberately accepts a greater dilution of its ownership in the firm, market participants may interpret this action as a costly commitment by the management. It is important to note that dilution also occurs if management decides to sell already existing shares. However, to better reflect the capital expenditure notion of Trueman's (1986) argumentation, we measure dilution as the outcome of the issuance of new shares. Consequently, the degree of dilution of pre-IPO shareholders is proxied by the degree of share capital enlargement due to the issuance of new shares and is expected to be positively related to property performance.

H1b: Dilution is positively related to property performance

Booth and Smith (1986) propose a model in which prestigious underwriters are employed to certify that the issue price is consistent with inside information about future earnings prospects of the firm. Again, assuming that earnings prospects are mainly determined by the performance of the IPO firms' underlying assets, IPOs underwritten by prestigious underwriters are assumed to mainly invest in geographic areas with strong asset performance. Thus, a positive relation between underwriter ranking and property returns is expected.

H1c: Investment bank reputation is positively related to future property performance

Leland and Pyle (1977) argue that owners can reveal their knowledge of high future cash flows by retaining, at IPO, a higher stake in the company because the implied under-diversification cost is higher for firms having not many positive NPV projects. Further, underpricing levels are decreasing with the quality of venture capitalist services and with the degree of the venture capitalists' managerial involvement because the expected expertise of venture capitalists serves as signal itself. These implications are consistent with the empirical findings of Megginson and Weiss (1991), Barry et. al. (1990), and Gompers (1996). However, these two signals are excluded from analysis because (i) the signalling potential of inside ownership is subject to econometrical challenges which are discussed extensively in chapter 3 of this thesis and (ii) because data on venture capital involvement was not available and is generally not as important in the real estate sector as in other industries.

A major prerequisite for the signalling models discussed above is the presence of information asymmetry because in a transparent investment environment, signalling is not necessary (Grinblatt and Hwang (1989) and Welch (1989)). Underpricing is a widely accepted measure for the degree of information asymmetry. Average first day returns exceeding 40% for IPOs issued in the dot.com area are a prominent example for the high correlation of underpricing and information asymmetry. However, previous research on real estate IPOs revealed comparatively low first day returns (Ling and Ryngaert (1997), Buttimer et al. (2005), Hartzell et al. (2005), Freybote et al. (2008)). A way to test for the presence of asymmetric information in a signalling context goes back to Welch (1989) who argues that ex ante uncertainty variables should be positively related to first day returns, given that information asymmetry is present. Welch argues that uncertainty about firm value is related to the market's belief that the firm is high quality. This belief is related to underpricing because a decrease in market's belief of the firm's high quality reduces the incentive of firms to play a pooling equilibrium issuance pricing. Thus, ex ante uncertainty variables are expected to be positively related to initial returns.

H2: Ex ante uncertainty proxies are positively related to underpricing

Overall, the argumentation presented above is analysed with a sample of European property companies. In the following section, the suitability of the sample to test the proposed hypotheses will be described, followed by the description of the methodology and the results.

2.3 RESEARCH DESIGN

2.3.1 Sample selection and data source

The sample contains IPOs of European property companies from 1997 to 2007, where European property companies are defined as operating real estate companies with a property-backed business model and with geographic investment foci covering Western Europe (Austria, Belgium, France, Germany, Italy, Portugal, Spain, Switzerland, UK), the Nordic countries (Denmark, Finland, Norway, Sweden) and Central and Eastern Europe (CEE) (Bulgaria, Croatia, Czech Republic, Estonia, Hungary, Latvia, Lithuania, Poland, Romania, Russia, Serbia, Slovakia, Slovenia, Ukraine). This particular data set shows characteristics that are specifically suitable to test our hypotheses. In order to analyse if signalling mechanisms of IPO firms do reveal any information about the quality of the industry, the following sampling requirements are key: (1) there must be a need for signalling for the sample firms and (2) assumptions of the signalling model need to be fulfilled.

(1) Need for signalling: The sample comprises European property companies without REIT regime that issued unseasoned equity between 1997 and

2007. The average firm age is 3.2 years and thereby shows that the sample firms have no long track record which aggravates the determination of a fair market value. In addition, 36 companies focused on real estate markets in the CEE where potentially instable political and economical situations increase investment risk. Lastly, our sample comprises only property companies without REIT regime. Thus, we can expect that these firms are subject to a sufficient degree of information asymmetry, which is needed to achieve separation via signalling.

(2) Assumption of the signalling model: The first assumption is that insiders have an informational advantage over outside investors. Due to long-term investment horizons and less pressure to produce immediate, Sirmans (1999) and Ooi (2000) argue that real estate companies have an increased likelihood to suffer from negative consequences of managerial opportunism. In combination with the relative ease of valuing underlying properties (Eichholtz et al. (2008)), it seems reasonable to argue that information is asymmetric between managerial insiders and outside investors. A further critical assumption of all signalling IPO models is that issuing firms follow a two-stage sale strategy as selling shareholders must be compensated for the costly signal of the unseasoned offering. Frye (2004) shows that inside ownership levels significantly decrease within a three year post-IPO period. In fact, paper 3 shows that the property companies analysed in this thesis only divest 1%, suggesting that further stakes a sold in a second stage sale. Thus, key signalling assumptions are met in the current IPO sample.

The target sample contains 242 IPOs which represent all European companies classified by the SIC code for real estate companies (SIC 65) of the Dealogic database. From this preliminary sample, several companies had to be excluded because company and/or stock market characteristics did not match the definition of a European property company as described above. More specifically, excluded firms from the sample include (1) companies with investment focus outside of Western Europe, the Nordic countries or CEE, (2) companies with no property-backed business model (such as real estate service companies or real estate agents), and (3) companies with no information on operating business and/or stock prices. The latter represents the largest group of excluded companies mainly because double checking Dealogic data with IPO prospectuses and company press releases revealed significant discrepancies. As the limited data availability, reliability, and comparability can be owed to large differences in accounting practices, tax regimes, and disclosure requirements of the 20 different legislative systems the sample firms operate in, we decided to only include IPOs for which the admission documents are available in either language of German, English, Spanish or French, offer prices and first day closing prices have been double checked and stock price information is available on Datastream. By these control steps, any biases due to local disclosure standards or accounting practices are expected to be minimised. As a consequence, the final data sample consists of 141 IPOs.

To guarantee representativeness of the sample we discussed each IPO with real estate experts in France, Germany and UK and were confirmed that the final sample consists of all companies that are regarded as characteristic for the European property company universe. Excluded IPOs are mainly small and rather unknown. In the course of this study, the sample size sums to 120 companies as for 21 companies, the target real estate investment markets could not be identified. An inspection of the data identified very few extreme values so we applied the winsorisation technique as a correction. This technique takes the non-missing values of a variable and generates a new variable identical except that the h highest and h lowest values are replaced by the maximum of five times the mean absolute deviation of all observations for this variable.

2.3.2 Methodology

In order to test whether underpricing and other IPO characteristics are potentially employed as signals for expected industry's underlying asset performance, empirical tests are undertaken based on the following logic. If firm quality of property company IPOs is mainly determined by the general property market performance in the firm's preferred geographic investment area, rather than by the individual performance of selected properties in the firm's portfolio, signals are expected to be positively related to the combined performance of real estate investments in corresponding European countries. These market sector performance measures of direct real estate are the main dependent variable of interest in this study. OLS regressions are employed to test the proposed relationships as stated in subsection 2.2.3.

In general, return analyses for direct real estate are suffering from general data poverty and from differences of the attributes and characteristics of the scarce data available. Previous literature proposed a variety of return measures to overcome these paucities, which, despite individual calculation differences, agree on using either *total return* or *yield* measures. The latter measures are usually calculated by dividing stabilised current income by an estimated value amount of the property. In contrast, total return measures are comprised of an income component and a property value price change component. The property value can be either based upon cost or market value where the latter is more common practice. Although using fair market values seems to be an appealing method, the common practice of deriving of a "fair" value via property appraisals raises concerns regarding the consequences of appraisal smoothing. Grissom and DeLisle (1998) note that relying on property appraisals, rather than on market transactions, may distort the measurement precision of the actual real estate distribution, thereby underestimating real estate's volatility. This is confirmed by Geltner (1989, 1991) and De Wit (1993), among others, who show that appraisal smoothing bias is especially significant when it comes to *change* calculations as it is the case for the capital component of the total return measure. In contrast, using yield ratios, such as income over capital value where the capital value itself is is based on current income, we expect the appraisal smoothing bias to be of minor importance. Nevertheless, for the sake of completeness, both yield and total return measures are used as dependent variables.

The main independent variables in this study are initial stock price returns, the amount of enlarged share capital, and the underwriter reputation ranking. All three variables are expected to be positively related to future property performance. In order to analyse the impact of the hypothesised signals, OLS regressions with YIELD and TOTRET as dependent variables are performed. To control for signalling theory's prediction that signalling is less required in times of reduced information asymmetry, we include an interaction term SIGNALS(c)NUMIPO as it is assumed that many issuings reveal much information that helps investors and issuers of following IPOs to better determine fair offer prices. This results in the following regression equation.

(2.1) $$PROPERTYRETURN = \beta_0 + \beta_1 SIGNALS + \beta_2 SIGNALS * NUMIPO$$

As mentioned before, Allen and Faulhaber (1989) argue that signalling is not necessary if information asymmetry is low. In order to test for information asymmetry, UNDERPRICING is regressed on various ex ante uncertainty variables that are expected to be of significant explanatory power, if information asymmetry is present. This leads to the second regression equation tested in this paper.

(2.2) $$UNDERPRICNG = \beta_0 + \beta_1 EXANTEUNCERTAINTY + \beta_3 CONTROLS$$

Finally, robustness checks, as presented in subsection 2.4.2.3, use variations in variable definitions of property return performance and signals in order to confirm the validity of the results.

2.3.3 Measures of variables

This section describes the variables employed in the regression equations 2.1 and 2.2. An overview of the definitions is presented in Table 2.1.

The main variables of interest are yield and total return measures for direct real estate in European countries. In order to assign each property IPO an individual property return measure, IPO prospectuses with regard to the company's geographic investment focus are examined. Having identified the IPO firms geographic target markets, each IPO is assigned the yield and total return measures of the corresponding national property markets, taken from the IPD multinational index spreadsheet. For companies diversifying geographically, return figures are weighted respectively, as long as investment ratios are mentioned. Yields (YIELD) are calculated as the rent passing as a percentage of the capital value at the same date where capital value is the market value of the properties as of year-end, supplied by internal or external valuers. Although the yields provided by IPD follow local market conventions and practice and thus are not directly comparable, the differences in the yield calculation employed are rather small and thus are unlikely to bias the result, especially because yields are not directly compared against each other. Total returns (TOTRET) are calculated as annual compounded rate of monthly capital appreciation, net of capital expenditure, plus monthly net income received expressed as a percentage of monthly capital value employed. One issue that has to be accounted for is the fact that IPD data is only available on a yearly basis. This might be problematic since IPOs take place around the year. For example, a company that issues in January 2006 is more dependent on the return measures of 2006 whereas a company which issues in December 2006 is rather dependent on the return measures of 2007. Thus, yields and total return figures need to measure a 12 month post-IPO period. As monthly or quarterly data on yields and total returns is not available, annual return measure are transformed in three month return figures, assuming quarterly compounding. Consequently, the assigned property return for an IPO that is issued in the fourth quarter of 2006 consists out of the combination of one quarter of 2006 returns and three quarters of 2007 returns. By undertaking this transformation, yield and total return measures reflect the performance of direct property for twelve month post-IPO periods.

The main signalling variables of interest are measured as follows: Initial returns (UNDERPRICING1) are determined by calculating the percentage change between the offer price and the closing price of the first trading day, adjusted for the benchmark return on the IPO date. The benchmark return is taken from the FTSE/EPRA Europe index.

EPRA also provides country specific index series. However, many of the companies used to calculate these indices are included in our sample. Thus, to avoid an autocorrelation bias, we use for all sample firms the general Europe index as benchmark return although results do not differ either way. Following Below et al. (1995), market-adjusted returns over the five day post IPO period are also calculated in order to avoid any biases because of aftermarket support by underwriters and also to allow the market for issues with low trading values to adequately adjust the price. The degree capital requirement (DILUTION) is measured as the ratio of new shares issued in relation to the amount of existing pre-IPO shares. Lastly, underwriter reputation (IBREPU) is a measured, in line with Derrien and Kecska (2007), via a dummy variable which equals one if the respective underwriter is a global investment bank and zero otherwise.

TABLE 2.1: OVERVIEW OF VARIABLES

Variable name	Definition	Source
DEAL	Deal volume measured as the number of new shares issued at IPO times the offer price	Dealogic, Datastream, IPO prospectus
DEBT	Pre-IPO total debt to total assets	IPO prospectus
DILUTION	Capital increase at the IPO measured as a percentage of issued share capital excluding over-allotment option relative to the pre-IPO share capital	IPO prospectus
DILUTIONGREEN	Capital increase at the IPO measured as a percentage of issued share capital including over-allotment option relative to the pre-IPO share capital	Dealogic, IPO prospectus
GROWTHPREMIUM	Growth opportunities measured as the difference between the offer price and the net tangible book value per share where the latter is calculated as total assets minus total debt plus cash proceeds of the offering. Figures are standardised by the offer price	IPO prospectus
IBREPU	Dummy variable that equals one if the issuing firm's underwriter or nominated broker is a global investment bank	IPO prospectus
IBREPUCOUN	Dummy variable that equals one if the issuing firm's underwriter or nominated broker is an investment bank with offices only in one country	IPO prospectus
NOPORT	Dummy variable that equals one if the issuing firm has no initial property portfolio at the time of the issuing	IPO prospectus
PIPELINE	Dummy variable that equals one if the issuing firm fully or at least partially specifies the properties it intends to acquire with the IPO proceeds and zero otherwise	IPO prospectus
TOTRET	Total returns of direct property investments are calculated as annual compounded rate of monthly capital appreciation, net of capital expenditure, plus monthly net income received expressed as a percentage of monthly capital value employed	Investment Property Database
TYPOSPEC	Dummy variable that equals one if the issuing firm's investment strategy focuses on one specific property type	IPO prospectus
UNDERPRICING1	Initial day return measured as the natural logarithm of the closing price of the first trading day and the issue price of the IPO divided by the issue price and adjusted for the market return of the EPRA Europe index on the IPO day	Datastream, IPO prospectus, Press releases
UNDERPRICING5	Initial day return measured as the natural logarithm of the closing price of the fifth trading day and the issue price of the IPO divided by the issue price and adjusted for the market return of the EPRA Europe index on the IPO day	Datastream, IPO prospectus, Press releases
VOLATILITY	Standard deviation of stock returns for an aftermarket period of 240 trading days	Datastream
YIELD	Yields of direct property investments are calculated as the rent passing as a percentage of the capital value at the same date where capital value is the market value of the properties as of year-end, supplied by internal or external valuers	Investment Property Database

As control variable, overall IPO activity is included as, among others, Lowry and Schwert (2002) and Jain and Kini (2006) argue that in times of many issuings, information asymmetry is expected to be lower because a high issuing activity reveals proprietary information that helps issuers and investors to derive more precise estimates of successive IPOs' valuations. As a consequence, signals are expected to be lower in times of hot issue markets as the reduced information asymmetry lessens the need to achieve separation. To test for this prediction, the interaction terms of each signalling variable and the number of IPOs 30 days before an issuing (NUMIPO) are included in the regression models. The interaction terms are expected to be negatively related with YIELD and TOTRET, if information asymmetry is reduced in periods of issuing activity.

Having explained the signalling variables, the following paragraphs present the reasoning and the definitions of the ex ante uncertainty variables employed in equation 2.2:

Our sample firms consist of European property companies without REIT regime. Thus, we expect these companies to have higher growth opportunities since they do not have to pay out the majority of their income as it is the case with most REIT regimes. A model that links growth opportunities with initial day returns has been developed by Chung et al. (2005). The authors show that returns for IPO investors reflect at least in part risk premia for investing in uncertain growth opportunities. The authors assume that the first day closing price reflects two components of the firm value: the value of assets in place - represented by the firm's net tangible book value - and the value of growth opportunities.

These growth opportunities are measured as the difference between the offer price and the net tangible book value per share where the latter is calculated as total assets minus total debt plus cash proceeds of the offering. Since most property companies try to raise capital for further real estate investments, the firm's admission documents are screened for valuation reports about already existing property portfolios and the assumed value of the pipeline portfolio that is intended to be acquired via the proceeds from the offering. If companies have disclosed valuation figures about their existing real estate portfolio, market values instead of book value figures have been used. In the case that there is specification about a property portfolio which the firm intends to buy with the cash proceeds of the offering, the future value (as stated in the prospectus) of the properties is calculated by subtracting approximated debt that in turn is derived from the target debt ratio in relation to the IPO proceeds. To make the growth premium measure comparable across IPOs, all figures are calculated as percentage of the offer price. GROWTHPREMIUM is expected to be positively related with underpricing.

Beatty and Ritter (1986) find that larger IPOs are often undertaken by firms with a longer operating history. The authors assume that these companies have less risky growth opportunities. Brounen and Eichholtz (2002) assume that the larger the issue the more professionally it is likely to be managed and the more information about the true value will be available. Thus, information asymmetry is reduced and lower first day returns are to be expected. To test for this relationship, deal volume (DEAL), which is defined as the product of number of the shares issued and the offer price, is employed.

James and Wier (1990), Habib and Ljungqvist (2001) and Schenone (2004) argue that firms, which raise private debt before an IPO, signal to the market that they are of high quality. Thus, the higher the debt ratio (DEBT), measured as total debt divided by total assets at IPO, the lower the expected information asymmetry and thus a negative relationship between DEBT and underpricing is expected.

Volatility (VOLATILITY), calculated as the standard deviation of the market adjusted stock returns for the first 20-trading day period, is also included since Ritter (1987) argues that firms, whose market value is highly uncertain before the offering, are characterised by volatile aftermarket share price performance. A better measure of ex ante uncertainty would be only unsystematic risk rather than also including market risk. However, since market movements of sample firms explain less than 6% of the daily returns during the first 20 trading days, total volatility as uncertainty proxy is employed. This procedure is analogous to Ritter (1984). A positive relationship between VOLATILITY and underpricing is expected.

A more real estate specific measure for ex ante uncertainty is sector specialisation. By investing in one property type, investors are assumed to have fewer difficulties in deriving a fair value of the company as empirically confirmed by Brounen and Eichholtz (2002). Sector specialisation is measured with the dummy variable TYPOSPEC, which equals 1 if the firm's investment strategy focuses on one specific property type and equals zero if the firm's investment strategy follows a diversified approach. A positive relationship between TYPOSPEC and underpricing is expected.

Further, Wang et al. (1992) and Leone et al. (2007) argue that the level of specification of the properties, which the issuing firms intend to acquire with the IPO proceeds, reduces investor's uncertainty about management's investment strategy. Thus, firms that provide detailed information about property type, its size, location, major tenants, and other property specific characteristics are expected to have lower underpricing. In contrast to industrial companies that are typically reluctant to be too specific about the intended use of proceeds, real estate companies do not have to fear competitive disadvantages by disclosing property specific information so long as they have appropriate purchase options on the properties they intend to acquire with the IPO proceeds (Londerville (2002)). In order to account for this argumentation, the dummy variable PIPELINE is created which equals 1 if a company states in its prospectus a money amount of the properties it intends to acquire with the IPO proceeds and zero otherwise. PIPELINE is expected to be positively related with initial day returns.

The last company-specific proxy for ex ante uncertainty is a dummy variable (NOPORT) that measures the investor's valuation uncertainty. At the offering stage, some European property companies have no assets and thereby complicate the determination of a precise company valuation. This problem is common among closed-end funds that, in general, also do not have pre-existing assets. Surprisingly, several studies have found that closed-end funds have nearly no underpricing. For example, Weiss (1989) and Peavy III (1990) report that new issues of closed-end mutual funds average a zero return on their first day of trading but register a negative abnormal return in the subsequent 100 trading days. However, the difference between EPCs and closed-end funds is that these vehicles normally invest in stocks with observable market values, making it easier for investors to price such a fund. In contrast, this study's sample contains only companies whose main assets are are not traded daily but are valued on a semi-annual or even annual basis. This ex ante uncertainty about the true value of the (in this case missing) underlying suggests that EPCs with no pre-existing asset should have higher initial returns as compensation for the high information asymmetry at the time of the IPO. Thus, NOPORT is expected to be positively related with underpricing.

2.4 Results

2.4.1 Descriptive statistics and correlations

Descriptive statistics of the various variables used in this paper are presented in Table 2.2. Property yields of the real estate markets analysed average 8%, with maximum values of 11% and minimum values of 2%. In contrast, total return measures are more volatile as indicted by a standard deviation of 9% and minimum and maximum values of -5% and 19% respectively. Total return figures average to 15%. Initial IPO returns are 6% which is higher to the underpricing levels found by REIT studies but in line with empirical results for property companies without REIT regime (Sahi and Lee (2001), Brounen and Eichholtz (2002), Freybote et al. (2008)).

Further, EPCs diluted their existing share capital by 44% and thereby raised on average EUR 125 million of cash proceeds. 38 companies were underwritten by a global investment bank that mainly provided their services for companies with lower growth premia, as indicated by the negative correlation coefficient.

TABLE 2.2: SUMMARY STATISTICS

	N	Mean	Median	Max	Min	Std.Dev.	Skewness	Kurtosis
DEAL	120	125.56	73.73	516.56	0.48	135.48	1.22	3.62
DEBT	120	0.47	0.53	0.70	0.00	0.19	-1.31	3.67
DILUTION	120	0.44	0.29	1.00	0.00	0.36	0.56	1.74
GROWTHPREMIUM	120	0.22	0.20	1.69	-1.77	0.61	-0.26	2.92
IBREPU	120	0.38	0.00	1.00	0.00	0.49	0.51	1.26
NOPORT	120	0.25	0.00	1.00	0.00	0.44	1.13	2.27
NUMIPO	120	5.75	5.00	12.00	1.00	3.62	0.38	1.87
PIPELINE	120	0.27	0.00	1.00	0.00	0.45	1.03	2.05
TOTRET	120	0.15	0.19	0.27	-0.05	0.09	-0.63	1.96
TYPOSPEC	120	0.45	0.00	1.00	0.00	0.50	0.21	1.04
UNDERPRICING1	120	0.06	0.05	0.31	-0.14	0.09	0.92	3.94
UNDERPRICING5	120	0.07	0.05	0.40	-0.30	0.12	0.73	4.77
VOLATILITY	120	0.02	0.01	0.05	0.00	0.01	1.36	1.20
YIELD	120	0.08	0.08	0.11	0.02	0.01	-1.38	3.22

The positive correlation coefficient between the variables UNDERPRICING1, DILUTION, and IBREPU and the real estate performance measures YIELD and TOTRET provide a first indication that firms potentially employ signalling to indicate their expectation about industry quality.

Other interesting relationships are as follows: On average, 22% of the offer price consists of growth opportunities. This means that European property companies valued their market value, on average, 22% above the fair value of their underlying properties. 25 companies issued equity without having a portfolio on the offer date as measured by the variable NOPORT. Interestingly, NOPORT is positively related with YIELD. This might imply that for these companies, the IPO is a financing tool in order to finance investments in real estate markets with promising yields.

Also interesting is that the correlation coefficient for NOPORT and TOTRET is not statistically significant which leaves the impression that European property companies, that seek primary market financing to fund investments, base their investment decisions on expected yield and not on expected total return figures.

TABLE 2.3: CORRELATION MATRIX

	YIELD	TOTRET	UNDERPRICING1	UNDERPRICING5	DILUTION	IBREPU	NUMIPO	GROWTHPREMIUM	DEBT	VOLATILITY	DEAL	TYPOSPEC	PIPELINE	NOPORT
YIELD	1.00													
TOTRET	0.34	1.00												
UNDERPRICING1	0.26	0.16	1.00											
UNDERPRICING5	0.25	0.18	0.82	1.00										
DILUTION	0.33	0.02	-0.02	0.08	1.00									
IBREPU	-0.06	-0.13	0.01	-0.09	-0.11	1.00								
NUMIPO	0.08	0.01	0.00	0.03	-0.06	-0.04	1.00							
GROWTHPREMIUM	0.23	0.16	0.28	0.23	-0.09	-0.17	0.09	1.00						
DEBT	-0.01	-0.13	-0.03	-0.04	-0.05	-0.06	0.06	0.26	1.00					
VOLATILITY	0.10	0.04	0.14	0.15	0.24	0.13	0.01	-0.11	0.00	1.00				
DEAL	0.07	-0.08	0.00	-0.06	0.08	0.38	-0.11	-0.13	0.13	0.42	1.00			
TYPOSPEC	0.00	-0.21	0.01	-0.02	-0.17	0.10	0.06	0.27	0.08	0.02	0.06	1.00		
PIPELINE	0.03	-0.04	-0.13	-0.08	0.30	0.22	-0.06	-0.57	-0.10	0.15	0.19	-0.07	1.00	
NOPORT	0.28	0.06	0.07	0.14	0.84	-0.12	-0.15	0.05	0.09	0.21	0.14	-0.16	0.32	1.00

2.4.2 Regression results

In the following subsections, the results of the empirical analysis are described. All performed regressions are OLS regressions for which standard errors are corrected for heteroscedasticity by using White's (1980) method. Subsection 2.4.2.1 presents the results of the main part of the analysis where direct property return measures are regressed on IPO signals in order to test for their information revelation potential. In subsection 2.4.2.2, underpricing is regressed on ex ante uncertainty variables in order to confirm the preconditioned existence of information asymmetry. Lastly, in subsection 2.4.2.3, variable definitions are changed in order to test for overall sensitivity of results.

2.4.2.1 OLS regression of property returns

This subsection discusses the results of regression equation 2.1 which is designed to examine whether European property companies employ IPO signals to reveal proprietary information about the expected performance of their target real estate investment markets. Real estate performance is measured by YIELD and TOTRET which therefore enter as dependent variables in the regressions performed. The results are presented in Table 2.4.

The description of the results starts with model I where country specific property yields (YIELD) are regressed on the proposed signals underpricing (UNDERPRICING1), capital expenditures (DILUTION) and underwriter reputation (IBREPU). The variables generate an adjusted R^2 of 0.14, thereby showing a generally high explanatory power of the model specification. The Ramsey-RESET test confirms the model is correctly specified and a maximum VIF factor of 1.02 indicates no multicollinearity problems.

Regarding the signals' impact on YIELD, it can be observed that the coefficients of UNDERPRICING1 and DILUTION are positive and significant at the 1% level. In contrast, the coefficient of IBREPU is negative and statistically insignificant.

The picture changes in model II when TOTRET is used as dependent variable. The adjusted R^2 drops to 0.01 and, although the RESET-test indicates that the model still is correctly specified, the F-statistic looses significance. UNDERPRICING1 is still significant at the 10% level, whereas DILUTION looses significance. IBREPU remains insignificant too.

The results let us imply the following: The YIELD model is significantly better specified compared to the TOTRET model. As both measures are designed to reflect direct real estate performance but only one of them, YIELD, seems to be explained by the regressions performed, we might infer that the measurement of TOTRET is likely to be biased, as already mentioned in subsection 2.3.2. This implication is checked for robustness in subsection 2.4.2.3.

Regarding the impact of the individual variables on real estate market return measures, we can note that initial day returns are, as hypothesized, positively related to both future direct property performance measures. Thus, it seems that European property companies which are of higher quality, where quality is assumed to be mainly determined by the performance of the underlying industry, seem to employ underpricing as a signal to reveal proprietary information about their expectation of the industry's prospects in their geographic main target markets.

Models III and IV include the number of IPOs (NUMIPO) to control for the signalling models' prediction that information asymmetry should be lower in times of increased number of issuings.

Referring to the positive relation of DILUTION to YIELD in model III, we can observe that DILUTION is also positively related to NUMIPO, a result that is rather contradictory to DILUTION's expected signalling function. The result rather implies that European property companies raise more funds with an increasingly favourable investment environment.

To more thoroughly address the question whether these relationships stem in fact from the motivation to signal industry prospects, models III and IV include the interaction terms UNDERPRICING1(c)NUMIPO, DILUTION(c)NUMIPO, AND IBREPU(c)NUMIPO which test for the assumption that periods of high issuing activity reduce information asymmetry which in turn requires lower levels of costly signals.

In fact, the coefficient of the interaction variable UNDERPRICING1(c)NUMIPO is significant and negatively related to YIELD and TOTRET. This shows that strong growth companies that have issued in a hot IPO market phase underprice less compared to strong growth companies that have issued in a cold IPO market phase. This result implies that IPO industry clusters seem to reduce information asymmetries which in turn allows follower IPOs to use a lesser amount of costly signals such as underpricing. Thus, H1a can be accepted.

DILUTION(c)NUMIPO is unrelated to either YIELD or TOTRET. This implies that European property companies seem to dilute pre-IPO share capital independently of IPO market heat. Although costly signalling via dilution would be less required in hot IPO markets, DILUTION(c)NUMIPO is not significantly related to both property performance measures. This implies that property companies deliberately dilute their shareholdings to raise more funds. Thus, it may be argued that DILUTION is not used for signalling purposes but primarily as financing avenue. Consequently, H1b needs to be rejected.

TABLE 2.4: OLS REGRESSION OF PROPERTY RETURNS ON SIGNALLING VARIABLES

	I (YIELD)					II (TOTRET)					III (YIELD)					IV (TOTRET)				
	Coef	Std. Err	t-stat	Prob		Coef	Std. Err	t-stat	Prob		Coef	Std. Err	t-stat	Prob		Coef	Std. Err	t-stat	Prob	
C	0.00	0.09	0.00	1.00		0.00	0.09	0.00	1.00		0.00	0.08	0.02	0.99		0.00	0.09	-	0.99	
DILUTION	0.30	0.09	3.27	0.00	(a)	0.00	0.09	0.01	0.99		0.30	0.09	3.24	0.00	(a)	-	0.09	-	0.83	
DILU-											-	0.09	-	0.81		-	0.09	-	0.36	
IBREPU	-	0.09	-	0.88		-	0.10	-	0.16		0.01	0.10	0.09	0.93		-	0.10	-	0.21	
IBREPU(c)NUMIPO											0.06	0.10	0.63	0.53		-	0.09	-	0.42	
NUMIPO											0.11	0.08	1.27	0.21		-	0.08	-	0.94	
UNDERPRICING1	0.27	0.09	2.90	0.00	(a)	0.16	0.09	1.71	0.09	(c)	0.25	0.09	2.95	0.00	(a)	0.16	0.09	1.76	0.08	(c)
UNDERPRIC-											-	0.08	-	0.11		-	0.07	-	0.04	(b)
Number of obs.	120					120					120					120				
F-statistic	4.69					1.67					2.92					2.11				
Prob. F-statistic	0.00					0.17					0.01					0.06				
Adj. R-squared	0.14					0.01					0.14					0.02				
Ramsey RESET test	0.23					0.39					0.83					0.35				
Max. VIF	1.02					1.02					1.04					1.04				

Notes: (c),(b), and (a) indicates significance at the 10, 5, and 1% level

IBREPU and IBREPU(c)NUMIPO is insignificantly related in all four model specifications. Under the assumption that IPO firms choose their underwriter (Titman and Trueman (1986), Habib and Ljungqvist (2001)), this result lets one suspect that IPO firms accept higher costs associated with prestigious underwriters for other reasons than for certification purposes.

Regarding the notion that prestigious investment banks only underwrite high quality IPOs (Chemmanur and Fulghieri (1994)), the insignificant relationships with market return measures lets one suspect that underwriters do not consider real estate market prospects when evaluating firm quality. Overall, investment bank reputation seems to have no signalling power for industry prospects and thus H1c needs to be rejected.

2.4.2.2 OLS regression of underpricing on ex ante uncertainty variables

This section analyses whether general and real estate specific ex ante uncertainty proxies have an effect on initial day returns in order to confirm the signalling models' implicitly assumed presence of information asymmetry. The dependent variables employed in models I and II in Table 2.5 are initial IPO returns measured over a one and a five day period respectively. Overall, both model specifications are significant and the RESET test shows that results are unlikely to be biased by specification failures. Adjusted R^2 values are, compared to other underpricing studies with similar sample sizes, relatively high, which gives a first indication that ex ante uncertainty variables seem to have explanatory power among European property companies.

The results of model I show that the coefficient of GROWTHPREMIUM is positive and significant at the 1% level. This implies that, as expected, companies with higher uncertain growth opportunities seem to be more risky and investors require higher underpricing to be compensated for higher risk.

DEBT is negatively related to UNDERPRICING1 and only closely fails to reach significance at the 10% level. In line with James and Wier (1990), Habib and Ljungqvist (2001) and Schenone (2004), higher debt levels seem to reduce information asymmetry as more levered companies are expected to be of higher quality because the firm deliberately accepts higher bankruptcy risk. Similarly, DEAL is also, as hypothesised by Beatty and Ritter (1986) and Brounen and Eichholtz (2002), negatively related with underpricing because larger companies are less exposed to risky growth projects and benefit from better management. Finally, the coefficient of VOLATILITY is also, as expected, positive and significant at the 1% level and thereby finally confirms that company specific risk is a major determinant of underpricing levels.

This result shows that capital market participants investing in European property companies are exposed to investment risk which is similar to the investment risk of industrial company IPOs. In addition, this result also imply that the low under underpricing levels of US REITs documented by Ling and Ryngaert (1997) and Buttimer et al. (2005), among others, can be explained by the reduced valuation uncertainty associated with the US REIT regime rather than by any lower risk characteristics associated with the asset class real estate.

TABLE 2.5: OLS REGRESSION OF FIRST DAY RETURNS ON EX ANTE UNCERTAINTY VARIABLES

	I (UNDERPRICING1)					II (UNDERPRICING5)				
	Coef	Std. Err	t-stat	Prob		Coef	Std. Err	t-stat	Prob	
C	0.21	0.09	2.38	0.02	(b)	0.24	0.12	1.98	0.05	(c)
DEAL	-0.01	0.01	-2.21	0.03	(b)	-0.01	0.01	-1.84	0.07	(c)
DEBT	-0.04	0.03	-1.41	0.16		-0.07	0.05	-1.35	0.18	
GROWTHPRE-	0.05	0.02	2.68	0.01	(a)	0.05	0.02	2.14	0.03	(b)
NOPORT	0.01	0.02	0.40	0.69		0.03	0.02	1.30	0.20	
PIPELINE	0.01	0.02	0.37	0.71		0.01	0.03	0.28	0.78	
TYPOSPEC	-0.01	0.01	-0.78	0.44		-0.01	0.02	-0.69	0.49	
VOLATILITY	0.01	0.00	2.95	0.00	(a)	0.01	0.00	2.41	0.02	(b)
Number of obs.	120					120				
F-statistic	4.55					3.41				
Prob. F-statistic	0.00					0.00				
Adj. R-squared	0.12					0.09				
Ramsey RESET test	0.23					0.29				
Max. VIF	2.11					2.11				

Notes: (c),(b), and (a) indicates significance at the 10, 5, and 1% level

Although the general ex ante uncertainty proxies show a significant relationship with IPO underpricing, interestingly, none of the real estate related ex ante uncertainty proxies do. This further supports the notion that issuing firms do not employ signals to convince investors about the firm's quality based on individual firm characteristics but rather to communicate their expectations about industry prospects. The intuition is as follows: If firms have no initial property portfolio, which is an intuitive proxy for valuation uncertainty risk, but do not use underpricing as signal to overcome this uncertainty as evidenced by the insignificant coefficient of NOPORT in Table 2.5, this either shows that underpricing is not used as investor risk compensation or IPO firms do not signal firm specific characteristics but industry prospects. Consequently, if property specific information as measured by NOPORT is not related to UNDERPRICING but to YIELD, as already stated in subsection 2.4.1, one might interpret this as further evidence that underpricing is used for signalling industry prospects rather than for signalling individual firm quality.

2.4.2.3 Robustness test: OLS regression with variations in variable definitions

This section presents the results of various robustness checks which have been conducted in order to confirm the validity of the results. These include checks for the general sensitivity of the results to variations in variable definitions of property return performance measures and of IPO signals as well as particular sensitivity checks to rationalise the stark discrepancy between the well fitted YIELD model specification and the poorly fitted TOTRET model specification.

Table 2.6 shows the regression results based on the following variable changes: First, UNDERPRICING1 is replaced by UNDERPRICING5 which measures initial IPO returns over a five day period. Further, the enlarged share capital ratio now includes the number of shares of the over-allotment option (DILUTIONGREEN). Finally, investment bank reputation now categorises all underwriters that have offices in more than one country (IBREPUCOUN). Models I and II show that the results are not substantially different compared to the results from subsection 2.4.2.1. Thus, it seems reasonable to argue that the relationships are valid and not sensitive to changes in variable definitions.

To more thoroughly examine potential reasons for the contrasting model fits described in subsection 2.4.2.1, variations of YIELD and TOTRET definitions are tested too. First it is examined whether the stark decrease of UK total return figures explain the discrepancy of the two models' fit. UK total return reached with 18% record highs in 2006 but then dropped to negative -3% in 2007. However, a re-estimation of the regression models without UK focused property companies reveals that the results remain unchanged. Further, YIELD and TOTRET are calculated with average values of the IPO year and the year after the IPO year. However, results do not change significantly. Lastly, total return figures are lagged by 6 months and by 12 months in order to control for potentially lagged appraisal values (Edelstein and Quan (2006)). Again, results do not change, i.e. the regression model fit for the YIELD specification remains strong whereas the model fit for the TOTRET specification remains particularly weak.

A final possibility that might explain the model's differences is that the majority of sample firms analysed pursue a business strategy that favours income generating investments over appreciating capital investments. Gerbich et al. (1999) note that investment firms invest in cash flow generating properties whereas real estate development firms rather depend on properties with strong capital appreciation potential. The authors use a rent to earnings ratio in order to distinguish between property investment and property development companies and find the latter to have significantly lower long-run stock returns following the IPO. The authors explain their finding with the higher valuation uncertainty of development companies. Unfortunately, rent data is not available for many sample firms. Thus, admission documents have been analysed with regard to the issuing firms' description of their investment strategy. Companies that describe their main business strategy as 'income investing' are assigned investment status whereas companies that generate profits by development activities or by frequently trading properties are assigned development status. A dummy variable (DEVELOPMENT) is created and is included in the model specifications of table Table 2.6.

TABLE 2.6: ROBUSTNESS CHECKS

	I (YIELD)					II (TOTRET)				
	Coef	**Std. Err**	**t-stat**	**Prob**		**Coef**	**Std. Err**	**t-stat**	**Prob**	
C	0.00	0.08	0.03	0.98		-	0.09	-	0.95	
DEVELOPMENT	0.16	0.08	1.95	0.05	(c)	-	0.10	-	0.75	
DILUTIONGREEN	0.29	0.09	3.28	0.00	(a)	-	0.10	-	0.71	
DILUTIONGREEN(c)NUMIPO	-	0.09	-	0.70		-	0.10	-	0.59	
IBREPUCOUN	0.03	0.09	0.35	0.73		-	0.10	-	0.22	
IBREPUCOUN(c)NUMIPO	0.06	0.09	0.68	0.50		-	0.09	-	0.31	
NUMIPO	0.10	0.08	1.18	0.24		-	0.09	-	0.89	
UNDERPRICING5	0.20	0.10	1.99	0.05	(b)	0.19	0.09	2.07	0.04	(b)
UNDERPRICING5(c)NUMIPO	-	0.08	-	0.07	(c)	-	0.07	-	0.74	
Number of obs.	120					120				
F-statistic	2.46					1.91				
Prob. F-statistic	0.01					0.31				
Adj. R-squared	0.15					0.00				
Ramsey RESET test	0.40					0.39				
Max. VIF	1.14					1.14				

Notes: (c),(b), and (a) indicates significance at the 10, 5, and 1% level

The results show that the coefficient of DEVELOPMENT is positive and statistical significant in the YIELD specification but not in the TOTRET specification. This finding unexpectedly shows that development companies, compared to investment companies, more carefully align their investment decisions with the prospects of their target real estate markets, at least on a yield basis. A rationalisation of this finding might be that development companies are more dependent on general industry performance whereas investment companies are, in line with the notion of the resource based view, better able to create value added via superior management of their investments. This argumentation would reduce the power of the industry signalling argument however.

The results of model II show that the DEVELOPMENT coefficient is not significantly related to TOTRET. Referring to the fact that YIELD and TOTRET are both designed to measure real estate market performance and that development companies are dependent on capital appreciation which is included in the total return measure, the insignificant coefficient of DEVELOPMENT lends further support to the assumed incapability of total return measures to accurately reflect direct real estate performance.

2.5 Conclusion

The goal of the present study is to analyse whether IPO signals reveal proprietary information about the prospects of an issuing firms' underlying industry. The study's motivation stems from the ambiguous results of previous empirical studies that let one infer that company specific performance characteristics might be a weak dependent variable to use when analysing the signalling hypotheses proposed by Allen and Faulhaber (1989), Grinblatt and Hwang (1989), and Welch (1989). Further, Jain and Kini (2006) note that IPOs from one industry tend to cluster in time which implies that pioneering IPOs must signal some information that let follower IPOs either accelerate or rethink their issuing decision. As the latter strand of research proposes some relation between IPO signals and industry, no study so far has measured the relationship of IPO signals and industry quality. The common problem of finding a suitable proxy for industry quality is alleviated by using performance measures of direct property investments in various real estate markets within Europe.

The first part of the empirical analysis regresses real estate market performance, measured as yields and total returns, on variables which have been found to have signalling power in previous research, i.e. initial IPO returns, the degree of dilution due to the issuance of new shares and underwriter reputation. The results show that underpricing and dilution have a positive impact on twelve months post IPO property yields whereas underwriter reputation has no explanatory power. Whereas the model fit of the yield specification is relatively strong, R^2 values drop significantly when the same signalling variables are regressed on total return figures. Nevertheless, underpricing sustains its significant impact, confirming its expected signalling function. Results also show that dilution is not used as a signal but as financing avenue to meet issuing firms' capital needs. Underwriter reputation is generally unrelated to real estate market performance. Robustness checks confirm that insignificant results for total return specification remain after controlling for different measurement periods, which lends either support to the notion that appraisal based returns measures are biased in general or that property companies base investment decisions on yields and not on total returns. The empirical section also analyses the degree of information asymmetry at the time of the IPO. Firm specific ex ante uncertainty variables show a significant relationship with initial IPO returns whereas real estate specific ex ante uncertainty proxies do not. This result shows that capital market participants investing in European property companies are exposed to investment risk which is similar to the investment risk of industrial company IPOs.

Overall, results imply that the degree of IPO underpricing signals information about the prospects of the issuing firm's underlying industry, i.e. real estate market performance. A direction for possible future research could be an empirical analysis which examines the relation of IPO signals and industry performance in other industries which thereby would shed further light on the question whether the results of this study are real estate specific or can be generalised.

3 LONG-RUN IPO PERFORMANCE, MARKET TIMING, AND REAL ESTATE MARKET TRANSPARENCY

3.1 INTRODUCTION

The short-run stock price performance of newly listed property companies shows return patterns that are significantly more moderate than general findings of cross-industry studies. This observation might explain why most initial public offering (IPO) analyses explicitly exclude property IPOs. However, when the long-run cross-industry studies exclude property IPOs and when the short-run returns of property IPOs are different compared to other industries, what can we expect from the long-run performance of property IPOs? Remarkably little is known about this feature, and little evidence from still developing European real estate markets hardly exists. Given the increasing number of European property companies seeking access to capital markets, the long-run performance of IPOs from the real estate sector is of crucial importance.

Overall, evidence regarding long-run IPO behaviour is mixed. Ritter (1991) shows in his seminal paper for a large sample of industrial IPOs that the *relative* performance of issuing firms is negative, i.e., issuing firms underperform a benchmark, but the degree of underperformance is subject to substantial variations across industries and across time. More precisely, Ritter (1991) provides evidence that those IPOs issued in times of general high issuing activity tend to be of poorer quality, as compared to those IPOs issued during times of low issuing activity. In contrast, Buttimer et al. (2005) focuses particularly on real estate investment trusts (REITs) and find that the relative long-run performance is *not* worse, as compared to a sample of matching firms during a three-year post-IPO period. In addition, they document only small differences in the quality of firms that issue in a hot market and those that issue in a cold market. Wang et al. (1992) suggest that REIT IPOs behave differently from industrial IPOs because REITs hold special assets, i.e., properties. Since there is evidence that the risk-return relationship of real estate investments is different from stocks in general, real estate holdings may explain the difference in IPO performance. Thus, is it true that real estate companies are a different species? First doubts are casted by Chan et al. (2001), who show that real estate companies in Hong Kong have first day returns that are comparable to those of industrial companies. However, they are not able to provide a rationale that explains the findings. A thorough understanding of why these variations in IPO performance patterns arise is still missing. Therefore, this study follows the suggestion of Chan et al. (2001) to explore possible explanations of the abnormal IPO performance of real estate companies by analysing a hand-collected data set of European property companies (EPCs).

Thus far, the literature on long-run IPO performance of real estate companies is scarce and concentrates primarily on companies operating in highly mature and established real estate markets such as in the US (Wang et al. (1992), Ling and Ryngaert (1997), Buttimer et al. (2005)), Australia (Dimovski and Brooks (2006)) or Hong-Kong (Chan et al. (2001)). Hartzell et al. (2005) particularly take advantage of the relative transparency of the US real estate market in order to document how the time-varying supply and demand for the underlying assets influence real estate firms' decisions to go public. As main finding they illustrate that IPO volume and initial day returns are related to the state of the underlying real estate market but, consistent with Buttimer et al. (2005), there is no direct evidence of variations in firm quality across the IPO cycle. Hartzell et al. (2005) attribute their findings (i) to REITs' relative transparency, which helps the market to have a higher confidence in its estimate of a REIT IPO's value, and (ii) to the REIT management's ability to time the issuing with times of increased demand for real estate investments.

However, what can we expect from property companies without a highly regulated REIT regime operating in real estate markets characterised by a lower degree of transparency - for example, countries in Central and Eastern Europe (CEE)? Remarkably, the impact of varying degrees of real estate market transparency has been neglected thus far in explaining divergences in IPO performance. To close this research gap, the focus of this paper is to develop an understanding of the impact of underlying real estate market transparency on long-run IPO performance. The reasoning is as follows: It is assumed that the finding of Buttimer et al. (2005) of no long-run underperformance and of Hartzell et al. (2005) of no differences in firm quality among IPO cycles is a result for the US real estate market's high transparency. High market transparency (i) allows investors to rather precisely analyse the issuing firm's prospects and (ii) allows the issuing firms' management to concretely forecast supply and demand for real estate. As Europe is characterised by highly heterogeneous real estate markets, one can expect, with a lesser degree of market transparency, precise decision making to be limited. This higher degree of uncertainty might induce less rational valuation levels. According to Aggarwal and Rivoli (1990), bounded rationality leads to the emergence of fads that cause investors to be over-optimistic about the prospects of newly listed firms. Consequently, initial trading prices are overvalued. Loughran et al. (1994) argue that firms can predict when over-optimism is most likely to occur and intentionally take advantage of this window of opportunity. Over time, initial overvaluation is revised, and long-run underperformance develops. Thus, with a lesser degree of transparency, investors are expected to have difficulties performing proper investment analysis due to, for example, language boundaries or a lack of knowledge of local particularities. On behalf of the issuing firm, with a lesser degree of transparency, managers are expected to be over-optimistic about the value of future investment opportunities that, in the long run, emerge as negative net present value projects.

The sample of EPCs is particularly suitable for analysing the hypotheses stated above: First, Europe is characterised by heterogeneous real estate markets that show a broad variation in transparency needed to distinguish between high and low transparency regimes. Second, the strong increase in EPC issuings during the years 2005 to 2007 makes it possible to distinguish in the period of 1997 and 2007 between hot and cold IPO phases in order to analyse whether market transparency has an impact on firm quality across IPO cycles.

The results show that the supposed influence of market transparency on market timing and IPO performance can be at least partly confirmed. EPCs have timed their IPO to coincide with times of favourable market conditions and with times of positive exogenous shocks. We also show that with a lesser degree of market transparency, investor over-optimism is more likely to develop than among capital market participants investing in transparent markets. In contrast, the results do not support the idea that timing occurs due to manager over-optimism. In general, EPCs are characterised by a high degree of long-run underperformance. Companies that used their informational advantage to time their issue with the presence of sentiment investors, significantly underperform. In contrast, results weakly show that firms which timed the equity issuing with a positive external exogenous shock outperform the benchmark over a 24-month aftermarket period, suggesting that the management is correctly anticipating growth opportunities. Robustness checks confirm the validity of the results.

By analysing the long-run performance of EPCs, this paper contributes to the extant real estate finance literature by shedding light on the ongoing debate regarding whether real estate is significantly less risky than industrial companies are. In terms of IPO investing, the results suggest that the special risk-return profile has *no* positive impact on the IPO performance of real estate companies. Instead, EPC's IPO performance is comparable to long-run IPO returns of industrial companies.

The rest of the paper is organised as follows. Section 3.2 first reviews the literature for cross-industry and real-estate-related empirical findings of the long-run underperformance phenomenon, followed by the development of the hypotheses. Section 3.3 covers the research design, which includes a justification of the sample selection, an explanation of the chosen methodology and a definition of the measurement of the chosen variables. Empirical results are presented in section 3.4, which includes the descriptive statistics, followed by negative binomial and OLS regressions, and ends finally with robustness checks of the results. Section 0 concludes.

3.2 Literature review and hypothesis development

3.2.1 Evidence of the long-run underperformance phenomenon

A number of studies have examined the long-run returns of IPOs in various countries. Many of these analyses are summarised by Jenkinson and Ljungqvist (2001, table 2.2). Ritter (1991) analyses a sample of 1,526 companies that went public in the US between 1975 and 1984 and demonstrates that these companies underperform a peer-group portfolio over a period of three years. He shows that small issues and young companies, which tend to achieve the highest first-day returns, also generate the lowest benchmark-adjusted returns in the long-run. Schuster (2003) reported significant long-run underperformance for seven continental European countries for IPOs from 1988-1998. For all seven countries (France, Germany, Italy, the Netherlands, Spain, Sweden and Switzerland), he reports negative 36-month cumulative market-adjusted returns varying from -12% in Germany to -42% in Italy.

Wang et al. (1992) examine REIT long-term performance for the period of 1971-1988 and find significant overpricing due to a lack of informed investors. Ling and Ryngaert (1997) report that US REIT IPOs outperform the market over the 100-day- and 200-day-interval post-IPO, respectively. Buttimer et al. (2005) analyse monthly returns of REIT IPOs in the US between 1980 and 2001 in a Fama and French factor model and find no long-run underperformance. Brounen and Eichholtz (2002) study 54 British, French and Swedish property companies and report that British and French companies only marginally underperform their benchmark over a 12-month period subsequent to the IPO. Swedish IPOs outperform significantly. Gerbich et al. (1999) focus their sample on 101 property development and property investment firms and present, for the latter, no significant long-run underperformance over a 36-month post-IPO period.

In sum, the empirical evidence reveals that investors in industrial IPOs have faced significant long-run underperformance, while results regarding real estate companies are mixed. Most REIT studies do not detect any long-run underperformance. Sparse literature for property companies has shown that long-run performance is more comparable to industrial IPO performance. This casts doubt on the special risk-return relationship to be responsible for long-run real estate IPO returns.

3.2.2 Investor sentiment, exogenous shocks and market timing

Managers prefer to take firms public when market conditions are favourable. As a consequence, in a bullish market, the number of IPOs tends to increase whereas in a bearish market IPO activity tends to decline. These hot and cold IPO phases develop and end periodically, as described by Ibbotson and

Jaffe (1975) and Ibbotson et al. (1988, 1994). European evidence on this phenomenon is provided by Gajewski and Gresse (2006), who use IPO statistics from 15 European countries from 1995 to 2004. Overall, studies consistently report that there are pronounced cycles in the number of offerings and in the size of deal volumes. However, Lowry and Schwert (2002, p. 1173) state that "we have little understanding of the factors that drive these fluctuations." Boutron et al. (2007) rationalise the development of hot IPO phases as being the results of favourable market conditions that make the placement of stocks easier, reduce the risk of failure of an IPO and exhibit overall higher securities prices. However, predominantly hot IPOs show long-run underperformance, which strongly challenges the idea of informationally efficient markets and has led to a variety of theoretical models that attempt to explain this phenomenon.

One major focus of research specifically relaxes the assumption of investor rationality and claims that long-run underperformance is the result of *irrational investors*. Aggarwal and Rivoli (1990), for instance, argue that there are fads in the IPO market, with investors initially being over-optimistic about the prospects of newly listed companies and bidding up initial trading prices beyond fair value. Similar arguments are provided by Ritter (1991), who argues that investors, in particular, tend to be overly optimistic about an IPO firm's earning potential. Empirical evidence by Mikkelson et al. (1997) further supports this notion: The significant long-run underperformance for a sample of 283 companies that failed to sustain their pre-listing levels of operating performance indicates that investors were surprised by the decline in profitability. Brav and Gompers (1997) show that underperformance is concentrated among small, non-venture-backed IPOs, which are more likely to be owned by retail investors who may be more easily influenced by fads.

In general, this strand of research argues that the presence of market investors can be either the result of general over-optimism or the result of external shocks. Both notions and their consequences for long-run IPO performance are discussed in the following paragraphs.

Timing due to over-optimism and its consequences for long-run performance: Loughran et al. (1994) argue that firms may even be able to *predict* when over-optimism is most likely to occur and intentionally take advantage of this window of opportunity. The argument which is supported by the curious coincidence of years in which many firms go public and overall investor sentiment is high. This coincidence implies that firms seem to time their flotations in periods during which particularly favourable offer prices can be obtained. Over time, more information becomes available, leading to a correction in the initial overvaluation, and, in the end, results in poor long-run performance. While Loughran et al. (1994) derive their argument from observing previous empirical studies, Schultz (2003) presents a formal model that provides a semi-rational explanation of firms' ability to time the market. He argues that firms go public when they expect to receive a high price for their shares. As a result, more companies go public at peak valuations. This process continues until the markets suddenly fall and listing activity dries up. Schultz (2003) documents also that there are more offerings at peak valuations than at lower prices. This is what he calls "pseudo market timing". The clustering of new issues during an (over)heated market leads to underperformance of the last large group of IPOs. Measuring the long-run return of the entire IPO population using equal weights, the high volume periods will carry a larger weight, resulting in underperformance of the whole sample.

Evidence for the market timing hypothesis is extensive. Ritter (1984), Lerner (1994) and Baker and Wurgler (2000) document that IPOs cluster when equity valuations are high and employ private financings when values are lower, suggesting firms' ability to correctly use favourable windows of opportunity. Further support is provided by Rajan and Servaes (1997), who analyse IPO firms' pre and post earnings and long-term growth prospects. They find more US companies going public when analysts are particularly over-confident about recent IPOs in the same industries. Nevertheless, long-run underperformance as a result of initial over-valuation is mixed. In line with Schultz's (2003) prediction, Rajan and Servaes (1997) show that IPOs with low forecast growth rates subsequently outperform IPOs with high forecast growth rates. This is consistent with the reports of Ritter (1991) and Loughran and Ritter (1995), who note that subsequent stock performance is significantly lower for companies going public in hot markets. Hot issues tend to be of poorer quality, implying that particular bad quality companies exploit times of over-optimism. However, Jenkinson and Ljungqvist (2001) doubt the persistence of issuing firms' ability to predict time variation in investor sentiment. In fact, Helwege and Liang (2004) find little difference between firms that issue in a hot market and those that issue in a cold market.

Timing due to external shocks and its consequences for long-run performance: Another body of literature argues that firms are able to predict when exogenous shocks are most likely to occur and intentionally take advantage of this window of opportunity. In previous research, several economy-wide and industry factors have been identified as drivers of a private firm's demand for public equity and, in turn, IPO volume. As an example of industry factors, Pastor and Veronesi (2005) name the arrival of innovations, and Choe et al. (1993) provide evidence that more firms issue seasoned equity if overall economic conditions are better, an example of economy-wide factors. Additionally, Lowry (2003) shows that the capital demand of private firms is an important driver of IPO volume. However, Loughran et al. (1994) and Breinlinger and Glogova (2002), using Swedish and European IPOs, respectively, cannot detect any impact of the business cycle on the IPO cycle. Yung et al. (2008) argue that the key features of hot IPO markets follow from time variations in adverse selection. A positive shock to the economy will improve investment opportunities that, in turn, raise the price at which a fixed cohort of firms can sell securities. Higher prices increase the temptation of bad firms to pool. Consequently, as the IPO market heats up, bad quality companies may go public due to the positive shock (e.g., strong increase in demand for real estate), resulting in a decline in the quality of average issuers. At equilibrium, more bad firms do pool, and on average, poor long-run underperformance is the result.

The hot market of 1998–2000 may be a good illustration of the evolution of issuer quality over the IPO market cycle. According to Ljungqvist and Wilhelm (2003), 62% of firms listing in the United States in 1997 have 12-month track records of earnings; by 1999, this ratio has fallen to just 24%. In contrast, Buttimer et al. (2005) show that there was no discernable difference in the quality of REIT IPO firms, as measured by returns and sensitivities to economic risk factors, which entered the market during a hot IPO phase from those that existed prior to the hot IPO phase. The findings are interpreted in a way that this behaviour is the result of an increased economic opportunity which provides growth opportunities for the whole REIT industry, not only for IPOs. In addition, Hartzell et al. (2005) specifically examine the quality of REIT IPO firms in "hot" and "cold" markets. Similar to Buttimer et al. (2005), lagged IPO proceeds are related to future sector-wide asset growth and to capacity utilisation. These results collectively suggest that REIT IPO cycles are driven by the demand for investment capital rather than adverse selection. While this result is consistent with demand for underlying assets driving IPO cycles, there is no difference in operating performance (their measure of issuer quality) between hot-market and cold-market issuers. Buttimer et al. (2005) conclude that REITs appear to raise money in advance of growth in the real estate sector.

In summary, empirical evidence provides no consistent findings in terms of the issuer quality during IPO cycles. However, the models and empirical findings described above imply that companies are able to time their IPO by intentionally exploiting a window of opportunity in the form of the sentiment of investors or expected growth opportunities. Long-run underperformance develops if investors' sentiment and the potential of growth opportunities are based on over-optimism, and over time, initial overvaluation is corrected, resulting in long-run underperformance.

As stated above, previous real estate IPO studies have analysed companies whose investment focus was one of the most mature and most transparent real estate markets in the world (Buttimer et al. (2005) – US, Chan et al. (2001) – Hong Kong, Ling and Ryangaert (1997) – US, etc.). Consequently, investors had only few difficulties in deriving a fair value of the company because they comparably could easy obtain information regarding prospects of property yields and future rent development. In contrast, the common European real estate markets are characterised by highly heterogeneous national markets that may hinder rational evaluation and decision making of investors or firm management. For the sake of brevity, IPOs of property companies with (less) transparent target real estate investment markets are termed (in)transparent companies interchangeable throughout the rest of the paper.

Thus, it is expected that with a decreasing degree of transparency, investors might have difficulties performing proper investment analysis e.g., due to national particularities or language boundaries. Thus, managers are able to exploit their informational advantage and specifically issue equity when the market overvalues the IPO firm's assets. This leads to the first hypothesis analysed:

H1a: Investor over-optimism is negatively related to issuing activity in transparent markets

Conversely, it can be argued that managers only issue equity when industry prospects are favourable. Assuming, as hypothesised above, that market intransparency negatively affects adequate evaluation by managers, it can be expected that an over-optimism proxy for managers is positively related to the number of IPOs in less transparent markets.

H1b: Manager over-optimism is negatively related to issuing activity in transparent markets

As H1a and H1b only test whether over-optimism is a function of real estate market transparency and whether it leads to market timing in general. It remains the question whether market timers are, on average, of lower quality, and whether the lack of market transparency leads to pooling of poor quality companies, i.e., companies that take advantage of market timing in order to exploit over-optimistic expectations. Therefore, we expect that long-run IPO performance is negatively related to market timing proxies because disclosure requirements of publicly listed companies will reveal previously private information which helps market investors to derive the true value of the firm which leads to a revision of a potential over-valuation at IPO (Loughran et al. (1994) and Yung et al. (2008)).

H2: Large market timing proxies are negatively related to long-run IPO performance for a lesser degree of market transparency

In addition, it is expected that, with a decreasing degree of real estate market transparency, the existence of sentiment investors or the presence of a positive exogenous shock increases the likelihood of poor quality issues as management either uses its information advantage to exploit investor over-optimism or as management itself is over-optimistic about investment opportunities. Again, assuming both that poor quality companies underperform the benchmark in the IPO aftermarket to a larger degree than good quality companies and that precise decision making is limited with a decreasing degree of real estate market transparency, proxies for investor sentiment and for investment opportunities are expected to be negatively related to long-run performance.

H3a: Large investor optimism variables are negatively related to IPO long-run performance for a lesser degree of market transparency

H3b: Large manager optimism variables are negatively related to IPO long-run performance for a lesser degree of market transparency

In sum, the hypotheses developed above are designed to rationalise why previous real estate IPO studies have found no long-run underperformance, a phenomenon that is rather common among industrial IPOs. It is argued that, with an increasing degree of market in-transparency, adequate IPO evaluation and financial decision making becomes increasingly difficult, and over-optimism is more likely to develop. This allows poor quality companies to issue equity above their true value. Consequently, initial valuation is too high, and long-run stock performance is expected to underperform the benchmark. Thus far, no study has analysed this reasoning, although empirical research has convincingly shown that real estate IPO performance is different, but has been unable to analyse the reasons.

3.2.3 Alternative mechanisms explaining long-run underperformance

One major criticism of the over-optimism hypothesis is the *persistent irrational* behaviour of investors and issuers. This idea not only challenges the efficient market hypothesis but also raises two intuitive questions, as summarised by Jenkinson and Ljungqvist (2001, p. 152): "(i) why don't investors learn from past mistakes? and (ii) why don't issuers take full advantage of investor's over-optimism by raising offer prices until there is no longer a price jump?" To also control for a rational explanation of the long-run underperformance phenomenon as proposed by Miller (1977), we test for investor heterogeneity. Miller (1977) argues that investors have heterogeneous expectations regarding the true value of a firm at the IPO. Among these investors, there are some investors particularly optimistic about the future growth prospects of the IPO firm. It is this minority of over-optimistic investors that initially sets market prices above fundamental values in a market with restricted short selling. Over time, as the variance of opinions decreases and short-selling constraints are loosened, the marginal investor's valuation will converge towards the mean valuation, and its price will fall. In the end, more pessimistic investors will enter the market, resulting in a stock price decline. This argument works better when the free float is small and not too many investors are required. This is consistent with the drop in share price at the end of the lockup period (when more public shares become available to the public), as documented by Bradley et al. (2001), Field and Hanka (2001) and Brav and Gompers (2003).

Miller's prediction of a negative relationship of long-run performance and initial extent of divergence of opinion has found extensive empirical support. Krigman et al. (1999) approximate divergence of opinion by calculating the ratio of sell-initiated, large block trading volume to total volume traded on the first day in what they call the flipping ratio. IPOs that are flipped more on the first trading day underperform low-flipping IPOs over the next 12 months. Aggarwal and Conroy (2000) argue that time-to-first-trade serves as another proxy for divergence of opinion. Empirical evidence for this hypothesis is provided by Houge et al. (2001), who show that late-opening IPOs significantly underperform over the subsequent three years. Further evidence is provided by Rajan and Servaes (1997), who document that more firms go public at times when analysts are overly optimistic. U.S. firms perform poorly over the first four years after their IPO, when analysts are more optimistic about their long-term growth potential.

All these findings are consistent with Miller's hypothesis that diverging opinions are the result of heterogeneous expectations of a company's value and its future growth prospects. Expectations can diverge when there is no clarity about the underlying firm characteristics that are used in the valuation process. A reduction in investors' asymmetric information of a firm's value reduces the heterogeneity of investor opinions and, thus, narrows the gap between diverging opinions. As a result, less long-run underperformance can be expected, if Miller's explanation holds true. Thus, proxies for information asymmetry are expected to be negatively related to long-run IPO performance.

H4a: Large information asymmetry proxies are negatively related to long-run IPO performance

In addition, the literature suggests that signalling mechanisms are often used as a mean to overcome information asymmetry. For example, a firm might compensate large information asymmetries in the form of valuation uncertainty with strong signals. Therefore, companies with large signalling proxies are expected to have better long-run performance.

H4b: Large signalling proxies are positively related to long-run IPO performance

The measurement and the reasoning of the asymmetric information and signalling proxies employed in this study to test Miller's (1977) hypothesis is described in subsection 3.3.3.3.

3.3 Research design

3.3.1 Sample selection and data source

The sample contains IPOs of European property companies from 1997 to 2007, where European property companies are defined as operating real estate companies with a property-backed business model and with geographic investment foci covering Western Europe (Austria, Belgium, France, Germany, Italy, Portugal, Spain, Switzerland, UK), the Nordic countries (Denmark, Finland, Norway, Sweden) and Central and Eastern Europe (CEE) (Bulgaria, Croatia, Czech Republic, Estonia, Hungary, Latvia, Lithuania, Poland, Romania, Russia, Serbia, Slovakia, Slovenia, Ukraine). The reasoning for using this particular data set is as follows: in order to analyse the impact of market in-transparency, three sampling requirements have to be fulfilled: (1) different degrees of transparency have to be present in the national sample markets, (2) hot and cold IPO phases should be clearly identifiable, and (3) post-IPO measurement period should be sufficiently long.

(1) Transparency: Transparency of the underlying real estate market must be measurable. The above definition of European property companies already gives an intuitive overview of the sample's heterogeneity in terms of real estate market transparency. In addition, Jones Lang LaSalle annually publishes since 1999 its Global Transparency Index study that analyses five categories (performance measurement, market fundamentals, listed vehicles, legal and regulatory environment and transaction process) to measure market transparency of real estate markets. We use this data of cross-border market transparency as objective measures.

(2) Identification of hot IPO market phase: It is important that the sample falls within an IPO wave in order to clearly indentify a hot IPO phase. IPOs of property companies in Europe were a rare event before 1994. In fact, the Dealogic database only returned 3 IPOs between 1989 and 1993. Issuing activity increased slightly during 1994 and 2003 whereas the years from 2005 until 2007 were characterised by a boom of real estate IPOs. More specifically, the number of IPOs increased by 65% from 139 listed companies in 2003 to 230 listed companies in 2007. Thus, the sample clearly includes a hot and a cold IPO phase as illustrated in Figure 3.1.

(3) Length of post-IPO measurement period: Sufficient data must be available to calculate long-run returns. Literature proposes time periods to calculate long-run aftermarket returns ranging from 12 months to 36 months. Since the majority of the sample firms went public between 2005 and 2007, a 36-month aftermarket analysis period would reduce the sample too much. Therefore, 24 months aftermarket IPO returns are used as the main dependent variable of interest.

The target sample contains 242 IPOs which represent all European companies classified by the SIC code for real estate companies (SIC 65) of the Dealogic database. From this preliminary sample, several companies had to be excluded because company and/or stock market characteristics did not match the definition of a European property company as described above. More specifically, excluded firms from the sample include (1) companies with investment focus outside of Western Europe, the Nordic countries or CEE, (2) companies with no property-backed business model (such as real estate service companies or real estate agents), and (3) companies with no information on operating business and/or stock prices. The latter represents the largest group of excluded companies mainly because double checking Dealogic data with IPO prospectuses and company press releases revealed significant discrepancies. As the limited data availability, reliability, and comparability can be due to large differences in accounting practices, tax regimes, and disclosure requirements of the 20 different legislative systems in which the sample firms operate, we decided to only include IPOs for which the admission documents are available in either language of German, English, Spanish or French, offer prices and first day closing prices have been double checked and stock price information is available on Datastream. By these control steps, any biases due to local disclosure standards or accounting practices are expected to be minimised. Consequently, the final data sample consists of 141 IPOs.

FIGURE 3.1: THREE-MONTH MOVING AVERAGE OF IPO VOLUME

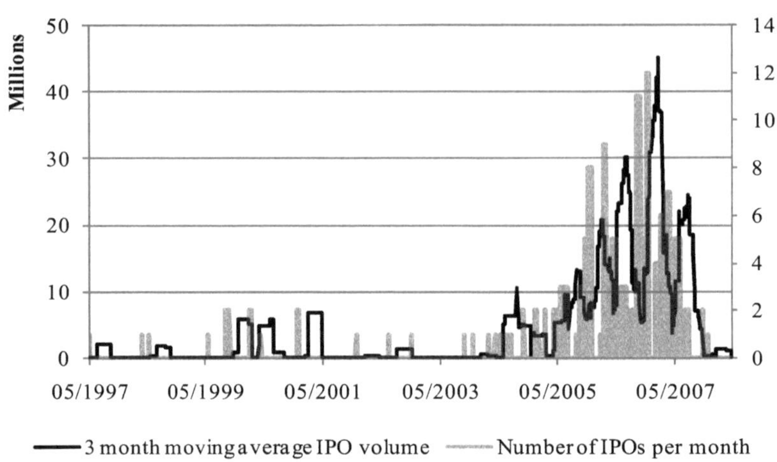

To guarantee representativeness of the sample we discussed each IPO with real estate experts in France, Germany and UK and were confirmed that the final sample consists of all companies that are regarded as characteristic for the

European property company universe. Excluded IPOs are mainly small and rather unknown. In the course of this long-run performance study, the sample size used in this study sums to 99 companies as the aftermarket stock prices information for the remaining companies was not available for at least 24 months. An inspection of the data identified very few extreme values so we applied the winsorisation technique as a correction. This technique takes the non-missing values of a variable and generates a new variable identical except that the h highest and h lowest values are replaced by the maximum of five times the mean absolute deviation of all observations for this variable.

3.3.2 Methodology

In order to test whether market transparency increases the likelihood of over-optimism and, consequently, can explain the long-run underperformance of EPCs, we use empirical tests based on the following logic:

First, when firms time the market by exploiting a window of opportunity due to investor over-optimism, this behaviour results in a long-run underperformance of poor quality companies that pool in times when irrational investors overvalue the firm at IPO. If poor quality firms are able to predict investor over-optimism, the extent of long-run underperformance should be influenced by the degree of over-optimism of primary market investors. This influence is positive if appropriate decision making by investors is limited and negative if rational decision making is simple. Assuming transparency of the underlying real estate market to proxy investors' ability for rational decision making, we expect that, with a decreasing degree of transparency, investors are more *over*-optimistic (because investors have difficulties analysing less transparent real estate markets). As a result, long-run underperformance develops.

Second, firms time the market by exploiting a window of opportunity caused by exogenous shock: It is assumed that long-run underperformance is a result of poor quality companies that pool in times of improving investment opportunities because CEOs are over-optimistic about investment opportunities. If poor quality firms are able to time their IPO with a positive exogenous shock (which raises the price at which firms can, on average, sell their securities), the extent of long-run underperformance should be influenced by the degree of the exogenous shock (i.e., the greater the exogenous shock, the more poor quality companies go public). Assuming transparency of the underlying real estate market to proxy a manager's ability for adequate valuation and precise financial decision making, we expect that, with a decreasing degree of transparency, managers are more *over*-optimistic. As a result, long-run underperformance develops.

Applying the logic presented above, the market timing hypothesis is analysed in two steps. First, we test the assumption that, with a decreasing degree of transparency, EPCs actually time the market by exploiting a window of opportunity. To do this, we measure whether favourable market conditions in general and investor and manager optimism in particular lead to an increase in the number of IPOs per month (NUMIPO). We thereby distinguish between IPOs with transparent and in-transparent real estate market focus to account for our assumption that over-optimism is more likely to develop in less transparent markets. A negative binomial regression model is employed in order to properly measure the counting characteristics of the dependent variable NUMIPO. The independent variables consist of proxies for market valuation (MARKETLEVEL) and favourable investment environment (GDPGROWTH) and two proxies for investor (OVEROPTI_INV) and management (OVEROPTI_MGT) over-optimism.

(3.1) $$NegativeBinomial(NUMIPO) = \beta_0 + \beta_1 MARKETLEVEL + \beta_2 GDPGRWOTH + \beta_3 OVEROPTI\_INV + \beta_4 OVEROPTI\_MGT$$

As the negative binomial regression analysis only shows whether market timing occurred, it leaves open the question whether timers are, on average, of good or bad quality. Loughran et al. (1994) and Yung et al. (2008) argue that firms which issue in a window of opportunity will under-perform the benchmark as initial over-valuation is revised when more information about true value of the firm is revealed. Therefore, OLS regressions are performed where long-run IPO performance (MV24) is regressed on market timing proxy (NUMIPO) in order to test the assumption of market timers being over-valued. Further, the real estate market transparency proxy (TRANSPARENCY) together with proxies measuring the potential presence of investor and management optimism (OPTIMISM) are included in order to specifically analyse the main goal of this paper, i.e. whether market transparency can explain why European property companies, in contrast to REITs, have high long-run underperformance. By analysing the interaction terms of the OPTIMISM variables and TRANSPARENCY, we can show whether limited decision making increases the risk of over-optimism which ultimately leads to long-run underperformance. Additional variables are asymmetric information (ASYMINFO) and signalling (SIGNAL) proxies. All variables are described in more detail in section 3.3.3.

(3.2) $$MV24 = \beta_0 + \beta_1 NUMIPO + \beta_2 OPTIMISM * TRANSPARENCY + \beta_3 ASYMINFO + \beta_4 SIGNAL$$

The robustness checks conducted in subsection 3.4.3.3 employ a quantile regression model in order to ensure that the regression of mean values is a reasonable approach to explain long-run returns and that the results are not biased by outliers.

3.3.3 *Measures of variables*

3.3.3.1 Measurement of long-run IPO performance

There is a variety of methods that have been used in previous research to determine long-run stock performance. The debate among researchers is ongoing about the methodology that correctly measures long-run performance. Thus, the following paragraphs provide a short summary of the methodologies used in previous studies in order to rationalise the method employed in the present analysis. Generally, there are three main methods used for measuring abnormal long-term stock price performance: cumulative abnormal returns (CAR), buy-and-hold abnormal returns (BAHRs) and returns based on the calendar-time portfolio approach. The CAR method can be formally written as:

$$CAR_{i,T} = \sum_{t=1}^{T}\left(R_{i,t} - R_{b,t}\right),$$

where $R_{i,t}$ is the month t simple return on sample firm i and $R_{b,t}$ is the month t simple return of an appropriate benchmark b . Ritter (1991) was among the first to use CARs in a long-term IPO performance analysis. However, Barber and Lyon (1997) show that CARs overestimate abnormal returns in the case of underperformance. Alternatively, they suggest the BAHR method.

$$BHAR_{i,[t,T]} = \prod_{t=1}^{T}\left(1 + R_{i,t}\right) - \prod_{t=1}^{T}\left(1 + R_{b,t}\right),$$

where $R_{i,t}$ is the month t simple return on sample firm i and $R_{b,t}$ is the month t simple return of an appropriate benchmark b . Barber and Lyon (1997) document that the derivation of the benchmark is critical. The application of some indices can induce serious biases. The use of reference portfolios such as equally weighted market indices or size decile portfolios as benchmarks is problematic, as they lead to mis-specified test statistics. The calculations are specifically driven by three biases: a positive new listing bias, a rebalancing bias, and a skewness bias.

However, Lyon et al. (1999) show that, by using carefully constructed reference portfolios, matched by size and book-to-market ratios, the new listing and rebalancing bias can be eliminated. Skewness can be controlled for by using skewness-adjusted t-statistics. The third methodology commonly applied by long-term performance studies is, as suggested by Fama (1998), the use of calendar time portfolio returns. This method captures the effects of the return correlation across event firms by the time series variation of the monthly abnormal portfolio returns. As Lyon et al. (1999) point out, the calendar time portfolio approach eliminates the problem of cross-sectional dependence among sample firms, but unlike buy-and-hold abnormal returns, the abnormal return measure does not precisely measure investor experience. Since this study only analyses one-sector IPO performance, i.e., the sector of real estate, and since the study particularly concentrates on the measurement of the investor experience of buying an IPO stock and holding it for a longer period of time, the BHAR is the appropriate method to choose (Stehle et al. (2000), Eckbo and Norli (2005), Jaskiewicz et al. (2005), Akhigbe et al. (2006)).

The next important issue is the correct specification of the benchmark. As Lyon et al. (1999) point out, the selection of an appropriate benchmark is crucial in long-term performance studies. Therefore, three equally and value-weighted benchmarks are employed: For equally weighted returns, we follow the approach of Barber and Lyon (1997) and calculate size-based portfolios that are reconstituted in July of each year. Reference portfolios calculations are based on data from all listed real estate companies (SIC 65) provided by the Dealogic database for the time period 1997 to 2007, excluding the firms used in this study. In June of year t, all reference firms are ranked based on the market value of equity. Size deciles are then created based on these rankings. In a next step, sample firms are placed in the appropriate reference firm size decile, based on their June market value of equity. Monthly returns are calculated for each of the ten size reference portfolios by averaging the monthly returns across all securities in a particular size decile. Since firms are ranked in June of each year, firms are allowed to change size deciles once each year.

The calculation of the size benchmark return is equal to a strategy of investing in an equally weighted size decile portfolio with monthly rebalancing. We also create ten reference portfolios with the help of book-to-market (BTM) ratios. Barber and Lyon (1997) additionally combine size and BTM portfolios. However, due to data restrictions on the BTM data and the generally small universe of 250 sample firms, there is not sufficient data for creating size/BTM reference portfolios. In order to avoid the new listing bias, we exclude all firms of the IPO sample for the calculation of the size- and BTM-matched portfolios.

Data restrictions prevent us from applying the matching firm approach. This methodology's advantage over reference portfolios is to avoid all of the misspecification biases. As there is only a small total number of control firms which are small in size (the median market value of all sample firms was EUR 28 million) and rather illiquid. It was too often not possible to find a suitable match. Therefore, due to a lack of alternatives and data restrictions and as a double check, the EPRA NAREIT index is employed. Although the use of this index might suffer from the new listing and rebalancing bias, it is a commonly used representative benchmark of the listed real estate universe widely used by practitioners and investors.

The final step in analysing long-term IPO performance is to assess their statistical significance. The nature of the BHAR distribution, which is positively skewed, prevents the use of conventional t-tests. Therefore, we follow Lyon et al. (1999) and employ a bootstrapped skewness adjusted t-test.

3.3.3.2 Measures used in market timing analysis

This subsection presents the definitions and measures of variables employed to test the timing hypothesis. Since the dependent variables were discussed in the previous subsection, we focus on the main independent variables concerning market conditions, investor and management over-optimism, and market transparency. An overview of the variable definitions is given in Table 3.1.

Favourable stock market conditions, which are expected to induce firms to time their IPO with periods characterized by generally high company valuations, are proxied by the market level of the FTSE EPRA NAREIT Europe index (MARKETLEVEL) and are expected to be positively related to NUMIPO.

Favourable investment conditions are proxied by the growth rate of the gross domestic product (GDP) of the issuing firm's target investment market. This is consistent with the notion of Yung et al. (2008) that hot IPO markets are a function of positive shocks to the economy. An increase in a country's economic power is often accompanied with an increase in its citizens' purchasing power and its citizens' demand for new and more expensive real estate. This is particularly true for Eastern European countries, which have suffered from a lack of state-of-the-art housing and commercial properties. Overall, economic growth is measured as the relative change in growth The GDP growth development (GDPGROWTH) is therefore calculated as the difference of the firm's target country GPD in the year after the IPO and the GDP in the IPO year divided by the GDP in the IPO year. The growth rates are adjusted in a way that they measure an annualized 12 month post-IPO period. GDPGROWTH is expected to be positively related to pooling and negatively related to long-run performance.

In order to proxy for investor *over*-optimism (OVEROPTI_INV), a dummy variable is constructed. It equals 1 (zero otherwise) if the company has the attributes associated with the NOPORTPIPE variable and additionally belongs to the lowest quintile of the 24-month aftermarket performance of the sample firms analysed. OVEROPTI_INV is expected to be positively related to pooling.

As an alternative proxy for manager *over*-optimism (OVEROPTI_MGT), a further dummy variable is created that equals 1 (zero otherwise) if the company has the attributes associated with the DILUTION variable *and* additionally belongs to the lowest quintile of the 24-month aftermarket performance of the sample. A positive relation for OVEROPTI_MGT and pooling is expected.

Finally, in order to analyze whether real estate market transparency has an impact on the likelihood of the development of over-optimism on either investor or management side, we use the degree of transparency (TRANSPARENCY) of the firm's target real estate investment market. We expect that, with a decreasing degree of transparency, investors might have difficulties in performing proper investment analysis (due to language barriers, and so on), and managers are able to exploit this informational advantage and only issue equity when the market overvalues their assets. Conversely, managers might be over-optimistic about the value of future investment opportunities that, in the long run, emerge as negative net present value projects. We search the target investment markets within the IPO prospectus of each IPO firm. In order to assign each geographic investment market a broadly accepted measure of in-transparency, the respective Jones Lang LaSalle Global Real Estate Transparency Index is employed. The index ranges from 1 to 5, in order of increasing in-transparency. We expect TRANSPARENCY to affect over-optimism variables in such as way that they are positively related to NUMIPO in transparent markets and negatively related in less-transparent markets.

3.3.3.3 Measures used in long-run IPO performance analysis

Next, the variables used in the regression analysis are described. The variables are designed a) to confirm the notion of the market timing hypothesis that market timers are of lower quality and thereby to provide a rationalization of the long-run underperformance phenomenon, b) to more thoroughly address the impact of real estate market transparency on the development of optimism, and c) to control for other potential long-run underperformance explanations as found by previous research.

As validation of the assumption that market timers are the reason for long-run underperformance, MV24 is regressed on NUMIPO which we expect to be negatively related.

Further, as we want to measure the influence of real estate market transparency on rational decision making, we analyze the interaction terms of TRANSPARENCY and proxies for the potential presence of investor and manager optimism, which are described in the following:

The measurement of investor or manager optimism imposes some difficulties as proxying for sentiment stages is generally difficult to obtain due to limited data availability. Applied proxies for investor sentiment in previous research are closed-end-fund discounts (Lee et al. (1991)), grey market prices (Cornelli et al. (2006)) or pre-offer IPO publicity (Cook et al. (2006)). As our access to this kind of data is limited, we follow Derrien and Kecska (2007), who use the market level of a representative stock index to proxy for investor sentiment among AIM-listed companies. Consequently, we split the variable MARKETLEVEL, as described above, into quintiles and create a dummy variable HOT which equals 1 during months in which the market level is in the top quintile and zero otherwise. By using the variable HOT, we particularly address the likelihood of over-optimism induced by particularly high market valuations. We expect, independent of market transparency, hot IPO market investors to suffer from over-optimism and thus expect HOT and its interaction with TRANSPARENCY to be negatively related to MV24.

A further investor optimism variable is a portfolio-related dummy variable (NOPORTPIPE) which specifically accounts for the particularity of real estate companies. The variable equals 1 (zero otherwise) if the company has no initial property portfolio at the time of the IPO and if the company provides no specific information of the properties they intend to buy with the IPO proceeds. It is argued that investors having bought these companies at IPO have no precise information about the fair value of the company and, thus, can only roughly approximate how the firm's intended investment objective can be realised. The valuation problem is expected be even higher in less transparent real estate markets. Therefore, we expect NOPORTPIPE itself but also its interaction with TRANSPARENCY, to be negatively related to long-run performance.

Among the manager optimism variables, we include the economic growth of the IPO firm's target investment country (GDPGROWTH) for which we expect in transparent markets a positive relationship with MV24 and in less transparent markets, a negative relationship as managers are not expected to be able accurately analyse the true growth potential with an decreasing degree of transparency.

Similar to the latter argument, we also include new share capital issued at IPO (DILUTION) which is measured as the percentage of capital increase at the IPO relative to the pre-IPO share capital. Companies that dilute their existing share capital to a greater degree are expected to intentionally take advantage of possible investment opportunities. Thus, we expect a positive relationship of DILUTION and MV24. However, with a decreasing degree of transparency, we expect managers to be over-optimistic about the actual capital needs and therefore a negative relation for the interaction term of DILUTION and TRANSPARENCY.

Control variables include those for asymmetric information and signalling mechanisms, as discussed in the following:

Among the asymmetric information variables, firm size (SIZE) is included. Brounen and Eichholtz (2002) argue that larger property companies are expected to have better long-run performance because larger companies are managed more professionally. Another intuition is provided by Brav and Gompers (1997) who argue that the smallest IPO firms significantly underperform because they are bought mainly by retail investors, who are more easily affected by fads. Supporting empirical evidence provided by Brav et al. (2000) show that the IPO's underperformance is concentrated primarily in small issuing firms with low book-to-value ratios.

TABLE 3.1: OVERVIEW OF VARIABLES

Variable name	Definition	Source
AGE	Age of the firm at the IPO measured as the natural logarithm of the difference of the IPO firm's offer year and its year of incorporation	IPO prospectus
DILUTION	Capital increase at the IPO measures as a percentage of issued share capital relative to the pre-IPO share capital	IPO prospectus
GDPGROWTH	Growth rate of the gross domestic product of the firm's target country measured as the difference of the GDP in the year after the IPO and the GDP in the IPO year divided by the GDP in the IPO year, annualized to measure a 12 month post IPO period	International Monetary Fund
HIGHTRANS	Dummy variable that equals one if the respective company invests in real estate markets that have a transparency measure which is higher than the median value of all transparency measures in this study and zero otherwise	Jones Lang LaSalle
HOT	Dummy variable that equals one during months in which the market level is in the top quintile of the EPRA/NAREIT Europe index	EPRA
IBREPU	Dummy variable that equals one if the issuing firm's underwriter or nominated broker is a global investment bank	IPO prospectus
MARKETLEVEL	Daily closing price of the EPRA/NAREIT Europe index	EPRA
MV24	Equal weighted buy-and-hold returns calculated over a 24 month holding period and adjusted for the performance of size matched reference portfolios, excluding initial day returns	Datastream
MV24_OFFER	Equal weighted buy-and-hold returns calculated over a 24 month holding period and adjusted for the performance of size matched reference portfolios, including initial day returns	Datastream
NOPORTPIPE	Dummy variable that equals one if the issuing firm has no initial property portfolio at the time of the issuing and if the company provides no specific information of the properties they intend to buy with the IPO proceeds	IPO prospectus
NUMIPO	Number of IPOs per month	Dealogic
OVEROPTI_INV	Dummy variable that equals one if the issuing firm has no initial property portfolio at the time of the issuing and belongs the lowest quintile of all sample firms in terms of 24 months size matched IPO performance	IPO prospectus, Datastream
OVEROPTI_MGT	Dummy variable that equals one if the issuing firm belongs to the top quintile of all sample firms in terms of capital increase at IPO and belongs to the lowest quintile of all sample firms in terms of 24 months size matched IPO performance	Dealogic, Datastream
REGULATED	Dummy variable that equals one if the issuing firm is not listed on a stock exchange lower than prime standard, i.e. AIM, Marché Libre, Entry Standard, Open Market and others	IPO prospectus
SIZE	Firm size measured as the natural logarithm of market value of outstanding shares at the end of the first trading day	Dealogic, Datastream, IPO prospectus
TRANSPARENCY	Real estate transparency index ranking ranging from one to five, in order of increasing in-transparency	Jones Lang LaSalle
TYPOSPEC	Dummy variable that equals one if the issuing firm's investment strategy focuses on one specific property type	IPO prospectus
UNDERPRICING	Initial day return measured as the natural logarithm of the closing price of first trading day and the issue price of the IPO divided by the issue price and adjusted for the market return of the EPRA Europe index on the IPO day	Datastream, IPO prospectus, Press releases

Overall, both arguments suggest that size is positively related to long-run performance. Thus, SIZE, the natural logarithm of the market value of outstanding shares valued at the issue price at the IPO, is expected to be positively related with long-run performance.

Further, firm age (AGE) is included as it has been employed persistently in previous literature (Allen and Faulhaber (1989), Welch (1989), Grinblatt and Hwang (1989)). Muscarella and Vetsuypens (1989) argue that a higher amount of publicly available information associated with older firms reduces information asymmetry among investors. Thus, AGE serves as a proxy for reputation and the availability of a track record. Track record and experience of management are particularly important for real estate companies due to long-term investment horizons. Therefore, AGE, which is measured as the number of years since the firm's incorporation and the offer year, is expected to be positively related to long-run performance.

Further, a proxy for the strength of listing requirements is included for which a positive relation with long-run IPO performance is expected because a strict regulatory framework is found to reduce information asymmetry (Alli et al. (1994), Buttimer et al. (2005)). The proxy REGULATED is a dummy variable that equals one if the issuing firm is listed on a stock exchange equal to prime standard and not on less regulated stock exchanges such as AIM, Marché Libre, Entry Standard, Open Market and others.

Finally, a real estate specific measure for information asymmetry is sector specialisation. By investing in one property type, investors have fewer difficulties in deriving an estimate about the fair value of the company. Brounen and Eichholtz (2002) provide evidence that companies who specialise in a single property sector have unexpectedly higher initial day returns, as compared to diversified companies. Sector specialisation is measured with the dummy variable TYPOSPEC, which equals 1 if the firm's investment strategy focuses on one specific property type and equals zero if the firm's investment strategy follows a diversified approach. Sector specialisation is expected to be positively related with long-run performance.

Among the signalling variables, investment bank reputation and first day returns are included: Beatty and Ritter (1986) propose that the reputation of the underwriting investment bank was a strong signal. Investment banks have a mediating role in IPO transactions. Their reputation is highly important for both issuers and investors. According to Titman and Trueman (1986), the quality of agents, e.g., underwriters, involved in the IPO process provides information about the value of a firm. The quality of an agent can have signalling information if a) an agent of high quality is more expensive for issuers or if b) the agent has a greater reputational capital at risk. It is argued that, particularly in hot IPO market phases, good quality firms deliberately tolerate higher listing expenses by employing a highly reputable underwriter. Good quality firms thereby want to signal their superior quality to investors. Investment bank reputation (IBREPU) is measured as a dummy variable and equals 1 if the firm's underwriter or nominated broker (which usually plays the role of an underwriter when AIM-listed firms sell securities) at IPO is prestigious and zero otherwise. We thereby follow Derrien and Kecska (2007), who classified an investment bank or broker as prestigious if it is a global investment bank. IBREPU is expected to be positively related with long-run performance.

Lastly, underpricing is included as an additional signalling proxy, as proposed by Allen and Faulhaber (1989), Welch (1989), Grinblatt and Hwang (1989). The reasoning is based on the assumption that underpricing is costly for the issuer and can only be recovered by high quality firms at a later stage, i.e., in the aftermarket or with seasoned equity offerings. Underpricing (UNDERPRICING) is measured as the first day stock return, adjusted for the EPRA market return of the IPO day. Long-run performance of the firm is expected to be positively related to underpricing, assuming that good quality firms have high long-run returns.

3.4 RESULTS

3.4.1 Descriptive statistics and correlations

Descriptive statistics of the various variables used in this study are presented in Table 3.2, while the corresponding correlations are presented in Table 3.3. All results of the regression analysis part are based on 99 observations after excluding IPOs for which less than 24 months post-IPO stock prices are available.

Overall, the long-run performance of the sample firms is, on average, negative with a mean 24-month size-matched IPO performance of -14% and a median of -18%. Large differences between the minimum value of MV24 of -130% and the maximum value of 123% indicate great performance differences. The extreme values for long-run returns, including initial day returns (MV24_OFFER), shift from less negative to more positive but, on average, are still negative. Both MV24 and MV24_OFFER are only marginally skewed so that transformation is not necessary. In contrast, AGE, has a relatively high positive skewness coefficient of 4.78. In order to minimise the impact of right-skewed data, AGE is transformed with the natural logarithm, which reduces the skewness significantly.

TABLE 3.2: SUMMARY STATISTICS

	N	Mean	Median	Max	Min	Std.Dev.	Skew-ness	Kurto-sis
AGE	99	6.53	3.00	31.30	0.00	8.64	1.56	4.43
DILUTION	99	0.45	0.32	1.00	0.00	0.37	0.42	1.61
GDPGROWTH	99	0.03	0.03	0.08	-0.01	0.02	0.52	2.73
HOT	99	0.22	0.00	1.00	0.00	0.42	1.34	2.79
IBREPU	99	0.34	0.00	1.00	0.00	0.48	0.66	1.43
LOG(1+AGE)	99	1.38	1.39	3.48	0.00	1.16	0.25	1.74
MARKETLEVEL	99	1979.60	2000.92	2702.44	924.90	530.92	-0.53	2.10
MV24	99	-0.14	-0.18	1.23	-1.30	0.46	0.73	4.86
MV24_OFFER	99	-0.03	-0.11	1.60	-0.97	0.57	1.04	4.12
NOPORTPIPE	99	0.15	0.00	1.00	0.00	0.36	1.94	4.78
NUMIPO	99	4.58	3.00	11.00	1.00	3.42	0.70	2.07
OVEROPTI_INV	99	0.22	0.00	1.00	0.00	0.42	1.34	2.79
OVEROPTI_MGT	99	0.03	0.00	1.00	0.00	0.17	5.48	31.03
REGULATED	99	0.53	1.00	1.00	0.00	0.50	-0.10	1.01
SIZE	99	258.00	148.00	1060.00	1.81	282.00	1.33	3.68
TRANSPARENCY	99	1.59	1.50	3.50	1.00	0.65	0.99	2.97
TYPOSPEC	99	0.45	0.00	1.00	0.00	0.50	0.18	1.03
UNDERPRICING	99	0.08	0.05	0.34	-0.13	0.09	0.97	3.89

MARKETLEVEL shows, with an increase of almost 300%, the strong growth of the EPC universe during the sample period.

Additionally, NUMIPO, which measures the number of IPOs per month, ranges from 1 to 11 and thereby confirms the presence of a hot and cold market period. Interestingly, measures for market heat, i.e., NUMIPO and MARKETLEVEL, show much stronger negative correlation coefficients with MV24_OFFER. This implies that hot market issues not only have lower underpricing but also perform significantly worse. The correlation with UNDERPRICING and MV24 is negative but becomes positively correlated with MV24_OFFER. This shows that first-day returns in the sample "pulls" the average long-run performance for a longer time above benchmark returns.

Consistent with the market timing hypothesis, NUMIPO and MARKETLEVEL have a strong positive correlation coefficient. In contrast, the relationship between GDPGROWTH and NUMIPO is still positive, but the correlation degree is significantly lower. Surprisingly, GDPGROWTH is positively correlated with TRANSPARENCY, implying that European countries with intransparent real estate markets experienced strong economic growth between

1997 and 2007. The availability of a property portfolio at IPO (NOPORTPIPE) is highly correlated with a number of variables.

TABLE 3.3: CORRELATION MATRIX

	NUMIPO	MAR-KETLEVEL	GDPGROWTH	OVER-OPTI_INV	OVER-OPTI_MGT	MV24	MV24_OFFER	TRANS-PAR-ENCY
NUMIPO	1.00							
MAR-	0.68	1.00						
GDPGROWTH	0.19	0.17	1.00					
OVER-	-0.11	0.14	-0.08	1.00				
OVER-	0.02	0.05	-0.06	0.05	1.00			
MV24	0.03	-0.04	0.11	-0.49	-0.22	1.00		
MV24_OFFER	-0.26	-0.38	0.08	-0.50	-0.10	0.78	1.00	
TRANSPAR-	0.12	0.08	0.68	-0.09	-0.12	0.04	0.02	1.00
REGULATED	0.29	0.17	-0.22	-0.20	-0.07	0.17	0.02	-0.34
HOT	0.42	0.60	0.06	0.18	0.05	-0.04	-0.35	0.02
NOPORTPIPE	0.13	0.04	0.29	-0.23	0.25	-0.26	-0.03	0.28
SIZE	0.00	0.06	0.06	-0.04	-0.14	0.26	0.08	-0.02
DILUTION	0.05	0.05	0.31	-0.17	0.11	-0.13	0.01	0.33
IBREPU	0.05	0.10	0.03	-0.18	-0.13	0.36	0.24	0.05
AGE	-0.03	-0.06	-0.13	0.11	-0.12	0.27	0.20	-0.22
LOG(1+AGE)	0.02	0.01	-0.16	0.14	-0.14	0.24	0.09	-0.21
UNDERPRIC-	0.04	0.08	-0.12	0.17	0.10	-0.11	0.10	0.01
DEBTRATIO	0.07	0.07	-0.23	0.12	-0.11	0.01	-0.08	-0.10
TYPOSPEC	0.16	0.06	-0.04	0.00	-0.04	-0.10	-0.16	0.01

	REGU-LATED	HOT	NOPORT PIPE	SIZE	DILU-TION	IBREPU	AGE	LOG(1+AGE)
REGULATED	1.00							
HOT	0.10	1.00						
NOPORTPIPE	-0.16	-0.23	1.00					
SIZE	-0.12	0.12	-0.22	1.00				
DILUTION	-0.20	-0.26	0.55	-0.29	1.00			
IBREPU	-0.01	0.18	-0.19	0.27	-0.15	1.00		
AGE	0.09	0.15	-0.30	0.20	-0.50	0.12	1.00	
LOG(1+AGE)	0.22	0.23	-0.43	0.19	-0.72	0.13	0.90	1.00
UNDERPRIC-	-0.14	0.11	0.13	-0.10	-0.05	0.07	-0.06	-0.06
DEBTRATIO	-0.15	0.07	-0.19	-0.01	-0.31	0.10	0.28	0.34
TYPOSPEC	-0.03	0.10	-0.05	0.03	-0.16	0.15	0.12	0.12

	UNDER-PRIC-ING	DEB-TRATIO	TYPO-SPEC
UNDERPRIC-	1.00		
DEBTRATIO	0.05	1.00	
TYPOSPEC	0.01	0.05	1.00

The strongest correlation is between NOPORTPIPE and the degree of capital expenditure of the issuing company (DILUTION). It appears that companies increasingly issued to fund future acquisitions. Similarly, REGULATED is negatively correlated with variables measuring the presence of sentiment investors (NUMIPO and NOPORTPIPE) as well as with variables measuring the presence of exogenous shocks (GDPGROWTH and DILUTION). This implies that firms that have timed the market due to over-optimistic investors or due to positive exogenous shocks increasingly opted to list on stock exchanges with low listing requirements, suggesting that firms deliberately choose unregulated listing markets because they are either of low quality which would deter from being listed on regulated markets.

3.4.2 Long-run IPO performance

This subsection describes the results of long-run IPO performance in more detail in order to show that results differ with regard to measurement period and method as well as benchmark used but that the overall conclusion of the presence of significant long-run underperformance remains. The results in Table 3.4 reveal, independently of the benchmark used, the existence of abnormal returns which are positive but statistically not significant in the first year of stock trading.

TABLE 3.4: EQUAL AND VALUE WEIGHTED BUY-AND-HOLD RETURNS

Benchmark	Holding period	N	Equal-weighted %		Value-weighted %	
	One year	114	-3.40	(b)	0.45	
EPRA	Two years	99	-19.23	(a)	-5.81	(b)
	Three years	45	-33.03	(a)	-4.69	(c)
	One year	88	-5.53	(a)	-1.55	
BTM	Two years	69	-27.02	(a)	-5.11	(c)
	Three years	39	-31.91	(a)	-0.25	
	One year	114	-6.45	(b)	-1.33	(c)
MV	Two years	99	-14.43	(a)	-2.84	(b)
	Three years	45	-22.02	(a)	0.07	

Notes: (c),(b), and (a) indicates significance at the 10, 5, and 1% level

However, the 24 and 36 months time horizon shows the existence of significantly negative abnormal returns with values between -14% and -27% for the 24 month horizon and with -22% and -33% for the 36 month horizon. Value weighted returns are far less significant, which indicates that size is an important determinant for long-run IPO performance.

Figure 3.2 plots the equal weighted buy-and-hold returns adjusted for benchmark returns of reference portfolios matched by size, EPRA, and book-to-market ratios over a 36-month period with the the initial day return being included. The figure shows that over a 24-month or 36-month period, issuing firms generate a negative performance for IPO investors, even when taking mostly positive initial day returns into consideration. Underperformance relative to the offer price has also been evidenced by Ritter (1991). According to the model of Ljungqqvist et al. (2006), this seems reasonable because the offer price will exceed the fundamental value by an amount equal to the issuer's share in the surplus extracted from the sentiment investors.

FIGURE 3.2: EQUAL WEIGHTED BUY-AND-HOLD RETURNS INCL. FIRST DAY RETURNS

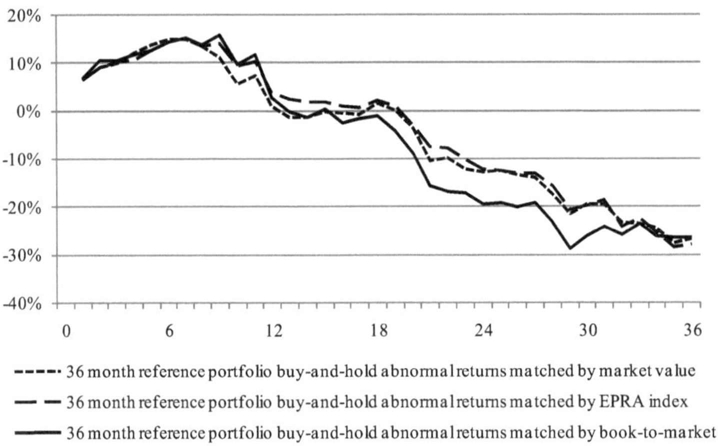

3.4.3 Regression results

The regression analyses performed in this section include negative binomial regressions to test the timing hypothesis (subsection 3.4.3.1) and OLS regressions to specifically examine the impact of market transparency, over-optimism, and asymmetric information as well as signalling proxies on long-run underperformance (subsection 3.3.3.2). To account for heteroscedasticity, standard errors in all regressions are adjusted using White's (1980) covariance matrix. Results are tested for robustness in subsection 3.4.3.3.

3.4.3.1 Negative binomial regression of number of IPOs

This subsection presents the results of the binomial regression analysis with NUMIPO as the dependent variable in order to test whether a decreasing degree of real estate market transparency creates over-optimism of investors or firm management which in the end causes an increase in IPO activity. The corresponding results are presented in Table 3.5.

Model I, with NUMIPO as the dependent variable, only includes transparent IPOs which are identified as companies with transparency measures higher than the median value. Model II includes firms investing in less transparent real estate markets which are companies with transparency measures lower than the median value. Both models show a high specification with an adjusted R^2 of 0.54 and 0.31, respectively. Additionally, LR statistics are highly significant for both models. As stated above, it is hypothesised that it is more difficult for investors and managers to accurately analyse the industry and firm's growth prospects in in-transparent markets. Thus, one might expect to find irrational behaviour either on the side of investors, of managers or on both sides.

In model I, the variables MARKETLEVEL and GDPGROWTH are both significantly and positively related to NUMIPO. The positive relation of MARKETLEVEL to NUMIPO gives a first indication that firms investing in transparent real estate markets have timed their IPO to favourable market conditions. The positive relation of GDPGROWTH and NUMIPO is plausible in the view that issuing firms' managers have also timed the IPO with an exogenous shock. The same relation is true for model II, which includes only IPO firms investing in less transparent real estate markets. These results imply that, irrespective of the degree of market transparency, European property companies have IPO timing skills but the results cannot explain whether irrational behaviour, i.e. overoptimism, is more likely to be present among companies mainly investing in less transparent real estate markets.

TABLE 3.5: NEGATIVE BINOMIAL REGRESSION ON NUMBER OF IPOS

	I (NUMIPO) High transparency					II (NUMIPO) Low transparency				
	Coef.	**Std. Err.**	**z-stat.**	**Prob.**		**Coef.**	**Std. Err.**	**z-stat**	**Prob.**	
C	-1.09	0.28	-3.97	0.00	(a)	-1.14	0.50	-2.29	0.02	(b)
GDPGROWTH	16.86	4.75	3.55	0.00	(a)	20.90	4.71	4.44	0.00	(a)
MARKETLEVEL	0.00	0.00	11.63	0.00	(a)	0.00	0.00	3.76	0.00	(a)
OVEROPTI INV	-0.48	0.09	-5.41	0.00	(a)	0.28	0.21	1.24	0.18	
Log likelihood	-148.60					-104.77				
Number of obs.	72.00					27.00				
LR statistic	108.76					47.53				
Prob. LR statistic	0.00					0.00				
Adj. R-squared	0.54					0.31				

Notes: (c),(b), and (a) indicates significance at the 10, 5, and 1% level

The variable OVEROPTI_INV addresses this question. The variable shows a significant negative relationship to NUMIPO in model I and a positive but insignificant relationship to NUMIPO in model II. This variable measures the degree of investor over-optimism and shows that, in transparent markets, investors are decreasingly over-optimistic about firms' prospects. In contrast, the variable's positive relation for firms investing in less transparent markets shows that investors are increasingly over-optimistic about firms' prospects. Nevertheless, the latter relationship has to be interpreted with caution since the variable is not statistically significant but given the relatively high z-statistic of 1.24, H1a can be accepted.

The OVEROPTI_MGT variable which measures the presence of manager over-optimism is not displayed because only three cases fulfilled the requirements described in subsection 3.3.3.2. This already shows that it is unlikely that the degree of market transparency affects IPO firm managers' ability to make precise investment decisions. In fact, the results even support the notion that EPCs anticipate future investment opportunities correctly and thereby provides support for the benefits of indirect real estate investing. Consequently, H1b needs to be rejected.

In sum, the results provide evidence that EPCs have timed their IPO to coincide with times of favourable market conditions and positive exogenous shocks, independent of the degree of real estate market transparency. It is also shown that, with a decreasing degree of market transparency, investor over-optimism is more likely to develop which is realized by companies and consequently leads to an increased issuing activity. In contrast, the results do not support the assumption of manager over-optimism, i.e. the assumption that more IPOs are issued because a decreasing degree of real estate market transparency has impaired the investment analysis of managers, leading them to be over-optimistic about the effect of the exogenous shock. However, the results do not explicitly rationalize why European property company IPOs underperform in the long-run. This question will be addressed in the following.

3.4.3.2 OLS regression of long-run returns on optimism variables

This subsection presents the results of OLS regressions with long-run IPO performance as dependent variables in order to test whether market timing variables in fact underperform their peers in the long-run and whether long-run underperformance is a function of over-optimism, created by a decreasing degree of real estate market transparency. Finally, asymmetric information and signalling proxies are included as control variables.

The description of the results starts with MV24 as the dependent variable: Overall, model I is statistically significant and has an adjusted R^2 of 0.25. The Ramsey RESET test shows that the regression is sufficiently specified. The maximum variance of inflation factor (VIF) at 4.26 is relatively low, suggesting that the results are not biased due to multicollinearity of the independent variables.

Model I starts with the description of the impact of the market timing proxy NUMIPO on long-run IPO performance. The variable is positively related to MV24 which is not in line with the market timing hypothesis. However, the relationship is statistically not significant.

Regarding the investor optimism proxies, the coefficient of HOT shows a significant and negative relationship to MV24, implying that IPO firms that have issued in a hot IPO phase have, on average, lower long-run returns. Similar results are obtained when using MARKETLEVEL instead of HOT. However, HOT is included in order to particularly emphasise the influence of hot IPO markets. Thus, it seems that the offer price of hot market IPOs is over-priced which leads to long-run underperformance once market participants have processed the new and publicly available information.

Further, it can be noted that NOPORTPIPE is, as hypothesized, significantly negatively related to MV24. This implies that IPO firms that only hinge on investor's beliefs about the successful implementation of their investment strategy perform worse. These findings already show that shareholders who invest in property companies with high valuation uncertainty risk suffer from declining aftermarket stock returns, independent of the degree of market transparency, implying that offer prices have been set too high at IPO.

The variables included to measure the potential presence of manager optimism show, without considering the impact of real estate market transparency, that over-optimism by managers is not present: More specifically, results show that GDPGROWTH is positively related to long-run returns although it does not reach the level of statistical significance. As can be inferred from subsection 3.4.3.1, more companies pursue an IPO as the degree of exogenous shocks increases. The finding of the OLS regression weakly shows that firms seem to correctly interpret the potential for investment opportunities. Similarly, the positive coefficient of DILUTION implies that firms with a higher need for capital also have, on average, higher long-run IPO performance.

Still, the question remains whether the coefficient signs of these variables change for companies investing in less transparent real estate markets? Interestingly, the single impact of TRANSPARENCY on MV24 is positive but not significantly related to long-run IPO performance, suggesting market transparency per se is not a determinant of long-run underperformance.

However, the interaction term NUMIPO(c)TRANSPARENCY is negative and with a t-statistic of -1.36 only closely fails to reach statistical significance at the 10% level. This shows that intransparent property companies, having issued in times where the number of property IPOs per month was high, underperform the benchmark. Thus, H2 (Larger market timing proxies are negatively related to long-run IPO performance for a lesser degree of market transparency) can be accepted. Similarly, HOT(c)TRANSPARENCY is negative and statistically significant at the 1% level thereby provides supporting evidence that intransparent companies, having issued in a market phase with generally high company valuation levels, perform worse. This result finally confirms that firms, timing high company valuation levels, significantly underperform.

In contrast, the NOPORTPIPE(c)TRANSPARENCY is not statistically significant, implying that companies with high valuation uncertainty risk have long-run underperformance, independent of real estate market transparency. This result implies that market transparency does not lead to over-optimism but provides evidence that valuation uncertainty alone explains long-run underperformance of European property companies. Nevertheless, given the significant results of HOT, H3a can be partly accepted.

Referring to the interaction term of GDPGROWTH(c)TRANSPARENCY, an almost significant and positive relationship with MV24 can be observed, implying that countries with less transparent real estate markets have experienced strong economic growth during the sample period analysed. This finding rejects the hypothesis that the degree of market transparency affects managers' investment decisions and rather lends supporting evidence to IPO firm's management correct anticipation of investment opportunities.

DILUTION(c)TRANSPARENCY is negatively related and with a t-statistic of -1.13 only closely fails to reach statistical significance at the 10% level. This result implies that firms which dilute their pre-IPO holdings to a larger degree with the intention to invest the raised capital in less transparent real estate markets, have worse long-run IPO stock performance. This finding is, in contrast to the positive coefficient of GDPGROWTH(c)TRANSPARENCY, supportive of the manager over-optimism hypothesis. Thus, H3b can be partly accepted.

With regard to the impact of information asymmetry proxies on the long-run IPO performance, the following relationships are revealed. First, the positive coefficient of SIZE indicates that smaller issues have significantly worse long-run performance than their larger counterparts. On the one hand, this result is consistent with the notion of Brav and Gomper (1997) that small issues are easily subject to over-optimism because they are dominantly targeted by retail investors. On the other hand, it can be argued that larger property companies have better financial resources to accomplish risk management through diversification. Because direct real estate investment is normally capital intensive, smaller companies are more prone to cluster risks as they only have financial resources for a small number of properties. Unfortunately, an empirical observation of this explanation could not be undertaken because prospectus information about individual property information was irregular or completely missing.

TABLE 3.6: OLS REGRESSION OF LONG-RUN IPO PERFORMANCE

	I (MV24)					I (MV24_OFFER)				
	Coef	Std.Err	t-stat	Prob		Coef	Std.Err	t-stat	Prob	
C	-0.03	0.16	-0.16	0.87		-0.07	0.15	-0.43	0.67	
AGE	0.29	0.16	1.78	0.08	(c)	0.29	0.15	1.91	0.06	(c)
DILUTION	0.14	0.13	1.13	0.26		0.18	0.13	1.37	0.18	
DILUTION(c)TRANSP~	-0.14	0.12	-1.17	0.25		-0.07	0.12	-0.57	0.57	
GDPGROWTH	0.12	0.15	0.81	0.42		-0.14	0.13	-1.05	0.30	
GDPGROWTH(c)TRANSP~	0.26	0.15	1.77	0.08	(c)	0.30	0.14	2.07	0.04	(b)
HOT	-0.25	0.10	-2.40	0.02	(b)	-0.37	0.11	-3.49	0.00	(a)
HOT(c)TRANSP~	-0.22	0.10	-2.25	0.03	(b)	-0.17	0.10	-1.69	0.10	(c)
IBREPU	0.32	0.10	3.27	0.00	(a)	0.29	0.09	3.03	0.00	(a)
NOPORTPIPE	-0.24	0.11	-2.18	0.03	(b)	-0.06	0.09	-0.64	0.53	
NOPORTPIPE(c)TRANSP~	0.03	0.09	0.32	0.75		-0.02	0.08	-0.29	0.78	
NUMIPO	0.09	0.09	0.95	0.34		-0.17	0.09	-1.86	0.07	(c)
NUMIPO(c)TRANSP~	-0.11	0.08	-1.36	0.18		-0.07	0.08	-0.99	0.33	
REGULATED	0.08	0.09	0.91	0.36		0.05	0.10	0.51	0.61	
SIZE	0.21	0.11	1.93	0.06	(c)	0.13	0.11	1.13	0.26	
TRANSPARENCY	-0.12	0.16	-0.72	0.48		-0.02	0.16	-0.11	0.91	
TYPOSPEC	-0.15	0.09	-1.71	0.09	(c)	-0.15	0.09	-1.74	0.09	(c)
UNDERPRICING	-0.04	0.09	-0.41	0.68		0.18	0.09	1.96	0.05	(c)
Number of obs.	99					99				
F-statistic	5.02					5.06				
Prob. F-statistic	0.00					0.00				
Adj. R-squared	0.25					0.24				
Ramsey RESET test	0.16					0.18				
Max. VIF	4.26					4.26				

Notes: (c),(b), and (a) indicates significance at the 10, 5, and 1% level

The positive and significant coefficient of AGE implies that younger firms experience worse long-run performance compared to more established firms, implying that information asymmetry is reduced for older firms because more information is available.

The variable REGULATED is statistically significant at the 1% level in both specifications. The positive coefficient implies that companies, opting to list on stock exchanges with low listing requirements, underperform in the long-run. This lends further support to the ability of EPCs to time the market when investment opportunities are anticipated. Moreover, the positive relationship confirms the assumption that low listing requirements facilitate equity issuing for poor quality companies.

The last proxy for information asymmetry is sector specialisation (TYPO-SPEC) which is negatively related to MV24, implying that diversified companies have a better long-run IPO performance. This finding is in contrast to the reduced valuation uncertainty argument of specialised companies, put by Brounen and Eichholtz (2002). The positive relation rather implies that diversified companies are less prone to cluster risks and can take advantage of diversification benefits. Overall, the results of the information asymmetry proxies are generally in line with Miller's (1977) divergence of opinion argument and H4a can thus be accepted.

Regarding the signalling variables, investment bank reputation (IBREPU) has a strong positive influence on long-run returns, implying that companies underwritten by prestigious underwriters significantly outperform the benchmark in the long-run. The findings are in line with Titman and Trueman (1986), who suggest that more prestigious investment bankers underwrite less risky IPOs. The significant coefficients of REGULATED and NOPORTPIPE, both risk measures, confirm this notion. If highly reputable investment banks only underwrite good quality companies, then IBREPU should explain away these poor quality variables. In contrast, the variables remain significant. This implies that companies underwritten by IBREPU do not commonly share characteristics measured by REGULATED and NOPORTPIPE. This in turn suggests that prestigious investment banks particularly choose low risk companies.

UNDERPRICING is negatively related to long-run returns, showing that companies with high initial day returns perform worse in the long run. As expected, the negative relation is not in line with signalling models because it is argued that EPC's long-run underperformance is the result of over-optimism. The signalling models in Allen and Faulhaber (1989), Welch (1989) and Grinblatt and Hwang (1989) suggest that, in order to signal their good quality, IPO firms are intentionally underpriced. Ljungqqvist et al. (2006) explain this relation as the result of gradual sale of IPO shares by institutional investors to sentiment investors. The authors argue that the relation is negative if the probability of the hot market ending is small. In fact, the correlation coefficient between UNDERPRICING and MV24 is -0.16 and is less negative for IPOs issued in the first half of the hot IPO period, as compared to the correlation coefficient of -0.25 for IPOs issued in the second half of the hot IPO period. In sum, H4b can be partly confirmed.

Model II repeats the regression analysis with MV24_OFFER as the dependent variable which allows for analyses of the stronger claim of underperformance relative to the issue price. By including first-day returns in the long-run return calculation, we specifically test two major assumptions with regard to underpricing. In their signalling hypotheses, Allen and Faulhaber (1989), Grinblatt and Hwang (1989), and Welch (1989) suggest that underpricing is a positive function of firm quality because only high quality firms are assumed to be able to underprice their IPO because they thereby create a costly signal in form of forgone IPO proceeds which cannot be sustained by poor quality firms. Thus, high quality issues are predicted to have, on average, higher underpricing.

In contrast, Rock's (1986) adverse selection model suggests that informed investors only invest in high quality companies because uninformed investors cannot distinguish between good or poor quality issuers, and so they will only be allocated a fraction of the most desirable new issues and will be allocated all of the least desirable new issues. Thus, poor quality issues have, on average, higher underpricing in order to attract a sufficient number of uninformed investors for whom underpricing serves as a compensation for their informational disadvantage.

In general, there exist three possibilities how results with MV24_OFFER as dependent variable differ from the results with MV24 as dependent variable. First, results do not change, which means that underpricing is not used in the sense of signalling or adverse selection theory.

Another situation is that variables change from being insignificant in the MV24 specification and become significant in the MV24_OFFER specification. This result would be supporting evidence for the signalling hypothesis as only the constellation of companies with better long-run performance and high underpricing causes MV24_OFFER to become significant.

The last situation is that variables change from being significant in the MV24 specification and become insignificant in the MV24_OFFER specification. This result would be supporting evidence for the adverse selection hypothesis as only the constellation of companies with worse long-run performance and high underpricing causes MV24_OFFER to become insignificant.

Noteworthy changes compared to model I are as follows:

The coefficient of NUMIPO changes from being not statistically significant in the MV24 specification in model I to being statistically significant at the 10%

level in the MV24_OFFER specification in model II. This result is supportive of the signalling hypothesis, i.e. companies that issue in times of generally high issuing activity have higher underpricing and higher long-run IPO performance, suggesting that these IPOs used underpricing as a signal to inform outside investors about their prospects.

In contrast, the negative coefficient of NOPORTPIPE changes from being significant to being insignificant in the MV24_OFFER specification. This result rather suggests that firms with high valuation uncertainty employ underpricing as a means to attract uninformed investors. Thus, this result is supportive of our previous results that NOPORTPIPE firms are of lower quality.

The same relation can be observed for SIZE, implying that smaller IPOs are characterized by higher information asymmetry which requires higher underpricing as risk compensation. The positive relationship implies that firm size is a decisive determinant in long-run IPO performance of European property companies.

3.4.3.3 Robustness test: Quantile regression of long-run IPO performance

Finally, the robustness of the results is checked via a quantile regression approach. The results are presented in Table 3.7. Quantile regression allows us to examine the whole distribution of long-run IPO returns rather than solely analysing average return values.

Consequently, the relative importance of explanatory variables at different points of the distribution of firms' performance can be evaluated. Overall, the quantile regression results confirm the robustness of the OLS regression results. Among the main variables of interest, all quantile regression coefficients show the same sign as the OLS regression coefficient. However, differences in terms of their impact on firms with different levels of long-run returns are detected.

Regarding the impact of the previously examined variables on long-run IPO performance, there is only small variation in the magnitude and sign of the estimated coefficients as one moves up the conditional distribution.

None of the variables with significant coefficients change signs throughout the analysed quantiles, suggesting that the impact of variables does not change within the distribution of long-run IPO returns. Further, it can be observed that independent variables have a significant impact on MV24 at the 0.10 and 0.90 quantiles, a normal situation for generally skewed IPO returns.

TABLE 3.7: QUANTILE REGRESSION

tau	0.10					0.25					0.5					0.75					0.90				
	Coef	Std. Err	t-stat	Prob		Coef	Std. Err	t-stat	Prob		Coef	Std. Err	t-stat	Prob		Coef	Std. Err	t-stat	Prob		Coef	Std. Err	t-stat	Prob	
C	-0.90	0.14	-6.26	0.00	(a)	-0.63	0.16	-3.85	0.00	(a)	-0.13	0.15	-0.87	0.39		0.28	0.30	0.92	0.36		1.27	0.31	4.06	0.00	(a)
AGE	0.17	0.16	1.06	0.29		0.01	0.10	0.07	0.94		0.07	0.15	0.46	0.64		0.35	0.21	1.69	0.09	(c)	0.28	0.35	0.81	0.42	
DILUTION	0.12	0.16	0.79	0.43		0.01	0.12	0.11	0.91		-0.02	0.15	-0.11	0.92		0.17	0.27	0.61	0.54		0.37	0.30	1.22	0.23	
DILUTION(c)TRANSP~	-0.27	0.16	-1.68	0.10	(c)	-0.21	0.12	-1.82	0.07	(c)	-0.19	0.16	-1.16	0.25		-0.16	0.23	-0.70	0.49		-0.13	0.13	-1.03	0.31	
GDPGROWTH	-0.01	0.13	-0.05	0.96		0.04	0.13	0.31	0.75		0.01	0.13	0.08	0.94		0.06	0.23	0.28	0.78		0.39	0.22	1.78	0.08	(c)
GDPGROWTH(c)TRANSP~	0.29	0.12	2.52	0.01	(b)	0.30	0.15	1.95	0.05	(c)	0.15	0.13	1.17	0.25		0.45	0.26	1.75	0.08	(c)	-0.07	0.45	-0.16	0.87	
HOT	-0.28	0.07	-4.08	0.00	(a)	-0.14	0.09	-1.58	0.12		-0.13	0.09	-1.47	0.15		-0.27	0.16	-1.71	0.09	(c)	-0.47	0.25	-1.87	0.07	(c)
HOT(c)TRANSP~	-0.25	0.11	-2.24	0.03	(b)	-0.25	0.09	-2.76	0.01	(a)	-0.12	0.13	-0.86	0.39		-0.30	0.15	-2.03	0.05	(b)	-0.27	0.15	-1.85	0.07	(c)
IBREPU	0.14	0.08	1.65	0.10		0.18	0.08	2.11	0.04	(b)	0.23	0.09	2.69	0.01	(a)	0.36	0.18	1.99	0.05	(c)	0.61	0.19	3.17	0.00	(a)
NOPORTPIPE	-0.29	0.10	-2.73	0.01	(a)	-0.27	0.15	-1.75	0.08	(c)	-0.11	0.13	-0.84	0.40		-0.17	0.26	-0.67	0.51		-0.49	0.29	-1.70	0.09	(c)
NOPORTPIPE(c)TRANSP~	0.08	0.06	1.23	0.22		0.09	0.09	0.98	0.33		0.04	0.13	0.31	0.76		-0.10	0.21	-0.49	0.63		0.14	0.18	0.78	0.44	
NUMIPO	0.33	0.11	2.87	0.01	(a)	0.09	0.11	0.85	0.40		-0.01	0.08	-0.07	0.95		-0.04	0.18	-0.19	0.85		0.15	0.31	0.47	0.64	
NUMIPO(c)TRANSP~	-0.18	0.06	-2.99	0.00	(a)	-0.12	0.08	-1.52	0.13		-0.03	0.06	-0.56	0.57		-0.02	0.18	-0.13	0.90		0.04	0.09	0.38	0.70	
REGULATED	0.24	0.08	2.83	0.01	(a)	0.13	0.10	1.34	0.18		0.15	0.09	1.63	0.11		0.11	0.14	0.78	0.44		0.03	0.16	0.18	0.86	
SIZE	0.30	0.10	2.91	0.00	(a)	0.16	0.08	2.00	0.05	(b)	0.00	0.09	0.01	1.00		0.08	0.22	0.37	0.71		0.56	0.20	2.76	0.01	(a)
TRANSPARENCY	0.16	0.23	0.67	0.50		-0.07	0.20	-0.36	0.72		0.02	0.20	0.07	0.94		-0.20	0.22	-0.90	0.37		-0.37	0.34	-1.09	0.28	
TYPOSPEC	-0.15	0.09	-1.69	0.09	(c)	-0.04	0.07	-0.53	0.60		-0.08	0.07	-1.17	0.25		-0.14	0.14	-1.02	0.31		-0.32	0.07	-4.68	0.00	(a)
UNDERPRICING	-0.05	0.13	-0.38	0.71		-0.20	0.09	-2.14	0.04	(b)	-0.08	0.09	-0.91	0.37		-0.06	0.15	-0.38	0.70		0.05	0.10	0.50	0.62	
Number of obs	99					99					99					99					99				
Quasi-LR statistic	0.33					32.7					40.7					30.6					52.5				
Prob. Quasi-LR statistic	0.00					0.01					0.00					0.02					0.00				
Pseudo R-squared	0.26					0.07					0.07					0.11					0.33				

Notes: (c),(b), and (a) indicates significance at the 10, 5, and 1% level

Further noteworthy changes are as follows: NUMIPO is only significant for the lowest decile of the return distribution, implying that following IPOs have tried to imitate successful pioneering IPOs but were not able to generate sufficient operating performance. In contrast, HOT and HOT(c)TRANSPARENCY are both statistical significant throughout the whole return distribution and thereby provide supporting evidence that firms which time their IPO with times of high valuation levels are generally overpriced.

SIZE is significant at the extreme return distributions, suggesting that particularly small companies perform particularly bad and vice versa whereas SIZE seems to have, for normally sized companies, no predictive power for long-run IPO performance.
Lastly, the impact of investment bank reputation on long-run IPO performance shows a large variation in the magnitude of the estimated coefficients. While IBREPU enters with an insignificantly positive and low coefficient at the lower quantiles, it becomes significant and increases in magnitude in the 90th quantile. This shows that prestigious underwriters seem to be able to positively influence long-run returns, with the precondition that the company is of high quality. In contrast, for low quality firms, prestigious underwriters seem to be only of little help. This strengthens the notion that prestigious investment banks particularly choose low risk companies.

3.5 CONCLUSION

The motivation of this paper is to rationalise why previous real estate IPO studies document no long-run underperformance, a phenomenon that is rather common among industrial IPOs. One explanation is provided by Wang et al. (1992) who assume that the special risk-return relationship of the asset class real estate might be one of the reasons. However, Chan et al. (2001) show that real estate companies in Hong Kong have first-day returns which are comparable to first-day returns of industrial companies and thereby provide evidence that seems to contradict the presumption of Wang et al. (1992).

This paper introduces market transparency as an alternative explanation. Most prior studies base their empirical analyses on data of property companies operating in mature and transparent real estate markets, such as the US, Australia, and Hong-Kong. We assume that these markets' high transparency enables market participants to perform elaborate investment analyses whereas we assume that a lesser degree of transparency rather hinders investors conducting a sophisticated valuation breakdown. We hypothesise that with a decreasing degree of real estate market transparency, profound investment analyses are increasingly difficult to perform, leading to the emergence of over-optimism among investors and/or among managers. Since over-optimism provides an opportunity for poor quality companies to issue equity, we expect these poor quality issuings to perform worse than the market and pull down the sample performance. The heterogeneity of the real estate market transparency of European property companies presents an ideal setting to explore this issue.

The results provide evidence that at least partly support the supposed influence of market transparency on market timing and IPO performance. We show that European property companies time their IPO to coincide with favourable market conditions and with positive exogenous shocks. We also show that investor over-optimism is more likely to develop among companies investing mainly in less transparent real estate markets. In contrast, the results do not support the assumption that the degree of market transparency has an effect on the ability of management to correctly identify investment possibilities.

Further, we document that IPOs of European property companies significantly underperform either equal or value-weighted benchmark portfolios in the long-run. More specifically, companies that issue equity at the peak of the market or have no initial property portfolio at the time of the IPO are among the companies with the highest underperformance levels, implying that these companies specifically take advantage of sentiment investors who initially overvalued the IPO firm's assets. In contrast, firms that time their equity issuing with a positive external exogenous shock outperform the benchmark over a 24-month aftermarket period, suggesting that the management is correctly anticipating growth opportunities. Finally, in line with previous studies, smaller firms tend to underperform more than larger companies. Supporting evidence for the small-firm effect, as detected by a variety of studies with industrial companies, provides additional evidence that the special risk-return characteristics of real estate are unlikely to be of explanatory power for IPO performance.

In summary, the findings support the notion that the transparency of the underlying real estate markets can affect rational decision making by investors. Low quality companies use their informational advantage to time their issue accordingly, which, on average, leads to long-run underperformance. Thus, accounting for real estate market transparency seems to explain why previous real estate IPO studies, using data of IPO firms that operate mainly in mature real estate markets, do not find long-run underperformance. Future research should be directed at developing other transparency measures that can also be employed in more homogenous real estate markets in order to verify the results presented in this study.

4 DO INVESTORS PAY A PREMIUM FOR IPOS IN THE REAL ESTATE INDUSTRY DEPENDING ON CORPORATE GOVERNANCE QUALITY?

4.1 INTRODUCTION

An initial public offering (IPO) represents the point in time when ownership becomes separated from control (Berle and Means (1932)). As a consequence, insiders' control rights are diluted and agency costs increase (Jensen and Meckling (1976)). Many control mechanisms have been proposed in the literature to mitigate this potential shareholder-manager conflict: Jensen and Murphy (1990) theoretically and empirically show the disciplinary power of compensation contracts, Hermalin and Weisbach (2003) review the role of the board, and Field and Karpoff (2002) propose anti-takeover amendments to decrease the agency cost. Nevertheless, there is continuing debate on the effect of these control mechanisms in firm valuation and firm performance. In particular, the impact of managerial ownership on valuation is open for debate: Jensen and Meckling (1976) propose that higher ownership retention by managers reduces their incentives to undertake non-value maximising projects, and thus has a positive effect on the market value of the firm. Supporting empirical evidence is provided by Morck et al. (1988), who find that managerial ownership is positively related to firm value, as measured by Tobin's Q. In contrast, Fama and Jensen (1983) highlight the problem of managerial entrenchment, suggesting that high managerial ownership may encourage management to undertake non-value maximising behaviour due to a misuse of their decision-making power. In addition, Himmelberg et al. (1999) even debate the possibility that the relationship between managerial ownership and firm value is subject to endogeneity. Overall, a vast number of empirical studies on large samples of industrial companies provide convincing evidence that favours either one of the proposed relationships. Consequently, some controversy on the relationship between managerial ownership and firm value remains.

Other researchers propose that besides the degree of management alignment, there are a variety of other control mechanisms with the potential to reduce agency costs and to affect firm value. Shleifer and Vishny (1986) argue that large shareholders have a monitoring effect on management because they, in contrast to atomistic shareholders, are able to capture a large fraction of the wealth gains resulting from a potential takeover. Jensen (1986) refers to the disciplinary role of debt. When firms have excess cash and low investment opportunities, leverage may serve as a disciplinary device because interest payments and principal repayments are not at the management's discretion. If the obligations are not met, creditors can demand that a firm be declared bankrupt. A variety of additional control mechanisms are summarised by Shleifer and Vishny (1997).

One major consequence of the large variety of disciplinary devices that might decrease agency problems between managers and shareholders is summarised by Pound (1995), who argues that effectively governed corporations ensure a balance of power between managers and shareholders. He suggests that establishing a system of corporate governance is the most effective way to create this balance. Such a monitoring system would include a combination of governance mechanisms rather than relying on one disciplinary device. In fact, Agrawal and Knoeber (1996) find that alternative control mechanisms are interdependent, i.e. a decrease in monitoring from one area is offset by an increase in monitoring from another area. Thus, the impact of a single control mechanism is probably misleading.

The purpose of this study is to provide further evidence of the interrelationship among common control mechanisms and to analyse whether investors are willing to pay premia for the control mechanisms' implementation at IPO. Tobin's Q is employed as a proxy for initial stock market valuation, which mitigates the need for risk adjustment (Lang and Stulz (1994)). In general, the theoretical framework of the study is an agency perspective, which suggests that investors are expected to pay a lower IPO price for a company the lower the quality and strength of the firm's corporate governance mechanisms. The reasoning is that a lower quality of control mechanisms increases the likelihood that shareholders will get expropriated or that their funds will be invested in non-value maximising or high-risk projects. Thus, less stringent monitoring mechanisms are expected to increase agency costs, and consequently should translate to lower market valuations.

The focus of this study is based on the valuation at the time of a firm's initial public offering (IPO), as it is assumed that a lower valuation at this time primarily affects insiders via lower cash proceeds from the offering. Hence, the expected negative relationship between less stringent monitoring results and firm valuation reflects insiders' willingness to trade higher managerial freedom for lower funds raised. Furthermore, we expect that corporate governance mechanisms of IPO firms are not yet employed in a firm value maximising manner, as it is assumed to be the case for well established form (Demsetz and Lehn (1985)). In fact, Petersen (2007) finds that insiders only divest a small proportion of their investment in the company, which exposes them to a significant under-diversification risk. Thus, by analysing the effect of control mechanisms for IPO firms, it is possible to analyse whether and how insiders employ corporate governance mechanisms to maximise firm value.

The sample used to analyse the issues addressed above is a set of European property companies (EPCs). Sirmans (1999) and Ooi (2000) argue that firms with substantial exposure to real estate risks are even more prone to the problems associated with the separation of ownership and control. In particular, Sirmans (1999) argues that real estate companies need a special set of control mechanisms because they are more prone to empire building, have less pressure to produce immediate results, and are generally more prone to the existence of managerial opportunism. Given these characteristics, European property companies might use monitoring and incentive alignment mechanisms differently when compared to industrial companies. There is a strong need for inside control via managerial ownership to ensure a proper alignment of interests, since the firm's performance is highly dependent on the management team. On the other hand, outside control is necessary to avoid managerial opportunism, given the high degree of managerial freedom in EPCs' management. Hartzell et al. (2004) perform the sole study to analyse the controlling effect of corporate governance mechanisms in a real estate IPO setup. The authors analyse a sample of 107 US real estate investment trusts (REITs) and find that REITs with stronger governance structures not only have higher average Tobin's Q, but also outperform their peers in terms of abnormal operating performance. However, the legal restrictions that come with the REIT regime might lessen the need for control mechanisms, and although the relationships have been found to be positive, they might be the results of other causes. But what can we expect from companies without a REIT regime? Remarkably, this question has not yet been addressed.

In order to solve this issue, we employ a hand-collected sample of 88 European property company IPOs during the time period from 1997 to 2007. This sample is well suited to address the study's research aim because the majority of the property companies issued within this time period are non-REITs, mainly because most European countries adopted REIT regimes in 2007 and later.

The corporate governance variables analysed in this paper are managerial ownership, outside blockholders, and financial leverage. The results confirm an interdependent relationship. More specifically, managerial ownership is negatively related to outside blockholders, which confirms their expected substitution relationship. Furthermore, debt is positively related to managerial ownership and blockholders, which leads one to suspect that debt is employed as a disciplinary device for European property companies. The results further show that concentrated ownership seems to negatively affect IPO valuation, regardless of whether the large stakes are held by management or by outside investors. Finally, debt has a positive effect on IPO valuation after allowing for simultaneous equation estimation. Lastly, no evidence for reverse causality is found, suggesting that the valuation of IPO firms does not impact the usage of corporate governance mechanisms in an IPO setting.

The remainder of this paper is organised as follows. Section 4.2 discusses previous literature regarding managerial ownership, large shareholdings, financial leverage, and firm value. The most relevant interrelationships are summarised and testable hypotheses are developed. Section 4.3 covers the research design, which includes a justification of the sample selection, an explanation of the selected methodology, and a definition of the measurement of the chosen variables. Empirical results are then presented in section 4.4, which includes the descriptive statistics followed by regression analyses, including basic and piecewise OLS regression, and ends with simultaneous system estimation to assess the robustness of the results. Section 4.5 concludes the paper.

4.2 Literature review and hypothesis development

4.2.1 Control mechanisms in an IPO setting

Because most corporate governance studies refer to well-established firms, it is first necessary to discuss the effects of control mechanisms in an IPO setting.

Because complete contracts are technically infeasible, managers end up with substantial residual control rights which leave them with sufficient discretion to allocate funds as they choose, thereby increasing the likelihood of managerial opportunism, i.e. managers can entrench themselves and expropriate or misallocate funds. Managerial opportunism in either form makes it difficult for companies to raise capital, as investors are less willing to finance the firm when facing the possibility of expropriation or misallocation of funds (Williamson (1985), Grossman and Hart (1986)). Thus, companies are in strong need of control mechanisms to assure investors that their funds are not expropriated or wasted on unattractive projects, and thus to minimise agency conflicts.

The monitoring mechanisms of companies prior to their IPO differ greatly from the documented monitoring mechanisms of well-established firms. Demsetz and Lehn (1985) argue that markets know about all the costs and benefits of monitoring mechanisms and will choose the structure that maximises firm value. They argue that there is an optimal level of monitoring mechanisms for well-established firms. Since all firms are in equilibrium, no significant relationship between ownership and performance is predicted. In contrast, IPO firms are typically young and small companies, characterised by a high degree of asymmetric information (with the informational advantage being on the side of the insiders, i.e. the management). Thus one can expect that the optimum level has not yet been reached. For example, Frye (2004) shows that inside ownership significantly decreases five years after an IPO has taken place, probably to decrease the under-diversification risk. On average, insiders only sell a small fraction of their stake in the company at IPO (Petersen (2002)). Under the assumption that the IPO firm is the insiders' major investment, this creates a paradoxical under-diversification problem. Rock (1986) notes: "An IPO means teeing the company for a future sale", suggesting that inside ownership following the IPO may still be higher than the preferred ownership structure, and thus inside holdings will continue to decrease. Although lock-up periods are designed to prevent insiders from selling their shares immediately after the IPO, it seems reasonable to argue that a high valuation and hence high IPO proceeds are beneficial for future projects of the company, which in turn increases the likelihood that the company will still be highly valued after the expiration of the look-up period.

In sum, the analysis of control mechanisms' impact on firm valuation at IPO allows us to pay particular attention on whether investors are willing to pay a premium for high quality corporate governance.

4.2.2 Real estate characteristics and the need for corporate control

Governance is more problematic when there is a high degree of asset specificity, when it is ex ante difficult to write complete contracts, and when there is higher information asymmetry. Any of these three problems can lead to managerial opportunism. As real estate companies invest in most of the time non-substitutable assets, i.e. properties, the general asset specificity is high. Furthermore, investing in real estate requires a high degree of local market knowledge, which increases the difficulty of pre-determining the tasks and duties of the management by contract. Lastly, the general absence of REIT-regimes in Europe significantly increases the information asymmetry among firm management and investors. Sirmans (1999) and Ooi (2000) allude to two further characteristics that leave property managers with numerous opportunities for expropriating investors and thereby support the relevance of strong corporate governance mechanisms in property companies. First, the long-term investment horizons of real estate investments put less pressure on managers for immediate reporting. Second, property managers might be more inclined towards empire building and reputation enhancement given the prominent media coverage of major property deals. In combination with sufficient control rights, this leaves managers much discretion about how to allocate investors' funds, and thereby leaves the investor with an increased likelihood of suffering from managerial self-dealing.

Hence, in order to analyse whether investors are willing to pay premia for the implementation of potentially agency cost reducing corporate governance mechanisms, the following subsections will critically review the previous literature by analysing whether and how corporate governance mechanisms can reduce agency costs, and then summarise the relationships in an inter-dependent theoretical framework that will serve as a guideline for the empirical analysis portion.

4.2.3 Interrelation of control mechanisms and IPO valuation

The following subsections concentrate on the interrelationships of various monitoring mechanisms in general and on how they affect firm value in particular. For a better understanding, it is first useful to clarify the definitions of the main dependent variables.

As a proxy for *inside control*, we follow Morck et al. (1988) and Short and Keasey (1999) and employ retained managerial ownership, which is defined as the percentage of total share capital after flotation owned by members of the management and their families. The distribution of shares among family members is often due to tax reasons and to increase the amount of divestment possible without triggering a directors' dealings announcement. Thus, family members are expected to have the same level of information as the active manager, and can therefore be included in the measurement of managerial ownership. Throughout this paper, the terms inside ownership and managerial ownership are used interchangeably. *Outside control* is measured by outside blockholders and is defined analogous to that reported by Agrawal and Knoeber (1996), as the percentage of shares held by owners other than those of the inside control proxy and those who hold 5% or more of outstanding the shares following admission. The *contracting* mechanism, as in the work presented by Frye (2004), is represented by financial leverage, i.e. the debt-to-assets ratio. Finally, Tobin's Q is used as a measurement of firm valuation in general and of growth opportunities in particular. Klapper and Love (2003) and Durnev and Kim (2005) note that firms with better investment opportunities have greater incentives to adopt better governance practices. In other studies, Q is sometimes referred to as a performance measure. However, as performance in IPO studies is measured by analysing aftermarket stock price quotation via buy-and-hold returns, the terms *valuation* and *growth opportunity* are used in connection with Q, although performance would be equivalent.

4.2.3.1 Inside control

Managerial ownership as a determinant of firm valuation: In their seminal paper, Jensen and Meckling (1976) show that inside ownership can help to reduce agency problems that arise from the separation of ownership and control. By retaining a stake in the company, managers bear the wealth consequences of their actions, which serve to align the interests of managers and investors. As EPCs are normally internally managed, the management has the ultimate control of the firm's investment decisions. A more IPO-specific argument for the interrelationship of managerial ownership and firm value is provided by Leland and Pyle (1977). The authors assume that an entrepreneur's personal wealth is tied up in an under-diversified portfolio, i.e. the firm. In order to reduce the risk associated with this sort of under-diversification, the entrepreneur can disperse some of the firm-specific risk and obtain a better-balanced portfolio by selling a part of the company via an IPO. In order to convince the market of the quality of the company, the manager can send a signal to the market by *retaining* part of his equity, which keeps him attached to firm-specific risk. Thus, the market values managerial ownership as a costly signal for potential investors, and thereby helps them to infer the true value of the shares. Hence, according to Leland and Pyle's signalling model, agency costs induced by managerial opportunism can be alleviated in IPOs if the management retains a larger stake in the issuing company. Empirical support in favour of Leland and Pyle (1977) is provided by Downes and Heinkel (1982) and Hughes (1989) for U.S. companies. However, in Europe, Keasey and Short (1997) find no supporting results for the Leland and Pyle model. Another line of research argues that inside ownership actually has a negative impact on firm valuation. Fama (1980), Fama and Jensen (1983), and Demsetz (1983) hypothesise that high information asymmetry increases the likelihood that managers will pursue projects that benefit them rather than investors or that managers entrench themselves and, for instance, stay on the job even if they are no longer qualified to run the firm (Shleifer and Vishny (1989)). Stulz (1988) provides a formal model in which he shows that firm value is negatively related to managerial ownership because large shareholdings by top management act as a deterrent for takeovers because of the greater ability to oppose a hostile bid or drive up premiums to the point where bidders no longer view the target company as a positive net present value investment. Israel and Israel (1992) and Stulz et al. (1990) provide supporting evidence for Stulz's model and show that sufficiently high managerial ownership will decrease the possibility of a tender offer by raiders. Morck et al. (1988), McConnell and Servaes (1990), and Hermalin and Weisbach (1991) find that "alignment of interest" occurs at low levels of managerial ownership, but that "entrenchment" occurs at high levels. Chen (2006) documents that for firms with low levels of managerial ownership, there is a negative relationship between managerial ownership and firm valuation. Lastly, Demsetz (1983) argues that there should be no systematic relationship between the ownership structure and the performance of a company. Demsetz and Lehn (1985) confirm this by accounting for the endogeneity of a firm's ownership structure, and find no relationship between the ownership concentration and the corporation profits. The authors argue that when the ownership structures of well-established firms are analysed, these ownership structures most suit the conditions under which firms operate. Thus, there is an optimal ownership structure that is accounted for by the market of well-established firms.

Managerial ownership as a determinant of blockholders: Stoughton and Zechner (1998) and Benveniste and Spindt (1989) argue that large shareholders are favoured during the allocation process of IPO shares because of it may be value-enhancing as large outside investors are able to monitor managerial actions. On the other hand, Brennan and Franks (1997) argue that, by favouring small shareholders, managers reduce the block size of new shareholdings, which decreases the incentive for outside shareholders to monitor because of the two free rider problems. First, Shleifer and Vishny (1986) argue that atomistic investors get a free ride on the monitoring attempts of large blockholders, resulting in insufficient monitoring as blockholders internalise only the gains for their stake. Second, Grossman and Hart (1980) argue that incumbent managers opt for dispersed ownership because it reduces the threat of hostile takeovers. Alavi et al. (2008) find that managers are reluctant to allocate shares to large new shareholders when management's pre-IPO stake in the company offers them control over the company. For companies with low pre-IPO managerial ownership, the emergence of large new blockholders is more likely.

Managerial ownership as a determinant of debt: Jensen and Meckling (1976) argue that inside ownership aligns interests and thereby reduces the bankruptcy risk that comes along with high debt levels. This makes the company more attractive to the lender, i.e. the lender can provide better interest rates and managers can rely more heavily on debt financing. Similarly, Stulz (1988) argues that greater leverage allows managers to increase their voting power for a given level of equity. Thus, debt serves as a way to relax the wealth constraints that a small group of investors face when they try to gain voting control of a company. Thus, Jensen and Meckling (1976) and Stulz (1988) predict a positive relationship. In contrast, Friend and Lang (1988) find a negative relationship between inside ownership and debt. The authors interpret this as the desire of managers to minimise the non-diversifiable risk associated with high debt ratios and add that the management of closely held companies seem to have the greatest power (compared to that of publicly held companies) to adjust the corporate debt levels according to its own interests.

4.2.3.2 Outside control

Blockholders as determinants of firm valuation: Large shareholders are believed to be an important component of effective governance and "the most direct way to align cash flow and control rights of outside investors" (Shleifer and Vishny (1997), p. 754). In addition, Jensen and Meckling (1976) argue that substantial shareholders are expected to monitor management carefully, as their wealth is tied to the firm's financial performance. As a consequence, large investors are expected to have a controlling effect on managerial opportunism, which in turn positively affects the firm value. Furthermore, Huddart (1993) argues that shareholders that have a large stake in a firm will monitor management carefully and encourage better management performance by modifying incentive contracts. Shleifer and Vishny (1986) argue that takeovers can only be successful when the bidder has already acquired a large minority ownership position in the firm. The potential takeover threat that large blockholders can exert works as an effective device for monitoring management. Whereas small atomistic shareholders cannot benefit from costly monitoring, holders of large blocks can benefit because they are able to capture a large fraction of the wealth gains that result from a takeover. Thus, Shleifer and Vishny (1986) predict that, all else being equal, the presence of a large outside blockholder will have a positive effect on the market value of the firm. Denis and McConnell (2003) argue that blockholder ownership has a more positive effect on firm value in countries with lower levels of investor protection, because it is more necessary to counter managerial agency problems in these countries. They find that this is broadly consistent with a review of the empirical evidence outside the US and the UK. In contrast, empirical evidence by Holderness and Sheehan (1988) and McConnell and Servaes (1990) do not support this hypothesis. Researchers have also raised some arguments suggesting that the existence of an outside blockholder may result in decrease in value as they may abuse their position of dominant control at the expense of minority shareholders (Stiglitz (1985), La Porta et al. (1999)). Whatever the identity of blockholders, they may have strong incentives to divert resources in ways that make them better off at the expense of other shareholders (Wruck (1989). La Porta et al. (1998) suggest that in this environment, firms with concentrated owners would face difficulty raising equity finance since minority investors would fear expropriation by managers and concentrated owners. Furthermore, Brickley et al. (1988) note that outside blockholders might be obliged to vote with the management in order to maintain the company's business. Pound (1988) argues that outside blockholders and management might form strategic alliances as they may find it mutually beneficial to cooperate. Similarly, Stulz (1988) assumes that the presence of manager-friendly blockholders has a negative impact on firm value because management's voting rights are increased, which in turn reduces the threat of a takeover. Overall, the *empirical evidence* on the effects of large blockholders on firm value is mixed. Supporting evidence is provided by Bathala et al. (1994), who find a positive relationship between outside blockholdings and firm value. Mikkelson and Ruback (1985) document positive abnormal returns for the acquired firm following the announcement of the acquisition of a 5% or greater stake in one firm by another firm. Similarly, McConnell and Servaes (1990) find a positive relationship between institutional ownership and Tobin's Q. In contrast, Demsetz and Lehn (1985) find no cross-sectional relationship between the concentration of shareholdings and the accounting rates of return.

Blockholders as determinants of managerial ownership: Blockholders have the incentive and the means to monitor the management in a cost effective way and, if necessary, to intervene to correct value-destructive actions by using their voting rights to remove managers who fail to maximise their wealth (Mikkelson and Ruback (1985)). Thus, the presence of blockholders may discourage managerial initiative and thus, although ex post beneficial, may be undesirable ex ante (Burkhart et al. (1997)). In other words, the manager is less inclined to show initiative, like searching for new investment projects, when shareholders are likely to interfere, leading to a trade-off situation between the gains from monitoring and those from managerial initiative. Following this argumentation, the presence of large blockholders might lead to lower managerial ownership. Alavi et al. (2008) note that if pre-IPO managerial ownership is low, the need for outside monitoring becomes stronger. In order to avoid agency costs in the form of a weak demand for IPO shares, management deliberately allocates large amounts to new shareholders in order to ensure sufficient monitoring. Thus, IPO firms with high outside blockholdings are expected to have lower managerial holdings.

Blockholders as determinants of debt: It is hypothesised that large blockholders use their power and influence to elicit high debt ratios, which are expected to reduce the resources available for perquisite consumption by management. However, Grier and Zychowicz (1994) propose that the presence of large blockholders rather acts as a substitute for debt's disciplinary role, and in fact find evidence that when institutional ownership, which is their measure for large blockholders, is prevalent, firms are characterised by lower degrees of debt in their capital structures. Thus, it can be argued that outside blockholders do not require debt as a monitoring device, but rather monitor themselves, which suggests a negative relationship between outside blockholdings and debt. Empirical evidence is provided by Ferris et al. (2001), who find a substitution effect of managerial ownership and debt, i.e. firms with higher levels of managerial ownership have low levels of debt. In contrast, Zwiebel (1996) argues that managers will not increase leverage voluntarily. In his view, managers aim to avoid leverage, but can be forced by other governance mechanisms to increase leverage, which serves as the ultimate disciplinary device to reduce over-investment behaviour. In line with this intuition, Friend and Lang (1988) find that corporations with large non-managerial investors have debt ratios that are significantly higher than the debt ratios in companies with no principal stockholders. The authors suggest that the presence of outside blockholders might lead to a tax-shield-induced optimal level from the viewpoint of diversified investors.

4.2.3.3 Contracting

Debt as a determinant of firm value: Another monitoring effect is associated with debt. Debt is a contract in which the borrower agrees with the lender to pay a pre-specified stream of future payments in exchange for receiving a certain amount of funds that the borrower can use at his discretion (Shleifer and Vishny (1997), p. 761). The controlling effect stems from the borrower's agreement not to violate a range of covenants (Smith and Warner (1979)). In the case that these covenants are breached, the lender can exercise certain rights such as the ability to repossess the debt's collateral, which is employed as security in the case of bankruptcy (Hart and Moore (1998)). In line with this argumentation, Grossman and Hart (1982) and Jensen (1986) argue that debt serves as a disciplinary mechanism to increase the likelihood that firm management is actually acting in a shareholder-value maximising manner. The authors point out that in the presence of managerial opportunism, debt pre-commits the disposition of free-cash flows and thus reduces the likelihood of value destroying investment decisions by the management. Empirical evidence of the effectiveness of debt as a control mechanism is mixed. Lang and Ofek (1996) provide empirical evidence that leverage restricts investments by firms with poor investment opportunities. McConnell and Servaes (1995) find evidence in favour of the disciplining power of debt. Similarly, Stulz (1990) shows that debt can reduce managers' tendency to over-invest, whereas Agrawal and Knoeber (1996) find no impact on firm valuation. In contrast, Myers (1977) refers to the underinvestment problem of debt financing and shows that debt levels that are too high induce managers to forego positive net present value projects. In contrast, Bathala et al. (1994) argue that debt levels that are too high subject the firm to risk shifting, i.e. managers might have a tendency to prefer riskier projects because they need only to pay the debt holders the contracted rate and can capture the surplus if the riskier project is successful. As these studies mainly concentrated on the US market, further studies focusing on European companies find, on average, evidence against the disciplinary role of debt. In fact, De Jong (2002) finds limited evidence to support the disciplining role of debt for a set of Dutch companies. Similarly, Harvey et al. (2004) also find no impact of debt on valuation for a survey of 18 emerging economies in 1995-1996.

Debt as a determinant of managerial ownership: Gilson (1989) argues that debt holders are important non-equity stakeholders whose influence is even strong enough to have a controlling impact on management turnover. In fact, the author finds that more than half of his sample of 409 US firms experience management turnover if they are either in default on their debt, bankrupt, or privately restructuring their debt to avoid bankruptcy. A rather logical argument concerning the impact of debt structure on the degree of managerial ownership is proposed by Jensen and Meckling (1976), who argue that the use of debt lessens the need for external capital, and thus raises the proportion of managerial ownership in the firm.

Debt as a determinant of blockholders: Ross (1977) argues that firms use debt as a signalling device. Assuming that outside blockholdings and debt are substitutable, then outsiders think that monitoring via debt sufficiently diverts away the free cash flow problem, and thus they do not need to invest heavily.

4.2.3.4 Firm value

Firm value as a determinant of managerial ownership: As mentioned before, the relationship between managerial ownership and firm valuation might be endogenously related, i.e. there may be two-way causality. Starting with a one-way causation relationship assuming all variables to be exogenous and then estimating simultaneous equations with endogenous variables, Agrawal and Knoeber (1996) and Cho (1998) find that most of the previously significant results disappear. The authors conclude that the equilibrium assumption of Demsetz (1983) prevails. In contrast, Loderer and Martin (1997) and Cho (1998), using simultaneous regressions, reveal that causation is reversed, i.e. that corporate value affects the ownership structure, but not vice versa. This suggests that ownership may not be an effective incentive mechanism to induce managers to make value-maximising investment decisions. In addition, Demsetz and Villalonga (2001) find, using a 2SLS method, that inside ownership has no impact on firm valuation, but that valuation has a negative impact on inside ownership.

Firm value as a determinant of blockholders: La Porta et al. (2002) argue that a positive impact of firm valuation on blockholder ownership occurs if blockholders are more inclined to be in control since a higher market price makes it possible to finance a given level of investment by issuing a smaller amount of stock to outside owners. Therefore, if current shareholders hold on to a larger fraction of the shares in high value companies, firm value can be inferred to have a positive effect on the fraction of shares held by the current blockholders.

Firm value as a determinant of debt: Jensen (1986) notes in his free-cash flow hypothesis that when firms have more internally generated funds than positive net present value investment opportunities, the presence of debt in the firm's capital structure forces managers to pay out funds that might otherwise have been invested in negative net present value projects. In other words, firms with low growth opportunities are likely to be leveraged in order to avoid potential over-investment. According to Ooi (2000), property companies have an increased likelihood of suffering from the negative effect of over-investment given the high popularity associated with trophy-building investments. Finally, Myers' and Majluf's (1984) pecking-order hypothesis argues that an increase in share price and firm value allows insiders (managers and blockholders) to finance a given level of investment in the firm by issuing fewer shares while relying more on debt and internally generated funds. However, this argument has less explanatory power in an IPO context.

4.2.4 Summary of previous literature and hypotheses

As can be inferred from this brief survey of the previous literature, there are a variety of mechanisms that theoretically and also practically seem to reduce agency costs. It also seems reasonable that these mechanisms are not exclusive, i.e. firms are likely to employ more than one of these monitoring systems. Figure 4.1 presents a simplified summary of the interdependencies and causal relationships in question. The figure shows that each variable can have an impact on the other variables. Nevertheless, not all relationships are expected to be relevant in the context of IPOs of EPCs. Thus, the following paragraphs discuss the relationships that are most important for European property companies, and testable hypotheses are derived.

First, consistent with the positive monitoring effect of blockholders, we expect managerial ownership and outside blockholders to be negatively related. Although Holderness and Sheehan (1988) and McConnell and Servaes (1990) argue that the presence of ineffective monitors imply a non-negative relationship of managerial ownership and blockholders, we expect managerial ownership and outside blockholders to be negatively related because companies are investing in real estate, which, in contrast to high-tech products, for example, is easy to value and hence makes blockholders effective monitors. Thus, we expect a negative relationship between managerial ownership and outside blockholders.

FIGURE 4.1: SUMMARY OF THE RELATIONSHIPS OF FIRM VALUATION AND CONTROL MECHANISMS

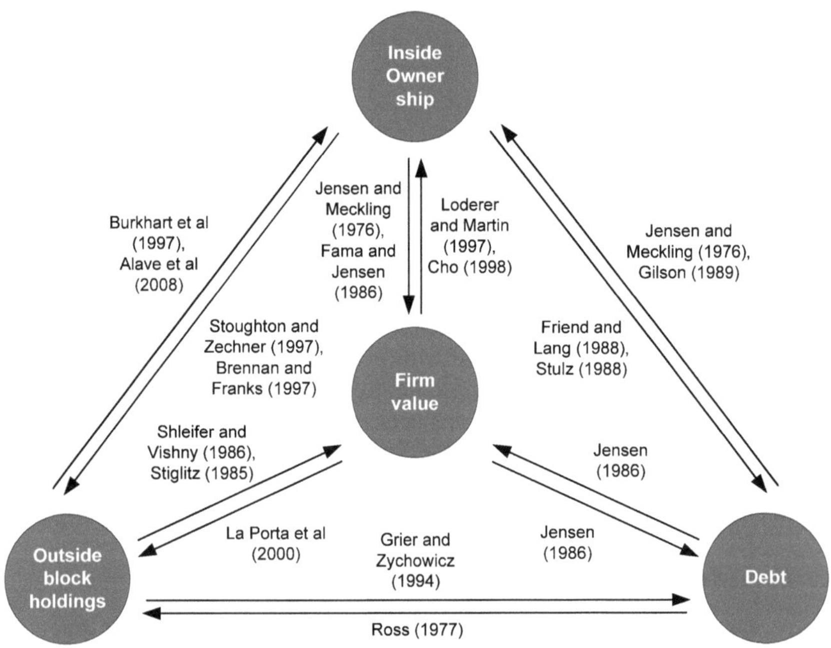

H1: Managerial ownership and outside blockholders are negatively related

The relationship of managerial ownership and debt cannot be predicted ex ante. On the one hand, managers of EPCs might be unwilling to dilute their control, and thus prefer to rely on bank debt financing. Thus, a positive relationship between managerial ownership and debt financing is expected. On the other hand, considering the under-diversification problem that a heavily invested manager faces, a negative relationship would be expected as debt levels that are too high increase the risk of bankruptcy.

H2a: Managerial ownership and debt are positively related

H2b: Managerial ownership and debt are negatively related

The relation between outside blockholders and debt is expected to be negative. As noted by Ooi (2000), the management of property companies has less pressure to produce immediate results. Thus, higher debt financing is a strong way to restrict the options of the manager to divert excess cash. The negative relationship is expected to be even stronger for companies investing in non-transparent real estate markets, as the monitoring potential of outside blockholders for such is limited. Therefore, in line with Grier and Zychowicz (1994), we expect the importance of the disciplinary role of debt to be diminished when a large outside equity holder is prevalent. Thus, a negative relationship between outside blockholders and debt is expected.

H3: Outside blockholders and debt are negatively related

Managerial ownership is expected to affect firm valuation nonlinearly, due to the competing effects of the incentive alignment argument according to Jensen and Meckling (1976) and the managerial entrenchment argument proposed by Fama and Jensen (1983). Hartzell et al. (2004) include the squared value of inside ownership to account for nonlinearity, and in fact find the relationship to be non-monotonic. This is interesting, as the strict REIT regime itself acts as a strongly controlled environment and is expected to divert any possibility for managerial entrenchment. we expect a sample of EPCs to have a non-monotonic relationship between inside ownership and IPO valuation, as characteristics of EPCs suggest both the need for incentive alignment and the possibility of managerial entrenchment.

H4: Managerial ownership is non-monotonically related to firm value

The relationships of blockholdings and debt to firm valuation can be inferred from the hypothesis H1 - H3. Hence, no additional hypotheses are formulated.

The last hypothesis is that firm valuation and control mechanisms are *not* jointly determined. Referring to the potentially interrelated causal relationships of firm value with corporate governance mechanisms and to the findings of Chen and Steiner (2000), who find for well-established firms that analyst coverage, managerial ownership, and firm valuation are jointly determined, this study tests whether the same is also true for IPO firms. We expect to find no joint determination, as it is expected that in IPO firms the management has relatively strong power over the issue price, choosing ownership structures that follow admission and issuing debt.

H5: Firm valuation and control mechanisms are *not* jointly determined

Due to the embedded two-way causality, the last hypothesis requires the construction and solution of a system of simultaneous equations. To our knowledge, this is the first study to analyse the potentially endogenous interrelationship of firm value, managerial ownership, outside blockholdings, and debt in an IPO context.

4.3 RESEARCH DESIGN

4.3.1 Sample selection and data source

The sample contains IPOs of European property companies from 1997 to 2007, where European property companies are defined as operating real estate companies with a property-backed business model and with geographic investment foci covering Western Europe (Austria, Belgium, France, Germany, Italy, Portugal, Spain, Switzerland, UK), the Nordic countries (Denmark, Finland, Norway, Sweden) and Central and Eastern Europe (CEE) (Bulgaria, Croatia, Czech Republic, Estonia, Hungary, Latvia, Lithuania, Poland, Romania, Russia, Serbia, Slovakia, Slovenia, Ukraine). The reasoning for using this particular data set is as follows: in order to analyse the impact of managerial ownership on property company IPO valuation, the following sampling requirements have to be fulfilled: (1) the calculation of Tobin's Q must be based on reasonable data and (2) information on shareholder structure has to be available.

(1) Tobin's Q: As IPO companies are normally young and have only a short operating history and limited accounting information. In particular sample firms that completed their IPO in the years 2006 and 2007 have been relatively young companies with no or only very small assets in their balance sheets leading to unreasonable high Q ratios. Thus, all companies with Q ratios of more than 3 times the sample's standard deviation and all companies with no asset value at all have been excluded

(2) Shareholder structure: Second, information on shareholder structure has to be available. Most European countries demand from their issuing companies that they must disclose the expected ownership structure before and after the IPO. Thus, ownership information is available for most of the companies.

The target sample contains 242 IPOs which represent all European companies classified by the SIC code for real estate companies (SIC 65) of the Dealogic database. From this preliminary sample, several companies had to be excluded because company and/or stock market characteristics did not match the definition of a European property company as described above. More specifically, excluded firms from the sample include (1) companies with investment focus outside of Western Europe, the Nordic countries or CEE, (2) companies with no property-backed business model (such as real estate service companies or real estate agents), and (3) companies with no information on operating business and/or stock prices. The latter represents the largest group of excluded companies mainly because double checking Dealogic data with IPO prospectuses and company press releases revealed significant discrepancies. As the limited data availability, reliability, and comparability can be owed to large differences in accounting practices, tax regimes, and disclosure requirements of the 20 different legislative systems the sample firms operate in, we decided to only include IPOs for which the admission documents are available in either language of German, English, Spanish or French, offer prices and first day closing prices have been double checked and stock price information is available on Datastream. By these control steps, any biases due to local disclosure standards or accounting practices are expected to be minimised. As a consequence, the final data sample consists of 141 IPOs.

To guarantee representativeness of the sample we discussed each IPO with real estate experts in France, Germany and UK and were confirmed that the final sample consists of all companies that are regarded as characteristic for the European property company universe. Excluded IPOs are mainly small and rather unknown. In the course of this long-run performance study, the final sample sums to 88 companies as balance sheet information and pre and post-IPO shareholder structure was not meaningful or not available. An inspection of the data identified very few extreme values so we applied the winsorisation technique as a correction. This technique takes the non-missing values of a variable and generates a new variable identical except that the h highest and h lowest values are replaced by the maximum of five times the mean absolute deviation of all observations for this variable.

4.3.2 Methodology

The analysis of corporate governance is subject to methodological challenges. In order to account properly for non-linearity and potential endogeneity issues, the empirical analysis involves the following steps. First, basic OLS regressions are estimated in order to analyse the interrelationship between managerial ownership, outside blockholdings, and debt. Second, Tobin's Q is regressed on control mechanisms in order to determine their ability to explain IPO valuation. Furthermore, Durbin-Wu-Hausman tests are conducted to test whether endogeneity issues led to biased OLS results, followed, if necessary, by a set of simultaneous equations to correct for the bias. The following paragraphs discuss the relevant steps in greater detail.

The first step involves OLS regression of control mechanisms. In order to analyse their interrelationship, three regression models are constructed with one of the three main variables of interest, i.e. RETAIN_MGT, BLOCK_OUT, and DEBT is used as a dependent variable, and the remaining other two as independent variables. Additional variables include variables derived from the previous literature that are also expected to have explanatory power for each equation. For an overview of the definitions of the variables, see Table 4.1 in Subsection 4.3.3. Heteroscedasticity-consistent standard errors are reported throughout all regressions using White's (1980) method. The first set of regressions is as follows:

(4.1) $$INSIDE = \beta_0 + \beta_1 OUTSIDE + \beta_2 CONTRACT + \beta_3 CONTROLS$$

(4.2) $$OUTSIDE = \beta_0 + \beta_1 INSIDE + \beta_2 CONTRACT + \beta_3 CONTROLS$$

(4.3) $$CONTRACT = \beta_0 + \beta_1 INSIDE + \beta_2 OUTSIDE + \beta_3 CONTROLS$$

The next block of the analysis also incorporates the Tobin's Q as a measure for firm value at IPO. Tobin's Q is defined as the market valuation of equity at the time of the IPO plus any debt divided by the replacement costs of the firm's assets. In this paper, the market value of equity, as employed in the calculation of Tobin's Q, is measured both as outstanding shares times the offer price (QISSUE) and as outstanding shares times the closing price (Q1). Looking at both definitions of the IPO valuation, one can analyse the impact of control mechanisms on the pricing of the IPO by both the issuers and the market. The equation is as follows:

(4.4) $$TOBINSQ = \beta_0 + \beta_1 INSIDE + \beta_2 OUTSIDE + \beta_3 CONTRACT + \beta_4 CONTROLS$$

Nonlinearity is a further issue that must be addressed when analysing the relationship of inside ownership and firm value, as the incentive hypothesis predicts a positive effect of inside ownership on valuation, whereas the entrenchment hypothesis predicts a countervailing effect. For a first assessment, RETAIN_MGT also appears as squared and cube values in Equation 4.4. Furthermore, firm value is also estimated in a piecewise regression where up to two breakpoints of RETAIN_MGT are tested. In order to derive the breakpoints, a simple grid-search technique similar to that of Cho (1998) is employed. First, the level of insider ownership that produces the most significant slope coefficient for the first insider ownership variable in the regression is calculated. This level is fixed, and then the second ownership level that yields the most significant slope coefficients for the second and third insider ownership variables in the regression is derived with the aid of an iterated search technique.

As discussed before, the causality of control mechanisms among each other and in relationship to the firm value might run in both directions or even act simultaneously. In other words, determinants of the potentially endogenous variable also affect the dependent variable, which causes the potentially endogenous variable to be correlated with the error term of the equation. This violates the assumption of OLS regression that all independent variables must be uncorrelated with the error term, and thus the OLS results would be biased. Systems of simultaneous equations can alleviate this problem by introducing instrumental variables (IV) that are correlated with the endogenous variable, but are not correlated with the error term. Demsetz and Lehn (1985), Agrawal and Knoeber (1996), Loderer and Martin (1997), Cho (1998), and Demsetz and Villalonga (2001), among others, use 2SLS to estimate a system of simultaneous equations. 2SLS is a single equation method, which means that over identifying restrictions in other equations are not taken into account in estimating the parameters of a particular equation, resulting in estimates that are not asymptotically efficient. Thus, 2SLS applies only to a single equation within the system of equations, and does not account for the cross-equation correlation among errors. 3SLS is the natural extension of 2SLS and estimates all coefficients of the model to form weights, and then and re-estimates the model using the estimated weighting matrix. The first two stages of 3SLS are the same as those in 2SLS, but the third stage involves the application of feasible generalised least squares to the equations in the system. The 3SLS procedure accounts for cross-equation error correlations, and thereby can be more efficient than 2SLS, which is the major advantage of 3SLS over 2SLS. However, the disadvantage of 3SLS is that in the case of system specification error, the error will affect all equations because 3SLS estimates them contemporaneously. However, for small sample sizes, 2SLS might be better. For the sake of completeness, both methods are employed.

One of the major challenges confronted with instrumental variable estimation is the detection of a valid set of IVs. The problem is how many instruments to use and which ones. The minimum required number of instruments is equal to the number of endogenous variables. Increasing the number of instruments would improve asymptotic efficiency of the estimation, but at the same time increases the finite sample bias (Johnston and DiNardo (1997). The choice of IVs is based on economical and statistical grounds. As statistical requirements are far more stringent, the first constraint is based on statistical reasons, and then double-checked with economical reasoning. The strong interrelationship of the corporate governance variables and the limited sample size make it difficult to find valid instruments. This leads to the result that almost any instrument variable identified for the one variable will plausibly (based on theory and/or empirical evidence) be related to at least one of the other potentially endogenous variables. Bhagat and Bolton (2008) make a similar point. In order to find reasonable instruments, the literature suggests testing for the strength and validity of the IVs.

Strength: The instruments should be strong, i.e. there should be a high correlation between the instrument and the corresponding endogenous variable. Stock et al. (2002) recommend that the first-stage F statistic should be greater than 8.96 for one instrumental variable. Based on this intuition, the following IVs can be identified: FOUNDER is chosen as the instrument for the managerial ownership equation. Besides strong empirical evidence, FOUNDER is also economically unlikely to be affected by the firm's debt policy or by the firm's IPO valuation. Furthermore, the strong correlation of FOUNDER with RETAIN_MGT and its low correlation with DEBT and QISSUE make FOUNDER a strong IV for managerial ownership. For the debt equation, the maximal borrowing power (MAXLEV) of the company is employed.

Table 4.3 confirms the strong correlation. Finally, UNDERPRICING is identified as a strong instrument for firm value. In line with the signalling argument of Leland and Pyle (1977), the degree of underpricing is highly correlated with firm value at IPO. As noted above, no IV could be identified for outside blockholders, which are therefore excluded from the simultaneous equation estimation.

Validity: The instruments must be orthogonal to the error term of the respective equations, i.e. the instruments must be truly exogenous. Sargan (1964) proposes a test statistic to test this robustness, which is calculated as the sample size times the R^2 value obtained from a regression of the residuals of a 2SLS estimation on all instruments included in the system. This statistic is distributed as chi-squared, with degrees of freedom equal to the number of instruments included in the system less the number of regressors in the respective equation. Due to the restriction on the number of degrees of freedom, this is not testable in exactly identified models, i.e. models with as many instruments as endogenous variables. Nevertheless, due to the fact that the above-identified instruments are each mostly correlated with the assigned endogenous variable and are far less correlated with the other endogenous variables, one can already give a first indication that the identified instruments are valid.

Before testing for reverse causality with simultaneous equation estimation, it is necessary to analyse whether endogeneity is actually inherent. To test for endogeneity, Durbin-Wu-Hausman (Hausman (1978)) tests are conducted. Employing system estimation without endogeneity can lead to biased results (Rhodes and Westbrook (1981)). Having confirmed that the regressions might be subject to endogeneity problems, 2SLS and 3SLS regressions are conducted. Equations 4.1 - 4.4 form the system of simultaneous equations to measure the reverse and two-way causality of IPO valuation and control mechanisms:

4.3.3 *Measures of variables*

4.3.3.1 Measures of control variables of control mechanisms

In the following section, various control variables included in equations 4.1 – 4.4 are described and the reasoning of their expected impact on the four main dependent variables of interest is discussed:

Managerial ownership equation: First, firm age (AGE) is included. Eichholtz et al. (2008) find that hostile takeovers are a very rare phenomenon in the real estate sector. More specifically, only two out of 95 analysed takeovers are hostile. This suggests that the management turnover rate of property companies might be lower compared to other industries where hostile takeovers are more prevalent. Consequently, one can expect the management of property companies to have longer tenure periods. In general, tenure is positively related to managerial ownership (Agrawal and Knoeber (1996)), which implies that older firms are expected to have long-lasting management-firm relationships. Hence, it is expected that management is less willing to dilute its ownership compared to more recently established firms, where the bonding relationship is less pronounced. Therefore, AGE and managerial ownership are expected to be positively related. As the under-diversification cost of large shareholdings is important for individuals because it is assumed that a great part of these individuals' wealth is tied to their stake in the firm, we include, following Agrawal and Knoeber (1996), firm size (ASSET) and volatility (VOLATILITY), measured as the standard deviation of stock returns, to measure these costs. In line with Chen and Steiner (2000), ASSET is expected to negatively impact managerial ownership, as wealth constraints hinder management's ability to obtain large stakes in the company. Loderer and Martin (1997) argue that stock volatility is positively associated with inside ownership as stock volatility increases the power of stock compensation packages and the value of inside information. Demsetz and Lehn (1985) argue that a firm's control potential is directly associated with the degree of asymmetric information for the environment in which it operates. Thus, regulation should also have a negative impact on managerial ownership, as regulation may restrict managerial freedom per se, and thus reduces the need for any control mechanisms. In fact, Booth et al. (2002) find that to the extent to which regulations reduce the impact of managerial decisions on shareholder wealth, effective internal monitoring of managers becomes less important in controlling agency conflicts. Thus, a negative relationship between REGULATED and managerial ownership is expected. In addition, the underlying real estate market's transparency (TRANSPARENCY) is included as a further asymmetric information variable, in line with the argument of Demsetz and Lehn (1985). Europe is characterised by real estate markets that differ significantly in terms of maturity and transparency.

TABLE 4.1: OVERVIEW OF VARIABLES

Variable name	Definition	Source
AGE	Age of the firm at the IPO measured as the natural logarithm of the difference of the IPO firm's offer year and its year of incorporation	IPO prospectus
ASSET	Pre-IPO total assets	IPO prospectus
BLOCK_OUT	Outside blockholdings measured as the percentage of shares held by owners of 5% or more of the equity following admission	IPO prospectus
DEBT	Pre-IPO total debt to total assets	IPO prospectus
DILUTION	Capital increase at the IPO measured as a percentage of issued share capital relative to the pre	IPO share capital.
DIVEST_MGT	The divestment of insiders relative to the pre IPO holdings	IPO prospectus
EPRA	Return of the FTSE/EPRA Europe index 12 months before the offering	EPRA
FOUNDER	Dummy variable that equals one if management holds 100% of the firm's pre-IPO equity	IPO prospectus
GDPGROWTH	Growth rate of the gross domestic product of the firm's target country measured as the difference of the GDP in the year after the IPO and the GDP in the IPO year divided by the GDP in the IPO year	International Monetary Fund
IBREPU	Dummy variable that equals one if the issuing firm's underwriter or nominated broker is a global investment bank	IPO prospectus
MAXLEV	The maximal allowed borrowing power of the company	IPO prospectus
NEWBLOCK_OUT	New outside blockholdings measured as the percentage of shares held by new owners of 5% or more of the equity following admission	IPO prospectus
OFFSHORE	Dummy variable that equals one if the company is incorporated in a legal regime which benefits from a corporate tax-exempt status, e.g. the British Islands	IPO prospectus
PIPELINE	Dummy variable that equals one if the issuing firm fully or at least partially specifies the properties it intends to acquire with the IPO proceeds and zero otherwise.	IPO prospectus
PW1-3	Interval of retained inside ownership in a piecewise regression	IPO prospectus
Q1	Market value of equity measured at the first day closing price plus the book value of debt divided by the book value of total assets	IPO prospectus, Dealogic, Datastream
QISSUE	Market value of equity measured at the IPO issue price plus the book value of debt divided by the book value of total assets	IPO prospectus, Dealogic, Datastream
REGULATED	Dummy variable that equals one if the issuing firm is not listed on a stock exchange lower than prime standard, i.e. AIM, Marché Libre, Entry Standard, Open Market and others	IPO prospectus
RESID~	Residuals of first stage Hausman regressions	Calculated
RETAIN_MGT	Cumulated retained inside ownership of management, board, and their families in percent at the IPO	IPO prospectus
SQRRETAIN_MGT	Squared value of cumulated retained inside ownership of management, board, and their families in percent at the IPO	IPO prospectus
TRANSPARENCY	Real estate transparency index ranking ranging from one to five, in order of increasing in-transparency	Jones Lang LaSalle
TYPOSPEC	Dummy variable that equals one if the issuing firm's investment strategy focuses on one specific property type	IPO prospectus
UNDERPRICING	Initial day return measured as the natural logarithm of the closing price of first trading day and the issue price of the IPO divided by the issue price and adjusted for the market return of the EPRA Europe index on the IPO day	Datastream, IPO prospectus, Press releases
VOLATILITY	Standard deviation of stock returns for an aftermarket period of 240 trading days	Datastream

While the real estate market in the UK is one of the most mature markets globally, countries in Eastern Europe are characterised by young economies where the implementation of corporate governance issues still has room for development. Political and economical instabilities as well as exchange rate risks make capital-intensive real estate investments difficult. Thus, it is highly important for real estate managers to have a large amount of knowledge of local real estate markets. Thus, we expect companies investing in non-transparent markets to have higher managerial ownership ratios. Thus a positive relationship between RETAIN_MGT and TRANSPARENCY is expected. Furthermore, management of real estate companies is expected to have in-depth market knowledge of the firm's main target real estate markets. We expect that the management is able to correctly anticipate the future growth of the underlying real estate markets. Thus, management is expected to use their information advantage and maintain a higher stake in the company when they expect industry prospects to be promising. Thus, we expect GDPGROWTH and managerial ownership to be positively related. On the other hand, it can be argued that management is less invested in these companies as the growth potential of certain regions is easy to forecast, which reduces information asymmetry and thus requires less investment by the management, which thereby reduces its under-diversification risk. Finally, the overall heat of the market (EPRA) is included as a further control variable to capture potential timing effects. Previous literature has found that issuers use their informational advantage about their firm and time their IPO (Baker and Wurgler (2000), Lowry (2003)). Rock (1986) argues that an IPO tees a company for a future sale, and Ibbotston (1975) argues that firms set offer prices below the true firm value in order to leave a good taste in investors' mouths. Thus, we expect that in times of high valuations, managers will only sell a small fraction of their stake in the company and continue to keep a high proportion in the company, as they intend to achieve higher proceeds in a secondary sale. Additionally, at an IPO, management ownership and divestment act as a signal. Thus, the market may interpret high divestments of managers in times of hot IPO phases as management's pure exit strategy, and thus reduce IPO valuation. Therefore, we expect EPRA and managerial ownership to display a positive relationship.

Outside blockholding equation: Stoughton and Zechner (1998) and Brennan and Franks (1997) argue the firms employ underpricing as a means to influence aftermarket shareholder ownership. Both studies suggest, although in diametrically opposite directions, a significant influence of underpricing on outside blockholders. Unfortunately, this relationship cannot be tested in this study, as data on post-IPO ownership structure are not available. Property companies can choose whether they want to disclose the future property portfolio that the management is going to acquire with the help of the proceeds from the IPO. By doing so, information asymmetries are reduced, which in turn encourage outside investors to acquire larger stakes in the company. Thus, a positive relationship between PIPELINE and BLOCK_OUT is expected. Similarly, regulated firms are expected to reduce information asymmetry, which motivates investors to accumulate larger stakes in the company. Thus, a positive relationship between REGULATED and outside blockholdings is expected. Similar to the under-diversification argument by Agrawal and Knoeber (1996), we expect proxies designed to measure this risk, i.e. AGE and ASSET, to be negatively related to outside blockholdings. Demsetz and Lehn (1985) argue that stock price volatility makes it more difficult for small shareholders to monitor managers' decisions. As proposed by Jensen and Meckling (1976), unmonitored managers are more likely to indulge in self-serving behaviour, which enforces the agency problem and negatively affects stock prices. Therefore, as mentioned by Demsetz and Lehn (1985), more risky firms increase the value of outside monitoring. Lower stock prices create incentives for outsiders to assemble larger blocks of shares and to enforce the management to make more shareholder-friendly decisions, thereby reaping a share of the associated positive stock price revaluation. Thus, the greater the stock price volatility (VOLATILITY), the larger the outside blockholdings. Similarly, firms investing in mainly in-transparent markets may discourage investors from buying large blocks of equity at the IPO. Assuming that outside investors are particularly interested in gaining exposure to a geographic region where they cannot invest by themselves because they possess insufficient market knowledge, such investors cannot be good monitors and thus have no incentive to buy large shareholding blocks. Thus a negative relationship between TRANSPARENCY and BLOCK_OUT is expected.

Debt equation: Companies opt for debt financing not only for monitoring reasons, but also because financial leverage can help to increase company's financial performance due to positive valuation effects stemming from a tax shield of debt (Modigliani and Miller (1958)). In a world of efficient markets, a permanently leveraged firm has a higher value than an identical but unleveraged firm. This surplus of firm value is equal to the value of the corporate tax shield of debt. Thus, companies that do not pay corporate tax seem to gain no benefit from debt financing. Considering the increased risk associated with leverage ratios, one would expect the debt level to be lower for companies benefiting from the status of being exempt from corporate taxation. Thus, a negative relationship between OFFSHORE and the firm's financial leverage is assumed. Rajan and Zingales (1995) argue that larger and older firms are more visible, and thus face fewer problems associated with information asymmetry. Thus, small and young companies are expected to experience more difficulty in raising debt financing, and thus a negative relationship of firm size (ASSET) and firm age (AGE) with debt is expected. Myers (1977) and Kim and Sorensen (1986) argue that the quantity of debt that a firm will take on is a negative function of the firm's business risk. Thus, a negative relationship of VOLATILITY and DEBT is expected. Furthermore, as stated above and in line with Demsetz and Lehn (1985) and Booth et al. (2002), the dummy variable REGULATED is included since regulated firms are expected to have lower agency problems, which in turn would imply lower debt levels because the need for monitoring is reduced. Thus, REGULATED and Tobin's Q are expected be negatively related. The same logic applies to the asymmetric information variable TRANSPARENCY and TYPOSPEC.

4.3.3.2 Measures of control variables of firm valuation

In addition to the main variables of interest, a set of additional variables is included, which have been found to be significant determinants of Tobin's Q in previous studies.

In the context of IPOs, several signalling variables have been identified in previous research to have explanatory power over firm valuation at IPO. First, underpricing (UNDERPRICING) is considered as a major signal in IPOs. By setting the offer price below the actual true value of the firm, as perceived by the market post-IPO, the issuer creates a costly signal that he intends to recover at a later stage through a seasoned equity offering. Following this notion, Allen and Faulhaber (1989) and Welch (1989) argue that firm value and underpricing should be positively related. Trueman (1986) argues that management can use the degree of dilution (DILUTION) i.e. the capital increase at IPO, as a costly signalling device. As the degree of enlarged capital raised through the IPO is generally used for capital expenditures, a larger fraction of dilution signals that high project returns are expected. Titman and Trueman (1986) argue that the quality of the underwriting investment bank (IBREPU) provides information about firm value, as high quality agents are more expensive and can only be afforded by high quality companies. Carter et al. (1998) show that the certification role of the underwriting investment bank can positively influence the IPO's initial pricing and performance. Thus, a positive relationship is expected. Size effects are captured by firm size (ASSET). In line with Agrawal and Knoeber (1996), a negative relationship between firm size and Tobin's Q is expected, as growth opportunities should be lower for larger firms. Rajan and Zingales (1995) argue that larger firms are more visible, and thus face fewer problems associated with information asymmetry. Similarly, Muscarella and Vetsuypens (1989), argue that firm age reduces information asymmetry, as older firms are assumed to be associated with a larger amount of publicly available information. Therefore, firm age (AGE), measured as the number of years since the firm's incorporation and the offer year, is included and expected to be positively related to firm valuation. In addition, the influence of the founder's presence is included, as it is expected that founders retain a stronger commitment to their firm (Wasserman (2006)). In fact, Jayaraman et al. (2000) find that founder management is positively related to stock performance among smaller and younger companies. Thus, a positive relationship can be expected. However, founders may also be more likely, or better able, to promote managerial entrenchment (Chang and Hertzell (2004)). Thus, a negative relationship can be expected. In order to test for the proposed relationship, FOUNDER, a dummy variable, is created for firms with 100% managerial ownership. Since managers of such fully owned firms are more likely to be the founders, we expect the 100%-ownership dummy to capture the effect of founder ownership relative to non-founder ownership. We assume this to be true because the founder-companies are, on average, older, which implies that in companies that are older but still owned by 100% of the management, it is rather impossible for a non-founding manager to acquire such high stakes that he also holds 100% of the company. In order to test the expected agency cost-reducing effect of a stricter regulatory frameworks, REGULATED is included. Furthermore, an information asymmetry variable, which measures the IPO investor's uncertainty about management's investment strategy, is included. Following Wang et al. (1992), a dummy variable, PIPELINE, is constructed that equals one if the company fully or at least partially specifies the properties it intends to acquire with the IPO proceeds and zero otherwise. As a specification reveals additional information and thus reduces information asymmetry, a positive relationship with IPO valuation is expected. Similarly, we expect companies with an investment strategy focusing on transparent real estate markets to possess less information asymmetry, and therefore expect a positive relationship between TRANSPARENCY and firm valuation. Next, future GDP growth (GDPGROWTH) is included in order to test whether Tobin's Q is a correct estimator for a company's growth potential. Lang and Stulz (1994) find firm size to be negatively related to firm valuation. The authors argue that larger firms are more diversified, which in turn negatively affects the firm value. Capozza and Seguin (1999) find empirical evidence that unfocused REITs, especially those diversified by property type, are more expensive to manage and less successful. In order to test this argumentation, a dummy variable, TYPOSPEC, is created that has a value of 1 if a company specializes in one property type. Thus, we assume TYPOSPEC to be positively associated with firm valuation.

4.4 Results

4.4.1 Descriptive statistics and correlations

In the following subsection, descriptive statistics of the various variables used in this paper are described. Table 4.2 provides a summary statistics table and Table 4.3contains a correlation matrix. All calculations are based on 88 companies. The data are winsorized: thus, the maximum and minimum data might not represent the true values. However, the number of cases in which extreme values are winsorised amounts to a maximum of five, depending on the variable, and thus minimises any bias when drawing conclusions from descriptive statistics.

Overall, the Tobin's Q measured at IPO prices (QISSUE) indicates that, on average, European property companies are valued 2.66 times their replacement costs, and thereby indicates relatively high valuation levels. Intuitively, Q values measured for the first day closing price (Q1) are even higher. Smaller median values and relatively large difference between minimum and maximum values imply a distribution that is skewed to the right. As this is, to the best of the author's knowledge, the first study to analyse IPO valuation of property companies without REIT regime, it is difficult to put the results of QISSUE and Q1 into context in terms of reasonability. For a sample of US REITs, Hartzell et al. (2004) report average Q values of 1.27, which is half the value of those found in the present study. However, this seems to be reasonable, as REIT regulations force companies to possess an established property portfolio before opting for the REIT regime, whereas EPCs have more flexibility in terms of the choice of their underlying portfolio.

TABLE 4.2: SUMMARY STATISTICS

	N	Mean	Median	Max	Min	Std. Dev.	Skewness	Kurtosis
AGE	88	8.04	6.00	30.14	0.00	7.76	1.30	4.00
ASSET	88	293.47	121.32	1344.68	0.72	365.64	1.50	4.15
BLOCK OUT	88	0.31	0.30	0.89	0.00	0.28	0.27	1.69
CONTROL50 MGT	88	0.27	0.00	1.00	0.00	0.45	1.02	2.04
DEBT	88	0.61	0.67	1.00	0.00	0.26	-0.93	3.08
DILUTION	88	0.29	0.25	0.96	0.00	0.24	1.23	4.05
DIVEST MGT	88	0.01	0.00	1.09	-1.00	0.35	1.15	7.40
EPRA	88	0.13	0.14	0.41	-0.28	0.15	-0.83	3.68
FOUNDER	88	0.22	0.00	1.00	0.00	0.41	1.38	2.91
GDPGROWTH	88	0.03	0.03	0.08	0.00	0.02	0.81	3.13
IBREPU	88	0.40	0.00	1.00	0.00	0.49	0.42	1.17
MAXLEV	88	0.34	0.00	1.00	0.00	0.48	0.67	1.45
NEWBLOCK OUT	88	0.02	0.00	0.20	0.00	0.05	2.86	9.58
OFFSHORE	88	0.19	0.00	1.00	0.00	0.40	1.55	3.42
PIPELINE	88	0.19	0.00	1.00	0.00	0.40	1.55	3.42
Q1	88	2.84	1.91	9.79	0.90	2.34	1.65	4.52
QISSUE	88	2.66	1.86	8.51	0.88	2.08	1.65	4.49
REGULATED	88	0.60	1.00	1.00	0.00	0.49	-0.42	1.17
RETAIN MGT	88	0.26	0.12	0.93	0.00	0.28	0.61	1.89
TRANSPARENCY	88	1.54	1.50	3.25	1.00	0.64	1.13	3.09
TYPOSPEC	88	0.49	0.00	1.00	0.00	0.50	0.05	1.00
UNDERPRICING	88	0.07	0.05	0.35	-0.14	0.10	0.99	3.93
VOLATILITY	88	0.02	0.01	0.06	0.00	0.02	1.46	4.50

Referring to the corporate governance variables managerial ownership, outside blockholders, and debt, the following characteristics can be observed. Managerial ownership after the IPO averages 26% compared to 40% pre-IPO ownership. Interestingly, the average divestment rate of management is only 1%. However, the variable is characterised by extreme values. Some management bought more than 100% of their initial stake in new shares, whereas others divested their total pre-IPO investment. Furthermore, we were able to identify 22 companies for which the founder was still on board at the time of the IPO. As expected, FOUNDER is negatively associated with DIVEST_MGT, suggesting that founders are less willing to sell their stake in the company than non-founding management.

Outside blockholders hold, on average, 31% of the post-IPO equity, and thus serve as a considerable counterweight to the 26% of the managerial ownership. Field and Sheehan (2004) study blockholders in an IPO setting for a sample of 952 IPOs from 1988-1992 and find mean blockholdings to be 30%, which is comparable to our data. The average debt level amounts to 61%, which is relatively high compared to previous studies focusing on REITs but consistent with Ross's (1977) argument that firms with a greater need for monitoring, i.e. firms without a REIT regime, employ debt to align management's interests with shareholders'.

In terms of signalling variables, the sample of European property companies analysed in this chapter is 7%, with a median of 5%. Interestingly, first-day returns are highly positively correlated with both QISSUE and Q1. The high correlation with the latter is not surprising, as Q1 is calculated based on the firm's market valuation at the end of the first trading day.

Interestingly, however, there is also a high positive correlation with QISSUE, which is calculated based on the offer price. This provides a first indication that underpricing may be used as a signalling device to justify high IPO valuations. EPCs analysed in this sample dilute their pre-IPO equity, on average, by 29%. Interestingly, some companies offer a particularly high amount of new shares, which indicates strong capital needs. Interpreting Tobin's Q as a measure of growth opportunities (Min and Prather (2001)), the positive correlation of dilution with both measures of Tobin's Q is not surprising. Nearly half of all companies analysed are underwritten by a prestigious investment bank.

On average, European property companies are 8-years-old when they undertake an IPO. The oldest company is in business for more than 30 years, whereas more than 30% of the sample has an operating history of less than 3 years. This is rather surprising and could have been expected for start-up companies, for example during the dot.com boom, but not for property companies with a long investment horizon. One explanation is the strong capital market environment during 2005 and 2007 which incentivised young companies without a strong asset base to explore public equity as a financing alternative.

TABLE 4.3: CORRELATION MATRIX

	QISSUE	Q1	RETAIN_MGT	FOUNDER	DIVEST_MGT	NEWBLOCK_OUT	BLOCK_OUT	DEBT
QISSUE	1.00							
Q1	1.00	1.00						
RETAIN_MGT	0.20	0.20	1.00					
FOUNDER	0.22	0.21	0.54	1.00				
DIVEST_MGT	-0.05	-0.06	-0.18	-0.15	1.00			
NEWBLOCK_OUT	0.07	0.07	-0.16	0.03	-0.24	1.00		
BLOCK_OUT	-0.30	-0.29	-0.74	-0.53	0.04	0.05	1.00	
DEBT	-0.05	-0.06	0.34	0.21	-0.09	0.11	-0.28	1.00
MAXLEV	0.17	0.16	0.25	0.21	-0.15	0.20	-0.25	0.66
UNDERPRICING	0.32	0.40	0.16	0.11	-0.16	0.02	-0.09	0.04
DILUTION	0.31	0.29	-0.27	0.07	0.29	0.36	-0.13	-0.26
IBREPU	0.14	0.13	-0.08	-0.09	-0.06	0.03	0.15	-0.01
ASSET	-0.42	-0.41	-0.27	-0.24	0.02	-0.11	0.36	0.04
AGE	-0.15	-0.15	0.40	0.18	-0.11	-0.21	-0.15	0.15
VOLATILITY	0.25	0.25	0.12	0.11	-0.05	-0.20	-0.05	0.03
REGULATED	-0.24	-0.24	-0.12	-0.08	-0.04	-0.33	0.25	0.09
PIPELINE	0.04	0.03	-0.20	-0.12	-0.06	0.19	0.22	-0.05
OFFSHORE	0.16	0.15	-0.22	-0.12	0.16	0.31	0.04	-0.12
TYPOSPEC	0.04	0.04	0.10	0.04	-0.07	-0.05	-0.09	0.21
GDPGROWTH	0.36	0.36	-0.02	-0.03	0.05	0.08	-0.04	-0.17
TRANSPARENCY	0.36	0.35	0.04	-0.01	-0.06	0.09	-0.09	-0.17
EPRA	0.27	0.30	0.18	0.13	-0.07	0.04	-0.13	0.06
CONTROL50_MGT	0.15	0.14	0.84	0.48	-0.21	-0.21	-0.60	0.30

	MAXLEV	UNDERPRICING	DILUTION	IBREPU	ASSET	AGE	VOLATILITY	REGULATED
MAXLEV	1.00							
UNDERPRICING	0.05	1.00						
DILUTION	-0.07	-0.12	1.00					
IBREPU	0.10	0.06	-0.01	1.00				
ASSET	-0.10	-0.06	-0.22	0.34	1.00			
AGE	0.06	0.03	-0.30	-0.03	0.12	1.00		
VOLATILITY	0.11	0.10	-0.11	-0.04	-0.13	0.07	1.00	
REGULATED	0.00	-0.13	-0.21	0.04	0.33	0.28	0.13	1.00
PIPELINE	-0.05	-0.14	0.15	0.31	0.06	-0.11	-0.11	-0.07
OFFSHORE	-0.11	-0.03	0.27	0.01	-0.11	-0.32	-0.32	-0.43
TYPOSPEC	0.21	-0.02	-0.15	0.09	-0.01	0.04	-0.02	0.10
GDPGROWTH	-0.15	0.09	0.23	-0.07	-0.08	-0.04	-0.16	-0.16
TRANSPARENCY	-0.10	0.00	0.20	0.19	-0.14	-0.09	-0.13	-0.26
EPRA	0.04	0.31	0.05	-0.03	0.01	0.00	0.06	0.04
CONTROL50_MGT	0.26	0.01	-0.26	0.02	-0.17	0.44	0.13	0.08

	PIPELINE	OFFSHORE	TYPOSPEC	GDPGROWTH	TRANSPARENCY	EPRA	CONTROL50_MGT
PIPELINE	1.00						
OFFSHORE	0.13	1.00					
TYPOSPEC	0.04	-0.13	1.00				
GDPGROWTH	0.07	0.32	-0.22	1.00			
TRANSPARENCY	0.13	0.33	-0.15	0.71	1.00		
EPRA	-0.07	-0.02	-0.29	0.22	-0.01	1.00	
CONTROL50_MGT	-0.11	-0.17	0.22	-0.05	0.04	0.10	1.00

Furthermore, AGE is negatively correlated with DIVEST_MGT and DILUTION, which suggests that the management of older firms divest less and issue fewer new shares, which is consistent with the former argument. During the sample period analysed and contemplated ex post, EPCs invested in geographic areas whose next year's gross domestic product grew, on average, by 8%. Interestingly, the countries with the strongest GDP growth are characterised by generally less transparent real estate markets, as shown by the high correlation coefficient between GDPGROWTH and TRANSPARENCY. Both variables are also positively correlated with DILUTION, which shows that companies with high growth opportunities used the capital markets as a financing alternative, probably because debt financing was not available for companies investing mainly in less transparent real estate markets, as the negative correlation coefficients of the latter three variables with DEBT may lead to suspect. Finally, the average return FTSE/EPRA index 12 months before the offering amounts to 14%, which shows that the sample period analysed is characterised by an overall strongly growing universe of listed real estate companies in Europe.

4.4.2 Regression results

4.4.2.1 OLS regression of interrelated control mechanisms

The main dependent variables in the following regressions are RETAIN_MGT, BLOCK_OUT, and DEBT, which in turn also serve as independent variables. The results are presented in Table 4.4. Collectively, the models all show a relatively good global fit, with adjusted R^2 values ranging from 0.16 to 0.37. The Ramsey RESET test on the general specification of the linear regression models shows that the models are well specified, except for models II and III, which almost fail the test at the 10% level. Re-estimating both specifications without the managerial ownership variable significantly improves the RESET test values, which implies that the specification problem is caused by the strong interrelationship of RETAIN_MGT and NEWBLOCK_OUT and not by any missing relevant explanatory variables. Finally, all variances of inflation factors are below three, suggesting that multicollinearity is not an issue in the respective specifications.

Starting with model I, the strong negative relationship of managerial ownership and outside blockholdings implies that corporate blockholders have no incentive to accumulate high stakes in the company if managerial ownership is high. Similarly, model II shows that RETAIN_MGT also has a significant impact on NEWBLOCK_OUT, implying that managers with high ownership levels are reluctant to let outside investors accumulate larger blocks of shares. Hence, H1 can be accepted. Intuitively, managers are expected to have the highest power in determining the post-IPO ownership structure if management is in total control of the company. Thus, as a robustness check, model III is re-estimated by replacing the RETAIN_MGT variable with a dummy variable (CONTROL50_MGT) that equals one if the pre-IPO ownership of the management is larger than 50% and zero otherwise. As expected, this variable is negatively related to outside blockholders, with a t-statistic of -3.88, implying statistical significance at the 1% level. This finding is in line with those of Alavi et al. (2008), who find that if managers are in control, they tend to issue only a small proportion of shares, which are allocated (or marketed) in a way that prevents the post-listing emergence of large shareholders.

Next, DEBT is positively related with managerial ownership. As discussed above, there are a variety of reasons that might explain this positive relationship. As mentioned by Jensen and Meckling (1976), closely held companies with high managerial ownership might be beneficially valued in bank-internal stress tests and thereby allow these companies to attract favourable debt financing. Another explanation offered by Ross (1977) is based on the signalling function of debt issues. The management deliberately increases the indebtedness of its firm and thereby increases the risk of bankruptcy, which sends a costly and therefore valid signal to the market that tells potential investors about the management's confidence in the firm. Despite the fact that the results in Table 4.4 are in line with these intuitive rationales, the findings contradict the results of Capozza and Seguin (2003), who find that REITs with greater inside ownership choose capital structures with less debt. The authors assume that firm management opts for lower debt levels in order to reduce the bankruptcy risk and, at the same time, their own under-diversification risk. In addition, Hartzell et al. (2004) find leverage to be positively related to IPO valuation of US REITs. Thus, it seems that the REIT regime itself plays a disciplinary role and there is no need for debt as a disciplinary mechanism, whereas, for EPCs, debt has rather a controlling function. Therefore, H2a can be accepted and H2b can be rejected. Lastly, at the 5% level, DEBT is also positively related to NEW-BLOCK_OUT. Friend and Lang (1988) find a similar positive relationship between debt and large shareholdings for well-established firms, and argue that blockholders force management to employ higher debt levels in order to take advantage of tax-shield effects. However, the present study analyses IPO firms where the management is assumed to have discretionary power over allocating shares to *new* blockholders following admission. Thus, a tax-shield induced argumentation is probably no reasonable explanation for the positive relationship. It rather seems that the positive relationship can be best explained by Jensen and Meckling's (1976) monitoring function of debt. Outside blockholders are more willing to accumulate higher stakes in an IPO company if its debt levels are high. This finding is supportive of the supposed monitoring role of debt, as higher debt levels seem to incentivise investors to buy large blocks of shares, probably as higher debt payments are considered as an effective mechanism to reduce the free cash flow problem. Consequently, H3 is rejected.

TABLE 4.4: BASIC OLS REGRESSIONS OF CONTROL MECHANISMS

	I (RETAIN_MGT)					II (NEWBLOCK_OUT)					III (NEWBLOCK_OUT)					IV (DEBT)				
	Coef	Std. Err	t-stat	Prob		Coef	Std. Err	t-stat	Prob		Coef	Std. Err	t-stat	Prob		Coef	Std. Err	t-stat	Prob	
C	0.00	0.08	0.00	1.00		0.00	0.09	0.00	1.00		0.00	0.09	0.00	1.00		0.00	0.09	0.00	1.00	
AGE	0.40	0.08	5.14	0.00	(a)	-0.03	0.07	-0.39	0.70		-0.03	0.07	-0.42	0.68		-0.03	0.07	-0.47	0.64	
ASSET	-0.21	0.08	-2.71	0.01	(a)	-0.11	0.06	-1.75	0.08	(c)	-0.10	0.06	-1.60	0.11		0.15	0.06	2.53	0.01	(b)
CONTROL50_MGT											-0.31	0.09	-3.52	0.00	(a)					
DEBT	0.34	0.07	5.13	0.00	(a)	0.25	0.11	2.27	0.03	(b)	0.23	0.10	2.21	0.03	(b)					
DIVEST_MGT						-0.31	0.12	-2.47	0.02	(b)	-0.32	0.12	-2.60	0.01	(b)					
EPRA	0.23	0.07	3.26	0.00	(a)															
GDPGROWTH	-0.17	0.11	-1.60	0.11																
NEWBLOCK_OUT	-0.23	0.07	-3.47	0.00	(a)											0.25	0.11	2.18	0.03	(b)
OFFSHORE																0.03	0.10	0.34	0.73	
PIPELINE						0.07	0.11	0.64	0.52		0.09	0.11	0.82	0.42						
REGULATED	-0.27	0.09	-2.96	0.00	(a)	-0.35	0.12	-2.83	0.01	(a)	-0.30	0.11	-2.61	0.01	(b)	0.16	0.12	1.34	0.19	
RETAIN_MGT						-0.30	0.10	-2.97	0.00	(a)						0.44	0.09	4.64	0.00	(a)
TRANSPARENCY	0.18	0.11	1.73	0.09	(c)	-0.01	0.09	-0.15	0.89		-0.01	0.09	-0.15	0.88		-0.14	0.12	-1.14	0.26	
TYPOSPEC																0.14	0.10	1.46	0.15	
VOLATILITY	0.04	0.08	0.44	0.66		-0.12	0.07	-1.71	0.09	(c)	-0.12	0.07	-1.78	0.08	(c)	0.02	0.12	0.15	0.88	
Number of obs.	88					88					88					88				
F-statistic	12.81					2.01					2.00					4.42				
Prob. F-statistic	0.00					0.04					0.04					0.00				
Adj. R-squared	0.37					0.23					0.25					0.16				
Ramsey RESET test	0.31					0.13					0.11					0.99				
Max. VIF	2.35					2.35					1.43					1.59				

Notes: (c),(b), and (a) indicates significance at the 10, 5, and 1% level

Impact of control variables in model I: AGE is strongly positively related to managerial ownership. As the coefficients are standardised, an increase of one standard deviation in firm age will lead to an increase of 0.33 standard deviations in firm value. The AGE coefficient displays the second largest value compared to the rest of the variables, which indicates that for EPCs, firm age seems to be a major determinant of managerial ownership. It seems that early established firms are founder-led firms (the correlation between founder and age is positive and significant at the 10% level), whereas younger firms seem to be set up with the aim of seeking capital in the equity markets (the correlation between age and dilution is negative and significant at the 1% level) and to cash out, as indicated by the significant negative correlation of AGE with DIVEST_MGT. The coefficient of ASSET, which is included to capture the size effect, is negative as expected, which confirms the assumption that wealth constraints hinder management from possessing large stakes in companies with high market capitalisation. Interestingly, VOLATILITY is insignificantly related to RETAIN_MGT. Thus, it seems that stock price volatility is not an explanatory variable that captures under-diversification risk. From the significant negative coefficient of REGULATED, it seems that management does not maintain high stakes in more regulated companies. The question of whether this is because they are reluctant to work in a strongly regulated environment that limits their managerial freedom or whether it is a consequence resulting from market forces that otherwise would lead to a lower IPO valuation will be analysed in Subsection 4.4.2.2. In fact, the significant positive coefficient of TRANSPARENCY shows that managers maintain higher stakes in the company when they invest in in-transparent markets. Thus, it seems that the underlying real market transparency positively influences management ownership, which is in line with Demsetz and Lehn's (1985) information asymmetry argumentation. GDPGROWTH is negatively related to managerial ownership, which suggests that the higher the expected growth potential of the target investment country, the less is the managerial ownership. Thus, it seems that investment targets with strong growth potential are not especially difficult to forecast, and therefore do not require high incentive alignment by the management. EPRA is also positively related to managerial ownership. This implies that in times when the IPO market is high, managers do *not* use their information advantage by taking advantage of potential over-valuation, but rather stick to the company. The question of whether this has a positive effect on firm value will be analysed in Subsection 4.4.2.2.

Impact of control variables in models II and III: First, divestments of management (DIVEST_MGT) have a significant negative impact on the amount of shares accumulated by outside investors. In line with the signalling hypothesis of Leland and Pyle (1977), higher management divestiture seems to signal information that is negatively associated with outside investors, and thus gives them a new incentive to become large shareholders. In contrast to the low t-values obtained for the variables VOLATILITY and REGULATED in the managerial ownership specification, the variables in the outside blockholder equation are significant at the 10% and 1% levels, respectively. Thus, in line with Agrawal and Knoeber (1996), investors are more likely to accumulate large blocks of shares in companies for which the cost of holding an undiversified portfolio is lower. Similar results are revealed for the information asymmetry proxy PIPELINE, which is significantly positively related to outside blockholders. This implies that if investors are informed about the specific use of proceeds, i.e. which properties are intended to be bought in which geographic locations, investors are more willing to acquire larger blocks of shares as information asymmetry is reduced. TRANSPARENCY seems to have no influence on the presence of large shareholders. Thus, it might be argued that large shareholders do not see themselves as good monitors in in-transparent markets, which further justifies the almost significant relationship of TRANSPARENCY with managerial ownership, i.e. in in-transparent markets, local knowledge of management is key, and this requires high managerial ownership. Finally, AGE is not related to BLOCK_OUT and for firm size, as measured by ASSET, a negative influence can be observed, similar to the managerial ownership equation. Thus, outside investors seem to refrain from accumulating blocks of shares, either because wealth constraints hinder them from buying sufficiently large blocks of shares to have a monitoring influence or because of an aversion to being under-diversified.

Impact of control variables in model IV: Lastly, control variables for the debt equation reveal rather insignificant results, except for firm size, which is significantly positively related to debt. This implies that larger firms have higher debt levels and is consistent with Rajan and Zingales' (1995) argument that larger firms have easier access to the debt market. It also supports the significant positive impact of managerial ownership on debt, as it is assumed by Jensen and Meckling (1976) that managers employ higher debt values to maintain control over the company. Furthermore, OFFSHORE is insignificantly related to debt. This shows that the capital structure of EPCs is not determined by tax-shield benefits, and thus further supports the notion that debt is employed as a monitoring device for management. TRANSPARENCY is negatively related to debt, which implies that firms investing in in-transparent markets experience more difficulty raising debt capital and leads one to suspect that these companies seek the equity market as a financing alternative. In contrast, TYPOSPEC has an almost significant, positive impact on debt. Thus, it seems that specialising in one property type allows firms to have higher debt ratios, probably because banks are more willing to extend debt financing to less risky firms. AGE, as well as the under-diversification cost proxies VOLATILITY and REGULATED, is not found to have any impact on the firm's financial leverage.

To account for a potential endogeneity bias of the OLS results reported above, the Durbin-Wu-Hausman test (Hausman (1978)) is performed. The Hausman test involves two steps. First, the potentially endogenous variable is regressed in an OLS setup for all exogenous variables and the corresponding instrumental variable, and the residuals from this regression are retrieved (not reported). The residuals can be understood as the endogenous portion of the potentially endogenous variable. In the second step, the original equation is re-estimated by including the residuals from the first-stage regression as additional regressors (RESID~). Significant coefficients of the RESID~ variables indicate that the estimation of the respective dependent variable is subject to endogeneity and that the OLS results might be biased. However, Table 4.5 shows that the coefficients of RESID_MGT and RESID_DEBT are not statistically significant. Thus, one can conclude that the OLS estimates are correct.

In summary, the results reveal that the corporate governance variables analysed herein are highly interrelated. Managerial ownership and outside blockholders seem to have an interchangeable character, whereas managerial ownership and debt seem to be complementary. In addition, outside blockholders and debt are complementarily related. This shows that corporate governance mechanisms seem to be employed by European property companies. However, the major aim of this study is to analyse whether the respective use of the discussed variables yields the desired effect on firm valuation at the IPO. Therefore, in the following sections, basic and piecewise OLS regressions as well as systems of simultaneous equations are employed, and possible implications of the results are discussed.

4.4.2.2 Basic and Piecewise OLS regression of IPO valuation

The main dependent variable is the firm valuation at IPO, measured as Tobin's Q. The main independent variables consist of the control variables RETAIN_MGT, BLOCK_OUT, and DEBT plus additional control variables. The description of the results starts with model I in Table 4.6. Overall, high R^2 values show a good model fit and, according to the Ramsey RESET test, the models are correctly specified. In the following paragraphs, the impacts of the aforementioned corporate governance variables and additional control variables on IPO valuation are described.

First, model I shows that the coefficient of the retained managerial ownership variable is positive but closely fails to be statistically significant at the 10% level. Nevertheless, the positive relationship is in line with the argument of Jensen and Meckling (1976) that higher managerial ownership reduces potential agency problems, resulting in higher firm values. The results do not account for a possible non-linear relationship, as detected by Morck et al. (1988). This will be analysed in more detail in the following section. Model II shows that outside blockholdings at the 10% level are significantly negatively related to IPO valuation. This result is in line with the results from Subsection 4.4.2.1 in the sense that managerial ownership and outside blockholders have a strong substituting relationship.

TABLE 4.5: DURBIN-WU-HAUSMAN TESTS OF CONTROL MECHANISMS

	I (RETAIN_MGT)					II (DEBT)				
	Coef	Std.Err	t-stat	Prob		Coef	Std.Err	t-stat	Prob	
C	0.00	0.08	0.00	1.00		0.00	0.09	0.00	1.00	
AGE	0.38	0.08	4.65	0.00	(a)	-0.08	0.14	-0.59	0.55	
ASSET	-0.24	0.07	-3.29	0.00	(a)	0.14	0.07	1.96	0.05	(b)
DEBT	0.29	0.14	2.14	0.04	(b)					
EPRA	0.22	0.08	2.72	0.01	(a)					
GDPGROWTH	-0.19	0.11	-1.65	0.10						
OFFSHORE						0.09	0.12	0.75	0.46	
PIPELINE										
REGULATED						0.12	0.12	0.97	0.34	
RESID_DEBT	0.02	0.18	0.12	0.90						
RESID_MGT						-0.12	0.27	-0.45	0.65	
RETAIN_MGT						0.50	0.24	2.08	0.04	(b)
TRANSPARENCY	0.24	0.11	2.05	0.04	(b)	-0.16	0.12	-1.33	0.19	
TYPOSPEC						0.14	0.11	1.27	0.21	
UNDERPRICING										
VOLATILITY	0.05	0.09	0.59	0.56		-0.02	0.12	-0.15	0.88	
Number of obs.	88					88				
F-statistic	9.67					2.94				
Prob. F-statistic	0.00					0.00				
Adj. R-squared	0.29					0.10				
Ramsey RESET test	0.25					0.95				
Max. VIF	2.35					2.35				
IV	FOUNDER					MAXLEV				
First Stage F-statistic	10.91					12.65				

Notes: (c),(b), and (a) indicates significance at the 10, 5, and 1% level

The negative relationship implies that the presence of large blockholders reduces the valuation of EPC IPOs. This implies that the market seems to be reluctant to invest in real estate companies when large blockholders are present because of the fear that the blockholders can use their power to pursue their interest (Shleifer and Vishny (1986)). Next, model III shows that debt is positively related to QISSUE, but lacks statistical significance. Thus, an insignificant relationship of debt with IPO valuation rejects debt's supposed disciplinary effect, as argued by Jensen (1986), and rather supports the argument presented in Subsection 4.2.3.3 that higher managerial ownership is valued favourably by banks and, in line with the pecking order argument of Myers and Majluf (1984), bank debt is more commonly employed as a financing alternative. This relationship seems reasonable, as European firms use capital markets rather infrequently as an avenue for financing, and thus are much more reliant on bank debt. Finally, model IV regresses Tobin's Q on all three control mechanisms.

The results show that BLOCK_OUT loses its statistical significance, RETAIN_MGT keeps its positive sign and remains insignificant, and the coefficient of DEBT even changes from positive to negative, which can be attributed to the insignificant relationship.

Impact of control variables in models I – IV: Interestingly, the managerial ownership change at the IPO (DIVEST_MT) shows an insignificant impact on IPO valuation, although the negative sign of the coefficient supports Leland and Pyle's (1977) argumentation that divestiture by the management has a negative effect on IPO valuation. However, due to its lack of significance, this result must be evaluated with caution. An explanation for the insignificant result might be related to the large variations in divestiture volumes. Despite winsorisation, Table 4.2 shows that the median divestment by management is 0 and the mean is 0.9%, although the standard deviation is 35%. A larger sample size might have smoothed the variation in the data. UNDERPRICING is strongly positively related to Tobin's Q (QISSUE), although Q is not calculated by including the first day closing price, but by using the generally lower offer price. Regressing Tobin's Q, including initial day returns (Q1), on the same variables yields even higher R^2 values, and the joint significance also increases significantly. For the sake of brevity, these results are not reported. The significant positive impact on QISSUE is in line with Leland and Pyle's (1977) argument that underpricing is used as a signal by insiders, as QISSUE reflects the initial valuation, which is largely determined by the investment banks and the firm management. Although underpricing is also an indirect cost incurred by insiders, in line with the signalling theory.

EPCs seem to employ underpricing as a costly signal to justify the high firm valuation. Similarly, the amount of enlarged capital (DILUTION) exhibits a strong positive and significant influence on firm valuation, which is in line with Trueman's (1986) signalling effect of dilution. Thus, it seems that the market is willing to pay more for an IPO share of a European property company if the market expects the company to have positive net present value projects for which high project returns can be expected.

Moreover, the investment bank reputation (IBREPU) is significantly related to the firm valuation. Carter and Manaster (1990) and Carter et al. (1998) argue that firms underwritten by high reputation investment banks will leave less money on the table as information asymmetry is reduced. This is particularly relevant for risky and high-growth companies. The results show that firms with high valuations are underwritten by reputable investment banks. The question of whether it is at the issuing firm's discretion to choose which underwriter to employ for the offering or whether underwriters decide which issuers to serve is still open for discussion.

TABLE 4.6: BASIC OLS REGRESSION OF IPO VALUATION ON CONTROL MECHANISMS

	I (QISSUE)					II (QISSUE)					III (QISSUE)					IV (QISSUE)				
	Coef	Std.Err	t-stat	Prob		Coef	Std.Err	t-stat	Prob		Coef	Std.Err	t-stat	Prob		Coef	Std.Err	t-stat	Prob	
C	-0.39	0.06	-6.50	0.00	(a)	-0.39	0.06	-6.51	0.00	(a)	-0.39	0.06	-6.38	0.00	(a)	-0.39	0.06	-6.53	0.00	(a)
AGE	-0.09	0.07	-1.24	0.22		-0.06	0.06	-0.95	0.35		-0.03	0.06	-0.57	0.57		-0.08	0.07	-1.11	0.27	
ASSET	-0.13	0.05	-2.60	0.01	(b)	-0.14	0.05	-2.94	0.00	(a)	-0.16	0.05	-2.97	0.00	(a)	-0.14	0.05	-2.71	0.01	(a)
BLOCK OUT						-0.16	0.09	-1.86	0.07	(c)						-0.11	0.12	-0.88	0.38	
DEBT											0.05	0.05	0.87	0.39		0.01	0.06	0.12	0.90	
DIVEST MGT	-0.02	0.06	-0.35	0.73		-0.02	0.06	-0.31	0.76		-0.02	0.07	-0.25	0.80		-0.02	0.06	-0.34	0.73	
EPRA	0.15	0.08	1.99	0.05	(c)	0.16	0.08	2.08	0.04	(b)	0.18	0.08	2.42	0.02	(b)	0.15	0.08	2.00	0.05	(b)
FOUNDER	0.03	0.09	0.35	0.72		0.04	0.08	0.46	0.64		0.09	0.07	1.35	0.18		0.02	0.09	0.25	0.81	
GDPGROWTH	0.17	0.08	1.97	0.05	(c)	0.16	0.09	1.89	0.06	(c)	0.15	0.09	1.71	0.09	(c)	0.17	0.09	1.98	0.05	(c)
IBREPU	0.15	0.07	2.32	0.02	(b)	0.16	0.07	2.38	0.02	(b)	0.15	0.07	2.20	0.03	(b)	0.16	0.07	2.39	0.02	(b)
PIPELINE	-0.04	0.06	-0.64	0.52		-0.03	0.07	-0.43	0.67		-0.06	0.07	-0.89	0.38		-0.03	0.07	-0.47	0.64	
REGULATED	-0.03	0.07	-0.44	0.66		-0.03	0.07	-0.39	0.70		-0.07	0.07	-0.91	0.36		-0.02	0.07	-0.33	0.74	
RETAIN MGT	0.17	0.11	1.58	0.12												0.09	0.15	0.58	0.56	
TRANSPARENCY	0.15	0.09	1.62	0.11		0.15	0.09	1.68	0.10	(c)	0.18	0.09	1.93	0.06	(c)	0.15	0.09	1.62	0.11	
TYPOSPEC	0.15	0.07	2.19	0.03	(b)	0.15	0.07	2.05	0.04	(b)	0.17	0.07	2.43	0.02	(b)	0.15	0.07	2.04	0.05	(b)
UNDERPRICING	0.19	0.06	2.95	0.00	(a)	0.18	0.06	2.99	0.00	(a)	0.18	0.06	3.08	0.00	(a)	0.18	0.06	2.96	0.00	(a)
VOLATILITY	0.20	0.08	2.44	0.02	(b)	0.21	0.08	2.49	0.02	(b)	0.21	0.08	2.69	0.01	(a)	0.21	0.09	2.43	0.02	(b)
	0.28	0.07	4.10	0.00	(a)	0.21	0.07	3.19	0.00	(a)	0.24	0.07	3.56	0.00	(a)	0.25	0.08	2.90	0.00	(a)
Number of obs.	88					88					88					88				
F-statistic	10.50					9.86					8.86					9.40				
Prob. F-statistic	0.00					0.00					0.00					0.00				
Adj. R-squared	0.46					0.44					0.39					0.45				
Ramsey RESET test	0.77					0.94					0.82					0.25				
Max. VIF	2.79					2.76					2.73					2.92				

Notes: (c),(b), and (a) indicates significance at the 10, 5, and 1% level

Most likely, issuing firms and underwriters associate by mutual choice. Issuers do not choose underwriters randomly, nor do banks randomly agree on which companies to take public (Fernando et al. (2005)). Among the remaining control variables, firm size, measured by ASSET, has a significant negative impact on firm valuation, which confirms the notion that larger firms have lower growth opportunities. Similarly, AGE is also negatively related to Tobin's Q, although the coefficient lacks statistical significance. Interestingly, the coefficient of FOUNDER is positive, but statistically insignificant. This implies that the presence of the founder is not advantageous for IPO valuation. REGULATED and PIPELINE do not affect Tobin's Q, and thus can be considered as rather weak indicators of the valuation of EPCs. In contrast, TYPOSEPC has a significant positive impact on QISSUE and shows that diversified companies seem to have lower firm values. The findings are in line with Brounen and Eichholtz (2002) and consistent with the notion that typologically specified property companies are easier to manage, which is valued positively by the market. GDPGROWTH is positively related to Tobin's Q. Similarly, TRANSPARENCY has an almost significant positive impact on firm valuation. This is surprising, as transparency is a proxy for information asymmetry, i.e. with increasing uncertainty one would expect lower IPO valuations. One explanation is that in-transparent markets are countries with high economic growth, as suggested by the high correlation coefficient of 0.71. Despite the high correlation of these two variables, the variance of the inflation factor is below 3 for all regression specifications. Hence, the results do not seem to be biased because of potential multicollinearity issues. Overall, it seems that IPO valuation correctly captures favourable growth opportunities. In terms of the market variable proxies, the coefficient of EPRA shows the expected positive sign and is statistically significant at the 5% level.

Piecewise OLS regression: Although retained managerial ownership is positively related to Tobin's Q, Fama and Jensen (1983) expect a negative relationship with higher managerial ownership levels. In order to account for this possible non-linearity, two additional specifications are tested in this subsection. First, next to the plain value of RETAIN_MGT, its square (SQRRETAIN_MGT) and its cube (CUBRETAIN_MGT) are included in the regression. In addition, a grid search technique, as conducted by Cho (1998), is performed to determine one or more breakpoints in the managerial ownership variable. Table 4.7 shows the results.

Model I shows that including SQRRETAIN_MGT causes RETAIN_MGT, in contrast to the results from the basic regressions, to become statistically significant and positively related to QISSUE, whereas SQRRETAIN_MGT is significantly negatively related to QISSUE, implying that the relationship is V-shaped. Morck et al. (1988) find a U-shaped relationship and Cui and Mak (2002) even find three inflection or break points, implying a W-shaped relationship. In order to test for this relationship, we follow Short and Keasey (1999) and Faccio and Lasfer (2000), who utilise a cubic specification to model the corporate value–managerial holdings relationship. However, in contrast to their findings, inclusion of the cubed value of managerial ownership is not statistically significant, as shown in model III. As a model specification with squared and cubed values can only validate that the relationship of managerial ownership and Tobin's Q is non-monotonic, it cannot show *when* managerial ownership value begin to decrease. Therefore, a grid search technique, as proposed by Cho (1998), is employed. In the search for the most significant breakpoint, the managerial ownership stakes are, starting from zero, altered at 5% intervals, leading to a first breakpoint at 25%.

As reported in Table 4.7, both breakpoint dummy variables show the expected coefficient sign and are both significant at the 5% and 10% levels, respectively. Searching for a second breakpoint, implying a U-shaped relationship, the iterated search stops at 50%, which leaves us with three piecewise dummy variables. However, as model IV shows, piecewise regression with two breakpoints leads to insignificant results for the third piecewise dummy, which is in line with the insignificant results of the cubic regression.

Nevertheless, the general relationship of managerial ownership and debt is non-monotonic, and thus H4 can be accepted.

Another noteworthy result is that accounting for the non-linear relationship of managerial ownership and Tobin's Q significantly increases the economic importance of the managerial ownership variable. As opposed to the basic regression results, where RETAIN_MGT and BLOCK_OUT and DEBT have similarly low coefficients, managerial ownership now seems to have a much stronger effect on firm value than the other two corporate governance variables, supporting the overall expected strong importance of management for European property companies.

Overall, the results show that the relationship between managerial ownership and Tobin's Q is non-monotonic, and therefore H4 can be accepted. The results are in line with most of corporate governance literature, except that we find a V-shaped relationship between managerial ownership and firm valuation. Thus, there seems to be a general incentive effect for low ownership levels, which has a positive effect on firm value but also a general entrenchment effect for high ownership levels that could allow managers to extract private benefits which in turn has a negative effect on Tobin's Q. In summary, concentrated ownership seems to affect IPO valuation negatively regardless of whether large stakes are held by the management or by outside investors.

TABLE 4.7: SQUARED, CUBIC AND PIECEWISE REGRESSIONS

	I (QISSUE)					II (QISSUE)					III (QISSUE)					IV (QISSUE)				
	Coef	Std.Err	t-stat	Prob		Coef	Std.Err	t-stat	Prob		Coef	Std.Err	t-stat	Prob		Coef	Std.Err	t-stat	Prob	
C	-0.39	0.06	-6.70	0.00	(a)	-0.39	0.06	-6.77	0.00	(a)	-0.39	0.06	-6.79	0.00	(a)	-0.39	0.06	-6.74	0.00	(a)
AGE	-0.04	0.07	-0.61	0.54		-0.03	0.07	-0.45	0.65		-0.04	0.07	-0.56	0.58		-0.04	0.07	-0.52	0.60	
ASSET	-0.15	0.05	-2.87	0.01	(a)	-0.16	0.06	-2.82	0.01	(a)	-0.15	0.06	-2.74	0.01	(a)	-0.15	0.05	-2.73	0.01	(a)
BLOCK_OUT	-0.04	0.08	-0.54	0.59		-0.09	0.12	-0.70	0.48		-0.09	0.13	-0.73	0.47		-0.09	0.12	-0.72	0.47	
CUBRETAIN_MGT											-0.05	0.07	-0.69	0.48						
DEBT	0.01	0.06	0.12	0.91		-0.02	0.05	-0.35	0.72		-0.03	0.05	-0.54	0.59		-0.03	0.05	-0.51	0.61	
DILUTION	0.29	0.08	3.69	0.00	(a)	0.24	0.08	2.88	0.01	(a)	0.24	0.08	2.94	0.00	(a)	0.24	0.08	2.93	0.00	(a)
DIVEST_MGT	-0.04	0.07	-0.50	0.62		-0.03	0.05	-0.57	0.57		-0.04	0.06	-0.76	0.45		-0.04	0.06	-0.75	0.46	
EPRA	0.16	0.07	2.26	0.03	(b)	0.18	0.07	2.43	0.02	(b)	0.18	0.07	2.44	0.02	(b)	0.18	0.07	2.51	0.01	(b)
FOUNDER	0.06	0.09	0.67	0.50		0.05	0.09	0.55	0.59		0.05	0.09	0.54	0.59		0.05	0.09	0.53	0.60	
GDPGROWTH	0.16	0.09	1.83	0.07	(c)	0.16	0.09	1.85	0.07	(c)	0.16	0.09	1.82	0.07	(c)	0.17	0.09	1.91	0.06	(c)
IBREPU	0.15	0.07	2.25	0.03	(b)	0.15	0.06	2.35	0.02	(b)	0.15	0.07	2.37	0.02	(b)	0.15	0.07	2.34	0.02	(b)
PIPELINE	-0.02	0.06	-0.37	0.71		-0.01	0.07	-0.18	0.86		-0.01	0.07	-0.17	0.86		-0.01	0.06	-0.22	0.83	
PW1RETAIN_MGT						0.28	0.11	2.61	0.01	(b)						0.24	0.09	2.77	0.01	(a)
PW2RETAIN_MGT						-0.18	0.13	-1.62	0.10	(c)						-0.10	0.15	-0.64	0.53	
PW3RETAIN_MGT																-0.05	0.08	-0.65	0.52	
REGULATED	-0.03	0.08	-0.38	0.70		0.00	0.07	0.00	1.00		0.00	0.07	0.02	0.99		-0.01	0.07	-0.13	0.90	
RETAIN_MGT	0.62	0.25	2.52	0.01	(b)						1.22	0.43	2.84	0.01	(a)					
SQRRETAIN_MGT	-0.52	0.26	-1.97	0.05	(c)						-2.08	0.92	-2.25	0.03	(b)					
TRANSPARENCY	0.15	0.10	1.58	0.12		0.16	0.10	1.66	0.10		0.16	0.10	1.67	0.10	(c)	0.16	0.10	1.65	0.10	
TYPOSPEC	0.18	0.07	2.59	0.01	(b)	0.19	0.07	2.59	0.01	(b)	0.19	0.07	2.59	0.01	(b)	0.18	0.07	2.56	0.01	(b)
UNDERPRICING	0.16	0.06	2.72	0.01	(a)	0.15	0.06	2.62	0.01	(b)	0.15	0.06	2.62	0.01	(b)	0.15	0.06	2.51	0.01	(b)
VOLATILITY	0.19	0.08	2.30	0.02	(b)	0.19	0.08	2.35	0.02	(b)	0.19	0.08	2.44	0.02	(b)	0.20	0.08	2.50	0.01	(b)
Number of obs.	88					88					88					88				
F-statistic	9.17					8.57					8.30					9.28				
Prob. F-statistic	0.00					0.00					0.00					0.00				
Adj. R-squared	0.42					0.44					0.43					0.46				
Ramsey RESET test	0.20					0.51					0.67					0.48				

Notes: (c),(b), and (a) indicates significance at the 10, 5, and 1% level

4.4.2.3 Robustness test: System of simultaneous equations of IPO valuation

Having analysed the one-way causal relationship of corporate governance mechanisms on IPO value, this subsection tests whether the above results suffer from any endogeneity bias and reverse causality. For a first assessment, Durbin-Wu-Hausman-tests are conducted. In the case of multiple potentially endogenous regressors, i.e. managerial ownership and debt, each endogenous variable is regressed separately on all IVs and exogenous variables (not reported). The predicted residuals are then included in the second-stage regression of the Durbin-Wu-Hausman test. The corresponding results are presented in Table 4.8. The significant residuals for RESID_DEBT reveal that Tobin's Q and debt are potentially subject to an endogenous relationship, whereas the insignificant residuals for RESID_MGT show that Tobin's Q and managerial ownership are not.

Due to the potential endogeneity bias, IV regressions are estimated with MAXLEV as an instrument for debt, and UNDERPRICING as an instrument for Tobin's Q. The instruments employed can be considered, in line with Stock et al. (2002), as strong instruments, as indicated by the high first-stage F statistics of the Hausman test (Table 4.8).

In this specification, none of the results from the basic and non-linear specification regressions change significantly, although the t-statistic for the debt variable is increased but still cannot reject the null hypothesis at the 10% level. For the sake of brevity, only piecewise results are presented. However, as 2SLS cannot capture contemporaneous correlations of disturbances across equations, simultaneous 3SLS estimation of IPO valuation and debt is performed, resulting in the following impressions: overall, the 3SLS results seem to be valid. Tests for heteroscedasticity reveal that the null hypothesis of homoscedasticity cannot be rejected. Although the reported R^2 values are high, they are not statistically meaningful in the context of 2SLS and 3SLS, and can thus be neglected.

Some noteworthy changes to the OLS regressions are as follows. DEBT is still positively related to Tobin's Q, but gains significance at the 10% level. Thus, in contrast to the OLS results, the simultaneous equations indicate that debt positively affects IPO valuation. This demonstrates that the Hausman test for endogeneity correctly anticipates a bias in OLS results due to endogeneity. The economic conclusion is that managers have a good reason to self-restrict their managerial freedom by higher debt levels because it raises the market value of their shares. In contrast, Tobin's Q shows a negative but insignificant impact on DEBT. The negative sign shows that firms with low growth opportunities have higher debt levels in order to contain over-investment.

TABLE 4.8: DURBIN-WU-HAUSMAN TESTS OF IPO VALUATION AND CONTROL MECHANISMS

	I (QISSUE)					II (Q1)				
	Coef	Std.Err	t-stat	Prob		Coef	Std.Err	t-stat	Prob	
C	-0.39	0.06	-6.63	0.00	(a)	-0.38	0.06	-6.82	0.00	(a)
AGE										
ASSET	-0.17	0.05	-3.32	0.00	(a)	-0.16	0.05	-3.29	0.00	(a)
DEBT	0.21	0.08	2.47	0.02	(b)	0.18	0.08	2.26	0.03	(b)
DILUTION	0.31	0.07	4.21	0.00	(a)	0.29	0.07	4.07	0.00	(a)
DIVEST_MGT	-0.03	0.06	-0.50	0.62		-0.02	0.05	-0.41	0.68	
EPRA	0.17	0.08	2.05	0.04	(b)	0.19	0.08	2.36	0.02	(b)
FOUNDER										
GDPGROWTH	0.16	0.09	1.80	0.08	(c)	0.15	0.09	1.77	0.08	(c)
IBREPU	0.16	0.07	2.32	0.02	(b)	0.15	0.06	2.39	0.02	(b)
PIPELINE	-0.06	0.07	-0.98	0.33		-0.06	0.06	-0.93	0.36	
REGULATED	-0.07	0.07	-1.01	0.32		-0.08	0.07	-1.14	0.26	
RESID_DEBT	-0.31	0.12	-2.50	0.01	(b)	-0.31	0.12	-2.58	0.01	(b)
RESID_MGT	0.14	0.17	0.77	0.44		0.14	0.17	0.83	0.41	
RETAIN_MGT	0.04	0.12	0.31	0.76		0.03	0.11	0.30	0.77	
TRANSPARENCY	0.18	0.09	1.95	0.05	(c)	0.17	0.09	1.95	0.06	(c)
TYPOSPEC	0.14	0.07	2.18	0.03	(b)	0.13	0.06	2.14	0.04	(b)
UNDERPRICING	0.17	0.07	2.40	0.02	(b)	0.22	0.07	3.30	0.00	(a)
VOLATILITY	0.22	0.08	2.73	0.01	(a)	0.21	0.08	2.64	0.01	(b)
Number of obs.	88					88				
F-statistic	10.15					11.12				
Prob. F-statistic	0.00					0.00				
Adj. R-squared	0.48					0.50				
Ramsey RESET test	0.21					0.20				
IV	FOUNDER								MAXLEV	
First stage F-statistic	10.12					13.41				

Notes: (c),(b), and (a) indicates significance at the 10, 5, and 1% level

Ghosh (2007) finds empirical evidence in support of this argument. However, the insignificant impact reported in this study seems to be a reasonable result for a cross-sectional IPO study, as for non-public companies the determining power lies with the management instead of the market. Overall, it supports the notion that management chooses structures that enhance firm value. If management holds high stakes in the company, it seems that they deliberately employ higher debt ratios in anticipation that it will mitigate agency costs, which is valued positively by potential investors. As the 3SLS results show, their anticipation is correct as debt increases IPO valuation. Consequently, debt seems to be a successful control mechanism for European property companies. Overall, it seems that firm valuation does not impact any of the control mechanisms, and thus H5 can be accepted.

In order to ensure that the implications drawn from the 3SLS results are correct, additional robustness checks are conducted. One major challenge confronted with the system of simultaneous equations stems from the fact that inferences from a simultaneous equation model are quite sensitive to small changes in the regression specifications and to the identification of valid instruments, which are necessary to identify the system (Coles et al. (2007)).

First, the instrument's strength has been discussed in Subsection 4.3.2 and identified as strong. Another prerequisite for valid 3SLS results is that the instruments are uncorrelated with the error term of the respective equation. A first assessment can be obtained by comparing 2SLS and 3SLS results. If there is misspecification in these estimators, it spreads to all equations in 3SLS. Thus, if 2SLS and 3SLS are similar, then this evidence indicates that 3SLS is performed properly.

A more formal test is the Sargan misspecification test, as described in Subsection 4.3.2. If the Sargan test statistics are significantly larger than predicted by the null hypothesis, it is likely that the model is incorrectly specified and/or the instruments are invalid. However, the results in Table 4.9 for models III and IV reveal that the Sargan test cannot be rejected at the 10% level for both equations. Thus, it is reasonable to argue that the instruments are not correlated to the equations' error terms and that the results are valid.

4.5 Conclusion

This paper is motivated to shed further light on the contradicting evidence regarding the impact of corporate governance on valuation. The setting of an IPO is chosen because it permits examination of how insiders install corporate governance to maximise IPO valuation. It is assumed that insiders use corporate governance mechanisms in such a way so as to maximise valuation and thus IPO proceeds, as they are the ones who suffer the most from any negative valuation effects. The sample analysed is a set of 88 European property companies because the increased likelihood of managerial opportunism, inherent in property companies without REIT regime, promises to reveal different results as was found in previous studies.

The first part of the analysis concentrates on the interrelationship of managerial ownership, outside blockholdings, and financial leverage: Collectively, the results show that managerial ownership and outside blockholders are strongly interrelated, i.e. they act as substitutes for one another. Corporate blockholders seem to have no incentive to accumulate high stakes in the company if managerial ownership is high. Similarly, managers in absolute control are reluctant to let outside investors accumulate larger blocks of shares. Furthermore, the results reveal that managerial ownership and debt are positively related, supporting the signalling function of debt issues (Ross (1977)).

TABLE 4.9: 2SLS AND 3SLS REGRESSION

	I (2SLS – QISSUE)					II (2SLS – DEBT)					III (3SLS – QISSUE)					IV (3SLS – DEBT)				
	Coef	Std. Err	t-stat	Prob		Coef	Std. Err	t-stat	Prob		Coef	Std. Err	t-stat	Prob		Coef	Std. Err	t-stat	Prob	
C	-0.39	0.07	-5.72	0.00	(a)	0.08	0.18	0.42	0.68		-0.39	0.07	-5.67	0.00	(a)	-0.03	0.11	-0.30	0.77	
AGE	-0.04	0.09	-0.48	0.63		0.01	0.11	0.10	0.92		-0.03	0.09	-0.38	0.71		-0.01	0.09	-0.14	0.89	
ASSET	-0.17	0.08	-2.12	0.04	(b)	0.16	0.10	1.56	0.12		-0.17	0.08	-2.19	0.03	(b)	0.12	0.09	1.43	0.16	
DEBT	0.18	0.12	1.51	0.14							0.21	0.12	1.76	0.08	(c)					
DILUTION	0.30	0.09	3.42	0.00	(a)						0.25	0.08	3.01	0.00	(a)					
DIVEST_MGT	-0.02	0.08	-0.31	0.76							0.00	0.07	-0.01	0.99						
EPRA	0.15	0.08	1.88	0.06	(c)						0.16	0.08	2.06	0.04	(b)					
FOUNDER	0.04	0.09	0.42	0.68							0.06	0.08	0.69	0.49						
GDPGROWTH	0.17	0.12	1.45	0.15							0.16	0.11	1.44	0.15						
IBREPU	0.15	0.08	1.86	0.07	(c)						0.12	0.08	1.53	0.13						
LOG(1 + QISSUE)						0.19	0.41	0.47	0.64							-0.08	0.18	-0.44	0.66	
MAXLEV						0.57	0.11	5.31	0.00	(a)						0.61	0.09	6.94	0.00	(a)
OFFSHORE						0.04	0.12	0.37	0.71							0.12	0.10	1.30	0.20	
PIPELINE	-0.04	0.08	-0.51	0.61							-0.01	0.07	-0.15	0.88						
PW1RETAIN_MGT	0.50	0.28	1.82	0.07	(c)	0.23	0.12	1.87	0.07	(c)	0.62	0.27	2.33	0.02	(b)	0.28	0.10	2.81	0.01	(a)
PW2RETAIN_MGT	-0.43	0.27	-1.57	0.12							-0.59	0.26	-2.23	0.03	(b)					
REGULATED	-0.03	0.08	-0.38	0.71		0.10	0.10	0.98	0.33		-0.03	0.08	-0.33	0.75		0.11	0.09	1.19	0.24	
TRANSPARENCY	0.17	0.12	1.46	0.15		-0.16	0.16	-1.02	0.31		0.19	0.11	1.71	0.09	(c)	-0.08	0.10	-0.83	0.41	
TYPOSPEC	0.15	0.08	1.90	0.06	(c)	0.02	0.09	0.26	0.80		0.15	0.08	1.91	0.06	(c)	0.05	0.08	0.60	0.55	
UNDERPRICING	0.16	0.08	2.15	0.04	(b)						0.17	0.07	2.40	0.02	(b)					
VOLATILITY	0.20	0.07	2.82	0.01	(a)	-0.10	0.13	-0.78	0.44		0.20	0.07	2.73	0.01	(a)	-0.03	0.09	-0.30	0.77	
Number of obs.	88					88					88					88				
R-squared	0.41					0.35					0.44					0.36				
Root MSE	0.65					0.80					0.65					0.79				
Sargan	n.a.					n.a.					2.53					11.06				
Chisq (10%)											2.70					13.36				

Notes: (c),(b), and (a) indicates significance at the 10, 5, and 1% level

The management deliberately increases the indebtedness of its firm, and thereby increases the risk of bankruptcy, which sends a costly and therefore valid signal to the market that tells potential investors about the management's confidence in the firm. This is also supported by the complementary character of outside blockholders and debt. Outside shareholders seem to be increasingly willing to accumulate large blocks of shares if debt levels are high, supporting the expected disciplinary role of debt.

The second part analysed the actual effect of monitoring mechanisms on IPO valuation. Overall, the results show that the relationship between managerial ownership and Tobin's Q is non-monotonic. The detected relationship resembles a V-shaped relationship between managerial ownership and firm valuation. In general, the results imply that concentrated ownership seems to affect the IPO valuation of European property companies negatively, no matter whether the large stakes are held by the management or by outside investors. This is line with the hypothesis expressed by Sirmans (1999) and Ooi (2000) that due to characteristics associated with real estate investments, potential expropriation due to a high ownership concentration is more feared than the benefits of a high incentive alignment. Finally, 3SLS regression reveals that debt positively affects IPO valuation, whereas a reverse causality cannot be confirmed. Hence, market participants beneficially incorporate higher debt levels in their IPO estimation, which supports Jensen's (1986) notion of the disciplinary power of debt. Finally, signalling mechanisms are complementarily employed in addition to the corporate governance mechanisms analysed.

In summary, the findings show that corporate governance matters for the IPO valuation of European property companies. Financial leverage is beneficial for IPO valuation, whereas monitoring by concentrated owners is not. An explanation for the latter relationship might be the advent of REIT regimes in many European countries, which, like US REITs, do not allow concentrated ownership. A possible direction for future research would be to conduct follow-up analyses with a larger sample size by focusing in particular on valuation differences of property companies with and without REIT regimes. Further, it might be interesting to take a closer look at EPCs' ownership structures by distinguish among institutional, international and private equity investors whose respective presence might give information about the issuing firms' IPO performance.

5 SUMMARY, CONCLUSION, AND OUTLOOK

This final chapter summarizes the findings of the three papers presented in this thesis and provides some overall conclusions as well as a general outlook for future research within the field of property company IPO research.

The first paper (chapter 2), "IPO underpricing, signalling, and property returns", analyses whether IPO signals reveal proprietary information about the prospects of an issuing firms' underlying industry. The study's motivation stems from the ambiguous results of previous empirical studies that let one infer that company specific performance characteristics might be a weak dependent variable to use when analysing the signalling hypotheses proposed by Allen and Faulhaber (1989), Grinblatt and Hwang (1989), and Welch (1989). Following the argumentation of the industrial organization view that firm performance is mainly determined by the performance of the individual firm's underlying industry, we assume and test whether IPO firms employ signals to communicate their expectations about their industry's prospects. By analysing a sample of 120 European property company IPOs from 1997 to 2007, we take advantage of having a heterogeneous set of industry performance measures, i.e. yields and total returns of direct property investments in various European real estate markets, which can be clearly assigned to each individual IPO. The results reveal that the main signal of interest, underpricing, is in fact positively related to average property yields of a 12 month post IPO period, a result which supports our assumption. Other signals, as proposed in previous research, seem to inherit no information about the prospects of the IPO firm's target real estate investment market. We also show that total returns seem to be a biased measure for direct property performance. Further tests for the signalling model's preconditioned presence of information asymmetry among European property companies reveal that underpricing levels are a function of company specific ex ante uncertainty proxies. In contrast, real estate specific ex ante uncertainty proxies do not explain underpricing levels.

Paper 2 (chapter 3), "Long-run IPO performance, market timing, and real estate market transparency", analyses whether the degree of transparency of IPO firms' underlying market segments has an effect on investors' and/or managers' ability to perform thorough investment analyses and company valuations or whether a decreasing degree of transparency rather leads to the emergence of over-optimism. The motivation of this research question stems from the absence of long-run underperformance of real estate related IPOs in the US, Australia or Hong-Kong, as documented by Buttimer et al. (2005), Dimovski and Brooks (2006), and Chan et al. (2001), respectively. We assume that with a decreasing degree of real estate market transparency, profound investment analyses are increasingly difficult to perform, leading to the emergence of over-optimism among investors and/or among managers. Since over-optimism provides an opportunity for poor quality companies to issue equity, we expect these poor quality issuings to perform worse than the market and pull down the sample performance. In order to ensure a sufficiently heterogeneous set of real estate market transparencies, the empirical analysis is based on data from 99 European property company IPOs from 1997 to 2007. We show that these companies time their IPO to coincide with favourable market conditions and with positive exogenous shocks. We also show that investor over-optimism is more likely to develop among companies investing mainly in less transparent real estate markets. In contrast, the results do not support the assumption that the degree of market transparency has an effect on the ability of management to correctly identify investment possibilities. Further, we document that IPOs of European property companies significantly underperform either equal or value-weighted benchmark portfolios in the long-run. More specifically, companies that issue equity at the peak of the market or have no initial property portfolio at the time of the IPO are among the companies with the highest underperformance levels, implying that these companies specifically take advantage of sentiment investors who initially overvalued the IPO firm's assets. In contrast, firms that time their equity issuing with a positive external exogenous shock outperform the benchmark over a 24-month aftermarket period, suggesting that the management is correctly anticipating growth opportunities. Low quality companies use their informational advantage to time their issue accordingly, which, on average, leads to long-run underperformance.

Paper 3 (chapter 4), "Do investors pay a premium for IPOs in the real estate industry depending on corporate governance quality?" examines whether investors are willing to pay premia for the implementation of potentially agency cost reducing corporate governance mechanisms. By focusing on a sample of 88 European property company IPOs, we are able to analyse any controlling effects in an environment where managerial opportunism is expected to be high, as postulated by Sirmans (1999) and Ooi (2000). The results show that managerial ownership and outside blockholders are strongly interrelated and thus have substituting character. Corporate blockholders seem to have no incentive to accumulate high stakes in the company if managerial ownership is high. Similarly, managers in absolute control are reluctant to let outside investors accumulate larger blocks of shares. Furthermore, the results reveal that managerial ownership and debt are positively related, supporting the signalling function of debt. Outside shareholders seem to be increasingly willing to accumulate large blocks of shares if debt levels are high, supporting the expected disciplinary role of debt. Regarding the impact of control mechanisms on Tobin's Q, we can infer that concentrated ownership seems to affect the IPO valuation of European property companies negatively, no matter whether the large stakes are held by the management or by outside investors. Finally, we find evidence that higher debt levels are associated with higher IPO valuations, a finding which is supporting Jensen's (1986) notion of the disciplinary power of debt.

Having recalled the individual motivation and findings of the three papers in this thesis, the following paragraphs are designed to provide some overall conclusions and implications that might be relevant to both academic community as well as practitioners and to present possible avenues for future research.

First, our results show that the IPO behaviour of European property companies is similar to that of industrial company IPOs. This contrasts the findings of Wang et al. (1992), Ling and Ryngaert (1997), and Buttimer et al. (2005) who find that the IPO market of US property companies operating under REIT regime has not been characterized by the same degree of initial underpricing and long-run underperformance as the general IPO market. This discrepancy in performance patterns of companies which are operating in the same industry but differ in terms of their regulatory environment implies that the market has higher confidence in the pricing of highly regulated companies compared to IPOs with lower restrictions on investment policies and shareholder structure.

In line with this argument, a further overall conclusion of this paper relates to the documented strong relationship between information asymmetry proxies and IPO performance, implying that investors in European property companies IPOs face similar valuation uncertainty and general firm specific risks when compared to industrial IPOs. Thus, it seems that although the valuation of real estate is expected to be rather straight forward, the IPO valuation of a real estate company is influenced by additional factors than merely by the value of its underlying assets. One of these factors can be the prospects of the real estate markets the IPO firm is mainly investing in, as analysed in paper 2 (chapter 3). Other factors which might be worth analysing but which are left for future research is the impact of real estate specific information presented in the IPO prospectus, the influence of the management's investment skills and industry experience, or the optimal structure of internal and external control mechanisms that specifically account for the particularities of property companies.

In general, while referring to the interpretation of our results or to the suggestions we made for future research, one must bear in mind that the majority of our sample firms went public in the years 2005 and 2006 and that the EPRA index increased by more than 40% within the same time period. Thus, our results might be impacted by an increased presence of irrational investors taking advantage of the IPO market's exuberance during that time period. Although we made major efforts to control for these effects, future research might extend this thesis's analyses by using longer-time periods in order to decrease any effects stemming from over-weighting hot issue market years. With the introduction of REIT regimes in many European countries, issuing activity of property companies is expected to increase steadily and thereby provide researcher not only with enlarged sample sizes for short-run IPO performance analyses but also allows them to conduct direct comparison tests of REIT and non-REIT IPOs in a non-US environment.

BIBLIOGRAPHY

Adams, A., & Venmore-Rowland, P. (1990). Property share valuation. *Journal of Property Valuation and Investment, 8*(2), 127–142.

Aggarwal, R., & Conroy, P. (2000). Price discovery in initial public offerings and the role of the lead underwriter. *Journal of Finance, 55*(6), 2903-2922.

Aggarwal, R., & Rivoli, P. (1990). Fads in the initial public offering market? *The Journal of the Financial Management Association, 19*(4), 45-57.

Agrawal, A., & Knoeber, C. R. (1996). Firm performance and mechanisms to control agency problems between managers and shareholders. *Journal of Financial & Quantitative Analysis, 31*(3), 377–397.

Akhigbe, A., Johnston, J., & Madura, J. (2006). Long-term industry performance following IPOs. *The Quarterly Review of Economics and Finance, 46*(4), 638–651.

Akhigbe, A., Johnston, J., Madura, J., & Springer, T. M. (2004). Market signals associated with REIT IPOs. *Journal of Real Estate Finance & Economics, 28*(4), 355–367.

Alavi, A., Pham, P. K., & Pham, T. M. (2008). Pre-IPO ownership structure and its impact on the IPO process. *Journal of Banking & Finance, 32*(11), 2361–2375.

Alli, K., Yau, J., & Yung, K. (1994). The underpricing of IPOs of financial institutions. *Journal of Business Finance & Accounting*, 21(7), 1013–1030.

Amihud, Y., Hauser, S., & Kirsh, A. (2003). Allocations, adverse selection, and cascades in IPOs: Evidence from the Tel Aviv Stock Exchange. *Journal of Financial Economics, 68*(1), 137–158.

Baker, M., & Wurgler, J. (2000). The equity share in new issues and aggregate stock Returns. *Journal of Finance, 55*(5), 2219–2257.

Barber, B. M., & Lyon, J. D. (1997). Detecting long-run abnormal stock returns: The empirical power and specification of test statistics. *Journal of Financial Economics, 43*(3), 341–372.

Barry, C. B., Muscarella, C. J., Peavy III, J. W., & Vetsuypens, M. R. (1990). The role of venture capital in the creation of public companies: Evidence from the going-public process. *Journal of Financial Economics, 27*(2), 447–471.

Bathala, C., & Moon, K. P. (1994). Managerial ownership, debt policy, and the impact of institutional holdings: an agency perspective. *The Journal of the Financial Management Association, 23*(3), 38–50.

Beatty, R. P., & Ritter, J. R. (1986). Investment banking, reputation, and the underpricing of initial public offerings. *Journal of Financial Economics, 15*(1-2), 213–232.

Below, S., Zaman, M. A., & McIntosh, W. (1995). The pricing of real estate investment trust initial public offerings. *Journal of Real Estate Finance & Economics, 11*(1), 55–64.

Benninga, S., Helmantel, M., & Sarig, O. (2005). The timing of initial public offerings. *Journal of Financial Economics, 75*(1), 115–132.

Benveniste, L. M., Busaba, W. Y., & Wilhelm, W. J. (2002). Information externalities and the role of underwriters in primary equity markets. *Journal of Financial Intermediation, 11*(1), 61-85.

Benveniste, L. M., & Spindt, P. A. (1989). How investment bankers determine the offer price and allocation of new issues. *Journal of Financial Economics, 24*(2), 343–361.

Berle, A. & Means, G. (1932). *The modern corporation and private property.* New York: Harcourt, Brace & World.

Bhagat, S., & Bolton, B. (2008). Corporate governance and firm performance. *Journal of Corporate Finance, 14*(3), 257–273.

Booth, J. R., Cornett, M. M., & Tehranian, H. (2002). Boards of directors, ownership, and regulation. *Journal of Banking & Finance, 26*(10), 1973-1996.

Booth, J. R., & Smith, R. (1986). Capital raising, underwriting and the certification hypothesis. *Journal of Financial Economics, 15*(1/2), 261–281.

Boutron, E., Gajewski, J.-F., Gresse, C., & Labegorre, F. (2007). Are IPOs still a puzzle? a survey of the empirical evidence from Europe. *Revue Finance, 28*(2), 5–41.

Bradley, D. J., Jordan, B. D., Ha-Chin Yi, & Roten, I. C. (2001). Venture capital and IPO lockup expiration: an empirical analysis. *Journal of Financial Research, 24*(4), 465–493.

Brav, A., Gecy, C., & Gompers, P. A. (2000). Is the abnormal return following equity issuances anomalous? *Journal of Financial Economics, 56*(2), 209–249.

Brav, A., & Gompers, P. A. (1997). Myth or Reality? The long-run inderperformance of initial public offerings: evidence from venture and nonventure capital-backed companies. *Journal of Finance, 52*(5), 1791–1821.

Brav, A., & Gompers, P. A. (2003). The role of lockups in initial public offerings. *Review of Financial Studies, 16*(1), 1–29.

Breinlinger, L., & Glogova, E. (2002). *Initial Public Offerings in a macroeconomic context.* Working Paper, SSRN.

Brennan, M. J., & Franks, J. (1997). Underpricing ownership and control in initial public offerings of equity securities in the UK. *Journal of Financial Economics, 45*(3), 391–413.

Brickley, J. A., Lease, R. C., & Smith, C. W., JR. (1988). Ownership structure and voting on antitakeover amendments: the distribution of power among corporate managers, Shareholders, and Directors. *Journal of Financial Economics, 20*, 267–291.

Brounen, D., & Eichholtz, P. (2002). Initial public offerings: evidence from the British French and Swedish Property share markets. *Journal of Real Estate Finance & Economics, 24*(1/2), 103.

Burkart, M., Gromb, D., & Panunzi, F. (1997). Large shareholders, monitoring and the value of the firm. *Quarterly Journal of Economics, 112*(3), 693–728.

Buttimer, R. J., Hyland, D. C., & Sanders, A. B. (2005). REITs, IPO waves and long-run performance. *Real Estate Economics, 33*(1), 51–87.

Capozza, D. R., & Seguin, P. J. (1999). Focus, transparency and value: The REIT evidence. *Real Estate Economics, 27*(4), 587–619.

Capozza, D. R., & Seguin, P. J. (2003). Inside ownership, risk sharing and Tobin's Q-ratios: Evidence from REITs. *Real Estate Economics, 31*(3), 367–404.

Carter, R. B., Dark, F. H., & Singh, A. K. (1998). Underwriter reputation, initial returns, and the long-run performance of IPO Stocks. *Journal of Finance, 53*(1), 285–311.

Carter, R. B., & Manaster, S. (1990). Initial public offerings and underwriter reputation. *Journal of Finance, 45*(4), 1045–1067.

Chadwick, W. (1993). Equity REIT securities: new investment for pension funds? *Real Estate Finance Journal*, (3), 24–30.

Chan, S. H., Stohs, M. H., & Wang, K. (2001). Are real estate IPOs a different species? evidence from Hong Kong IPOs. *Journal of Real Estate Research, 21*(3), 201-220.

Chang, S., & Hertzel, M. (2004). Equity ownership and firm value: evidence from targeted stock repurchases. *Financial Review, 39*(3), 389–407.

Chemmanur, T. J., & Fulghieri, P. (1994). Investment bank reputation, information production, and financial intermediation. *Journal of Finance, 49*(1), 57–79.

Chen, C. R., & Steiner, T. L. (2000). Tobin's Q, managerial ownership, and analyst coverage: a nonlinear simultaneous equations model. *Journal of Economics and Business, 52*(4), 365–382.

Chen, M.-Y. (2006). Managerial ownership and firm performance: an analysis using switching simultaneous-equations models. *Applied Economics, 38*(2), 161–181.

Cho, M.-H. (1998). Ownership structure, investment, and the corporate value: an empirical analysis. *Journal of Financial Economics, 47*(1), 103–121.

Choe, H., Masilus, R., & Nanda, V. (1993). Common stock offerings across the business cycle: theory and evidence. *Journal of Empirical Finance, 1*(1), 3–31.

Chung, K. H., Li, M., & Yu, L. (2005). Assets in place, growth opportunities, and IPO returns. *Financial Management, 34*(3), 65–88.

Coles, J., Meschke, F., & Lemmon, M. (2007). *Structural models and endogeneity in corporate finance: the link between managerial ownership and corporate performance.* Working Paper, SSRN.

Cook, D. O., Kieschnick, R., & van Ness, R. A. (2006). On the marketing of IPOs. *Journal of Financial Economics, 82*(1), 35–61.

Cornelli, F., Goldreich, D., & Ljungqvist, A. (2006). Investor sentiment and pre-IPO markets. *Journal of Finance, 61*(3), 1187–1216.

Cui, H., & Mak, Y. T. (2002). The relationship between managerial ownership and firm performance in high R&D firms. *Journal of Corporate Finance, 8*(4), 313-336.

De Jong, A. (2002). The disciplining role of leverage in Dutch firms. *European Finance Review, 6*(1), 31–62.

De Wit, D. (1993). Smoothing bias in In-House appraisal-based returns of open-end real estate funds. *Journal of Real Estate Research, 8*(2), 157-170.

Demsetz, H. (1983). The structure of ownership and the theory of the firm. *Journal of Law & Economics, 26*(2), 375–390.

Demsetz, H., & Lehn, K. (1985). The structure of corporate ownership: causes and consequences. *Journal of Political Economy, 93*(6), 1155-1177.

Demsetz, H., & Villalonga, B. (2001). Ownership structure and corporate performance. *Journal of Corporate Finance, 7*(3), 209–233.

Denis, D. K., & McConnell, J. J. (2003). International corporate governance. *Journal of Financial & Quantitative Analysis, 38*(1), 1–36.

Derrien, F., & Kecska, A. (2007). The initial public offerings of listed firms. *Journal of Finance, 62*(1), 447–479.

Dimovski, W., & Brooks, R. (2006). The pricing of property trust IPOs in Australia. *Journal of Real Estate Finance & Economics, 32*(2), 185–199.

Downes, D. H., & Heinkel, R. (1982). Signaling and the valuation of unseasoned new issues. *Journal of Finance, 37*(1), 1–10.

Durnev, A., & Kim, E. (2005). To steal or not to steal: firm attributes, legal environment, and valuation. *Journal of Finance, 60*(3), 1461–1493.

Eckbo, B. E., & Norli, Ã. (2005). Liquidity risk, leverage and long-run IPO returns. *Journal of Corporate Finance*, 11(1/2), 1–35.

Edelstein, R., & Quan, D. (2006). How does appraisal smoothing bias real estate returns measurement? *Journal of Real Estate Finance & Economics, 32*(1), 41–60.

Eichholtz, P., Kok, N., & Otten, R. (2008). Executive compensation in UK property companies. *Journal of Real Estate Finance & Economics, 36*(4), 405–426.

Faccio, M., & Lasfer, M. (2000). Do occupational pension funds monitor firms in which they hold large stakes? *Journal of Corporate Finance, 6*, 71–110.

Fama, E. F. (1980). Agency problems and the theory of the firm. *Journal of Political Economy, 88*(2), 288–307.

Fama, E. F. (1998). Market efficiency, long-term returns, and behavioral finance. *Journal of Financial Economics, 49*(3), 283–306.

Fama, E. F., & Jensen, M. C. (1983). Separation of ownership and control. *Journal of Law & Economics, 26*(2), 301–326.

Fernando, C., Gatchev, V. A., & Spindt, P. A. (2005). Wanna dance? How firms and underwriters choose each other. *Journal of Finance, 60*(5), 2437–2469.

Ferris, S., Kim, K., & Kitsabunnarat, P. (2001). Is managerial equity ownership an alternative governance mechanism for Japanese firms? In M. Hirschey, K. John & A. K. Makhija (Eds.), *Advances in Financial Economics,* (Vol. 6, pp. 39–63). Amsterdam: Elsevier/JAI.

Field, L. C., & Hanka, G. (2001). The expiration of IPO share lockups. *Journal of Finance, 56*(2), 471–500.

Field, L. C., & Karpoff, J. M. (2002). Takeover defenses of IPO firms. *Journal of Finance, 57*(5), 1857–1889.

Field, L. C., & Sheehan, D. P. (2004). IPO underpricing and outside blockholdings. *Journal of Corporate Finance, 10*(2), 263-280.

Freybote, T., Rottke, N., & Schiereck, D. (2008). Underpricing of European property companies and the IPO cycle: a note. *Journal of Property Investment & Finance, 26*(5), 376–387.

Friend, I., & Lang, L. (1988). An empirical test of the impact of managerial self-interest on corporate capital structure. *Journal of Finance, 43*(2), 271–281.

Frye, M. B. (2004). *The evolution of corporate governance: evidence from initial public offerings.* Unpublished working paper.

Gajewski, J.-F., & Gresse, C. (2006). *A survey of the European IPO market.* ECMI Research Reports, No. 2, European Capital Markets Institute, August.

Garfinkel, J. A. (1993). IPO underpricing, insider selling and subsequent equity offerings: is underpricing a signal of quality? *The Journal of the Financial Management Association, 22*(1), 74–83.

Geltner, D. (1989). Estimating real estate's systematic risk from aggregate level appraisal-based returns. *Journal of the American Real Estate & Urban Economics Association, 17*(4), 463–481.

Geltner, D. M. (1991). Smoothing in appraisal-based returns. *Journal of Real Estate Finance & Economics, 4*(3), 327–345.

Gerbich, M., Levis, M., & Venmore-Rowland, P. (1999). Property investment and property development firm performance around initial public offerings and rights offerings: U.K. evidence, *Journal of Real Estate Finance & Economics, 18*(2), 207-238.

Ghosh, S. (2007). Leverage, managerial monitoring and firm valuation: A simultaneous equation approach. *Research in Economics, 61*(2), 84–98.

Gilson, S. C. (1989). Management turnover and financial distress. *Journal of Financial Economics, 25*(2), 241–262.

Gompers, P. A. (1996). Grandstanding in the venture capital industry. *Journal of Financial Economics, 42*(1), 133–156.

Grier, P., & Zychowicz, E. J. (1994). Institutional investors, corporate discipline, and the role of debt. *Journal of Economics & Business, 46*(1), 1-11.

Grinblatt, M., & Hwang, C. Y. (1989). Signalling and the pricing of new issues. *Journal of Finance, 44*(2), 393–420.

Grissom, T. V., & DeLisle, J. (1998). Alternative total return series for direct real estate investment. *Journal of Real Estate Portfolio Management, 4*(1), 17-33.

Grossman, S. J., & Hart, O. D. (1980). Takeover bids, the free-rider problem, and the theory of the corporation. *Bell Journal of Economics, 11*(1), 42–64.

Grossman, S. J., & Hart, O. D. (1982). Corporate financial structure and managerial incentives. In J. J. McCall (Ed.), *The economics of information and uncertainty,* (pp. 107–140). Chicago: Univ. Press.

Grossman, S. J., & Hart, O. D. (1986). The costs and benefits of ownership: a theory of vertical and lateral integration. *Journal of Political Economy, 94*(4), 691–719.

Gyourko, J. (1994). The long-term prospects of the REIT market. *Real Estate Review, 24*(1), 42-46.

Habib, M. A., & Ljungqvist, A. P. (2001). Underpricing and entrepreneurial wealth losses in IPOs: theory and evidence. *Review of Financial Studies, 14*(2), 433-458.

Hanley, K. W., & Wilhelm, W. J. (1995). Evidence on the strategic allocation of initial public offerings. *Journal of Financial Economics, 37*(2), 239–257.

Hart, O., & Moore, J. (1998). Default and renegotiation: a dynamic model of debt. *Quarterly Journal of Economics, 113*(1), 1–41.

Hartzell, J. C., Kallberg, J. G., & Liu, C. H. (2004). *The Role of corporate governance in initial public offerings: evidence from real estate investment trusts.* Working Paper.

Hartzell, J. C., Kallberg, J. G., & Liu, C. H. (2005). The role of the underlying real asset market in REIT IPOs. *Real Estate Economics, 33*(1), 27–50.

Harvey, C. R., Lins, K. V., & Roper, A. H. (2004). The effect of capital structure when expected agency costs are extreme. *Journal of Financial Economics, 74*(1), 3–30.

Hausman, J. (1978). Specification tests in econometrics. *Econometrica, 46*(6), 1251–1271.

Helwege, J., & Liang, N. (2004). Initial public offerings in hot and cold Markets. *Journal of Financial & Quantitative Analysis, 39*(3), 541–569.

Hermalin, B. E., & Weisbach, M. S. (1991). The effects of board composition and direct incentives on firm performance. *The Journal of the Financial Management Association, 20*(4), 101–112.

Hermalin, B. E., & Weisbach, M. S. (2003). Boards of directors as an endogenously determined institution: a survey of the economic literature. *Economic Policy Review, 9*, 7–26.

Himmelberg, C. P., Hubbard, R. G., & Palia, D. (1999). Understanding the determinants of managerial ownership and the link between ownership and performance. *Journal of Financial Economics, 53*(3), 353–384.

Holderness, C. G., & Sheehan, D. P. (1988). The role of majority shareholders in publicly held corporations: an exploratory analysis: the distribution of power among corporate managers, shareholders, and directors. *Journal of Financial Economics, 20*, 317–346.

Houge, T., Loughran, T., Suchanek, G., & Xuemin Yan (2001). Divergence of opinion, uncertainty, and the quality of initial public offerings. *Financial Management, 30*(4), 5–23.

Hughes, J. (1989). Discussion of "The valuation of initial public offerings". *Contemporary Accounting Research, 5*(2), 519–525.

Ibbotson, R. G. (1975). Price performance of common stock new issues. *Journal of Financial Economics, 2*(3), 235–272.

Ibbotson, R. G., & Jaffe, J. F. (1975). Hot issue markets. *Journal of Finance, 30*(4), 1027–1042.

Ibbotson, R. G., Sindelar, J. L., & Ritter, J. R. (1988). Initial public offerings. *Journal of Applied Corporate Finance, 1*(2), 37–45.

Ibbotson, R. G., Sindelar, J. L., & Ritter, J. R. (1994). The market's problems with the pricing of initial public offerings. *Journal of Applied Corporate Finance, 7*(1), 66–74.

Israel, R., & Israel, R. (1992). Capital and ownership structures, and the market for corporate control. *Review of Financial Studies, 5*(2), 181-198.

Jain, B. A., & Kini, O. (2006). Industry clustering of initial public offerings. *Managerial & Decision Economics, 27*(1), 1–20.

James, C., & Wier, P. (1990). Borrowing relationships, intermediation, and the cost of issuing public securities. *Journal of Financial Economics, 28*(1/2), 149–171.

Jaskiewicz, P., González, V. M., Menéndez, S., & Schiereck, D. (2005). Long-run IPO performance analysis of German and Spanish family-owned businesses. *Family Business Review, 18*(3), 179–202.

Jayaraman, N., Khorana, A., Nelling, E., & Covin, J. (2000). CEO founder status and firm financial performance. *Strategic Management Journal, 21*(12), 1215-1224.

Jenkinson, T., & Ljungqvist, A. (2001). *Going public* (2nd edition). Oxford: Oxford Univ. Press.

Jensen, M. C. (1986). Agency costs of free cash flow, corporate finance, and takeovers. *American Economic Review, 76*(2), 323-329.

Jensen, M. C., & Meckling, W. H. (1976). Theory of the firm: managerial behavior, agency costs and ownership structure. *Journal of Financial Economics, 3*(4), 305–360.

Jensen, M. C., & Murphy, K. J. (1990). CEO incentives -- it's not how much you pay, but how. *Harvard Business Review, 68*(3), 138–149.

Johnston, J., & DiNardo, J. (1997). *Econometric methods* (4th edition). New York, NY: McGraw-Hill.

Keasey, K., & Short, H. (1997). Equity retention and initial public offerings: the influence of signalling and entrenchment effects. *Applied Financial Economics, 7*(1), 75–85.

Kim, W. S., & Sorensen, E. H. (1986). Evidence on the impact of the agency costs of debt on corporate debt policy. *Journal of Financial & Quantitative Analysis, 21*(2), 131–144.

Klapper, L. F., & Love, I. (2003). Corporate governance, investor protection, and performance in emerging markets. *Journal of Corporate Finance, 10*(5), 703–728.

Koh, F., & Walter, T. (1989). A direct test of Rock's model of the pricing of unseasoned issues. *Journal of Financial Economics, 23*(2), 251–272.

Krigman, L., Shaw, W. H., & Womack, K. L. (1999). The persistence of IPO mispricing and the predictive power of flipping. *Journal of Finance, 54*(3), 1015–1044.

La Porta, R., Lopez-de-Silanes, F., & Shleifer, A. (1999). Corporate ownership around the world. *Journal of Finance, 54*(2), 471–517.

La Porta, R., Lopez-de-Silanes, F., Shleifer, A., & Vishny, R. (2002). Investor protection and corporate valuation. *Journal of Finance, 57*(3), 1147–1170.

La Porta, R., Lopez-de-Silanes, F., Shleifer, A., & Vishny, R. W. (1998). Law and finance. *Journal of Political Economy, 106*(6), 1113-1155.

Lang, L., & Ofek, E. (1996). Leverage, investment, and firm growth. *Journal of Financial Economics, 40*(1), 3–29.

Lang, L. H. P., & Stulz, R. (1994). Tobin's Q, corporate diversification, and firm performance. *Journal of Political Economy, 102*(6), 1248-1280.

Lee, C. M. C., Shleifer, A., & Thaler, R. H. (1991). Investor sentiment and the closed-end fund puzzle. *Journal of Finance, 46*(1), 75–109.

Leland, H. E., & Pyle, D. H. (1977). Informational asymmetries, financial structure and financial intermediation. *Journal of Finance, 32*(2), 371–387.

Leone, A. J., Rock, S., & Willenborg, M. (2007). Disclosure of intended use of proceeds and underpricing in initial public offerings. *Journal of Accounting Research, 45*(1), 111–153.

Lerner, J. (1994). Venture capitalists and the decision to go public. *Journal of Financial Economics, 35*(3), 293–316.

Levis, M. (1990). The winner's curse problem, interest costs and the underpricing of initial public offerings. *Economic Journal, 100*(399), 76–89.

Ling, D. C., & Ryngaert, M. (1997). Valuation uncertainty, institutional involvement, and the underpricing of IPOs: the case of REITs. *Journal of Financial Economics, 43*(3), 433–456.

Liow, K. (1996). Property companies' share price discounts and property market returns: the Singapore evidence. *Journal of Property Finance, 7*(4), 64–77.

Ljungqvist, A. P., Nanda, V., & Singh, R. (2006). Hot markets, investor sentiment, and IPO pricing. *Journal of Business, 79*(4), 1667–1702.

Ljungqvist, A. P., & Wilhelm, W. J. (2003). IPO pricing in the Dot-com bubble. *Journal of Finance, 58*(2), 723–752.

Loderer, C., & Martin, K. (1997). Executive stock ownership and performance tracking faint traces. *Journal of Financial Economics, 45*(2), 223–256.

Londerville, J. (2002). Canadian real estate investment trusts: a review of the IPO literature and preliminary analysis of Canadian REIT IPO pricing. *Canadian Journal of Administrative Sciences*, 19(4), 359-368.

Loughran, T., & Ritter, J. R. (1995). The new issues puzzle. *Journal of Finance, 50*(1), 23–51.

Loughran, T., Ritter, J. R., & Rydqvist, K. (1994). Initial public offerings: international insights. *Pacific-Basin Finance Journal, 2*(2-3), 165–199.

Lowry, M. (2003). Why does IPO volume fluctuate so much? *Journal of Financial Economics, 67*(1), 3-40.

Lowry, M., & Schwert, G. W. (2002). IPO market cycles: bubbles or sequential learning? *Journal of Finance, 57*(3), 1171–1200.

Lyon, J. D., Barber, B. M., & Tsai, C.-L. (1999). Improved methods for tests of long-run abnormal stock returns. *Journal of Finance, 54*(1), 165–201.

Mason, E. S. (1939). Price and production policies of large-scale enterprise. *American Economic Review, 29*, 61-74.

McConnell, J. J., & Servaes, H. (1990). Additional evidence on equity ownership and corporate value. *Journal of Financial Economics, 27*(2), 595–612.

McConnell, J. J., & Servaes, H. (1995). Equity ownership and the two faces of debt. *Journal of Financial Economics, 39*(1), 131–157.

McGuinness, P. (1992). An examination of the underpricing of initial public offerings in Hong Kong: 1980-90. *Journal of Business Finance & Accounting, 19*(2), 165–186.

Megginson, W. L., & Weiss, K. A. (1991). Venture capitalist certification in initial public offerings. *Journal of Finance, 46*(3), 879–903.

Michaely, R., & Shaw, W. H. (1994). The pricing of initial public offerings: tests of adverse-selection and signaling theories. *Review of Financial Studies, 7*(2), 279-319.

Mikkelson, W. H., Megan Partch, M., & Shah, K. (1997). Ownership and operating performance of companies that go public. *Journal of Financial Economics, 44*(3), 281–307.

Mikkelson, W. H., & Ruback, R. S. (1985). An empirical analysis of the interfirm equity investment process. *Journal of Financial Economics, 14*(4), 523–553.

Miller, E. M. (1977). Risk, uncertainty and divergence of opinion. *Journal of Finance, 32*(4), 1151–1168.

Min, J. H., & Prather, L. J. (2001). Tobin's Q, agency conflicts, and differential wealth effects of international joint ventures. *Global Finance Journal, 12*(2), 267–283.

Modigliani, F., & Miller, M. H. (1958). The cost of capital, corporation finance and the theory of investment. *American Economic Review, 48*(3), 261-297.

Morck, R., Shleifer, A., & Vishny, R. W. (1988). Management ownership and market valuation: an empirical analysis. *Journal of Financial Economics, 20*(1/2), 293–315.

Muscarella, C. J., & Vetsuypens, M. R. (1989). A simple test of Baron's model of IPO underpricing. *Journal of Financial Economics, 24*(1), 125–135.

Myers, S. C. (1977). Determinants of corporate borrowing. *Journal of Financial Economics, 5*(2), 147–175.

Myers, S. C., & Majluf, N. S. (1984). Corporate financing and investment decisions when firms have information that investors do not have. *Journal of Financial Economics, 13*(2), 187–221.

Ooi, J. T. (2000). Managerial opportunism and the capital structure decisions of property companies. *Journal of Property Investment & Finance, 18*(3), 316–331.

Pastor, L., & Veronesi, P. (2005). Rational IPO waves. *Journal of Finance, 60*(4), 1713–1757.

Peavy III, J. W. (1990). Returns on initial public offerings of closed-end funds. *Review of Financial Studies, 3*(4), 695–708.

Petersen, M. (2007). *Retained inside ownership, signaling, and the valuation of initial public offerings - evidence from Germany,* Working paper, SSRN.

Porter, M. (1980). *Competitive strategy.* New York: Free Press.

Pound, J. (1988). Proxy contests and the efficiency of shareholder oversight. *Journal of Financial Economics, 20*(1/2), 237–265.

Pound, J. (1995). The promise of the governed corporation. *Harvard Business Review, 73*(2), 89–98.

Rajan, R., & Servaes, H. (1997). Analyst following of initial public offerings. *Journal of Finance, 52*(2), 507–529.

Rajan, R. G., & Zingales, L. (1995). What do we know about capital structure? Some evidence from international data. *Journal of Finance, 50*(5), 1421–1460.

Rhodes, G., & Westbrook, M. D. (1981). A study of estimator densities and performance under misspecification. *Journal of Econometrics, 16*(3), 311–337.

Ritter, J. R. (1984). The "Hot Issue" market of 1980. *Journal of Business, 57*(2), 215–240.

Ritter, J. R. (1987). The costs of going public. *Journal of Financial Economics, 19*(2), 269–281.

Ritter, J. R. (1991). The long-run performance of initial public offerings. *Journal of Finance, 46*(1), 3–27.

Rock, K. (1986). Why new issues are underpriced. *Journal of Financial Economics, 15*(1-2), 187–212.

Ross, S. A. (1977). The determination of financial structure: the incentive-signalling approach. *Bell Journal of Economics, 8*(1), 23–40.

Rumelt, R. P. (1991). How much does industry matter? *Strategic Management Journal, 12*(3), 167–185.

Sahi, W., & Lee, S. L. (2001). The initial return performance of UK property company IPOs. *Journal of Property Investment & Finance, 19*(2), 127–139.

Sargan, J. (1964). Wages and prices in the United Kingdom: A study in econometric methodology. In P. Hart, G. Mills & J. Whitaker (Eds.), *Econometric analysis for national economic planning,* (pp. 25–63). London.

Schenone, C. (2004). The effect of banking relationships on the firm's IPO underpricing. *Journal of Finance, 59*(6), 2903–2958.

Schmalensee, R. (1985). Do markets differ much? *American Economic Review, 75*(3), 341-351.

Schultz, P. (2003). Pseudo market timing and the long-run underperformance of IPOs. *Journal of Finance, 58*(2), 483–518.

Schuster, J. (2003). *IPOs: Insights from seven European countries.* Working paper, London School of Economics.

Shleifer, A., & Vishny, R. W. (1986). Large shareholders and corporate control. *Journal of Political Economy, 94*(3), 461–488.

Shleifer, A., & Vishny, R. W. (1989). Management entrenchment. *Journal of Financial Economics, 25*(1), 123–139.

Shleifer, A., & Vishny, R. W. (1997). A survey of corporate governance. *Journal of Finance, 52*(2), 737–783.

Short, H., & Keasey, K. (1999). Managerial ownership and the performance of firms: Evidence from the UK. *Journal of Corporate Finance, 5*(1), 79–101.

Sirmans, C. F. (1999). *Governance issues in real estate investing: the case of REITs.* Working paper, University of Connecticut.

Smith, C. W., JR., & Warner, J. B. (1979). On financial contracting: an analysis of bond covenants. *Journal of Financial Economics, 7*(2), 117–161.

Stiglitz, J. E. (1985). Credit markets and the control of capital. *Journal of Money, Credit & Banking, 17*(2), 133–152.

Stehle, R., Ehrhardt, O., & Przyborowsky, R. (2000). Long-run stock performance of German initial public offerings and seasoned equity issues. *European Financial Management*, 6(2), 173-196.

Stock, J. H., Wright, J. H., & Yogo, M. (2002). A survey of weak instruments and weak identification in generalized method of moments. *Journal of Business & Economic Statistics, 20*(4), 518–529.

Stoughton, N. M., & Zechner, J. (1998). IPO-mechanisms, monitoring and ownership structure. *Journal of Financial Economics, 49*(1), 45–77.

Stulz, R. (1990). Managerial discretion and optimal financing policies. *Journal of Financial Economics, 26*(1), 3–27.

Stulz, R. (1988). Managerial control of voting rights: financing policies and the market for corporate control. *Journal of Financial Economics, 20*, 25–54.

Stulz, R. M., Walkling, R. A., & Song, M. H. (1990). The distribution of target ownership and the division of gains in successful takeovers. *Journal of Finance, 45*(3), 817–833.

Titman, S., & Trueman, B. (1986). Information quality and the valuation of new issues. *Journal of Accounting and Economics, 8*(2), 159–172.

Trueman, B. (1986). The Relationship between the Level of Capital Expenditures and Firm Value. *Journal of Financial & Quantitative Analysis, 21*(2), 115–129.

Wang, K., Chan, S. H., & Gau, G. W. (1992). Initial public offerings of equity securities. *Journal of Financial Economics, 31*(3), 381–410.

Wasserman, N. (2006). Stewards, agents, and the founder discount: executive compensation in new ventures. *Academy of Management Journal, 49*(5), 960–976.

Weiss, K. (1989). The post-offering price performance of closed-end funds. *The Journal of the Financial Management Association, 18*(3), 57–67.

Welch, I. (1989). Seasoned offerings, imitation costs, and the underpricing of initial public offerings. *Journal of Finance, 44*(2), 421–449.

Wernerfelt, B. (1984). A resource-based view of the firm. *Strategic Management Journal, 5*(2), 171–180.

White, H. (1980). A heteroskedasticity-consistent covariance matrix estimator and a direct test for heteroskedasticity. *Econometrica, 48*(4), 817–838.

Williamson, O. E. (1985). *The economic institutions of capitalism: firms, markets, relational contracting.* New York: Free Press.

Wruck, K. H. (1989). Equity ownership concentration and firm value: evidence from private equity financings. *Journal of Financial Economics, 23*(1), 3–28.

Yung, C., Colak, G., & Wei Wang (2008). Cycles in the IPO market. *Journal of Financial Economics, 89*(1), 192–208.

Zheng, S. X., & Stangeland, D. A. (2007). IPO underpricing, firm quality, and analyst forecasts. *Financial Management, 36*(2), 45–64.

Zwiebel, J. (1996). Dynamic capital structure under managerial entrenchment. *American Economic Review, 86*(5), 1197–1215.

Corporate Finance and Governance

Herausgegeben von Dirk Schiereck

Band 1 Sebastian Michael Gläsner: Return Patterns of German Open-End Real Estate Funds. An Empirical Explanation of Smooth Fund Returns. 2010.

Band 2 Patrick Ams: Directors' Dealings and Insider Trading in Germany. An Empirical Analysis. 2010.

Band 3 Joachim Vogt: Value Creation within the Construction Industry. A Study of Strategic Takeovers. 2011.

Band 4 Fabian Braemisch: Underpricing, Long-Run Performance, and Valuation of Initial Public Offerings. 2011.

www.peterlang.de

Philipp Mohl

Empirical Evidence on the Macroeconomic Effects of EU Cohesion Policy

Springer Gabler

Philipp Mohl
Heidelberg, Germany

Dissertation University of Heidelberg, 2013

ISBN 978-3-658-13851-6 ISBN 978-3-658-13852-3 (eBook)
DOI 10.1007/978-3-658-13852-3

Library of Congress Control Number: 2016937384

Springer Gabler

Printed on acid-free paper

This Springer Gabler imprint is published by Springer Nature
The registered company is Springer Fachmedien Wiesbaden GmbH

Empirical Evidence on the Macroeconomic Effects of EU Cohesion Policy

Acknowledgements

The research for this dissertation was to a large extent carried out at the Centre for European Economic Research (ZEW). I would like to thank several people without whom my thesis would not have been possible. First and foremost, I am indebted to Prof. Dr. Lars P. Feld for supervising my thesis and for giving valuable advice. I am also grateful to Prof. Dr. Axel Dreher, who kindly consented to be my second supervisor. Moreover, I feel privileged to have participated in the Ph.D. Programme of Economics of the University of Mannheim.

I greatly benefited from the support of Friedrich Heinemann, Head of the "Corporate Taxation and Public Finance" department of the ZEW, who provided a pleasant and inspiring work atmosphere and ensured an excellent cooperation in our research projects. Special thanks goes to my co-author Tobias Hagen for many enriching discussions and the fantastic teamwork. Moreover, I am grateful for the helpful suggestions from my ZEW colleagues: Alexander Kalb, Andreas Schrimpf, François Laisney, Markus Kappler, Qingwei Wang, Sarah Borgloh, Sebastian Hauptmeier and Steffen Osterloh. I am also grateful to Florian Meier for his research assistance, as well as to Heidi Schielke and the service team at the ZEW for facilitating my life in Mannheim.

Furthermore, I am grateful for valuable comments from various discussants and participants of the following conferences: DIW Macroeconometric Workshop (2008), European Public Choice Society (2006-2009), German Economic Association (2007- 2009), International Conference on Panel Data (2009), International Institute of Public Finance (2008-2009), Macroeconomic Research Meeting (2008), Silvaplana Workshop on Political Economy (2007), World Conference of Spatial Econometrics (2009) as well as participants of the European Commission workshop on public finances in the EU (2008) and of the internal seminars at the European Central Bank and at the ZEW.

Finally, I am indebted to my friends who supported me over the last years despite my time constraints. Many thanks to Thilo Hatzius who motivated me to seek a more profound understanding of economics. Last, but not least, I thank my parents, Inge & Wolfi, and Niloufar for their support.

Philipp Mohl

Table of Contents

List of Figures

List of Tables

Chapter 1

Introduction

1.1 Theme and Motivation

The largest part of the EU budget–more than one third of the total EU expenditures that correspond to 380 billion euros–is spent on EU Cohesion Policy (CP) within the Multiannual Financial Framework ranging from 2007–2013.[1] Its main purpose is to promote the "overall harmonious development" of the EU, to reduce disparities between the levels of development of the various regions, and to strengthen its "economic, social and territorial cohesion" (Art. 3(3) of the Treaty establishing the European Community (TEU)).

The relevance of EU Cohesion Policy has increased over the past decades. Before 1989, the EU budget was implemented annually and the Cohesion Policy was spent via several structural funds (SF), namely the European Social Fund (with its initial primary goal to support labour mobility), the European Agricultural Guidance and Guarantee Fund (to support the restructuring of rural areas) and the European Regional Development Fund (to correct regional imbalances). Following the implementation of the Single European Act in 1987, the EU budget has been allocated within multi-annual "programme periods"[2] and some additional financial instruments, among others the Cohesion Fund, were established. At the same time, the European Commission defined several allocation rules and guiding principles, in particular that EU funding has to be co-financed by the member states, it is a supplement and not a substitute for the public national investment and must not crowd out national public expenditures. Moreover, the European Commission introduced several

[1] In this book, the terms "EU Cohesion Policy" and "EU Regional Policy" are used synonymously. Both refer to the total expenditures in this policy field, which is used to (co-)finance national projects mostly funded via "structural funds" at the regional level or the "Cohesion Fund" at the national level.

[2] The first period ran from 1989 to 1993, the subsequent multi-annual frameworks comprise the following time periods: 1994-1999, 2000-2006 and 2007-2013.

so-called "objectives", which reflect the key priorities for EU expenditures. The most important objective by far is to support economically "less developed regions" (the so-called Objective 1 regions). The other objectives are targeted, *inter alia*, at areas affected by industrial decline (Objective 2) or at fighting long-term unemployment (Objective 3). Both the number and the definition of the objectives are not fixed over time and vary over the programme periods.

The number of funding criteria have increased significantly over the years. While EU aid has initially focused mainly on supporting national labour market policies, it has been extended, *inter alia*, to research and development projects, renewable energies as well as to support cultural activities and health and education systems. In this context, several studies conclude that the evolution of the EU expenditure (and revenue) side is clearly shaped by the veto power of EU member states and the impact of side payments in the political negotiation processes (for example, Blankart and Kirchner, 2003; Feld, 2005; Feld and Schnellenbach, 2007; Heinemann, Mohl and Osterloh, 2010). A prominent example is the establishment of the Cohesion Fund in 1994, which can be explained by the fact that the poor countries had to be compensated against losses of the single currency of the European Monetary Union (van der Beek and Neal, 2004). Similarly, while new funding criteria have been steadily created, the veto power of member states prevented the European Commission from phasing out old criteria (Heinemann, Hagen, Mohl, Osterloh and Sellenthin, 2010).

European Cohesion Policy is successful if disparities between regions decrease. Therefore, the convergence-process of EU regions is a question of high political importance and it has attracted the interest of several researchers. Generally, the empirical studies point to a small convergence effect of all or at least of some European regions (Barro and Sala-i-Martin, 1991; Sala-i-Martin, 1996). However, whether the potential success with regard to economic growth and convergence results from EU Cohesion Policy is an open question in applied econometric research. While some authors do find evidence of a positive impact of structural funds on economic growth (for example, Beugelsdijk and Eijffinger, 2005; Dall'erba, 2005; Ramajo, Márquez, Hewings and Salinas, 2008), others only find weakly-positive (for example, Esposti and Bussoletti, 2008), no statistically-significant (for example, Dall'erba and Le Gallo, 2008) or even a negative impact (for example, Eggert, von Ehrlich, Fenge and König, 2007). There are, however, several issues requiring further investigation.

First, the estimation results might be biased due to *limited data availability of EU funding*. The European Commission (1995, 1996a,b, 1997, 1998, 1999, 2000) only published data on regional structural funds payments for the 1994-1999 period, but restricted to the release of structural funds commitments before and of payments at the country level after that period. As structural funds commitments may be called up with a delay due to missing absorption capacity, the use of commitments instead of payments results in a *measurement error*. Owing to missing data availability, the current literature has focused on the time period before 2000 and has hardly analysed the effects of the different objectives defined by the European Commission in greater detail.

Second, the estimates might be biased due to *reverse causality*. The allocation criteria of EU funding are presumably correlated with the dependent variable of our empirical investigations–the regional economic growth rate and the employment level–due to two reasons. First, the size of Objective 1 funding depends on the ratio of the regional GDP per capita and the EU-wide GDP. Second, the allocation of Objectives 2 and 3 is based, *inter alia*, on the employment structure and the population density.

Third, insights of the new economic geography literature (Krugman, 1991; Krugman and Venables, 1995) indicate the *significance of spillover effects*, which is confirmed in several empirical studies at the regional level within the European Union (Abreu, de Groot and Florax, 2005; Arbia, Le Gallo and Piras, 2008). Applied to our research question, EU aid might affect the regional growth rate or employment level and these effects might, in turn, spill over into neighbouring regions. As a result, the estimation results are biased if the spillover effects cannot be separated from the "original" impulse. The existing studies analysing the growth effects of EU funding have focused on cross-section analyses (Dall'erba, 2005; Dall'erba and Le Gallo, 2008). Thus, no paper has used spatial econometric tools for panel data to address the effects of EU Cohesion Policy.

Fourth, the estimations might be biased as the current literature mostly relies on *(strict) functional form assumptions*. Although growth theory provides well-established suggestions for the estimation of growth relationships (see, among others Durlauf and Quah, 1999; Islam, 2003), it is ex ante not clear which economic growth model to use and which functional form is appropriate for the effect of SF payments (Durlauf, Kourtellos and Tan, 2008). There may be non-linearities and interactions with covariates, which may lead to biased estimates if they are not taken into account.

Apart from the methodological issues, the current literature analysing the effects of EU Cohesion Policy largely ignores the fact that *EU Cohesion Policy might also have an impact on other policy fields*.

First, the *employment effects* are key to understanding regional income disparities, since income differences are, among other factors, based on differences in the labour productivity and/or employment level. In addition, parts of the EU expenditures (in particular Objective 2 payments) directly aim at reducing disparities in the employment sector. Nevertheless, only a few papers have analysed the employment effects of this policy field. While some contributions find positive employment effects for EU countries (Bouvet, 2005), regions (Busch, Lichtblau and Schnabel, 1998) or Italian firms (Bondonio and Greenbaum, 2006), more recent evidence is rather disillusioning; pointing to no positive employment effects (Dall'erba and Le Gallo, 2007; Heinemann, Mohl and Osterloh, 2009; Becker, Egger and von Ehrlich, 2010). In this context, it has been disregarded that from a theoretical perspective, higher expenditures on EU funding do not necessarily increase the total employment level. Instead, its impact depends on whether structural funds are used as capital subsidies or as human capital investment and it is subject to the educational attainment of the population. All in all, the net effect on total employment is an empirical question.

Second, there are at least two reasons why the *impact on public investment* might be of special interest. First, according to the "principle of additionality" the member states are obliged to co-finance EU funded projects without crowding out investment spending elsewhere (European Commission, 2007a). Second, since a major part of the Cohesion Policy is spent on public investment (European Commission, 2004a), almost all empirical studies on the investigation of growth effects implicitly assume that Cohesion Policy increases investment, leading to a higher steady-state capital per capita, which, in turn, increases the GDP growth rate. Hence, an essential condition for the effectiveness of EU transfers is the degree to which they affect overall public investment. However, the impact of Cohesion Policy payments on national public investment has not yet been evaluated. The paper by Ederveen, Gorter, de Mooij and Nahuis (2002) might be most closely related to this research question. The authors analyse the impact of receiving Objective 1 funding for national regional support and conclude that one euro of additional EU aid crowds out 17 cents of national Regional Policy.

1.2 Main Research Questions and Results

Against this background, the aim of this doctoral thesis is to evaluate the macroeconomic effects of EU Cohesion Policy by applying econometric techniques. In particular, we account for several methodological issues which have so far not been addressed in the context of the investigation of the economic growth effects of EU funding and

- provide a new detailed dataset of EU regional structural funds payments for the period 1999-2006 to determine more precise measures of EU funding,

- control for spatial spillover effects in a panel context,

- take account of the endogeneity problem and
- avoid using strict functional form assumptions.

Obviously, given the current state-of-the-art econometric models and the available data, it is not possible to deal with all the problems mentioned above simultaneously. However, by taking into account the methodological issues and by comparing the results of several empirical approaches, one might get an idea about the range of the "true effect" of EU Cohesion Policy on growth.

Moreover, the current literature has hardly taken into account that EU funding might not only affect economic growth but also other policy fields. As a consequence, we extend the literature by analysing the impact of EU Cohesion Policy on

- employment and
- public investment.

The thesis shows that regional spillovers have a significant impact on regional growth rates and employment levels, which confirms the importance of regional interconnectivity within the European Union. In terms of the effects of EU aid on regional economic growth, our findings indicate that EU Cohesion Policy is only conditionally effective and its effectiveness depends on which Objective is analysed. To be more precise, only Objective 1 payments have a positive and statistically significant impact on the economic growth rates. Furthermore, in line with the theoretical predictions, we find no clear evidence that EU funding promotes regional employment levels per se. Instead, structural funds payments seem to be used as capital subsidies: they have a statistically positive impact on employment in regions with a low share of low-skilled population, and they have a negative impact on employment levels in regions with a high share of low-skilled population. Finally, our results show that EU Cohesion Policy payments do not significantly increase public investment in the EU countries, which points to a crowding out of national investment. Overall, the gained insights contribute to a more profound understanding of the macroeconomic effects of EU Cohesion Policy, which is essential to design a more effective and efficient EU spending system in the future.

1.3 Outline

The book combines articles analysing the macroeconomic effects of EU Cohesion Policy with empirical methods. Each chapter comprises a stand-alone analysis of the research question, includes an introduction, stresses the contribution to the existing literature and presents the methodological approach. All essays except for one were written in collaboration with a co-author and simultaneously prepared for submission to academic journals. More detailed information can be found at the beginning of each chapter. The thesis is structured as follows:

Chapter 2 provides an introduction to and an overview of how to measure the effectiveness of EU Cohesion Policy. The chapter forms an introduction to the institutional background, presents the theoretical framework used to evaluate the effectiveness of EU Cohesion Policy, discusses the main econometric issues and reviews the existing literature of this research field in order to shed light on the main reasons for the diverging results.

Chapter 3 evaluates the regional growth effects of EU structural funds payments. The empirical analysis is based on a new dataset of 126 NUTS-1 / NUTS-2 regions for the period 1995-2006, which was compiled by the European Commission in 2008. This allows for more precise measures of structural funds by distinguishing between Objective 1, 2 and 3 payments. The empirical results are based on panel econometric methods controlling for heteroscedasticity, serial and spatial correlation as well as for endogeneity.

The aim of *Chapter 4* is to evaluate the growth effects of SF payments by trying to avoid simple functional form assumptions. In this context, structural funds payments are interpreted as a continuous treatment and by applying the method of generalised propensity score. This method is applied to our new regional panel dataset.

Chapter 5 deals with an empirical investigation of the employment effects of EU structural funds using our new dataset. In particular, it explicitly takes into account the unambiguous theoretical propositions that higher expenditures on EU funding do not necessarily increase the total employment level. Instead, its impact depends on whether structural funds are used as capital subsidies or as human capital investment and it is subject to the educational attainment of the population.

Chapter 6 investigates whether, and to which extent, EU Cohesion Policy payments have an impact on national public investment. Put differently, the study evaluates whether cohesion payments are 'additional' or whether they only lead to a displacement of national public investment. To address this research question, a new comprehensive dataset comprising total EU Cohesion Policy payments for the EU-27 sample covering the period 1982-2006 is used.

Finally, *Chapter 7* summarises the main findings and concludes.

Chapter 2

Econometric Evaluation of EU Cohesion Policy: A Survey[1]

2.1 Introduction

The aim of this chapter is to provide a fundamental review of the econometric evaluation of EU Cohesion Policy in order to shed light on the reasons for the diverging results described in Chapter 1. To be more precise, this chapter forms an introduction to the institutional background, presents the theoretical framework used to evaluate EU Cohesion Policy, discusses the main econometric issues and surveys the existing literature. Note that this chapter does not include a discussion on the question of whether or not and to what extent the Cohesion Policy may be effective from a theoretical point of view. A more general discussion on Regional Policy can be found in Jovanovic (2009) or Baldwin and Wyplosz (2009).

The remainder of this chapter is structured as follows. Following this introduction, Section 2.2 starts with a brief overview of the institutional background, before Section 2.3 explains how the effectiveness of EU Cohesion Policy can be evaluated. This is followed by a review of the main econometric issues and an outline of potential solutions in Section 2.4, while Section 2.5 discusses the related literature against the background of Sections 2.3 and 2.4. Finally, Section 2.6 concludes.

---

1 This chapter is based on the following joint article with Tobias Hagen: Hagen and Mohl (2011): *Econometric evaluation of EU Cohesion Policy: A survey*, M.N. Jovanovic (ed.): International Handbook of Economic Integration, Edward Elgar: Cheltenham, p. 343–370. An earlier version appeared as: Hagen and Mohl (2009a): *Econometric Evaluation of EU Cohesion Policy: A Survey*, ZEW Discussion Paper No. 09-052, Mannheim.

2.2 Institutional Set-Up of EU Cohesion Policy[2]

EU Cohesion Policy started in 1975 with the introduction of the European Regional Funds (ERDF). The ERDF focused on expenditure for development projects in the poorer regions. Since that time, the Cohesion Policy has gained importance; several additional funds have been created and it has become the most important budget item comprising almost 36 per cent of the total EU budget in the 2007-2013 period (the second most important item is the Common Agricultural Policy).

The Cohesion Policy can be divided into at least two policy regimes: before and after 1989. Before 1989, the EU budget was implemented annually and the Regional policy focused on the European Social Fund (ESF), the Guidance Section of the European Agricultural Guidance and Guarantee Fund (EAGGF) and the European Development Fund (ERDF), where the main beneficiaries were Italy, the UK, France, and Greece. After the passage of the Single European Act in 1987, the regional policy was allocated within multi-annual 'programme periods', the first of which ran from 1989 to 1993.[3] Most importantly, the explicit purpose of the Cohesion Policy was established, namely to enhance cohesion and to reduce welfare disparities among the EU regions. The EU also introduced a number of further financial instruments such as the Cohesion Fund. In addition, several allocation rules and guiding principles were introduced. In our context, the main principle of Cohesion Policy is that the payments by the EU have to be co-funded by the member states and must not crowd out national/regional policy expenditures.[4]

Since 1989, European Cohesion Policy addressed regional problems under various so-called "objectives". These objectives reflect the key priorities for EU expenditures. They are listed for the last two financial periods in Table 2.1. The current Cohesion Policy (for the period 2007-2013) is not described here since it has not yet been taken into account in econometric studies.[5] The most important objective by far is to support lagging regions (the so-called Objective 1 regions), comprising approximately 75 per cent

---

[2] This section focuses on the expenditure side of the EU budget. An overview of the development of the revenue side of the EU budget can be found in (Feld and Schnellenbach, 2007; Heinemann, Mohl and Osterloh, 2008; Osterloh, Heinemann and Mohl, 2008).

[3] The subsequent multi-annual frameworks comprise the following time periods: 1994-1999, 2000-2006 and 2007-2013.

[4] A more detailed overview of the development of EU Cohesion Policy can be found, among others, in Allen (2005).

[5] Since 2007, the EU Cohesion Policy has revolved around three new (rearranged) objectives: (1.) Convergence (formerly Objective 1) (81.7% of total Cohesion Policy payments): support for growth and job creation in the least developed member states and regions (GDP per capita less than 75% of the EU average). (2.) Competitiveness and employment (formerly Objective 2) (15.8%): designed to help the richer member states to deal with economic and social change, globalisation and the transition to the knowledge based society. (3.) Territorial cooperation: to stimulate cross-border co-operation, the development of economic relations and the networking of member states.

of the total SF. The other objectives are targeted at areas affected by industrial decline (Objective 2), fighting long-term unemployment (Objective 3), adaptation to industrial change (Objective 4), reform of agricultural sectors (Objective 5a), rural areas (Objective 5b) and sparsely populated areas (Objective 6). Note that there is a clear-cut definition on what qualifies a region as an Objective 1 receiver (regional GDP has to be lower than 75 per cent of the EU average), while a clear allocation scheme is missing in the case of the latter two objectives. Table 2.1 shows that both the number and the definition of the objectives are not fixed over time, but rather that they may vary over the programme periods. For example, the number of objectives was reduced from six to three in the 2000-2006 financial framework in order to strengthen the concentration of EU support.[6] However, this rearrangement was purely cosmetic, as the same eligibility criteria continued under different labels. This corresponds precisely to one conclusion which can be drawn from the history of the Cohesion Policy: once introduced, a particular objective is rarely (completely) phased out in the future.

Table 2.1: Definition of the structural funds variables by Objective, 1994–2006

1994-1999		2000-2006	
Definition	**share of total SF**	**Definition**	**share of total SF**
Obj. 1: To promote the development and structural adjustment of regions whose development is lagging behind the rest of the EU	67.6%	**Obj. 1**: Supporting development in the less prosperous regions	69.7%
Obj. 6: Assisting the development of sparsely populated regions (Sweden & Finland only)	0.5%		
Obj. 2: To convert regions seriously affected by industrial decline	11.1%	**Obj. 2**: To support the economic and social conversion of areas experiencing structural difficulties	11.5%
Obj. 5b: Facilitating the development and structural adjustment of rural areas	4.9%		
Obj. 3: To combat long-term unemployment and facilitate the integration of young people and of persons excluded from the labour market into working life	9.4%	**Obj. 3**: To support the adaptation and modernisation of education, training and employment policies in regions not eligible under Obj. 1	12.3%
Obj. 4: To facilitate the adaptation of workers to industrial changes and to changes in production systems	1.6%		

Source: European Commission.

Figure 2.1 shows the historical development, including the total (nominal) EU Cohesion Policy payments[7] (vertical bars) and their shares relative to the EU-GNI (solid line) and to the public national spending (dotted line). It becomes clear that there is a long-term upward trend in payments when measured in absolute terms, which can be explained, *inter alia*, by the enlargement steps of the EU (1973: EU-9, 1981: EU-10, 1986:

6 There has been a recent discussion on whether further objectives should be introduced. Proposals focused on aid for regions/countries with climate change, environmental problems or strong demographic changes (European Commission, 2007c).

7 These are the ERDF, the ESF, the EAGGF, and the Financial Instrument for Fisheries Guidance (FIFG), as well as the Cohesion Fund and the Instrument for Structural Policies for Pre-accession (ISPA) for the accession countries.

EU-12, 1995: EU-15, 2004: EU-25, 2007: EU-27). By contrast, payments measured as per cent of EU-GNI or public national spending have remained almost constant since 1993. Furthermore, Figure 2.1 shows that–on average–SF payments do not seem to be particularly large compared to total public spending, with an EU-27 average of below 0.7 per cent in 2007.

Figure 2.1: Development of total EU Cohesion Policy payments since 1975

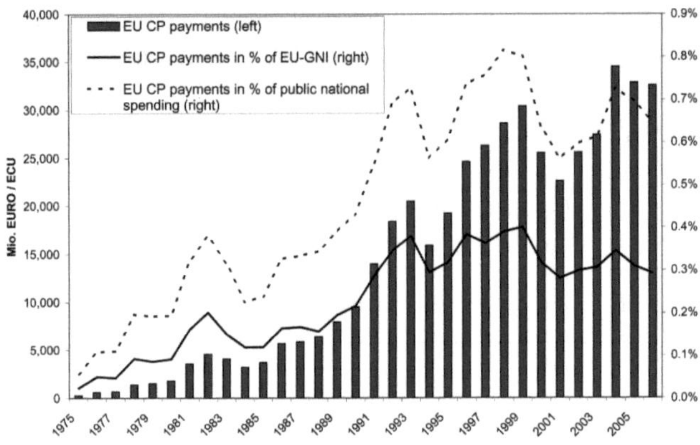

Source: European Commission (2008).

However, focusing on the relatively small EU-average share might obscure the fact that the EU Regional policy is quite important for some countries. Figure 2.2 compares the Cohesion Policy payments with the public investment in the member states. It becomes clear that EU spending is quite important for the poorest countries, that is, those countries receiving money from the Cohesion Fund, namely the so-called "old" (Spain, Greece, Ireland, and Portugal) and "new" (Eastern European countries) cohesion countries. In addition, focusing on the regional level, EU spending has a particularly high importance for some regions (for example, Extremadura received more than 2.7 per cent of EU support (as per cent of GDP) in 2002). Thus, these figures illustrate two aspects: First, EU policy matters at least in some regions and/or member states. Second, given the volume of the spending, it may indeed be difficult for some countries to absorb the transfers and to co-finance European projects without cutting expenses elsewhere.

Furthermore, it should be noted that ever since the introduction of the multiannual financial framework, the European Commission determines so-called "commitments", which do not have to be equal to the final flows of EU support, the so-called SF "payments". For example, due to missing absorption capability, the commitments may not be

Figure 2.2: Cohesion Policy payments and public investment (as % of GDP)

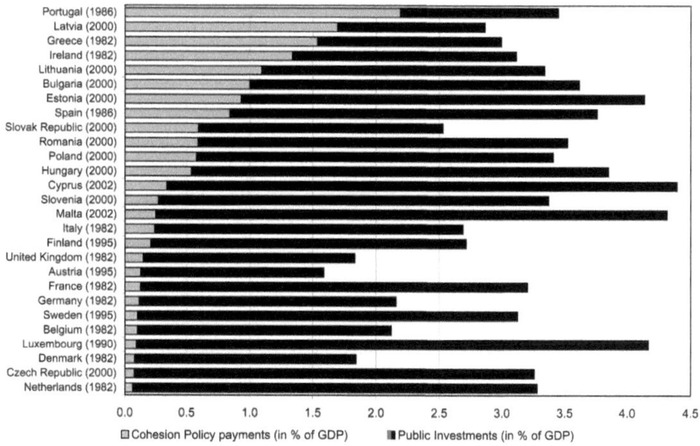

Note: The starting points of the time periods under observations differ between countries. The first year of observation is listed in brackets for illustrative purposes.
Source: European Commission and AMECO.

entirely depleted or may be called up with a delay of one or two years. In this context, the so-called "N+2 rule" states that SF payments have to be called up with a delay of two years at the latest. This introduces big time lags between the determination of the eligibility for EU funding and the final flows of EU money. Figure 2.3 clarifies this issue by using the current financial framework 2007-2013 as an example. The statistical data basis to determine which regions receive EU support is based on the annual averages of the years 2000 to 2002, whereas the list of supported regions is published in 2006. As the financial framework runs from 2007 to 2013, the latest possibility to call up EU support is in 2015 due to the N+2 rule. Hence, there is a gap of up to 15 years between the underlying statistical data and the calling up of EU support.

Finally, some studies conclude that the evolution of the EU revenue and expenditure side is shaped by the political bargaining power of the member states. To be more precise, Cohesion Policy is affected by the veto power of EU member states and by side payments which are necessary to find an agreement in the tough negotiation rounds (for example, Blankart and Kirchner, 2003; Feld, 2005; Feld and Schnellenbach, 2007; Heinemann, Mohl and Osterloh, 2010). In this context, van der Beek and Neal (2004) explain the establishment of the Cohesion Fund in 1994 with the fact that poor member states had to be compensated against losses of the foundation of a European Monetary

Figure 2.3: Selection criteria and payout of EU funding: a sluggish adaptation process

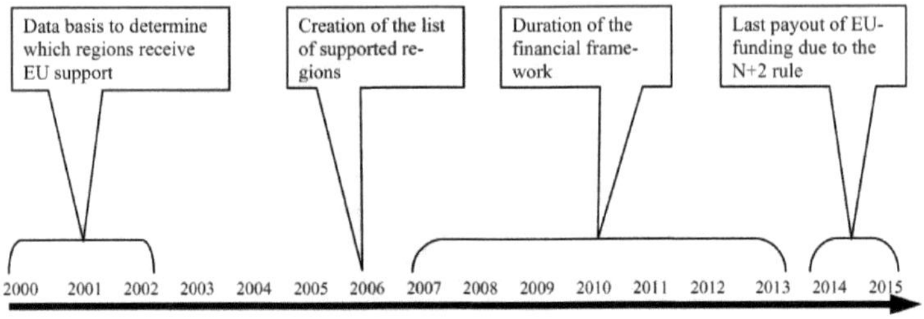

Source: Heinemann, Hagen, Mohl, Osterloh and Sellenthin (2010).

Union. Similarly, there is empirical evidence that political-economic factors affect the allocation of EU funding. The findings by Bodenstein and Kemmerling (2008) and Bouvet and Dall'erba (2010) indicate that the allocation of Objective 2 funding at the regional level is shaped by political factors, such as the electoral competition. The empirical evidence by Osterloh (2011) points out that politicians might spend regionally transfers strategically in order to increase the support of the citizens to the EU.

2.3 Measuring the Effectiveness of Cohesion Policy

There are several approaches to the evaluation of Cohesion Policy. One may distinguish between *ex ante* and *ex post* studies on the one hand, and *qualitative*, as well as *quantitative*, methods on the other hand. Qualitative studies are, for example, case studies. Since this type of study is beyond the scope of this chapter, a discussion is omitted here (see, for example, Davies, Bachtler, Gross, Michie, Vironen and Yuill, 2007; Milio, 2007). With regard to quantitative studies, one may distinguish between macroeconomic simulation studies (which can be used for ex ante as well as ex post evaluations; for example Bradley and Untiedt, 2007) on the one hand and (ex post) econometric studies on the other hand. The results of the simulation studies strongly depend on the–more or less–plausible assumptions. For example, in this respect it is often assumed that EU Cohesion Policy leads to an increase in investment and that these are profitable. However, this assumption typically leads to the result that all models indicate a positive effect of Cohesion Policy. Hence, the results of simulation models can be interpreted as an estimate of the *potential* of Cohesion Policy and should not be taken as empirical evidence in favour of its *effectiveness*.

As a consequence, we focus on (quantitative ex post) econometric studies here. In these studies the sample consists of EU countries or regions. Beyond this, there are microeconometric studies using individual level or firm level data evaluating the effects of single programmes (co-)financed by SF on various outcome variables at the micro-level. For example, Bondonio and Greenbaum (2006) analyse the effects of (Objective 2) business investment incentives on employment using firm-level data.

So far, theoretically founded econometric evaluations of the Cohesion Policy have mostly been based on the neoclassical growth theory.[8] In the following, it is shown how this theory is applied to panel data, although it was originally applied to cross-sectional data.[9]

The literature on the convergence of income levels (for example, GDP per capita) distinguishes between the so-called β– and σ–convergence. The former predicts that if countries have the same steady-state determinants converging to a common balanced growth path, then those countries with relatively low initial income levels grow faster than richer countries (Durlauf, Johnson and Temple, 2005, p. 585). Moreover, β–convergence can be easily evaluated in a linear regression context, for example of the neoclassical growth model. Assuming that β–convergence holds for $i = 1, ..., N$ regions, the natural logarithm of income y of region i at time t (for example, measured as GDP per capita) can be approximated by:

$$ln(y_{it}) = \alpha + (1 - \beta)\, ln(y_{it-1}) + u_{it}, \tag{2.1}$$

where $0 < b < 1$ and u_{it} is an i.i.d. error term (Sala-i-Martin, 1996; Young, Higgins and Daniel, 2008). Since is assumed to be constant across regions, the balanced growth paths are identical. Rearranging (1) yields to the more common version of the neoclassical growth model (Young, Higgins and Daniel, 2008):

$$ln(y_{it}) - ln(y_{it-1}) = \alpha + \beta\, ln(y_{it-1}) + u_{it}. \tag{2.2}$$

8 Roughly speaking, the theoretical approaches can be classified as growth theories and trade theories and one can distinguish between "new" and "traditional" approaches. These have diametric political implications (Heinemann, Hagen, Mohl, Osterloh and Sellenthin, 2010). For example, while traditional neoclassical growth theory (Solow, 1956; Swan, 1956) implies that regional policy have no long-term effects, the new economic geography (Krugman, 1991; Krugman and Venables, 1995) indicates positive effects on regional convergence under certain circumstances. Nevertheless, the latter also predicts a trade-off between growth and convergence. From the perspective of the new (endogenous) growth theory (Romer, 1986, 1990), regional policy may have long-term effects if it promotes R&D or human capital.

9 A more general survey which includes cross-section as well as time series data can be found in Magrini (2004).

Hence, $\beta < 0$ implies a negative correlation between growth and initial log income.[10]

The neoclassical growth model assumes that economies (countries or regions) with similar economic conditions converge with respect to their income level. *Absolute / unconditional convergence* refers to an inverse relationship between the growth of income and the initial level if control variables are absent, i.e., a significantly negative $\widehat{\beta}$ in the regression framework described above. Conditional convergence prevails if this relationship still holds after conditioning on further variables. Hence, the neoclassical growth model predicts a negative $\hat{\beta}$. Empirical studies provide evidence in favour of both hypotheses (Islam, 1995, 2003; Cuaresma, Ritzberger-Grünwald and Silgoner, 2008). The estimated convergence rates are typically a little lower in cross-section studies (approximately 2 per cent per year Barro and Sala-i Martin, 2004) than in panel studies (Lee, Pesaran and Smith, 1998).[11]

To make the distinction between conditional and unconditional convergence clear, we plug fixed regional or country effects into equation 2.2 and distinguish two simple regression equations for regional-level data (Ederveen, Gorter, de Mooij and Nahuis, 2002):

$$ln(y_{it}) - ln(y_{it-1}) = \alpha + \beta\, ln(y_{it-1}) + c_i + u_{it}, \tag{2.3}$$

$$ln(y_{it}) - ln(y_{it-1}) = \alpha + \beta\, ln(y_{it-1}) + \mu_i + u_{it}, \tag{2.4}$$

with c_i denoting country-specific fixed effects (a set of country dummies) and μ_i region-specific fixed effects (a set of region dummies).

While β in equation 2.2 is a measure of absolute convergence, 2.3 and 2.4 provide estimates of conditional convergence. To be precise, equation 2.3 analyses convergence conditional on whether a region lies in a particular country. Thus, it allows for differences in steady states of income between country 1 and country 2 (country-specific steady states). It assumes, however, that within countries, different regions receive equal income levels. Equation 2.4 assumes region-specific steady-states, that is, there may be income gaps between regions which are never bridged even within countries (for a more detailed discussion on this topic see Islam, 2003).

The concept of σ–convergence is a measure of statistical dispersion of income at period T (Barro and Sala-i-Martin, 1991, 1992). σ-convergence holds if the dispersion of income levels declines between t and $t+T$ (Durlauf, Johnson and Temple, 2005), that is, if:

$$\sigma^2_{ln\, y_t} - \sigma^2_{ln\, y_{t+T}} > 0. \tag{2.5}$$

10 y_{it} may also indicate the GDP per capita of the region i relative to the aggregate GDP per capita of all regions at time t. In doing so, common time effects are cancelled out.

11 For a critical review on the 2 per cent finding see Quah (1996).

The concepts of β– and σ–convergence are linked: β–convergence provides the necessary, but not the sufficient condition for σ–convergence. As a consequence, σ–convergence can only be achieved with β–convergence, whereas this does not hold the other way round. Hence, even if β–convergence can be observed (poorer regions grow faster than richer ones), the dispersion between the income levels of regions may increase, so that there would be no σ–convergence.

Almost all econometric studies analysing the growth effects of EU regional policy are based on a neoclassical growth model of the Solow (1956) and Swan (1956) type, that is, equation 2.2 is augmented by further theory-driven variables. In this context, SF payments are assumed to correspond to investment (Ederveen, de Groot and Nahuis, 2006; Bähr, 2008; Mohl and Hagen, 2008). A regression equation for regional data may be specified as:

$$\begin{aligned} ln(y_{it}) - ln(y_{it-1}) = &\alpha + \beta_1\, ln(y_{it-1}) + \beta_2\, ln(sf_{it-1}) + \beta_3\, ln(sav_{it-1}) + \\ &\beta_4\,(n_{it-1} + g + \delta) + \beta_5\, ln(educ_{it-1}) + \mu_i + \lambda_t + u_{it}, \end{aligned} \tag{2.6}$$

where sav_{it-1} is the saving rate, n_{it-1} is the population growth rate, g and δ stand for the technological progress and the time discount factor. Most authors follow the seminal paper by Mankiw, Romer and Weill (1992) and assume that g and δ are constant over time and region and jointly amount to 5 per cent. Furthermore, $educ_{it-1}$ measures the education level of the population (for example, per centage share of population with higher education). Finally, equation 2.6 includes fixed-region effects (μ_i) as well as fixed time effects (λ_t). The reasons for their inclusion will be discussed in Section 2.4.

The main variable of interest in this kind of literature is the SF variable (sf_{it-1}), which is expressed as payments as a share of nominal GDP (among others, Bähr, 2008) or as per cent of persons employed (for example, Esposti and Bussoletti, 2008). If the estimate of β_2 is positive and significantly different from zero, the SF payments positively affect the regions' steady-state growth rate, hence, they enhance the transitional growth rate of each region towards its own steady state (Dall'erba and Le Gallo, 2008).

Most papers only focus on the evaluation of the sign of the coefficient of SF and neglect the size of its impact. However, the latter should be of relevance since an expensive EU Regional policy with a tiny size effect might be effective but not "cost-efficient". Those authors who discuss the size effect usually interpret the short-term elasticity of the impact. Given that the variables of equation 2.6 are specified in logarithmic terms, a one per cent increase of the SF variable increases the growth rate by $\widehat{\beta_2}$ per cent. However, note that equation 2.6 equals the dynamic approach shown in equation 2.1, so that it is more convincing to interpret the long-term impact of variables, which can simply be calculated as $\widehat{\phi} = (\widehat{\beta}_2 / - \widehat{\beta}_1)$ in the case of SF payments. The long-term elasticity can be interpreted as showing that a one per cent increase of SF payments (as percentage of GDP) raises the real GDP per capita by $\widehat{\phi}$ per cent. Unfortunately, most studies do not discuss the quantitative long-term impact.

Note that regressions of the equation 2.6 type only allow for an estimation of the effect of SF payments on growth, and hence we cannot learn directly from $\widehat{\beta}_2$ whether or not a poor region A catches up with a rich region B. However, this is precisely one important aim of Cohesion Policy. What we learn from $\widehat{\beta}_2$ is "only" whether and to what extent SF promotes growth. Nevertheless, since the allocation criteria of the SF (in the case of Objective 1 payments, as well as total SF payments) imply a negative correlation between the level of GDP per capita and SF payments, a significantly positive $\widehat{\beta}_2$ can be interpreted as an indication for convergence at least.

In order to directly measure the effects of Cohesion Policy on convergence, Eggert, von Ehrlich, Fenge and König (2007) propose the following specification using regional data:

$$\begin{aligned} ln(y_{it}) - ln(y_{it-1}) = {} & \alpha + \beta_1 \, ln(y_{it-1}) + \beta_2 \, ln(sf_{it-1}) + \\ & c \, ln(y_{it-1}) \, ln(sf_{it-1}) + \ldots + u_{it}. \end{aligned} \tag{2.7}$$

This equation states that the estimated effect of SF payments depends on the initial income level. In this case $\widehat{\beta}_2$ indicates the impact of SF payments given an initial income level (y_{it-1}) equalling zero, which is obviously of no use as there are no regions with a GDP of zero. Given a positive $\widehat{\beta}_2$, a negative $\widehat{c}$ implies that this positive effect declines with an increasing initial income level, which, in turn, may be interpreted as a sign of convergence. One possibility of deriving meaningful quantitative conclusions from equation 2.7 is to calculate the marginal effects of SF payments across the observed range of initial income level (y_{it-1}) by: $\widehat{\beta}_2 + \widehat{c} \, ln(y_{it-1})$. Subsequently, these marginal effects might be illustrated graphically including confidence intervals around the slope to show the statistical significance level (Brambor, Clark and Golder, 2006).

Several studies, especially those using country-level data (for example, Ederveen, de Groot and Nahuis, 2006; Bähr, 2008), investigate whether the effectiveness of SF payments depends on institutional and economic aspects of the country, such as the quality of institutions,[12] the member states' federal structure (decentralisation) or the openness to trade. They use specifications similar to the following:

[12] Ederveen, de Groot and Nahuis (2006) use, for example, the World Bank governance indicators "political stability", "government effectiveness" and "rule of law".

$$\begin{aligned} ln(y_{it}) - ln(y_{it-1}) = &\alpha + \beta_1 \, ln(y_{it-1}) + \beta_2 \, ln(sf_{it-1}) + c_1 \, cond_{it} + \\ &c_2 \, cond_{it} \, ln(sf_{it-1}) + ... + u_{it}, \end{aligned} \tag{2.8}$$

where $cond_{it}$ denotes a variable including the aspects of the country i in year t and $cond_{it} \, ln(sf_{it-1})$ is an interaction term. Solid results should again be derived by calculating and illustrating the marginal effects as indicated above.

A further issue is the question through which channel SF payments affect growth. The assumption underlying virtually all empirical studies is that the Cohesion Policy increases regional investment leading to a higher steady-state capital stock per capita and, ultimately, to a higher GDP. This may be justified by the nature of SF spending which consists predominantly of investment. However, as pointed out by Bouvet (2005) or Esposti and Bussoletti (2008), SF payments may influence long-run growth in two more ways within the neoclassical growth model. First, it may increase the initial level or the growth of the regional total factor productivity (TFP). Second, it may affect the labour market, that is, the growth rate of the initial workforce. One problem here concerns the many neoclassical growth specifications, which (implicitly) assume full employment or constant employment rates over time, as well as across regions. Since the employment rates differ between European states and evolve differently over time, and since SF payments are likely to affect employment, Esposti and Bussoletti (2008) propose using growth of GDP per employment (which corresponds to average labour productivity) rather than growth of GDP per capita as a dependent variable. However, it may be argued that the goal of the Cohesion Policy is to promote convergence of GDP per capita, implying that this variable is more appropriate. Nevertheless, Esposti and Bussoletti's argument points to the fact that it is necessary to evaluate the labour market effects of the Cohesion Policy, an undertaking that has been neglected so far (exceptions are Bouvet, 2005; Dall'erba and Le Gallo, 2007; Becker, Egger and von Ehrlich, 2010).

2.4 Main Econometric Issues and Potential Solutions

When estimating the effects of SF payments on economic growth and convergence, several methodological issues have to be considered.

The estimation of the relationship between SF payments and the growth rates in regions or countries is complicated by the potential endogeneity problem, i.e., the fact that within a regression model such as equation 2.6, the covariance between at least one of the explanatory variables (for example, the SF variable) and the disturbance term is not equal to zero (Wooldridge, 2002). This endogeneity may be attributed to the following four issues:

First, there is the danger of biased estimates due to *reverse causality*, leading to an underestimation of the effectiveness. The allocation criteria of the SF commitments are likely to be correlated with the dependent variable "economic growth". First and foremost, the allocation of SF is based on the ratio of the regional GDP per capita in purchasing power parities (PPP) and the EU-wide GDP. If this ratio is below 75 per cent, the region is a so-called Objective 1 region, implying that it is eligible for the highest transfers relative to GDP. Furthermore, the allocation of Objectives 2 and 3 depends , *inter alia,* on the regional unemployment rate, the employment structure and the population density. Moreover, the effective payments by the Commission to the regions depend on the regions' or countries' abilities to initiate and to co-finance these projects. This ability may be higher in times of higher economic growth rates, for example, due to higher tax revenues. Nevertheless, some authors argue that the problem of reverse causality might be mitigated by the multi-annual programme periods, in which the determination of the eligibility for EU funding is made several years before the actual flows of EU spending (see in Section 2.2).

Second, there may be *unobserved variables* (unobserved heterogeneity) or (due to missing data availability) *omitted variables*, which have an impact on the regional growth rates, but which are not included in the equation and are thus part of the error term of the specification. If these omitted variables are correlated with one explanatory variable, this explanatory variable is endogenous. A special case of an omitted variable bias is the relevance of spillover effects: SF payments may increase the economic growth rate which, in turn, may affect the neighbour's growth positively. If these spillover effects cannot be separated from the "original" impulse, the estimated effect of SF payments is biased. This problem might be of less importance when using country data. By contrast, there is strong empirical evidence indicating that regional spillover effects do play a significant role at the regional level (Abreu, de Groot and Florax, 2005; Arbia, Le Gallo and Piras, 2008). Hence, the effects of Cohesion Policy in one region are obviously not limited to that region, since there are regional spillovers to other (neighbouring) regions. The fact that the European classification of regions is based on political, rather than on economic, criteria intensifies this problem.

Third, keeping the identity of equations 2.1 and 2.2 of Section 2.3 in mind, it is obvious that equation 2.3 equals a dynamic approach. Hence, simply applying a fixed effects estimator in a dynamic setup leads to a correlation of the lagged dependent variable and the error term results in an underestimation of the lagged dependent variable which is well-known as the *Nickell bias* (Nickell, 1981; Magrini, 2004).

A fourth problem is related to *measurement errors*. This problem is of special concern with regard to the SF variable at the regional level. The annual reports on SF published by the European Commission only comprise regional commitments and payments for the period 1994-1999. Unfortunately, since 2000, these reports contain data only at the country level. Furthermore, before 1994, only SF commitments are available. However, using SF commitments instead of payments might lead to biased results. Depending on the assumptions on how SF commitments and payments are correlated, SF commitments might be correlated with the error term. By contrast, the problem of data availability with regard to SF payments is less severe at the country level. Despite that, to the best of our knowledge, it is not possible to distinguish between the different objectives and funds for a long time period, at least there is information on the total EU Regional policy payments for the 1976-2007 period (European Commission, 2008).[13]

Apart from these endogeneity-related aspects, the estimations might be biased by a fifth issue. Although growth theory provides well-established suggestions for the estimation of growth relationships, it is ex ante not clear which economic growth model to use and which *functional form* is appropriate for the effect of SF payments (Durlauf, Kourtellos and Tan, 2008). There may be non-linearities and interactions with covariates, which may lead to biased estimates if they are not taken into account. Similarly, the "real" impact of EU regional policy on growth might be misspecified because the time structure of its effects is ex ante unknown. It may be argued that SF projects, such as infrastructure investment, only become effective for growth after some time lag.

Finally, a fundamental–but often ignored–sixth econometric problem is related to the choice of the *appropriate control variables*, i.e., which variables should be included in the right-hand side of the regression model. For example, one may derive from growth theory that growth of GDP per capita is affected by (private and public) investment and that an omission may bias the estimated results. However, the inclusion of the investment variable into the regression evaluating the growth effects of SF payments might lead to biased results. Since SF payments may stimulate growth through the channel "investment" (leading to a higher steady-state capital stock per capita), the inclusion of the investment variable might render it impossible to evaluate the investment increasing

[13] With respect to further economic and socio-demographic control variables included in estimations using regional data, Eurostat provides a relatively large database with the most relevant variables. However, for a longer time period, there are, to the best of our knowledge, no high-quality education data at the regional level like those proposed at the country level by Barro and Lee (2001); de La Fuente and Doménech (2006); Cohen and Soto (2007). Instead, there is only data available since 1999, which measures the population aged 15 years and over with a high, medium or low level of education. For this reason, Mohl and Hagen (2008) use the number of patents per million inhabitants as a proxy for the education variable.

effect of SF payments on growth. More generally: one should be careful not to include control variables which may also serve as a dependent variable of the Cohesion Policy (Angrist and Pischke, 2009, call these variables "bad controls").

Obviously, given the current state-of-the-art econometric models and the available data, it is not possible to deal with all the problems mentioned above simultaneously. However, by taking into account the methodological issues and by comparing the results of several empirical approaches, one might hope to get an idea about the range of the "true effect" of SF payments on growth. There exist at least a few potential approaches to coping with the issues presented above individually, as will be illustrated in the following.

First, using panel data helps to solve some problems. If (un-)observed omitted variables affecting growth are constant over time, they are eliminated by including fixed effects or by first-differencing. If these unobserved variables are not constant, methods such as instrumental variable (IV) estimators are necessary. Moreover, unobserved time effects (such as common macroeconomic shocks) influencing growth might be relevant (Bond, Hoeffler and Temple, 2001). A very common and flexible approach to avoiding parametric assumptions is to use a set of common (for example, annual) time dummies which can control for effects common to all regional units, such as pan-European business cycles (see equation 2.3). This may also reduce the problem of regional spillovers (Bronzini and Piselli, 2009). In order to avoid the fact that the use of time dummies leads to a significant loss of degrees of freedom (which is most relevant in the case of the popular general method of moments (GMM) estimators due to the matrix of instruments), one may transform the variables into deviations from time means (i.e., the mean across the N individual regions for each period) which is equivalent to the use of time dummies (Bond, Hoeffler and Temple, 2001). If necessary, time effects may be modeled in a more complex manner: for example, one may allow for country-time specific effects in regional data by defining country-specific annual dummies. Another approach is to define country-specific or region-specific time trends (Wooldridge, 2002; Hagen and Mohl, 2009b).

In order to deal with the first and second problem, an IV estimator combined with fixed effects or first differences seems to be the right choice. However, to the best of our knowledge, no convincing external IV has been proposed in the literature (exceptions may be the studies by Bouvet (2005) as well as Dall'erba and Le Gallo (2008) summarised in Section 2.5). Hence, identification has to be based on internal instruments via the GMM estimators (Arellano and Bond, 1991; Roodman, 2009b). In addition, GMM estimators are also suitable for dealing with the third issue introduced above, by instrumenting the initial income level (as well as further variables) by lagged values. On the one hand, there is evidence that the first-differenced GMM (FD-GMM) estimator by Arellano and

Bond (1991) has a large finite sample bias and poor precisions when the time series are persistent, so that the system GMM (SYS-GMM) estimator by Blundell and Bond (1998) should be preferred. On the other hand, some applications question the superiority of the SYS-GMM estimator because the additional instruments might not be valid (Lucchetti, Papi and Zazzaro, 2001). Hence, one might apply different estimators to draw well-founded conclusions. Note that the consistency of both GMM estimators is based on large N, which might not be given in the analyses using country-level data. However, there is preliminary evidence of Monte Carlo simulations showing that, given predetermined explanatory variables, the SYS-GMM estimator has a lower bias and higher efficiency than the FD-GMM or the fixed effects estimator (Soto, 2006). Nevertheless, country-level data (such as EU-15 data) may still be too small for GMM estimations.

One should be careful as regards the use of instruments when applying GMM estimators: using too many instruments can overfit instrumented variables (Roodman, 2009a), reduce the power properties of the Hansen test (Bowsher, 2002) and lead to a downward bias in two-step standard errors (Windmeijer, 2005).[14] One solution might be to include lag limits or to collapse the set of instruments (Mehrhoff, 2009).[15] Since an increasing number of studies on the effects of Cohesion Policy apply GMM estimators, these aspects are highly relevant and should be taken into account in order to avoid misleading estimation results.

Applying spatial panel econometric techniques helps to control for spatial spillover effects, which is of special concern when using region-level data (for a survey, see LeSage and Pace, 2009). The usual approach is to specify a weight matrix containing information on the number or distance of neighbours (Anselin, Florax and Rey, 2004). This is done by focusing on (i) the contiguity of each region, (ii) its k-nearest neighbours, or (iii) the geographical distance (for example, expressed in kilometers) to its neighbours. Sometimes the weight matrices are weighted by some economic variables (for example, using trade data between regions). However, often geographical distance based weight matrices are preferred because they are strictly exogenous. Nevertheless, the right choice of the weight matrix is of fundamental concern, as incorrectly specified weight matrices might lead to wrong conclusions (LeSage and Fischer, 2008).

Generally speaking, including a weight matrix does affect the efficiency and/or the consistency of the OLS estimator, leading to biased results. Hence, the spatial econometric estimations are usually estimated by Maximum Likelihood (Anselin, 1988; Anselin

14 Roodman (2009a, p. 156): "Perhaps, the lesson to be drawn is that internal instruments, though attractive as a response to endogeneity, have serious limitations".

15 However, the choice of the number of lags used as instruments or the possibility of collapsing the number of instruments might seem arbitrary.

and Hudak, 1992; Elhorst, 2010) or by GMM (Kelejian and Prucha, 1998, 1999; Bell and Bockstael, 2000). There are two predominant approaches to specifying the spatial model: one can either include a spatially weighted dependent variable ("spatial lag model") or a spatially-autocorrelated error ("spatial error model") in the regression model. These approaches were originally focused on cross-sectional (Anselin, 1988; Anselin and Bera, 1998; Anselin, 2006) and static panel datasets (Elhorst, 2003b) and they have been extended to the case of dynamic panel estimators (Badinger, Müller and Tondl, 2004; Yu, de Jong and Lee, 2008). Recently, further approaches have been introduced, such as including both spatial lag and spatial error simultaneously (Kelejian and Prucha, 1998; Lee, 2003) or including spatially weighted independent variables ("spatial Durban model", see, for example, Elhorst, Piras and Arbia, 2006; Ertur and Koch, 2007). Unfortunately, there is as yet no estimator that controls for both spatial spillover and endogeneity of further independent variables (besides the lagged dependent variable) within a panel data framework.

The fourth problem should be addressed by using SF payments instead of commitments. As mentioned above, the differences between payments and commitments can be sizable.

With regard to the fifth problem, almost all studies are based on a neoclassical growth model. Despite some criticism due to its strict assumptions (Dall'erba and Le Gallo, 2008), the use of the neoclassical growth model might be explained by the limited data availability at the regional level.[16] Possible approaches to this problem have been proposed by Becker, Egger and von Ehrlich (2010) as well as by Hagen and Mohl (2008), who avoid strict functional form assumptions by using treatment effect methods (for a recent survey for applied researchers see Austin, 2007). These studies will be summarised in Section 2.5 in greater detail.

In order to take into account that SF payments might be effective after some time lag, Rodríguez-Pose and Fratesi (2004) and Mohl and Hagen (2008) include past values of the SF variable besides contemporaneous values. For example, Mohl and Hagen (2008) start their empirical analyses by excluding any SF variable, and then gradually add the lagged SF payments, beginning with a lag of one year and ending up with a specification comprising SF with a lag of one to five years ($\sum_{j=1}^{5} ln\, SF_{i,t-j}$).[17]

[16] See Arbia, Le Gallo and Piras (2008) for a recent empirical comparison of different theoretical convergence models at the European regional level.

[17] Due to multicollinearity, the coefficients and standard errors of the SF variable cannot be interpreted if the variable is included into the regression with several lags. As a consequence, Mohl and Hagen (2008) calculate the joint sum of SF coefficients corresponding to the short-term elasticity and use a simple Wald test to determine whether this short-term elasticity is statistically different from zero. Based on this, it is possible to calculate the long-term elasticity as described above.

2.5 Review of the Empirical Evidence

The main aspects of the previous literature on the impact of the Cohesion Policy on economic growth are summarised in the following. We distinguish between studies using country-level data (Table 2.5), regional-level data in a multi-country framework (Table 2.5), and regional-level data within one county (Table 2.5).

Generally, EU regions are classified into three different groups by the European Commission according to the "Nomenclature des unites territoriales statistiques" (NUTS). These units refer to the country level (NUTS-0) and to three lower subdivisions (NUTS-1, NUTS-2 and NUTS-3) which are classified according to the size of population (Eurostat, 2007). The advantage of regional data for econometric analyses is the resulting large sample size which allows the application of methods based on a large number of cross-sections (N). Furthermore, regions (as opposed to countries) are usually the unit of interest for the Cohesion Policy. By contrast, using country-level data comes with the advantage of larger data availability but with the drawback of small sample sizes (EU-12, EU-15 etc.). Moreover, region-specific effects cannot be analysed by definition.

Apart from the choice of the appropriate sample, the studies differ in the time period covered, the econometric methods applied, the type of dataset used (cross-section versus panel) and the operationalisation of SF payments. With respect to the last, theory does not provide an unambiguous indication. While most studies operationalize SF as a continuous variable, some studies use a dummy variable to indicate whether a region is an Objective 1 region or not. The last case has the advantage that data on payments are not necessary, but it comes with the disadvantage that it is not possible to measure the real size effect of Regional policy. If SF are operationalised as a continuous variable, the studies differ with regard to the question of whether to express the SF as percentage of GDP, in PPP and/or in per capita terms. Moreover, not all studies use SF payments–some use data on SF commitments.

With respect to the econometric methods used, there are various approaches to dealing with the issues described in the last Section. Simple cross-sectional or pooled OLS estimators are based on the assumption that, after conditioning on further explanatory variables, many of the problems discussed in Section 2.4 (reversed causality, omitted/unobserved variables) are not relevant. Thus, it seems to be more convincing to rely on panel data methods which, in fact, most studies do. As mentioned in the last Section, using panel data enables the researcher to eliminate unobserved fixed effects affecting SF and growth simultaneously.

We start the survey with the studies based on *country-level data* (Table 2.5). Ederveen, Gorter, de Mooij and Nahuis (2002) analyse the effects at the national (EU-12) as well as at the regional (NUTS 2) level. The study only investigates the effects of the ERDF and applies a pooled OLS estimator: only conditionally positive growth effects for an EU-12 sample for the 1960-1995 period are found (implemented via an interaction term, see equation 2.8). In particular, cohesion support is more likely to be effective for member states with open economies (such as Ireland) and less likely to be effective in closed ones (such as Spain). According to the explanation of the authors, openness disciplines governments, which stimulates more productive investment of cohesion support.

Beugelsdijk and Eijffinger (2005) restrict their analysis to the programme period from 1995 to 2001. They focus on the dependency of the effectiveness from moral hazard behaviour and substitution effects by interacting the SF variable with a corruption index. According to the authors, the moral hazard effect matters because countries might be inclined not to raise the welfare level of those regions which are close to the critical value of getting EU support, as this would possibly imply a reduction in future financial EU support. Hence, it is possible that the resources are not used for projects that would have the largest direct and indirect impact, so that the moral hazard effect might lead to an inappropriate use of SF. The substitution effect means that SF payments lead to a crowding out of national spending. Using EU-15 data and different dynamic panel data estimators (including an FD-GMM in order to take endogeneity into account) they find that the hypothesis that SF contribute to fewer inter-regional disparities within the 15 European countries cannot be rejected. Furthermore, the results do not indicate that the more corrupt countries use their SF in a less efficient way.

Ederveen, de Groot and Nahuis (2006) analyse the effectiveness of the ERDF for the 1960-1995 period using dynamic panel approaches for an EU-13 sample. Among other econometric techniques, they apply FD-GMM and SYS-GMM estimators, assuming, however, that the SF payments are strictly exogenous. They find that SF as such do not improve the countries' growth performance. However, they find evidence that they only enhance growth in those countries with the "right" institutions, that is, countries with a high economic openness and high direct measures of institutional quality (such as low inflation and low public debt). From these findings, Ederveen, de Groot and Nahuis (2006, p. 25) derive consequences for a redesign of the EU regional policy: In the light of the EU enlargement process, the funds should be allocated first and foremost to institution building. Given institutions of a satisfactory quality, the EU regional policy may be effective in stimulating growth.

Recently, Bähr (2008) complemented these results by analysing whether the degree of decentralisation within countries mattered in the EU-15 during the 1975-1995 period. The hypothesis is that, given the sensitivity of EU Cohesion Policy to specific regional needs, member states with a higher degree of decentralisation should be able to implement more effective programmes. An interaction variable comprising SF and a decentralisation measure is introduced to the model, which is estimated by various panel estimators. Robustness checks are performed , *inter alia,* by instrumenting the SF variable with its own lagged values. While structural funding cannot be said to be unambiguously growth promoting in itself, Bähr finds a significantly positive effect of SF on growth in more decentralised countries. This is explained by the fact that regional authorities have better information on specific growth-inducing projects, so that there is a more effective regional implementation of the programs in traditionally decentralised countries.

Bradley and Untiedt (2008) criticise the approaches by Ederveen, Gorter, de Mooij and Nahuis (2002) as well as those by Ederveen, de Groot and Nahuis (2006) , *inter alia,* for the following reasons: First, the time period used includes the time before the fundamental reform of Cohesion Policy in 1989, a period in which payments were relatively low. Second, they point to misspecifications in the regression (especially with regard to the interaction of SF payments and institutional variables). Third, they criticise the assumption of exogeneity of Cohesion Policy and show that the econometric results are far from being robust (see Rodrik, 2005, for the expression of fundamental concerns on the evaluation of growth effects of public policies see).

Apart from these country analyses, some studies use more detailed data and focus on the *regional level* (Table 2.5). The conclusions of the analysis of Ederveen, Gorter, de Mooij and Nahuis (2002) for 183 NUTS-2 regions from 1981 to 1996 using pooled OLS depend on the convergence model used. Assuming that all regions finally catch up to the same income level (absolute convergence, that is, neither further explanatory variables nor country or regional dummies are included), they find a negative effect of SF on growth. By contrast, assuming that the convergence process is limited to convergence within countries (including country dummies and no further explanatory variables), they do not find a significant effect. Finally, when assuming region-specific steady-states, that is, including regional fixed effects, a significantly positive effect is found. The authors conclude from these results (p. 55) "...the more optimistic one is about convergence in the long run, the more pessimistic one should be about the impact of Cohesion Policy, and vice versa [...]. The somewhat grim conclusion must be: either Cohesion Policy is counterproductive, or regional differences will persist." However, one should keep in mind that there are good reasons to assume that omitting fixed effects (regional dummies) and further control variables results in biased estimates (see Section 2.4).

Table 2.2: Overview of econometric studies on the effects of Cohesion Policy using country data

Paper by	Central results: Impact of SF on economic growth	Operationalisation of structural funds	Time period	Units	Econometric methods used
Bähr (2008)	Only in countries with a high degree of decentralisation do SF have a positive impact on growth	ERDF payments (as % of GDP) [exogenous,endogenous]	1975-1995	13 EU countries	Panel: Pooled OLS, FE, FE-IV
Ederveen, de Groot and Nahuis (2006)	SF promote growth and convergence given the "right" institutional set-up	ERDF payments (as % of GDP) [exogenous]	1960-1995	12/13 EU countries	Panel: Pooled OLS, FE, FD-GMM
Beugelsdijk and Eijffinger (2005)	SF promote growth. More "corrupt" countries do not gain less from Cohesion policy with respect to growth	SF payments (as % of GDP) [endogenous]	1995-2001	15 EU countries	Panel: FD-GMM
Ederveen, Gorter, de Mooij and Nahuis (2002)	Only in open economies SF have a positive impact on growth	ERDF payments (as % of GDP) [exogenous]	1960-1995	12 EU countries	Panel: Pooled OLS

Notes: OLS = ordinary least squares, FE = fixed effects model, IV = instrumental variable, FD-GMM = first difference generalised method of moments estimator (Arellano and Bond, 1991).

Cappelen, Castellacci, Fagerberg and Verspagen (2003) focus on the question of whether the SF reform in 1989 has increased the effectiveness of the Cohesion Policy by dividing their sample period into two time periods (1980-1988 and 1989-1997). Using these two cross-sections and applying OLS, they find a positive impact on regional growth. The authors find evidence that SF are most effective in more developed regions (measured in terms of the unemployment rate, R&D spending etc), whereas the effectiveness is limited in "poorer" regions. Furthermore, it turns out that the reform of 1989 has increased the effectiveness.

Esposti and Bussoletti (2008) analyse the impact of Objective 1 spending on regional growth using a data set with 206 NUTS-2 regions covering the time period 1989-2000. They apply different estimation techniques (such as DIFF-GMM, SYS-GMM). However, it seems that SF payments are treated as strictly exogenous and only the lagged dependent variable is instrumented. They find a positive impact of SF on Objective 1 regions over the whole EU area, even though its size and statistical significance vary across alternative estimators. Generally, the impact is quite limited and becomes negligible or even negative in some regional cases. For instance, when regions are grouped by country, a negative effect may be observed for German, Greek, and Spanish Objective 1 regions. By contrast, the French Objective 1 regions show the highest policy treatment effect.

The study by Puigcerver-Peñalver (2007) is based on 41 NUTS-2-regions in the EU-12. It analyses whether Objective 1 payments to these regions promoted growth in the 1989-2000 period, with SF payments modelled as being affected by the TFP. Using a fixed effects model it is shown that the effectiveness depends on the time period. While the Cohesion Policy (Objective 1) had a positive impact in the 1989-1993 funding period, no significantly positive impact can be detected during 1994-1999.

Using a cross-sectional approach, de Freitas, Pereira and Torres (2003) analyse whether Objective 1 regions grow faster than non-Objective 1 regions between 1990 and 2001, assuming strict exogeneity of the Objective 1 status. They find evidence of conditional convergence among EU regions. Moreover, the quality of national institutions has a positive impact, while there is no evidence of a correlation between the eligibility for Objective 1 payments and faster convergence.

Rodríguez-Pose and Fratesi (2004) also focus on Objective 1 regions between 1989 and 1999. The study not only analyses the time lags of SF effects but also differentiates between Cohesion Policy categories, such as (a) support to agriculture and rural promotion, (b) business and tourism support, (c) investment in human capital and (d) investment in infrastructure and environment. However, the analysis is based on SF commitments instead of on SF payments. Applying fixed effects as well as pooled GLS estimators, they cannot find significant effects of SF on infrastructure or, to a lesser extent, on business support. By contrast, support for agriculture has positive short-term effects on growth, but these wane quickly; and only investment in education and human capital–representing only about one-eighth of the total commitments–show positive and significant returns.

The study by Bouvet (2005) goes one step further by not only investigating the impact of the ERDF spendings on economic growth but also analysing through which channels Cohesion Policy might work, that is, investment, TFP or employment (see Section 2.3). The database consists of 118 NUTS-2 regions in the EU-8 from 1975 to 1999. The SF payments (ERDF) are instrumented with political variables.[18] It turns out that the Cohesion Policy has a positive but modest effect on growth. The study does not find significant evidence that this positive effect works through an increase in regional investment. By contrast, it is found that the Cohesion Policy increases TFP and employment growth and that these are the channels through which the policy affects GDP growth.[19]

As mentioned in Section 2.4, a major econometric problem when using regional-level data results from omitting regional spillover effects, which may lead to biased results. Dall'erba and Le Gallo (2008)[20] is one of the few studies that try to cope with this problem. However, this comes with the drawback that other econometric issues (regional fixed effects, among others) are not taken into account. The authors use spatial econometric techniques for cross-sectional data for 145 regions in 1989-1999. The SF payments are instrumented , *inter alia,* with the regions' distances to Brussels using two-stage least squares. The results from Dall'erba and Le Gallo (2008) indicate that significant convergence takes place, but that the SF have no impact on it.

18 The following instrumental variables are used: the interaction term of the coincidence between local central governments and the coincidence between the central government and the president of the Commission, the interaction term of the local incumbent dummy and the coincidence between the central government and the president of the Commission, the coincidence between local central governments, the local-incumbent dummy and the national incumbent dummy.

19 Bouvet (2005) also examines the determinants of fund allocation. While more funds are allotted to regions with lower per capita incomes and structural deficiencies, some evidence of political interference in the allocation process is found.

20 In a preceding study, Dall'erba (2005) applies an exploratory spatial analysis and finds a positive relationship between SF payments and regional growth.

Table 2.3: Overview of econometric studies on the effects of Cohesion Policy using European-wide regional level data

Paper by	**Central results:** **Impact of SF on economic growth**	**Operationalisation of structural funds**	**Time period**	**Units**	**Econometric methods used**
Becker, Egger, von Ehrlich and Fenge (2010)	Positive and significant growth effect of Obj. 1 regions	Dummy variable = 1 for regions receiving Obj. 1 funding, 0 else [exogenous]	1989-1993, 1994-1999, 2000-2006	up to 3301 NUTS-3 regions (EU-12/25)	Panel: Regression discontinuity analysis
Mohl and Hagen (2010)	Obj. 1 payments promote growth, whereas Obj. 2 and 3 payments do not have a positive impact	Obj. 1,2,3,1+2+3 payments and remaining commitments from 1994-99 (as % in GDP) [endogenous,exogenous]	1995-2005	122 NUTS-1/2 regions (EU-15)	Panel: FE, SYS-GMM, spatial lag and error model
Dall'erba and Le Gallo (2008)	SF have no statistically significant impact on regional convergence	SF payments and remaining commitments from 1994-1999 (as % of GDP) [endogenous]	1989-1999	145 NUTS-2 regions (EU-12)	Cross-section: Spatial lag model with IV
Esposti and Bussoletti (2008)	Limited impact of SF on regional growth	Obj. 1 payments per capita (in PPS) [exogenous]	1989-1999	206 NUTS-2 regions (EU-15)	Panel: FD-GMM, SYS-GMM
Falk and Sinabell (2008)	SF have a marginal positive and significant growth impact	Dummy variable = 1 for regions receiving Obj. 1 funding, 0 else [exogenous]	1995-2004	1084 NUTS-3 regions (EU-15)	Panel: Pooled OLS, median regression approach, weighted least squares
Hagen and Mohl (2008)	SF have a positive, but not statistically significant impact on regional growth	Obj. 1+2+3 payments and remaining commitments from 1994-99 (as % of GDP) [exogenous]	1995-2005	122 NUTS-1/2 regions (EU-15)	Panel: Generalised propensity score approach
Ramajo, Márquez, Hewings and Salinas (2008)	Faster cond. convergence of relative income levels of regions belonging to Cohesion countries than in non-Cohesion regions	Separate regressions for regions belonging to Cohesion countries vs. non-Cohesion countries	1981-1996	163 NUTS-2 regions (EU-12)	Cross-section: Robust OLS, spatial lag model
Puigcerver-Peñalver (2007)	Positive effect of SF on growth rates of Obj. 1 regions in 1989-1993, but not in 1994-1999	Total SF (as % of GDP p.c.); total SF; SF of region i over total SF received by all regions [exogenous]	1989-1999, 1989-1993	41 NUTS-2 regions (EU-10)	Panel: pooled OLS, FE

Table 2.3: Overview of econometric studies on the effects of Cohesion Policy using European-wide regional level data (continued)

Paper by	**Central results: Impact of SF on economic growth**	**Operationalisation of structural funds**	**Time period**	**Units**	**Econometric methods used**
Bouvet (2005)	SF have a modest positive impact on regional growth rates	ERDF payments per capita [endogenous]	1975-1999	111 NUTS-1/2 regions (EU-8)	Panel: Pooled OLS, FE, IV
Dall'erba (2005)	Positive relationship between SF and regional growth	SF payments and remaining commitments from 1994-1999 (as % of GDP) [exogenous]	1989-1999	145 NUTS-2 regions (EU-12)	Cross-section Exploratory spatial data analysis
Cappelen, Castellacci, Fagerberg and Verspagen (2003)	SF have a positive and significant impact on the growth rates; they are more effective since 1988	Obj. 1, 2, 5b (as % of GDP) [exogenous]	1980-1997, 1980-1988, 1989-1997	105 NUTS-1/2 regions (EU-9)	Cross-section: OLS
Rodriguez-Pose and Fratesi (2004)	Limited impact of SF on growth; only SF funding on education and human capital have positive effects	Obj. 1 commitments (as % of GDP) [exogenous]	1989-1999	152 NUTS-2 regions (EU-8)	Cross-section & panel: OLS, pooled GLS FE
de Freitas, Pereira and Torres (2003)	Obj. 1 regions do not show faster convergence than non-Obj. 1 regions	Dummy variable = 1 for regions receiving Obj. 1 funding, 0 else [exogenous]	1990-2001	196 NUTS-2 regions (EU-15)	Cross-section: OLS
Ederveen, Gorter, de Mooij Nahuis (2002)	Results depend on the assumptions underlying the convergence model	SF + Cohesion Fund (as % of GDP) [exogenous]	1981-1996	183 NUTS-2 regions (EU-13)	Panel: Pooled OLS

Notes: OLS = ordinary least squares, FE = fixed effects model, IV = instrumental variable, FD-GMM = first difference generalised method of moments estimator (Arellano and Bond, 1991), SYS-GMM = system generalised method of moments estimator (Blundell and Bond, 1998).

Table 2.4: Overview of econometric studies on the effects of Cohesion Policy using regional data within single countries

Paper by	Central results: Impact of SF on economic growth	Operationalisation of structural funds	Time period	Units	Econometric methods used
Eggert, von Ehrlich, Fenge and König (2008)	SF accelerate a region's convergence, but reduce the average growth rate	SF payments (as % of GDP) [exogenous]	1989-1993, 1994-1999,	16 NUTS-1 regions (Germany)	Cross-section: Pooled OLS, Regress average growth of 1994-99 (2000-04) on average SF of 1989-93 (1993-99)
Soukiazis and Antunes (2006)	SF promote convergence; small positive impact on growth; more effective in coastal than in interior regions	ERDF per capita [exogenous]	1991-1999	30 NUTS-3 regions (Portugal)	Panel: Pooled OLS, FE, Random Effects
Percoco (2005)	SF induce a high level of volatility in the level of growth rates	Obj. 1 payments (as % of GDP) [endogenous]	1994-1999	6 NUTS-2 regions (Italy)	Panel: GMM-IV
Garcia-Milà and McGuire (2001)	Grants are not effective in stimulating private investment or improving the overall economies of the poorer regions	Grants = Eur. + national grants; Dummy var. = 1 for regions receives above-average grants, 0 else [exogenous]	1977-1981, 1989-1992	17 NUTS-2 regions (Spain)	Panel: OLS and difference-in-difference approach

Notes: OLS = ordinary least squares, FE = fixed effects model, IV = instrumental variable, FD-GMM = first difference generalised method of moments estimator (Arellano and Bond, 1991), SYS-GMM = system generalised method of moments estimator (Blundell and Bond, 1998).

Ramajo, Márquez, Hewings and Salinas (2008) apply cross-sectional spatial econometric techniques to estimate the speed of convergence for a sample of 163 regions in the EU-12 over the 1981-1996 period. First, they find evidence in favour of the existence of two spatial convergence clubs among European regions, namely, the presence of two significantly different spatial clusters formed by regions belonging to Cohesion (Ireland, Greece, Portugal and Spain) and non-Cohesion countries. The estimations indicate that throughout the period analysed, there is a faster conditional convergence in relative income levels of the regions belonging to Cohesion countries (5.3 per cent) than in the rest of the regions of the EU (3.3 per cent). Hence, the results provide support for policies that are explicitly designed to promote regional growth in the less-developed regions located in Cohesion countries.

Based on a sample of 1,084 NUTS-3 regions (EU-15) over the 1995-2004 period, Falk and Sinabell (2008) investigate the determinants of Objective 1 payments on the regional growth of GDP per capita in a cross-sectional analysis. As the Lagrange Multiplier test statistic does not hint at spatial spillover effects, they focus on robust OLS and weighted-least-squares procedures. The latter is used in order to control for outliers. In addition, Falk and Sinabell decompose the growth following the Blinder-Oaxaca decomposition (Oaxaca and Ransom, 1994) in order to check how much of the growth differential can be explained by observable differences between Objective 1 and non-Objective 1 regions. Their results indicate that there is a significant growth differential, which is, however, almost entirely due to the difference in characteristics such as initial GDP per capita, economic structure and population density. As a consequence, these results point to a low effectiveness of the EU funds.

Mohl and Hagen (2008) use a panel dataset of 124 NUTS-2 regions over the 1995-2005 time period, extending the literature with regard to the following aspects: First, they use more precise measures of SF by distinguishing between Objective 1, 2, 3 and 1+2+3 payments and by a more thorough investigation of the impact of time lags. Second, the time period of investigation is extended, using SF payments of the last financial framework 2000 to 2006 that have not been analysed before. Third, the paper examines the robustness of the results by comparing various econometric approaches. Apart from SYS-GMM (which allows for endogeneity of SF payments as well as of further variables), spatial panel econometric techniques are applied. The results show that Objective 1 payments in particular promote regional economic growth, whereas Objectives 2 and 3 do not have a positive and significant impact on the EU regions' growth rates. Furthermore, Mohl and Hagen find that time lags substantially affect the results, i.e., the growth impact does not occur immediately, but rather with a time lag of up to five years.

Finally, there are two papers that use treatment effect methods in order to deal with the problem of unknown functional form and parameter heterogeneity (Wooldridge, 2002, Ch. 18). Becker, Egger and von Ehrlich (2010) use up to 3,301 NUTS-3 regions and apply "regression discontinuity design" techniques.[21] They make use of the relatively clear-cut rule that defines an Objective 1 region: NUTS-2 regions with a GDP per capita level below 75 per cent of the EU average. This enables the authors to use regression discontinuity design techniques, which basically means estimating the effect by comparing "treated" and "non-treated" regions near the 75 per cent threshold. On average, the Objective 1 status raises per-capita income by about 1.8 per cent relative to similar "non-treated" regions. Since the authors do not find a positive employment effect, they conclude that the growth effect may work through an investment increasing effect. Furthermore, they provide a simple cost-benefit analysis: 1 euro spent on Objective 1 transfers leads to 1.21 euros of additional GDP in the eligible regions.

Hagen and Mohl (2008) interpret total SF payments (Objective 1+2+3) as a "continuous treatment" and apply the method of generalised propensity score which leads to the estimation of a dose-response function as proposed by Hirano and Imbens (2004). They use a sample of 122 NUTS-1 and NUTS-2 (EU-15) regions for the 1995-2005 time period and find a positive, but not statistically significant, impact on the regions' average three-year growth rates. This would imply that it does not matter which "dose" of SF payments a region receives.

Besides the studies presented above, there are further studies focusing on *regions within single countries* (see Table 2.5). Since their focus may be too narrow to draw a conclusion with regard to European integration, we do not discuss them here.

2.6 Conclusions

The Cohesion Policy of the European Union has gained importance over the recent decades, becoming the most important budget item and amounting to 36 per cent of the total EU budget in the 2007-2013 period. With its rising relevance, the attempts to evaluate this policy field have increased. Despite its primary goal to "reduce disparities among the regions", surprisingly, the focus of these studies is not so much on the question whether EU Cohesion Policy has decreased divergence, but rather whether EU support is growth enhancing. One reason for this might be that the question of convergence refers to a long-run concept, which is difficult to evaluate given the available empirical data.

[21] An introduction to regression discontinuity design can be found in the Journal of Econometrics 142 (2008); see especially Imbens and Lemieux (2008).

This chapter shows that the econometric evaluation of EU Cohesion Policy is hampered by several econometric issues, namely reverse causality, measurement error, omitted variables (including spatial spillovers), Nickell bias, strict functional form assumptions and the potential inclusion of inappropriate control variables. Based on these issues we present potential solutions for coping with these problems individually. Unfortunately, given the econometric methods and the available database, there is currently no method to control for all problems mentioned above simultaneously. As a consequence, by comparing the results of several approaches, one has to derive conclusions on the robustness of the results.

As the data availability for the EU Cohesion Policy payments has improved significantly over the last years, we would argue that meaningful results should be based on panel data, which reduces some of the main econometric problems. Moreover, it is advisable to use studies taking fixed effects into account and/or studies that attempt to solve the problem of reverse causality. With this in mind, we count 10 studies (including two papers applying treatment effects models) that consider these aspects.

At the country level, the most that can be concluded from empirical studies is that Cohesion Policy seems to be only conditionally effective. Given a good quality institutional setup (Ederveen, de Groot and Nahuis, 2006), or decentralised governmental structures (Bähr, 2008), the Cohesion Policy has a positive impact on growth. However, the methodological problems discussed in Section 2.4 should be kept in mind. For example, many studies do not allow for endogeneity of the Cohesion Policy. Hence, one should be careful when interpreting the results.

Using regional level data might be a preferable alternative because, first, EU Cohesion Policy focuses on the development and convergence of regions and, second, the robustness of the results is increased by the higher number of cross sections. One drawback is that structural funds data at the regional level is limited to the 1995-2006 time period. There are four studies controlling for the endogeneity problem using regional level data, three of which find at least a limited positive impact of structural funds payments. Moreover, using regional data without controlling for spatial spillover effects increases the problem of an omitted variable bias. There are three papers applying spatial techniques that find, again, weak evidence for a positive impact of structural funds. However, the disadvantage of these methods is that it is currently not possible to control for both spatial spillover effects and the endogeneity of several independent variables.

One explanation for the weak results might be the fact that almost all studies are derived from a neoclassical growth model assuming that EU Cohesion Policy increases investment, which ultimately raises the economic growth rate. However, the results by

Bouvet (2005) and Hagen and Mohl (2009b) suggest that EU Cohesion Policy may only have a modest impact on investment. These results might simply indicate that the EU support crowds out national investment. Moreover, we know very little about the labour market impact of the EU Cohesion Policy. Hence, one task for future studies will be to more thoroughly investigate the channels through this policy works.

Another reason for the inconclusive empirical results might be that the allocation of funds is at least partly determined by political-economic factors. In this context, the Cohesion Policy is not solely based on clear criteria. Hence, there is room for political bargaining and/or side payments which might result in the funding of politically feasible, and less economically efficient, projects.

Chapter 3

Impact on Regional Economic Growth I: Evidence from Panel Data[1]

3.1 Introduction

Investigating the impact of European structural funds on the economic growth and convergence process is a broad research topic. Nevertheless, the empirical evidence has provided mixed and contradictory results. While some authors do find evidence of a positive impact of structural funds on economic growth (for example, Dall'erba, 2005; Ramajo, Márquez, Hewings and Salinas, 2008), others only find a weakly positive (for example, Esposti and Bussoletti, 2008), no statistically significant (for example, Dall'erba and Le Gallo, 2008) or even a negative impact (for example, Eggert, von Ehrlich, Fenge and König, 2007; Checherita, Nickel and Rother, 2009). However, there are several issues requiring further investigation.

First, the estimation results might be biased due to the use of imprecise data. This problem is of special concern as the current literature often utilises structural funds commitments instead of actual payments. This results in a measurement error as commitments may not be entirely completed or be called up with a delay, for example due to missing absorption capacity. Furthermore, the existing literature has not investigated the impact of the different Objectives defined by the European Commission and the analyses have

[1] This chapter is based on the following joint article with Tobias Hagen: Mohl and Hagen (2010): Do EU structural funds promote regional growth? New evidence from various panel data approaches, *Regional Science and Urban Economics*, 2010: 40, 353–-365. An earlier version appeared as: Mohl and Hagen (2008): Does EU Cohesion Policy promote growth? Evidence from regional data and alternative econometric approaches, ZEW Discussion Paper, 08-086.

been restricted to the time period before 2000.

Second, there is the danger of biased estimates due to reverse causality. The allocation criteria of the structural funds are likely to be correlated with the dependent variable economic growth. First and foremost, the allocation of structural funds is based on the ratio of the regional GDP per capita (in PPS) and the EU-wide GDP. If this ratio is below 75 per cent, the region is a so-called "Objective 1" region, implying that it is eligible for the highest transfers relative to GDP. Moreover, the effective payments by the European Commission to the regions depend on the abilities of the regions or countries to initiate and co-finance these projects. This ability is presumably affected by the economic situation of the regions themselves (for example due to diverging tax revenues).

Third, there may be unobserved variables (unobserved heterogeneity) or–due to data availability–omitted variables, which have an impact on the regional growth rates but are not included in the specification. If the omitted variable is correlated with one explanatory variable, this explanatory variable is endogenous. For example, the request of funds by the regions may depend on political factors which, in turn, may affect growth. In this context, the results by Bouvet (2005) indicate that partisan affinity between the European Commission, the national governments and the regional governments has an impact on aid distribution.

In order to deal with the second and third problem, an instrument variable (IV) estimator combined with fixed effects or first-differences seems to be the right choice. In the literature two kinds of IVs have been suggested. Dall'erba and Le Gallo (2008) instrument structural funds payments by the regions' distance to Brussels, arguing that the spatial distribution of structural funds payments follows a center-periphery distribution. Bouvet (2005) uses partisan affinity as an instrument. However, while the first set of instruments shows no variation over time at all, the time variation of variables related to political affinity is low and in some regions even zero. Thus, their effect on structural funds payments is absorbed once regional fixed effects are controlled for, so they are not suitable for a panel fixed effects approach.

Finally, the results might be biased due to the omission of regional spillover effects: Structural funds payments may increase one region's growth which, in turn, may influence neighbouring regions' growth rates. In particular, the new economic geography (Krugman, 1991; Krugman and Venables, 1995) highlights the importance of regional spillovers. If these spillover effects cannot be separated from the "original" impulse, the estimated effect of structural funds payments is biased. To the best of our knowledge, only Dall'erba (2005) and Dall'erba and Le Gallo (2008) have controlled for spatial spillover effects investigating the growth effects of EU aid. However, they focus on cross-section analyses, so no paper has used spatial econometric tools for panel data.

Against this background, we extend the current literature by at least three aspects: First, we utilise a new structural funds dataset of 126 NUTS-1 / NUTS-2 regions, whereby our analysis consists of more precise measures of structural funds by distinguishing between Objective 1, 2 and 3 payments. In doing so we investigate the effect of time lags in greater detail and include the Financial Perspective 2000–2006, which has not been analysed before. Second, we address the problem of endogeneity in a panel context by basing the identification on internal instruments via a system GMM estimator (Blundell and Bond, 1998). Finally, we apply a spatial panel econometric estimator as recently proposed by Elhorst (2010), using a weight matrix containing information on the k-nearest neighbors of each region in order to control for spatial autocorrelation.

This paper is structured as follows. Section 3.2 briefly reviews the relevant literature. The data are then described in Section 3.3, followed by the presentation of the econometric specification in Section 3.4. The empirical results are discussed in Sections 3.5, before concluding in Section 3.6.

3.2 Literature Review

Roughly speaking, the theoretical approaches analysing the impact of economic integration and Cohesion Policy can be classified as growth theories and trade theories, distinguishing between "classical" and "new" approaches. In part, these approaches have diametric political implications (Martin, 1998; Dall'erba and Le Gallo, 2008; Heinemann, Mohl and Osterloh, 2009).

According to the neoclassical growth theory (Solow, 1956; Swan, 1956), regions with the same saving rate, depreciation rate and population growth and having access to the same technology will converge. When structural funds finance physical capital in capital-scarce regions, their growth is temporarily stimulated above the regions' usual steady state growth levels. However, due to the decreasing marginal product of capital, this policy only allows the economy to converge faster towards its steady state (Dall'erba and Le Gallo, 2008). Hence, as long as economic integration leads to an access to technology, it promotes convergence and there is no need for regional policy.

By contrast, the new economic geography (Krugman, 1991; Krugman and Venables, 1995) indicates that economic integration may lead to a spatial "core-periphery" pattern as a reduction in transportation costs could cause a spatial concentration of increasing returns to scale industries in the "core" and the concentration of constant returns to scale industries in the "periphery". Thus, integration may lead to divergence. In this case, regional policy may only have positive effects on regional convergence under certain circumstances. For example, applied to the question at hand, in the period 2000-2006 41% of Objective 1 funds were used for public infrastructure (European Commission, 2004b). Hence barriers and transport costs between core and peripheral regions were reduced. However, new economic geography theory predicts that a reduction of the transportation costs might be harmful for the economies of less developed regions by stimulating the agglomeration of economic activity in more developed "core" regions.[2]

From the perspective of the new (endogenous) growth theory (Romer, 1986, 1990), regional policy may have long-term effects if it will promote R&D or human capital resources. Investment in human capital are typically included under Objective 3, but also, to a lesser extent, under Objective 2. Furthermore, within the new growth theory public infrastructure may also affect growth if is an input in the production process (Barro, 1990).

Finally, the classical trade theory of comparative advantages suggests that countries (regions) specialise in sectors in which they have a comparative advantage. Hence, regional policy may be effective if it succeeds in promoting those comparative advantages.

Obviously, it is not possible to identify the "correct" theory for the evaluation of Cohesion Policy. The neoclassical growth model is theoretically well grounded in the convergence literature (Islam, 1995; Barro and Sala-i Martin, 2004) and it serves–especially in the econometric evaluation of Cohesion Policy–as a benchmark model (Durlauf, Johnson and Temple, 2005). It does, however, contain several shortcomings. From an econometric point of view, the use of regional datasets, in particular, increases the likelihood of spatial heterogeneity and spatial autocorrelation among regions (Baltagi, 2008). Therefore, the neglect of spatial dependence is of major concern and may lead to biased results (Badinger, Müller and Tondl, 2004; Arbia, Le Gallo and Piras, 2008). From a theoretical point of view, neoclassical convergence models were recently extended to control for spatial autocorrelation (López-Bazo, Vayá, Mora and Suriñach, 1999; Ertur and Koch, 2006). Furthermore, since a large part of structural funds finances transportation infrastructures, which may have industry relocation effects, the insights of the new economic geography highlighting the importance of spatial spillover effects have to be taken into account (Krugman, 1991; Krugman and Venables, 1995).

2 Our thanks to an anonymous reviewer for this remark about the potential "perverse" effects of Objective 1 payments from the perspective of new economic geography.

Table 3.1: Main results of the literature on the impact of structural funds on economic growth

Paper by	Central results: Impact of SF on economic growth	Operationalisation of structural funds	Time period	Units	Econometric methods used
Becker, Egger, von Ehrlich and Fenge (2010)	Positive and significant growth effect of Obj. 1 regions	Dummy variable = 1 for regions receiving Obj. 1 funding, 0 else [exogenous]	1989-1993, 1994-1999, 2000-2006	up to 3301 NUTS-3 regions (EU-12/25)	Panel: Regression discontinuity analysis
Hagen and Mohl (2010)	SF have a positive, but not statistically significant impact on regional growth	Obj. 1+2+3 payments and remaining commitments from 1994-99 (as % of GDP) [exogenous]	1995-2005	122 NUTS-1/2 regions (EU-15)	Panel: Generalised propensity score approach
Dall'erba and Le Gallo (2008)	SF have no statistically significant impact on regional convergence	SF payments and remaining commitments from 1994-1999 (as % of GDP) [endogenous]	1989-1999	145 NUTS-2 regions (EU-12)	Cross-section: Spatial lag model with IV
Esposti and Bussoletti (2008)	Limited impact of SF on regional growth	Obj. 1 payments per capita (in PPS) [exogenous]	1989-1999	206 NUTS-2 regions (EU-15)	Panel: FD-GMM, SYS-GMM
Falk and Sinabell (2008)	SF have a marginal positive and significant growth impact	Dummy variable = 1 for regions receiving Obj. 1 funding, 0 else [exogenous]	1995-2004	1084 NUTS-3 regions (EU-15)	Panel: Pooled OLS, median regression approach, weighted least squares
Ramajo, Márquez, Hewings and Salinas (2008)	Faster cond. convergence of relative income levels of regions belonging to Cohesion countries than in non-Cohesion regions	Separate regressions for regions belonging to Cohesion countries vs. non-Cohesion countries	1981-1996	163 NUTS-2 regions (EU-12)	Cross-section: Robust OLS, spatial lag model
Puigcerver-Peñalver (2007)	Positive effect of SF on growth rates of Obj. 1 regions in 1989-1993, but not in 1994-1999	Total SF (as % of GDP p.c.); total SF; SF of region i over total SF received by all regions [exogenous]	1989-1999, 1989-1993	41 NUTS-2 regions (EU-10)	Panel: Pooled OLS, FE
Eggert, von Ehrlich, Fenge and König (2007)	SF accelerate a region's convergence, but reduce the average growth rate	SF payments (as % of GDP) [exogenous]	1989-1993, 1994-1999,	16 NUTS-1 regions (Germany)	Cross-section: Pooled OLS, Regress average growth of 1994-99 (2000-04) on average SF of 1989-93 (1993-99)
Soukiazis and Antunes (2006)	SF promote convergence; small positive impact on growth; more effective in coastal than in interior regions	ERDF per capita [exogenous]	1991-1999	30 NUTS-3 regions (Portugal)	Panel: Pooled OLS, FE, Random Effects

Table 3.1: Main results of the literature on the impact of structural funds on economic growth (continued)

Paper by	Central results: Impact of SF on economic growth	Operationalisation of structural funds	Time period	Units	Econometric methods used
Bouvet (2005)	SF have a modest positive impact on regional growth rates	ERDF payments per capita [endogenous]	1975-1999	111 NUTS-1/2 regions (EU-8)	Panel: Pooled OLS, FE, IV
Dall'erba (2005)	Positive relationship between SF and regional growth	SF payments and remaining commitments from 1994-1999 (as % of GDP) [exogenous]	1989-1999	145 NUTS-2 regions (EU-12)	Cross-section Exploratory spatial data analysis
Percoco (2005)	SF induce a high level of volatility in the level of growth rates	Obj. 1 payments (as % of GDP) [endogenous]	1994-1999	6 NUTS-2 regions (Italy)	Panel: GMM-IV
Rodriguez-Pose and Fratesi (2004)	Limited impact of SF on growth; only SF funding on education and human capital have positive effects	Obj. 1 commitments (as % of GDP) [exogenous]	1989-1999	152 NUTS-2 regions (EU-8)	Cross-section & Panel: OLS, pooled GLS FE
de Freitas, Pereira and Torres (2003)	Obj. 1 regions do not show faster convergence than non-Obj. 1 regions	Dummy variable = 1 for regions receiving Obj. 1 funding, 0 else [exogenous]	1990-2001	196 NUTS-2 regions (EU-15)	Cross-section: OLS
Ederveen, Gorter, de Mooij Nahuis (2002)	Results depend on the assumptions underlying the convergence model	SF + Cohesion Fund (as % of GDP) [exogenous]	1981-1996	183 NUTS-2 regions (EU-13)	Panel: Pooled OLS
Garcia-Milà and McGuire (2001)	Grants are not effective in stimulating private investment or improving the overall economies of the poorer regions	Grants = Eur. + national grants; Dummy var. = 1 for regions receives above-average grants, 0 else [exogenous]	1977-1981, 1989-1992	17 NUTS-2 regions (Spain)	Panel: OLS and difference-in-difference approach

Notes: OLS = ordinary least squares, FE = fixed effects model, IV = instrumental variable, FD-GMM = first difference generalised method of moments estimator (Arellano and Bond, 1991), SYS-GMM = system generalised method of moments estimator (Blundell and Bond, 1998).

It is striking that almost all empirical studies investigating the impact of EU structural funds on regional economic growth are based on a neoclassical growth model, where structural funds mainly correspond to investment which are endogenous in the neoclassical growth framework.[3] Overall, despite a recently growing literature, the results have been ambiguous (for a summary of the main findings see Table 3.2). Moreover, in some cases the findings are conditioned by certain aspects. Rodríguez-Pose and Fratesi (2004) conclude that only expenditures for education and human capital have a positive effect in the medium term, whereas expenditures for agriculture do not. Ederveen, Gorter, de Mooij and Nahuis (2002) condition their key results on the assumptions of the convergence model. Assuming that all regions finally catch up to the same level, they find a positive effect. By contrast, assuming that the convergence process is limited to convergence within countries, they do not find a positive effect. Finally, some papers point to the significance of the time period of observation. Puigcerver-Peñalver (2007) finds the structural funds to had a positive impact on the growth rates for the period 1989–1993, but not for 1993–1999.

One key explanation for the diverging results is the poor data quality of structural funds. Most authors have no access to total structural funds, but focus on Objective 1 funding only (for example, Percoco, 2005) or on expenditures of the European Development Fund (ERDF) (for example, Bouvet, 2005; Soukiazis and Antunes, 2006). Some authors restrict their empirical analysis to structural funds commitments instead of payments (Rodríguez-Pose and Fratesi, 2004). Other authors limit to the use of dummy variables distinguishing between regions with and without EU support (Garcia-Milá and McGuire, 2001; de Freitas, Pereira and Torres, 2003; Becker, Egger, von Ehrlich and Fenge, 2008; Falk and Sinabell, 2008). Recently, Ramajo, Márquez, Hewings and Salinas (2008) derive the conclusions regarding the European regional convergence by running separate regressions for regions belonging to Cohesion and non-Cohesion countries.

The diverging results are also based on differences in the research design. While earlier papers largely use cross-section analyses (for example, Rodríguez-Pose and Fratesi, 2004), the recent findings are mostly based on panel data approaches (for example, Esposti and Bussoletti, 2008). In general, panel data provide more information as they contain less collinearity and more variation over time. Panel data increase the efficiency of the estimation results due to the greater availability of degrees of freedom (Elhorst, 2003b). Furthermore, even though Abreu, de Groot and Florax (2005) recently find that ignoring spatial effects leads to unreliable results, there have been only a few papers applying spatial econometric techniques (for a survey see Abreu, de Groot and Florax, 2005). In a

[3] Notable exceptions are Becker, Egger and von Ehrlich (2010) and Hagen and Mohl (2008) who avoid strict functional form assumptions by using treatment effect methods.

spatial cross-sectional setting omitting region fixed effects, Dall'erba (2005) and Dall'erba and Le Gallo (2007) show that spatial effects do play an important role when analysing the impact of EU funds. Finally, although there are several reasons why the assumption of exogeneity of structural funds seems too restrictive, only Bouvet (2005) and Dall'erba and Le Gallo (2008) have controlled for endogeneity. However, they focus on a cross-sectional setup, which does not take account of the advantages of a panel data approach.

3.3 Data

Unfortunately, data availability at the European regional level is limited with regard to both structural funds data and economic variables. Consequently, the choice of the time period of investigation and the sample of regions are pre-determined by the availability of suitable data. The annual reports on structural funds published by the European Commission (1995, 1996a,b, 1997, 1998, 1999, 2000) only comprise regional commitments / payments for the period 1994–1999. Unfortunately, since 2000, these reports have only consisted of aggregate data at the country level.

Our empirical analysis is based on a new dataset, as we were given access to the annual regional payments and commitments by the European Commission in Brussels. This dataset contains payments for the time period 2000–2006 that, to the best of our knowledge, have not been analysed before. It has to be taken into account that only payments of the period 2000–2006 are available in this dataset, i.e. remaining payments from the previous Financial Perspective 1994–1999 are excluded. In order to avoid an underestimation of the total amount of European structural funds, we allocate those commitments from the Financial Perspective 1994–1999 that had not been paid out by 1999 for the years 2000 and 2001. In doing so we calculate the residual amount of structural funds by subtracting the aggregated payments for 1994–1999 from the aggregated commitments in the same period. Assuming that all commitments finally lead to payments and taking into account the N+2 rule, which basically states that payments can be called up two years after they have been allocated as commitments, we allocate the remaining amount at a rate of 2:1 to the years 2000 and 2001 respectively.

In our analysis we concentrate on Objective 1, 2 and 3 payments. Note that they have different aims, which can be classified under three topics (see Table 2.1): (i) The highest share (approximately two-third) of total structural funds payments are spent on Objective 1 projects to promote development in less prosperous regions. The remaining part is shared almost equally among (ii) Objective 2 payments for regions in structural decline and (iii) Objective 3 payments to support education and employment policies.

Note that there is a clear-cut definition which regions qualify as an Objective 1 receiver (regional GDP has to be below 75% of the EU average), while a clear allocation scheme is missing in the case of the latter two Objectives. We follow the restructuring of the Objectives after the Financial Perspective 1994–1999 and add the Objective 6 payments to Objective 1, the Objective 5b payments to Objective 2 and the Objective 4 payments to Objective 3 (Table 2.1). Moreover, we are only interested in the impact of structural funds on the regional growth rates, so we restrict our analysis to those payments, that we are able to allocate to the regional level. Therefore, multi-regional programmes aiming at the national level (for example structural funds expenditures for education) are not considered. As a consequence, we can extend the period of investigation to the time period 1995–2005.

To present an overview of the regional distribution of the structural funds, Figure 3.1, 3.2 shows the quantile maps displaying the distribution of the funds over nine intervals by assigning the same number of values to each of the nine categories in the map. The payments are expressed as a share of population and are displayed as averages over the entire time period of observation (1995–2005). The darker the area, the higher the share of that region's payments of structural funds per capita. The figures show that Ireland, Eastern Germany, Greece, Southern Italy and Spain benefited most from Objective 1 payments, whereas France, the UK, Northern Spain and Sweden showed particularly high gains from Objective 2 and Objective 3 payments, respectively.

Moreover, Figure 3.3 displays the distribution pattern of GDP per capita, darker areas indicating that regions are wealthier than the EU-15 average. Following the logic of the European Cohesion Policy to reduce disparities among the European regions, regions with a lower GDP relative to the EU average should receive more structural funds, enabling these countries to catch up. A comparison of Figure 3.3 with Figure 3.1 indicates that the real GDP per capita is a good proxy for the allocation of Objective 1. Furthermore, it becomes clear that the receivers of Objective 1 payments often do not receive an equally large sum from Objectives 2 or 3 and vice versa.

Beyond the structural funds variable, the economic data is taken from the Regio database by Eurostat. Due to recent modifications in the accounting standards (from the European System of Accounting (ESA) 1979 to ESA 1995), we only use variables available in ESA 1995.

For the spatial econometrics analysis, we additionally need data to specify the spatial weight matrix. In this context, we were given access to the Gisco Eurostat dataset containing spherical coordinates measured in latitudes and longitudes of the European Union and of the candidate countries (Eurostat, 2007). We adjust the data according

Figure 3.1: Quantile maps: Obj. 1 payments per capita, 1995–2005

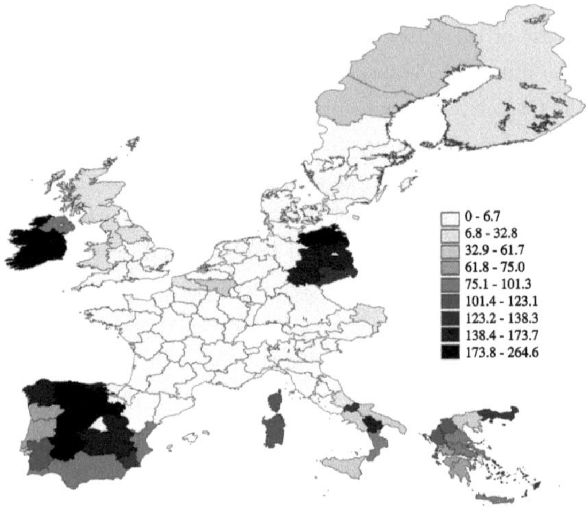

Notes: Own illustration. The payments of structural funds per capita do not include multiregional funding programmes. The darker the area, the higher the relative share of regions' payments of structural funds per capita.

Figure 3.2: Quantile maps: Total structural funds payments per capita, 1995–2005

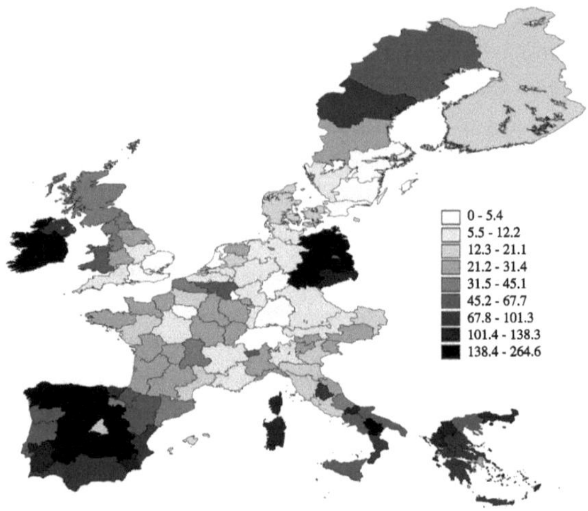

Notes: Own illustration. The payments of structural funds per capita do not include multiregional funding programmes. The darker the area, the higher the relative share of regions' payments of structural funds per capita.

Figure 3.3: Quantile map, GDP per capita (in PPS), 1995–2005

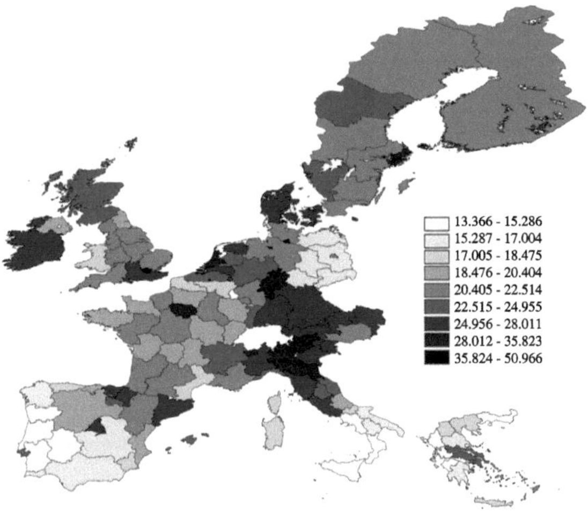

Source: Own illustration. The darker the area the wealthier is the region compared to the EU-15 average.

Table 3.2: Variables and data sources

Variable	Definition	Source
Real GDP p.c. growth (t)	Real GDP (PPS) per capita growth rate from t to t-1	
Real GDP p.c.	Real GDP (PPS) p.c.	
Investment	Gross fixed capital formation, as a share of nominal GDP	Eurostat Regio statistics
Pop. growth (t)	Population growth rate from t to t-1	
Innovation	Patents (per million inhabitants) (interpolated)	
Objective 1	Objective 1 payments per capita (in Euro)	Data for the period 1994–1999: European Commission (1995, 1996a, b, 1997, 1998, 1999, 2000); Data for the period 2000–2006 were accessed at the European Commission in Brussels on 24/25 November 2007.
Objectives 1+2+3	Objectives 1+2+3 payments per capita (in Euro)	

to the selection of our dataset, which comprises 126 NUTS-1 and NUTS-2 regions. As mentioned above, the selection of NUTS regions is predetermined mainly by the allocation of structural funds.[4] For a detailed description of the choice of the NUTS level, see Appendix A. Furthermore, all variables are described in Table 3.2.

4 There are only four regions for which we have structural payments, but the control variables are missing (see Appendix A).

3.4 Econometric Specification

In the first step, we apply the neoclassical Solow-Swan-type growth framework (Solow, 1956; Swan, 1956) as a benchmark. In the second step, we extend this model in order to account for regional spillovers. Hence, similar to the empirical approach of Ederveen, de Groot and Nahuis (2006) and Bähr (2008),[5] we estimate the following growth model:

$$\begin{aligned} ln(y_{i,t}) - ln(y_{i,t-1}) = & \beta_0 + \beta_1 \, ln(y_{i,t-1}) + \beta_2 \, ln(inv_{i,t-1}) + \beta_3 \, (n_{i,t-1} + g + \delta) \\ & + \beta_4 \, ln(innov_{i,t-1}) + \beta_5 \, ln(sf_{i,t-1}) + \mu_i + \lambda_t + u_{i,t} \end{aligned} \tag{3.1}$$

where the subscript $i = 1, ..., 126$ denotes the region and t indicates the time index of our sample ranging from 1995–2005. Moreover, $y_{i,t}$ is the real GDP per capita (in PPS) of region i at time t, $inv_{i,t-1}$ indicates the investment (in % of nominal GDP). $n_{i,t-1}$ is the population growth rate, g and δ stand for the technological progress and the time discount factor. Following Mankiw, Romer and Weill (1992), we assume that g and δ are constant over time and region and jointly amount to 5%.

Unfortunately, data availability of our explanatory variables is limited at the regional level. To the best of our knowledge, there are no high-quality education data to compare with that proposed at the country level by de La Fuente and Doménech (2006), Barro and Lee (2001) or Cohen and Soto (2007). Therefore, we assume that education is proxied by an innovation variable ($innov_{i,t-1}$), that measures the number of patents per million inhabitants. To test for robustness, we also ran the regressions using the number of high-tech innovations per million inhabitants. However, the results do not substantially differ.

Our main variable of interest is the structural funds payments variable ($sf_{i,t-1}$). We follow Esposti and Bussoletti (2008) and express it per total population.[6] The main argument against using structural funds payments per GDP is that simultaneity problems might bias the results, as GDP (growth) appears on both sides of the regression equation.[7] We are not only interested in analysing the growth impact of total regional structural funds payments, but we also wish to distinguish between Objective 1, 2 and 3 payments. Hence, we start with specifications including the total sum of Objectives 1+2+3 payments and then proceed investigating the impact of Objective 1 payments only.

---

[5] However, in contrast to our analysis, Ederveen, de Groot and Nahuis (2006) and Bähr (2008) use country data.

[6] We follow, among others, Ederveen, de Groot and Nahuis (2006) by adding 1 to the share of structural funds per capita, since some regions receive no EU funding at all and we want to include logged variables in our specification.

[7] As a sensitivity analysis, we re-run the estimations using structural funds payments per GDP. The results do not substantially differ and they are available upon request.

Moreover, we analyse in greater detail the impact of time lags. It may be argued that structural funds projects, such as infrastructure investment, only become effective after a certain time lag. Thus, as a reference, we first start our empirical analyses by excluding any structural funds variable, then we stepwise add the lagged structural funds payments beginning with a lag of one year and ending up with a specification comprising structural funds with a lag of between one and five years ($\sum_{j=1}^{5} ln(sf_{i,t-j})$). Due to multicollinearity the coefficients and standard errors of the structural funds variable cannot be interpreted if the variable is included into the regression with several lags. As a consequence, we calculate the joint sum of structural funds' coefficients (Obj. joint sign. (size)) corresponding to the short-term elasticity and use a simple Wald test to check whether this short-term elasticity is statistically different from zero (Obj. joint sign. (p-value)).

Note that the estimated specification displayed in equation (3.1) implicitly implies a dynamic approach, so it is more convincing to interpret the long-term impact of structural funds. We do so in the following and report the size (Obj. long-term elast. (size)) and the significance level (Obj. long-term elast. (p-value)) of the estimated long-term elasticities (ϕ) in the regression output tables.[8] The long-term elasticity indicates that a one per cent increase of structural funds per capita raises the regional real GDP per capita by ϕ%.

Finally, we include fixed regional effects (μ_i) as well as fixed (annual) time effects (λ_t), while $u_{i,t}$ is the i.i.d. error term of the specification. The summary statistics are listed in Table 3.3.

3.5 Empirical Results

3.5.1 "Classical" Panel Regression Results

As our set of regions is a non-random sample, which is possibly subject to common influences affecting our variables of interest, we omit the LSDV estimations using White

Table 3.3: Summary statistics

Variable	Mean	Std. dev.	Min.	Max.
Real GDP p.c. growth	0.018	0.032	-0.175	0.243
Ln real GDP p.c.	9.959	0.253	9.344	10.919
Ln investment	-1.720	0.344	-3.435	-0.680
Ln pop. growth (+0.05)	-2.938	0.105	-3.295	-2.487
Ln innovation (interpolated)	3.505	1.668	-2.419	6.595
Ln Objectives 1+2+3 p.c.	3.178	1.452	0.000	5.951
Ln Objective 1 p.c.	1.698	2.179	0.000	5.951

Notes: The number of observations is equal to 1096.

[8] Starting from a dynamic approach, the long-term elasticity is derived as follows: $ln\, y_{i,t} = \beta_1 ln\, y_{i,t-1} + \beta_2 ln\, sf_{i,t} + ... \Leftrightarrow ln\, y_{i,t} - ln\, y_{i,t-1} = (\beta_1 - 1) ln\, y_{i,t-1} + \beta_2 ln\, sf_{i,t} + ... \Leftrightarrow ln\, y_{i,t} - ln\, y_{i,t-1} = \alpha\, ln\, y_{i,t-1} + \beta_2 ln\, sf_{i,t} + ... \Leftrightarrow \phi = \beta_2/(1-\beta_1) = \beta_2/-\alpha$.

heteroscedasticity robust standard errors (White, 1980). Following the Wooldridge test results pointing to first-order autocorrelation (Wooldridge, 2002), we adjust the standard errors for heteroscedasticity, serial and spatial correlation by employing a non-parametric covariance matrix as proposed by Driscoll and Kraay (1998) (see Hoechle (2007) for a recent discussion).[9] In addition, we provide further evidence by running system GMM regressions following Blundell and Bond (1998) in order to control for endogeneity.

The regression results displayed in Table 3.4 are mostly consistent with the predictions of the neoclassical growth theory. We find–regardless of the empirical estimation approach–that the initial GDP variable is negative and strongly significant in most cases. Furthermore, the estimated size of the coefficients is comparable with that of the cross-sectional analysis by Dall'erba and Le Gallo (2008). In empirical investigations for longer time periods (for example, cross-section estimations for 10–100 years (see, among others, Barro and Sala-i-Martin, 1992; Sala-i-Martin, 1996; Arbia, Le Gallo and Piras, 2008) or for several 5-year averages (for example, Ederveen, de Groot and Nahuis, 2006)), the lagged initial GDP variable gives evidence for the conditional beta convergence, i.e., after controlling for other explanatory variables, this variable indicates whether poorer regions catch-up with richer ones. Note that from theoretical considerations this is only valid for more or less similar economies on their convergence paths (Islam, 2003; Barro and Sala-i Martin, 2004). This condition might be fulfilled as our sample consists of western European regions. However, the time period of investigation is too short to derive solid predictions about the convergence process. Nevertheless, the initial GDP is an important control variable in our panel as it determines the allocation of Objective 1 payments.

Furthermore, the coefficients of the population growth rate follow the predictions of the Solow growth model as it is in most cases negative and statistically significant. The investment variable is – apart from a few GMM specifications–in many cases positive but it is hardly statistically significant. Finally, the proxy for education, the innovation variable, shows positive coefficients in most specifications and it is highly significant in case of the GMM specifications.

The key variable of interest, however, is the structural funds variable. The results displayed in Table 3.4 show mixed findings with switching signs depending on the number of lags of the structural funds variable included in the specification. According to the short-term elasticity, structural funds are not statistically significant different from zero. As stressed above, it is more convincing to interpret the long-term elasticity. Table 3.4

[9] As a sensitivity check, we also controlled for serial correlation following Newey and West (1987) and by applying the Prais-Winsten transformation matrix to transform the AR(1) disturbances in the error term into serially uncorrelated classical errors. The results strengthen the robustness of our results and are available upon request.

shows that the sign of the long-term elasticity is not clear-cut and it is only significant when restricted to one lag only.

As discussed above, our results might be biased due to endogeneity of the explanatory variables. Hence, we estimate equation (1) using the two-step system GMM estimator proposed by Blundell and Bond (1998), assuming that all variables are endogenous. The standard errors are finite-sample adjusted following Windmeijer (2005). In order to guarantee a parsimonious use of instruments, we limit the number of instruments to four. The reason for this is that using too many instruments can overfit instrumented variables (Roodman, 2009b), reduce the power properties of the Hansen test (Bowsher, 2002) and lead to a downward-bias in two-step standard errors (Windmeijer, 2005). As a robustness check we also increased the number of instruments in the system GMM regressions. However, the results hardly differ.

Given this parsimonious specification, the estimation results show that the Hansen test of overidentifying restrictions is not statistically significant, i.e. the null hypothesis, which states that the instruments are not correlated with the residual cannot be rejected (see Table 3.5). Apart from the Hansen test, we also report the p-values for the tests of serial correlation. These tests are based on first-differenced residuals and we expect the disturbances $u_{i,t}$ not to be serially-correlated in order to yield valid estimation results. The regression output in Table 3.5 shows no second-order serial correlation (AR(2) (p-value)). Moreover, the short- and long-term elasticities have negative signs and they are statistically significant when including more than three lags. Against this background, we conclude that there are no clear-cut results regarding the impact of the sum of Objectives 1+2+3.

Alternatively, it might be more revealing to analyse more precise measures of structural funds by evaluating the single Objectives separately. Hence, we estimate the regressions by only including Objective 1 payments–which constitute the major part of Cohesion Policy–into the specification. The results displayed in Tables 3.6–3.7 show that the coefficients of both the short- and the long-term elasticities have positive signs. Furthermore, the long-term elasticities are statistically different from zero when more than three lags are included. The results indicate that a one per cent increase of Objective 1 payments per capita raises the regional GDP by at least 0.01% and by a maximum of 0.07%. This implies that EU aid for the less-developed regions are most effective in promoting economic growth.

Finally, we test the sensitivity of the appropriate choice of control variables. Even though it is theoretically well founded, the inclusion of the investment variable into the regression evaluating the growth effects of structural funds payments may lead to biased results. Since structural funds payments may stimulate growth through the channel "investment" (leading to a higher steady-state capital stock per capita), the inclusion of the investment variable may render it impossible to evaluate the investment increasing effect of SF payments on growth. More generally stated: One should be careful not to include control variables, which may also serve as a dependent variable of Cohesion Policy (Angrist and Pischke (2009) call these variables "bad controls"). As a consequence, we re-run the regressions excluding the investment variable. It is striking that this sensitivity analysis does not lead to different conclusions.[10]

3.5.2 Spatial Panel Analysis

Apart from adopting the standard errors according to the Driscoll and Kraay (1998) approach, we have so far neglected any sort of spatial correlation, which may lead to biased results. One might argue that part of our significant results is explained by regional spillover effects. Moreover, in our sample of 126 western European regions, those regions which are located next to each other might disclose a stronger spatial dependence than regions at a greater distance.

In order to take these factors into account, we apply spatial econometric techniques, where one key task is to specify a weight matrix W containing information about the connectivity between regions. This square matrix has N rows / columns corresponding to our sample of 126 regions. The diagonal consists of zeros, whereas each w_{ij} specifies the way region i is spatially connected to region j. To standardise the external influence upon each region, the weight matrix is normalised such that the elements amount to one. We follow the approach by Le Gallo and Ertur (2003) and Ertur and Koch (2006) and use a weight matrix consisting of the k-nearest neighbours computed from the distance between the centroids of the NUTS regions.[11] This weight matrix is based solely on geographical distance, which has the big advantage that its exogeneity is unambiguous. Generally, the k-nearest neighbours' weight matrix $W(k)$ is defined as follows:

$$W(k) = \begin{cases} w^*_{ij}(k) = 0 \text{ if } i = j \\ w^*_{ij}(k) = 1 \text{ if } d_{ij} \leq d_i(k) \text{ and } w_{ij}(k) = w^*_{ij}(k) / \sum_j w^*_{ij}(k) \\ w^*_{ij}(k) = 0 \text{ if } d_{ij} > d_i(k) \end{cases}$$

where w^*_{ij} is an element of the unstandardised weight matrix W and w_{ij} is an element of

10 The results based on the alternative specification excluding investment are available upon request.

11 We use the Matlab toolbox "Arc_Mat" (LeSage and Pace, 2004) to determine the centroids of the polygons (regions) expressed in decimal degrees. The 10 nearest neighbours of each region are then determined with the help of the Spatial Statistics Toolbox 2.0 (Pace, 2003).

the standardised weight matrix, $d_i(k)$ is the smallest distance of the kth order between region i and j such that each region i has exactly k neighbours. Following Ertur and Koch (2006) we set $k = 10$.[12]

Generally speaking, there are two possibilities to integrate this weight matrix into our estimation approach. One can either include a spatially weighted dependent variable (the so-called "spatial lag model") or a spatially autocorrelated error term ("spatial error model") into the regression model. We run Lagrange Multiplier tests as originally proposed for cross-sections by Anselin (1988) and implemented for panel data by Elhorst (2010) in order to decide which approach to use. They clearly favour the spatial lag approach,[13] so we estimate the following model, which includes the sample of 126 regions:

$$\begin{aligned} ln(y_{i,t}) - ln(y_{i,t-1}) = {} & \beta_0 + \rho W\big(ln(y_{i,t}) - ln(y_{i,t-1})\big) + \beta_1 \, ln(y_{i,t-1}) \\ & + \beta_2 \, ln(inv_{i,t-1}) + \beta_3 \, ln(innov_{i,t-1}) \\ & + \beta_4 \, (n_{i,t-1} + g + \delta) + \beta_5 \, ln(sf_{i,t-1}) + \mu_i + \lambda_t + u_{i,t} \end{aligned} \tag{3.2}$$

Apart from the inclusion of the lagged and spatially weighted dependent variable as an independent variable, the selection of variables remains the same as in equation (1).

The inclusion of a spatially lagged dependent variable into a panel fixed effects model generates an endogeneity problem because the spatially weighted dependent variable is correlated with the disturbance term (Elhorst, 2003b). In order to control for this simultaneity, the following results are based on a fixed effects spatial lag setup using the maximum likelihood (ML) estimator proposed by Elhorst (2010). Unfortunately, it is currently not possible to estimate a spatial panel lag model and to control simultaneously for endogeneity of other independent variables, for example within a system GMM approach. The reason for this is that introducing a spatial weight matrix creates a non-zero log-Jacobian transformation from the disturbances of the model to the dependent variable, while the system GMM procedure by Blundell and Bond (1998) is based on the assumption of no Jacobian term involved.

We start our spatial panel analysis by testing whether to use a fixed or random effects approach. The Hausman test clearly rejects the latter (-114.69, p-value: 0.000), so the results of the spatial panel fixed effects regressions are reported in Table 3.8. One measures

12 For example, the elements of the row / column vector of the weight matrix (W) for the region "Region de Bruxelles-capitale" (be) are all zeros with the exception of the ten nearest neighbours (be2, be3, fr10, fr21, fr22, fr30, fr41, nl2, nl3 and nl4) whose elements are 0.1.

13 The LM test statistic clearly rejects the null hypothesis of no spatial spatial model (test statistic: 8.878, p-value: 0.003), whereas it is not rejected for the null hypothesis of no spatial error model (test statistic: 1.897, p-value 0.168). As a sensitivity test, we also run spatial panel error regression. The results confirm our main conclusions and they are available upon request.

which indicates whether spatial effects are present is given by the coefficient of the weight matrix (ρ). The results show that ρ is positive throughout and highly significant. This implies that a one per centage point increase in the average of the GDP per capita of the ten nearest neighbours would tend to increase the growth rate in region i by between 0.458 to 0.602 per cent. The estimated size of the coefficient is in line with the related literature (for example Dall'erba and Le Gallo, 2008). Furthermore, it becomes clear that compared to the previous regression results the use of the spatial weight matrix slightly decreases the coefficients of the explanatory variables. Thus, it emerges that the explanatory power of these variables attributed to their in-region value is really due to the neighbouring locations, which is now allowed for by the coefficient of the spatially weighted dependent variable.

All in all, the results of the coefficients again follow the neoclassical growth predictions. We find a negative and highly significant impact of the real GDP variable and the population growth rate. The investment variable has a predominantly positive but hardly significant impact on the GDP growth rate. The innovation variable is mostly positive but scarcely statistically significant.

Most importantly, the results confirm our previous conclusions concerning the effectiveness of the structural funds. For the sum of Objectives 1+2+3 we receive no clear-cut results, as most of the short- and long-term elasticities have switchings signs and most of them are not statistically significant (Table 3.8). By contrast, Objective 1 payments seem to have a positive impact as both the short- and the long-term elasticities have a positive sign and all long-term elasticities are significant irrespective of the estimation approach. According to our findings, a one per cent rise of Objective 1 payments increases the real GDP per capita by 0.006–0.025% (Table 3.9). Hence, taking regional spillovers into account leads to smaller estimated effect of SF payments.

3.6 Conclusions

The aim of this paper is to evaluate the growth effects of European structural funds payments at the regional level. Our empirical results are based on a new dataset using panel methods controlling for heteroscedasticity, serial and spatial correlation as well as for endogeneity. In particular, using a spatial panel approach we find that regional spillovers do have a significant impact on the regional growth rates irrespective of which Objective and time lag is analysed. This finding confirms the importance of regional interconnectivity (for example Arbia, Le Gallo and Piras, 2008) implying that the growth performance of western European regions also depends on the GDP growth rate in the neighbouring regions.

Furthermore, we find empirical evidence that the effectiveness of structural funds in promoting growth is strongly dependent on which Objective is analysed. Our estimation results show that Objective 1 payments, in particular, have a positive and statistically significant impact on the regions' GDP. Broadly summarising, we find that a one per cent increase of Objective 1 payments, i.e. those funds used for the poorest regions, leads to a small but positive impact on the regional GDP per capita by approximately 0.05%. Hence, the potential "perverse" effect of transportation infrastructure on growth in poorer regions predicted by the new economic geography seems not to dominate the results. By contrast, the growth effects of the total amount of Objective 1, 2 and 3 payments are in most specifications not statistically significant, implying no effect or even negative effects of Objective 2 and 3 payments, respectively. Moreover, our results show that time lags play a key role in influencing the effectiveness. We find that the growth impact does not appear immediately but rather occurs with a time lag of more than three years.

Our findings that the total EU aid (including Objective 2 and 3) has no statistically significant or even negative impact on the regional growth rate may be explained by several aspects: First, in contrast to Objective 1 payments, Objective 2 and 3 payments are not solely based on clear criteria. Hence, there is room for political bargaining and side payments, respectively, which might result in funding of politically feasible projects to the detriment of economically efficient ones. Second, the structural funds payments have de jure to be co-financed. However, empirical studies using country data provide evidence that some crowding out of national public investment takes place (Ederveen, Gorter, de Mooij and Nahuis, 2002; Hagen and Mohl, 2009b). This, in turn, might have a negative impact on the regional GDP growth. Third, the underlying neoclassical growth model implicitly assumes full-employment. Given that Objective 2 and 3 payments directly affect the labour market and given that these effects are not (directly) reflected in the real GDP per capita figures, we cannot measure the impact of these consequences precisely. Therefore, further research should investigate the labour market effects of EU structural policy.

One might argue that the results presented above are influenced by the statistical "noise" of the annual growth rate. As our time period of investigation is relatively short due to data availability, we cannot follow, say, Islam (1995) and use 5-year averages as this would reduce our sample to two periods only. Furthermore, we do not wish to rely soley on a simple cross-section approach, as the fixed effects could then not be cancelled out, and this might lead to biased estimates (Durlauf, Johnson and Temple, 2005).

All things considered, our results support the recent conclusion by Ramajo, Márquez,

Hewings and Salinas (2008) that EU regional policy explicitly designed for the less-developed regions are most effective in promoting growth and that regional spillovers do, in fact, play an important role.

Acknowledgements

Special thanks go to Jose Madeira and Christian Weise (both European Commission) for their helpful support in acquiring the EU structural funds payments for 2000–2006. Moreover, we would like to thank Friedrich Schneider, François Laisney, James LeSage, the participants of the IIPF Annual Congress in Maastricht (23 August 2008), those of the Annual Meeting of the German Economic Association in Graz (25 September 2008) and those of the Panel Data Conference in Bonn (5 July 2009) for their helpful and inspiring comments and advice. In addition, many thanks to Florian Mayer for his excellent research assistance. Last but not least, we would like to thank two anonymous reviewers and the editor in charge for their valuable comments on the paper.

3.7 Appendix

3.7.1 Construction of the Dataset

This Section illustrates in more detail the construction of our database. The European regions are classified by the European Commission into three different groups called "Nomenclature des unités territoriales statistiques" (NUTS). These units refer to the country level (NUTS-0) and to three lower subdivisions (NUTS-1, NUTS-2 and NUTS-3) which are classified according to the size of population. Our dataset consists of both NUTS-1 and NUTS-2 regions. In order to guarantee the highest degree of transparency, this Section lists the abbreviations of the NUTS codes in brackets following the classification of the European Commission (2007b).

The choice of the NUTS level follows the data availability of structural funds payments. Generally, we try to use data on NUTS-2 level whenever possible. This is the case for France, Greece, Italy, Portugal, Spain, and Sweden. However, in case of Germany we have to use NUTS-1 level because the annual reports do not contain more detailed information. Moreover, in some countries there is no clear-cut distinction in the sense that in the annual reports of the structural funds are partly allocated to the NUTS-1 and partly to the NUTS-2 level. Finally, the annual reports of structural funds for 1995 and 1996 (European Commission, 1996b, 1997) for some countries only contain data at the NUTS-1 level. As a consequence, we choose the NUTS-1 level for Austria, Belgium, Finland, the Netherlands, and the United Kingdom.

For Denmark and Luxembourg subdivisions do not exist, so NUTS-0, NUTS-1 and NUTS-2 codes are the same. We regard those cases as NUTS-2 regions. In Ireland the labels of NUTS-0 and NUTS-1 level are identical, so that we classify Ireland as a NUTS-1 region. Please note that we do not consider the overseas regions of France (Départments d'outre-mer (fr9) consisting of Guadeloupe (fr91), Martinique (fr92), Guyane (fr93) and Réunion (fr94)), Portugal (Região Autónoma dos Açores (pt2, pt20), Região Autónoma da Madeira (pt3, pt30)), and Spain (Canarias (es7, es70)).

As a consequence, our dataset consists of 130 NUTS-1 and NUTS-2 regions for which we have structural funds payments. However, we have to exclude four regions for which the economic control variables of Eurostat are not completely available. These regions are Voreio Aigaio (gr41), Ciudad Autónoma de Ceuta (es63), Ciudad Autónoma de Melilla (es64) and Luxembourg (lu). Thus, our dataset consists of the following 126 NUTS-1 and NUTS-2 regions:

Belgium (3 NUTS-1 regions): Région de Bruxelles-capitale (be1), Vlaams Gewest (be2), Région Wallonne (be3);

Denmark (1 NUTS-2 region): Denmark (dk);

Germany (16 NUTS-1 regions): Baden-Württemberg (de1), Bayern (de2), Berlin (de3), Brandenburg (de4), Bremen (de5), Hamburg (de6), Hessen (de7), Mecklenburg-Vorpommern (de8), Niedersachsen (de9), Nordrhein-Westfalen (dea), Rheinland-Pfalz (deb), Saarland (dec), Sachsen (ded), Sachsen-Anhalt (dee), Schleswig-Holstein (def), Thüringen (deg);

Greece (12 NUTS-2 regions): Anatoliki Makedonia, Thraki (gr11), Kentriki Makedonia (gr12), Dytiki Makedonia (gr13), Thessalia (gr14), Ipeiros (gr21), Ionia Nisia (gr22), Dytiki Ellada (gr23), Sterea Ellada (gr24), Peloponnisos (gr25), Attiki (gr30), Notio Aigaio (gr42), Kriti (gr43);

Spain (16 NUTS-2 regions): Galicia (es11), Principado de Asturias (es12), Cantabria (es13), País Vasco (es21), Comunidad Foral de Navarra (es22), La Rioja (es23), Aragón (es24), Comunidad de Madrid (es30), Castilla y León (es41), Castilla-La Mancha (es42), Extremadura (es43), Cataluña (es51), Comunidad de Valenciana (es52), Illes Balears (es53), Andalucía (es61), Región de Murcia (es62);

France (22 NUTS-2 regions): Île de France (fr10), Champagne-Ardenne (fr21), Picardie (fr22), Haute-Normandie (fr23), Centre (fr24), Basse-Normandie (fr25), Bourgogne (fr26), Nord-Pas-de-Calais (fr30), Lorraine (fr41), Alsace (fr42), Franche-Comté (fr43), Pays-de-la-Loire (fr51), Bretagne (fr52), Poitou-Charentes (fr53), Aqui- taine (fr61), Midi-Pyrénées (fr62), Limousin (fr63), Rhône-Alpes (fr71), Auvergne (fr72), Provence-Alpes-Côte d'Azur (fr82), Languedoc-Roussillon (fr81), Corse (fr83);

Ireland (1 NUTS-1 region): Irland (ie);

Italy (21 NUTS-2 regions): Piemonte (itc1), Valle d'Aosta/Vallée d'Aoste (itc2), Liguria (itc3), Lombardia (itc4), Provincia autonoma Bolzano (itd1), Provincia autonoma Trento (itd2), Veneto (itd3), Friuli-Venezia Giulia (itd4), Emilia-Romagna (itd5), Toscana (ite1), Umbria (ite2), Marche (ite3), Lazio (ite4), Abruzzo (itf1), Molise (itf2), Campania (itf3), Puglia (itf4), Basilicata (itf5), Calabria (itf6), Sicilia (itg1), Sardegna (itg2);

The Netherlands (4 NUTS-1 regions): Noord-Nederland (nl1), Oost-Nederland (nl2), West-Nederland (nl3), Zuid-Nederland (nl4);

Austria (3 NUTS-1 regions): Ostösterreich (at1), Südösterreich (at2), Westösterreich (at3);

Portugal (5 NUTS-2 regions): Norte (pt11), Algarve (pt15), Centro (P) (pt16), Lisboa (pt17), Alentejo (pt18);

Finland (2 NUTS-1 regions): Manner-Suomi (fi1), Åland (fi2);

Sweden (8 NUTS-2 regions): Stockholm (se11), Östra Mellansverige (se12), Småland med öarna (se021), Sydsverige (se22), Västsverige (se23), Norra Mellansverige (se31), Mellersta Norrland (se32), Övre Norrland (se33);

UK (12 NUTS-1 regions): North East (ukc), North West (ukd), Yorkshire and the Humber (uke), East Midlands (ukf), West Midlands (ukg), East of England (ukh), London (uki), South East (ukj), South West (ukk), Wales (ukl), Scotland (ukm), Northern Ireland (ukn).

3.7.2 Regression Results

Table 3.4: Regression results using the Driscoll and Kraay estimator (Obj. 1+2+3)

	(1)	(2)	(3)	(4)	(5)	(6)
Ln real GDP p.c. (t-1)	-0.172**	-0.171**	-0.211**	-0.266*	-0.380**	-0.609***
	(-2.843)	(-2.825)	(-2.686)	(-2.571)	(-3.359)	(-12.27)
Ln investment (t-1)	0.00258	0.00335	0.00113	0.00771	-0.0110	0.000119
	(0.551)	(0.707)	(0.177)	(1.260)	(-1.849)	(0.0134)
Ln pop. growth +0.05 (t-1)	-0.0620*	-0.0638*	-0.0735*	-0.0745**	-0.0483*	-0.0797***
	(-2.278)	(-2.234)	(-2.472)	(-2.789)	(-1.983)	(-5.334)
Ln innovation (t-1)	-0.00148	-0.00152	-0.000648	8.56e-05	0.00260	0.00321
	(-0.593)	(-0.625)	(-0.245)	(0.0343)	(0.852)	(1.046)
Ln Objectives 1+2+3 p.c. (t-1)		0.00209	0.00262*	0.00248	0.00385***	0.00242
		(1.933)	(2.214)	(1.954)	(3.576)	(1.340)
Ln Objectives 1+2+3 p.c. (t-2)			-0.00178	-0.00212	-0.00277	0.00162
			(-0.797)	(-0.856)	(-0.914)	(1.192)
Ln Objectives 1+2+3 p.c. (t-3)				-0.000680	0.000620	0.00130
				(-0.540)	(1.207)	(0.969)
Ln Objectives 1+2+3 p.c. (t-4)					-0.00346***	-0.00351***
					(-5.998)	(-3.983)
Ln Objectives 1+2+3 p.c. (t-5)						-0.000993
						(-0.659)
Obj. 1+2+3 joint sign. (size)			0.000838	-0.000324	-0.00177	0.000842
Obj. 1+2+3 joint sign. (p-value)			0.711	0.894	0.477	0.842
Obj. 1+2+3 long-term elast. (size)		0.0123**	0.00397	-0.00122	-0.00465	0.00138
Obj. 1+2+3 long-term elast. (p-value)		0.0405	0.724	0.896	0.530	0.843
WT time dummies (p-value)	0.000	0.000	0.000	0.000	0.000	0.000
Wooldridge AR(1) (p-value)	0.000	0.000	0.000	0.000	0.000	0.000
No. of observations	1096	1096	979	864	745	622
No. of regions	126	126	126	126	126	126

Notes: Standard errors are adjusted according to Driscoll and Kraay (1998), t-statistics are reported in parentheses; * significant at 10%; ** significant at 5%; *** significant at 1%; constant and time dummies are not shown.

Table 3.5: Regression results using the two-step system GMM estimator (Obj. 1+2+3)

	(1)	(2)	(3)	(4)	(5)	(6)
Ln real GDP p.c. (t-1)	-0.00554	-0.0107	-0.0147	-0.0263	-0.0470**	-0.0508**
	(-0.366)	(-0.771)	(-1.175)	(-1.889)	(-2.920)	(-2.737)
Ln investment (t-1)	-0.0101*	-0.00825	-0.00883	0.00315	-0.00628	-0.00749
	(-2.360)	(-1.730)	(-1.779)	(0.490)	(-0.489)	(-0.508)
Ln pop. growth + 0.05 (t-1)	-0.00329	-0.00601	0.00143	0.00752	0.0104	-0.00413
	(-0.217)	(-0.390)	(0.0971)	(0.542)	(0.746)	(-0.262)
Ln innovation (t-1)	0.00368*	0.00340*	0.00362*	0.00598***	0.00453*	0.00391
	(2.256)	(2.148)	(2.414)	(3.620)	(2.391)	(1.597)
Ln Objectives 1+2+3 p.c. (t-1)		-0.000844	0.00582**	0.00919***	0.0103***	0.0114***
		(-0.369)	(2.858)	(4.127)	(3.532)	(3.846)
Ln Objectives 1+2+3 p.c. (t-2)			-0.00615***	-0.00800***	-0.00920***	-0.00852***
			(-3.897)	(-4.480)	(-4.668)	(-3.449)
Ln Objectives 1+2+3 p.c. (t-3)				-0.00290*	-0.00178	-0.00174
				(-1.964)	(-0.966)	(-0.826)
Ln Objectives 1+2+3 p.c. (t-4)					-0.00587**	-0.00816**
					(-2.788)	(-3.223)
Ln Objectives 1+2+3 p.c. (t-5)						-0.00154
						(-0.704)
Obj. 1+2+3 joint sign. (size)			-0.000331	-0.00171	-0.00651**	-0.00855*
Obj. 1+2+3 joint sign. (p-value)			0.896	0.550	0.0423	0.0510
Obj. 1+2+3 long-term elast. (size)		-0.0792	-0.0225	-0.0652*	-0.138***	-0.168***
Obj. 1+2+3 long-term elast. (p-value)		0.441	0.240	0.0589	0.00350	0.00619
WT time dummies (p-value)	0.000	0.000	0.000	0.000	0.000	0.000
AR(1) (p-value)	0.000	0.000	0.000	0.000	0.000	0.000
AR(2) (p-value)	0.909	0.942	0.843	0.910	0.386	0.108
Hansen (p-value)	0.203	0.855	0.937	0.965	0.908	0.619
No. of instruments	126	155	165	168	159	142
No. of observations	1096	1096	979	864	745	622
No. of regions	126	126	126	126	126	126

Notes: Standard errors are corrected using the approach by Windmeijer (2005); z-statistics are listed in parentheses. All variables are assumed to be endogenous. We instrument the endogenous variables with both its lags and its differenced lags restricting the laglimit to four. Calculations are done with *xtabond2* by Roodman (2009a).
significant at 10%; ** significant at 5%; *** significant at 1%; constant and time dummies are not shown.

Table 3.6: Regression results using the Driscoll and Kraay estimator (Obj. 1)

	(1)	(2)	(3)	(4)	(5)	(6)
Ln real GDP p.c. (t-1)	-0.172**	-0.175**	-0.217**	-0.275**	-0.385***	-0.619***
	(-2.843)	(-2.934)	(-2.778)	(-2.708)	(-3.388)	(-10.96)
Ln investment (t-1)	0.00258	0.00316	0.00141	0.00806	-0.00935	0.00239
	(0.551)	(0.691)	(0.231)	(1.264)	(-1.492)	(0.236)
Ln pop. growth +0.05 (t-1)	-0.0620*	-0.0586*	-0.0726*	-0.0760**	-0.0563*	-0.0877***
	(-2.278)	(-2.000)	(-2.577)	(-3.029)	(-2.467)	(-5.544)
Ln innovation (t-1)	-0.00148	-0.00162	-0.000825	0.000367	0.00320	0.00351
	(-0.593)	(-0.670)	(-0.307)	(0.145)	(1.099)	(1.171)
Ln Objective 1 p.c. (t-1)		0.00344***	0.00239*	0.00183*	0.00220	-0.000953
		(4.410)	(2.488)	(2.003)	(1.484)	(-1.023)
Ln Objective 1 p.c. (t-2)			0.000967	-0.000995	-0.000895	0.000937
			(0.396)	(-0.432)	(-0.334)	(0.601)
Ln Objective 1 p.c. (t-3)				0.00510***	0.00363***	0.00321*
				(3.455)	(4.019)	(2.354)
Ln Objective 1 p.c. (t-4)					-0.000941	-0.000533
					(-1.219)	(-0.564)
Ln Objective 1 p.c. (t-5)						0.00356*
						(1.989)
Obj. 1 joint sign. (size)			0.00336**	0.00593***	0.00400***	0.00622**
Obj. 1 joint sign. (p-value)			0.0483	5.76e-07	0.000494	0.0397
Obj. 1 long-term elast. (size)		0.0196**	0.0155	0.0216*	0.0104**	0.0101*
Obj. 1 long-term elast. (p-value)		0.0334	0.179	0.0509	0.0196	0.0553
WT time dummies (p-value)	0.000	0.000	0.000	0.000	0.000	0.000
Wooldridge AR(1) (p-value)	0.000	0.000	0.000	0.000	0.000	0.000
No. of observations	1096	1096	979	864	745	622
No. of regions	126	126	126	126	126	126

Notes: Standard errors are adjusted according to Driscoll and Kraay (1998), t-statistics are reported in parentheses; * significant at 10%; ** significant at 5%; *** significant at 1%; constant and time dummies are not shown.

Table 3.7: Regression results using the two-step system GMM estimator (Obj. 1)

	(1)	(2)	(3)	(4)	(5)
Ln real GDP p.c. (t-1)	-0.00728	-0.00633	-0.0176	-0.0381*	-0.0446*
	(-0.528)	(-0.464)	(-1.177)	(-2.355)	(-2.445)
Ln investment (t-1)	-0.0146**	-0.0155**	-0.00598	-0.0192	-0.0270
	(-2.697)	(-2.828)	(-0.870)	(-1.402)	(-1.674)
Ln pop. growth + 0.05 (t-1)	0.00989	0.0126	0.0252	0.0372*	0.0261
	(0.619)	(0.829)	(1.735)	(2.239)	(1.474)
Ln innovation (t-1)	0.00582***	0.00583***	0.00870***	0.00835***	0.00724**
	(3.685)	(3.737)	(5.131)	(4.115)	(2.774)
Ln Objective 1 p.c. (t-1)	0.00338**	0.00923***	0.00999***	0.0112***	0.0109***
	(2.584)	(4.621)	(3.767)	(4.231)	(3.734)
Ln Objective 1 p.c. (t-2)		-0.00614**	-0.00726**	-0.00605*	-0.00547
		(-2.695)	(-2.905)	(-2.278)	(-1.901)
Ln Objective 1 p.c. (t-3)			0.00122	0.00382	0.00420
			(0.570)	(1.379)	(1.265)
Ln Objective 1 p.c. (t-4)				-0.00622*	-0.00560
				(-2.089)	(-1.820)
Ln Objective 1 p.c. (t-5)					-0.00181
					(-0.755)
Obj. 1 joint sign. (size)		0.00309**	0.00395***	0.00278*	0.00226
Obj. 1 joint sign. (p-value)		0.0174	0.00171	0.0826	0.171
Obj. 1 long-term elast. (size)	0.465	0.488	0.224	0.0729**	0.0506**
Obj. 1 long-term elast. (p-value)	0.597	0.642	0.239	0.0185	0.0145
WT time dummies (p-value)	0.000	0.000	0.000	0.000	0.000
AR(1) (p-value)	0.000	0.000	0.000	0.000	0.000
AR(2) (p-value)	0.977	0.801	0.867	0.322	0.101
Hansen (p-value)	0.840	0.950	0.957	0.878	0.587
No. of instruments	155	165	168	159	142
No. of observations	1096	979	864	745	622
No. of regions	126	126	126	126	126

Notes: Standard errors are corrected using the approach by Windmeijer (2005); z-statistics are listed in parentheses. All variables are assumed to be endogenous. We instrument the endogenous variables with both its lags and its differenced lags restricting the laglimit to four. Calculations are done with *xtabond2* by Roodman (2009a).
* significant at 10%; ** significant at 5%; *** significant at 1%; constant and time dummies are not shown.

Table 3.8: Regression results using a spatial panel lag model (Obj. 1+2+3)

	(1)	(2)	(3)	(4)	(5)	(6)
Ln real GDP p.c. (t-1)	-0.1289***	-0.1277***	-0.1605***	-0.1947***	-0.2847***	-0.4264***
	(-9.6975)	(-9.6225)	(-10.7945)	(-11.5305)	(-14.428)	(-18.6113)
Ln investment (t-1)	0.0026	0.0029	0.0029	0.0069*	-0.011**	-0.0048
	(0.8936)	(0.9945)	(0.8979)	(1.8415)	(-2.0065)	(-0.7781)
Ln pop. growth + 0.05 (t-1)	-0.0351***	-0.0351***	-0.0403***	-0.0439***	-0.0306***	-0.0438***
	(-3.1184)	(-3.122)	(-3.3369)	(-3.3799)	(-2.2007)	(-2.9398)
Ln innovation (t-1)	-0.0002	-0.0002	0.0004	-0.0009	0.0010	0.0009
	(-0.1656)	(-0.1474)	(0.241)	(-0.4411)	(0.4981)	(0.4122)
Ln Objectives 1+2+3 p.c. (t-1)		0.0012	0.0015	0.0009	0.0021**	0.0018
		(1.4262)	(1.6303)	(0.9098)	(1.9972)	(1.5889)
Ln Objectives 1+2+3 p.c. (t-2)			-0.0004	-0.0008	-0.0014	0.0007
			(-0.5082)	(-0.8674)	(-1.388)	(0.6106)
Ln Objectives 1+2+3 p.c. (t-3)				-0.0003	0.0010	0.0013
				(-0.317)	(1.018)	(1.1641)
Ln Objectives 1+2+3 p.c. (t-4)					-0.0032***	-0.0042***
					(-3.3454)	(-3.8627)
Ln Objectives 1+2+3 p.c. (t-5)						-0.0022***
						(-2.3032)
ρ	0.589***	0.602***	0.594***	0.572***	0.55***	0.458***
	(17.3193)	(18.1349)	(17.1872)	(15.4772)	(14.1377)	(10.9579)
Obj. 1+2+3 joint sign. (size)			0.0011	-0.0002	-0.0015	-0.0027
Obj. 1+2+3 joint sign. (p-value)			0.3595	0.9075	0.4259	0.2738
Obj. 1+2+3 long-term elast. (size)		0.0091	0.0066	-0.0009	-0.0054	-0.0062**
Obj. 1+2+3 long-term elast. (p-value)		0.1601	0.2528	0.8596	0.1475	0.0163
LR-test spatial effects (size)	407.17***	409.26***	429.49***	424.70***	486.15***	582.92***
LR-test spatial effects (p-value)	0.000	0.000	0.000	0.000	0.000	0.000
R-squared	0.6009	0.6024	0.6259	0.6412	0.6844	0.7359
No. of regions	126	126	126	126	126	126
No. of observations	1260	1260	1134	1008	882	756

Notes: Calculations are done with the Matlab routine *sar_panel_FE* by Elhorst (2010); t-statistics are reported parentheses; * significant at 10%; ** significant at 5%; *** significant at 1%; constant and time dummies are not shown.

Table 3.9: Regression results using a spatial panel lag model (Obj. 1)

	(1)	(2)	(3)	(4)	(5)
Ln real GDP p.c. (t-1)	-0.1323***	-0.1657***	-0.2017***	-0.2833***	-0.4208***
	(-10.0031)	(-11.1457)	(-11.9946)	(-14.3143)	(-18.2267)
Ln investment (t-1)	0.0033	0.0033	0.0077**	-0.0083	-0.0018
	(1.1082)	(1.0221)	(2.0658)	(-1.5069)	(-0.2829)
Ln pop. growth + 0.05 (t-1)	-0.0327***	-0.0393***	-0.0463***	-0.0385***	-0.0551***
	(-2.9177)	(-3.2727)	(-3.6034)	(-2.7882)	(-3.7066)
Ln innovation (t-1)	-0.0003	0.0002	-0.0005	0.0014	0.0013
	(-0.2594)	(0.1408)	(-0.2472)	(0.6632)	(0.6136)
Ln Objective 1 p.c. (t-1)	0.0033***	0.0022**	0.0013	0.0019	0.0012
	(3.5301)	(2.1125)	(1.1618)	(1.6105)	(0.951)
Ln Objective 1 p.c. (t-2)		0.0015	0.0003	0.0005	0.0015
		(1.3834)	(0.2909)	(0.424)	(1.2867)
Ln Objective 1 p.c. (t-3)			0.0037***	0.0027**	0.0026**
			(3.1124)	(2.2505)	(2.1305)
Ln Objective 1 p.c. (t-4)				-0.0019	-0.0028***
				(-1.4603)	(-2.1379)
Ln Objective 1 p.c. (t-5)					0.0001
					(0.1118)
ρ	0.596***	0.597***	0.583***	0.562***	0.469***
	(17.7591)	(17.3282)	(16.0977)	(14.6175)	(11.3563)
Obj. 1 joint sign. (size)		0.0037***	0.0053***	0.0031	0.0026
Obj. 1 joint sign. (p-value)		0.0025	0.0005	0.1094	0.2609
Obj. 1 long-term elast. (size)	0.0251***	0.0223***	0.0263***	0.0109***	0.0061**
Obj. 1 long-term elast. (p-value)	0.0006	0.0007	0.000	0.0089	0.0357
LR-test spatial effects (size)	414.21***	435.85***	438.11***	479.05***	571.58***
LR-test spatial effects (p-value)	0.000	0.000	0.000	0.000	0.000
R-squared	0.6053	0.6283	0.6465	0.6833	0.7321
No. of regions	126	126	126	126	126
No. of observations	1260	1134	1008	882	756

Notes: Calculations are done with the Matlab routine *sar_panel_FE* by Elhorst (2010); t-statistics are reported parentheses; * significant at 10%; ** significant at 5%; *** significant at 1%; constant and time dummies are not shown.

3.7.3 Additional Robustness Tests

Using Structural Funds Per GDP Instead of Structural Funds Per Capita

As mentioned in footnote 7 of the paper, the main argument against using structural funds payments per GDP is that simultaneity problems may bias the results, as GDP (growth) appears on both sides of the regression equation. As the use of structural funds payments per GDP is widespread in the literature (for example Ederveen, de Groot and Nahuis, 2006; Dall'erba and Le Gallo, 2008), we re-run our estimations using structural funds payments per GDP (see Tables 3.10–3.13). Our results indicate no clear-cut results for the total sum of Obj. 1+2+3 payments. By contrast, Objective 1 payments, in particular, do promote regional growth. Furthermore, we find that time lags substantially affect the results. As a consequence, we conclude that the operationalisation of the structural funds variable (per capita versus per GDP) does not substantially affect the results.

Alternative Approaches to Control for Serial Correlation

As indicated in footnote 9 we used two additional alternative approaches to control for serial correlation. First, we estimated standard errors, which are robust not only to heteroskedasticity but also to first-order autocorrelation using the approach proposed by Newey and West (1987). The results displayed in Tables 3.14–3.15 show that the t-statistics of most coefficients are slightly increased and that the p-values of the short- and long-term elasticities are increased. Second, we also used the Prais-Winsten transformation matrix to transform the AR(1) disturbances in the error term into serially uncorrelated classical errors (Tables 3.16–3.17). Overall, the size and the significance levels remain very similar to those of the previous specifications.

Excluding the Investment Variable

As mentioned in Section 5.1 the selection of *appropriate control variables* plays a decisive role. In the main text we mention that the investment variable might be a "bad control" variable (Angrist and Pischke, 2009), since structural funds payments may stimulate growth through the channel "investment" (leading to a higher steady-state capital stock per capita), so that the inclusion of the investment variable might render it impossible to evaluate the investment increasing effect of structural funds payments on growth.

Tables 3.18–3.21 display the estimation results excluding the investment variable. However, our main conclusions regarding the effectiveness of the single Objectives do not differ.

Focus on Objective 2 and 3 Payments

Apart form the focus on Objective 1 payments, we additionally investigated the impact of Objective 2 and Objective 3 payments separately. The results show that Objective 2 payments have a negative but not statistically significant short- and long-term impact on the regional growth rates (Tables 3.22–3.23). Moreover, we find evidence that both short- and long-term elasticity of Objective 3 payments have in most cases negative coefficients which are statistically different from zero (Tables 3.24–3.25).

Spatial Panel Analyses

In order to guarantee replicability, Table 3.26 reports the centroids of the NUTS regions which are used to calculate the weight matrix. They are calculated using the Matlab toolbox "Arc_Mat" (LeSage and Pace, 2004) and they are converted to lattitude and longitude coordinates. Note that negative longitude values imply that the centroid of the region is located West of the Meridian (Greenwich) Line.

Moreover, as indicated in footnote 13, we estimated our specification using a spatial panel error model (Elhorst, 2010). The reported results in Table 3.27–3.28 make clear that the coefficient measuring spatial spillover effects (λ) is highly significant irrespective of which Objective and lag length are analysed. Furthermore, the estimation results do not differ substantially from the spatial panel lag model, which, in turn, strengthens our main findings.

Conclusions

In summary, these sensitivity analyses again confirm the main results of our paper. We find clear evidence that Objective 1 payments have a positive and significant impact on the regional growth rates in the EU-14. By contrast, there are no clear-cut results for the sum of Objective 1+2+3 payments.

Tables of the Additional Robustness Tests

Table 3.10: Regression results using the Driscoll and Kraay estimator (Obj. 1+2+3 per GDP)

	(1)	(2)	(3)	(4)	(5)	(6)
Ln real GDP p.c. (t-1)	-0.176**	-0.177**	-0.237***	-0.281**	-0.370***	-0.574***
	(-2.273)	(-2.254)	(-2.627)	(-2.285)	(-2.774)	(-5.744)
Ln investment (t-1)	0.00308	0.00356	0.00619	0.0140*	0.0257**	0.0439**
	(0.489)	(0.541)	(0.874)	(1.819)	(2.156)	(2.248)
Ln pop. growth + 0.05 (t-1)	-0.0130	-0.0123	-0.0133	-0.0226	-0.0276**	-0.0340**
	(-0.538)	(-0.487)	(-0.629)	(-1.193)	(-2.211)	(-2.301)
Ln innovation (t-1)	0.00137	0.00153*	0.00161	0.000646	0.00283**	0.00254
	(1.469)	(1.662)	(1.285)	(0.426)	(2.163)	(1.103)
Ln Objectives 1+2+3 per GDP (t-1)		0.000263	0.000308	7.11e-05	0.000212	0.000435
		(0.794)	(0.797)	(0.159)	(0.396)	(0.769)
Ln Objectives 1+2+3 per GDP (t-2)			0.000772*	0.000848*	0.000708	0.00126**
			(1.759)	(1.745)	(1.056)	(2.128)
Ln Objectives 1+2+3 per GDP (t-3)				-0.000460	7.99e-06	-0.000605*
				(-1.089)	(0.0202)	(-1.802)
Ln Objectives 1+2+3 per GDP (t-4)					-0.000242	-0.000778
					(-0.869)	(-1.552)
Ln Objectives 1+2+3 per GDP (t-5)						-0.000770
						(-1.527)
Obj. 1+2+3 joint sign. (size)			0.00108*	0.000459	0.000686	-0.000463
Obj. 1+2+3 joint sign. (p-value)			0.0807	0.645	0.473	0.369
Obj. 1+2+3 long-term elast. (size)		0.00149**	0.00456***	0.00164**	0.00185***	-0.000806***
Obj. 1+2+3 long-term elast. (p-value)		0.0259	0.00972	0.0241	0.00641	6.83e-08
WT time dummies (p-value)	0.000	0.000	0.000	0.000	0.000	0.000
No. of observations	1062	1062	943	826	705	584
No. of regions	124	124	124	124	124	124

Notes: Standard errors are adjusted according to Driscoll and Kraay (1998), t-statistics are reported in parentheses; * significant at 10%; ** significant at 5%; *** significant at 1%; constant and time dummies are not shown.

Table 3.11: Regression results using the two-step system GMM estimator (Obj. 1+2+3 per GDP)

	(1)	(2)	(3)	(4)	(5)	(6)
Ln real GDP p.c. (t-1)	-0.00506	-0.0209	-0.0112	-0.0174	-0.0185	-0.0180
	(-0.279)	(-1.583)	(-0.840)	(-1.073)	(-1.088)	(-0.846)
Ln investment (t-1)	-0.00330	-0.00386	-0.00285	0.00453	0.0103	0.0156
	(-1.088)	(-1.192)	(-0.669)	(0.773)	(0.730)	(0.923)
Ln pop. growth + 0.05 (t-1)	0.00931	0.0134	0.00973	0.00664	0.00194	-0.00648
	(1.016)	(1.522)	(1.137)	(0.737)	(0.183)	(-0.500)
Ln innovation (t-1)	-0.00105	0.000178	-0.000161	0.000313	0.000248	0.000368
	(-0.501)	(0.128)	(-0.101)	(0.190)	(0.119)	(0.149)
Ln Objectives 1+2+3 per GDP (t-1)		-0.000401	-0.000608	-0.000363	-0.000243	-0.000344
		(-0.808)	(-1.336)	(-0.780)	(-0.445)	(-0.586)
Ln Objectives 1+2+3 per GDP (t-2)			0.000682***	0.000458	0.000411	0.000607
			(2.622)	(1.496)	(0.957)	(1.291)
Ln Objectives 1+2+3 per GDP (t-3)				-0.000932***	-0.000855**	-0.000707
				(-2.938)	(-2.239)	(-1.431)
Ln Objectives 1+2+3 per GDP (t-4)					-0.000531	-0.000680
					(-1.094)	(-1.041)
Ln Objectives 1+2+3 per GDP (t-5)						-0.000281
						(-0.494)
Obj. 1+2+3 joint sign. (size)			7.45e-05	-0.000837	-0.00122*	-0.00140
Obj. 1+2+3 joint sign. (p-value)			0.885	0.230	0.0915	0.173
Obj. 1+2+3 long-term elast. (size)		-0.0192	0.00662	-0.0482	-0.0659	-0.0779
Obj. 1+2+3 long-term elast. (p-value)		0.113	0.401	0.283	0.277	0.398
WT time dummies (p-value)	0.000	0.000	0.000	0.000	0.000	0.000
AR(1) (p-value)	3.54e-09	5.38e-09	3.22e-08	9.94e-08	1.10e-06	5.45e-07
AR(2) (p-value)	0.0870	0.129	0.105	0.306	0.159	0.0989
Hansen (p-value)	0.0174	0.298	0.300	0.211	0.111	0.0461
No. of instruments	94	128	128	123	112	98
No. of observations	1062	1062	943	826	705	584
No. of regions	124	124	124	124	124	124

Notes: Standard errors are corrected using the approach by Windmeijer (2005); z-statistics are listed in parentheses; Endogenous variables are real GDP p.c., investment and Obj. 1+2+3, while all other variables are assumed to be exogenous. We instrument the endogenous variables with both its lags and its differenced lags restricting the laglimit to seven in order to prevent that the number of instruments exceeds the number of regions. Calculations are done with *xtabond2* by Roodman (2009a). * significant at 10%; ** significant at 5%; *** significant at 1%; constant and time dummies are not shown.

Table 3.12: Regression results using the Driscoll and Kraay estimator (Obj. 1 per GDP)

	(1)	(2)	(3)	(4)	(5)
Ln real GDP p.c. (t-1)	-0.179**	-0.232***	-0.280**	-0.366***	-0.553***
	(-2.360)	(-2.664)	(-2.434)	(-2.927)	(-5.110)
Ln investment (t-1)	0.00367	0.00564	0.0147**	0.0263**	0.0438***
	(0.599)	(0.841)	(2.150)	(2.598)	(2.650)
Ln pop. growth + 0.05 (t-1)	-0.00703	-0.0180	-0.0262	-0.0305	-0.0437*
	(-0.280)	(-0.764)	(-1.163)	(-1.514)	(-1.730)
Ln innovation (t-1)	0.00149	0.00159	0.00124	0.00325***	0.00335*
	(1.579)	(1.265)	(0.854)	(2.788)	(1.837)
Ln Objective 1 per GDP (t-1)	0.000875**	8.44e-05	-0.000262	-5.51e-05	-0.000119
	(2.296)	(0.243)	(-0.539)	(-0.123)	(-0.239)
Ln Objective 1 per GDP (t-2)		0.00113	-4.76e-05	-0.000349	0.000246
		(1.580)	(-0.0840)	(-0.399)	(0.291)
Ln Objective 1 per GDP (t-3)			0.00255***	0.00201***	0.00136***
			(3.252)	(2.620)	(2.673)
Ln Objective 1 per GDP (t-4)				0.000459	4.94e-05
				(1.034)	(0.118)
Ln Objective 1 per GDP (t-5)					0.000712**
					(2.302)
Obj. 1 joint sign. (size)		0.00122**	0.00224***	0.00207***	0.00225***
Obj. 1 joint sign. (p-value)		0.0177	3.48e-07	0.000	0.000921
Obj. 1 long-term elast. (size)	0.00489**	0.00525***	0.00801***	0.00564***	0.00407***
Obj. 1 long-term elast. (p-value)	0.0199	0.00876	0.0164	0.00408	1.20e-06
WT time dummies (p-value)	0.000	0.000	0.000	0.000	0.000
No. of observations	1062	943	826	705	584
No. of regions	124	124	124	124	124

Notes: Standard errors are adjusted according to Driscoll and Kraay (1998); t-statistics are reported in parentheses; * significant at 10%; ** significant at 5%; *** significant at 1%; constant and time dummies are not shown.

Table 3.13: Regression results using the two-step system GMM estimator (Obj. 1 per GDP)

	(1)	(2)	(3)	(4)	(5)
Ln real GDP p.c. (t-1)	-0.0216	-0.0226	-0.0186	-0.0393**	-0.0397*
	(-1.199)	(-1.154)	(-0.914)	(-2.058)	(-1.782)
Ln investment (t-1)	-0.00731	-0.00688	-0.000565	0.00196	0.00754
	(-1.495)	(-1.328)	(-0.0816)	(0.104)	(0.370)
Ln pop. growth + 0.05 (t-1)	0.0314***	0.0330**	0.0271**	0.0342**	0.0273*
	(2.976)	(2.568)	(2.098)	(2.359)	(1.890)
Ln innovation (t-1)	0.00543**	0.00534*	0.00621**	0.00525**	0.00420
	(2.140)	(1.770)	(2.282)	(2.107)	(1.202)
Ln Objective 1 per GDP (t-1)	0.00120*	0.00215***	0.00166**	0.00263***	0.00247**
	(1.920)	(2.590)	(2.523)	(2.596)	(2.292)
Ln Objective 1 per GDP (t-2)		-0.000991	-0.00117*	-0.00187**	-0.00170**
		(-1.594)	(-1.856)	(-2.322)	(-2.121)
Ln Objective 1 per GDP (t-3)			0.000768	0.00165	0.00174
			(1.605)	(1.457)	(1.610)
Ln Objective 1 per GDP (t-4)				-0.00189	-0.00130
				(-1.298)	(-0.795)
Ln Objective 1 per GDP (t-5)					-0.00116
					(-1.593)
Obj. 1 joint sign. (size)		0.00116*	0.00126*	0.000525	5.09e-05
Obj. 1 joint sign. (p-value)		0.0800	0.0829	0.326	0.919
Obj. 1 long-term elast. (size)	0.0554	0.0511	0.0675	0.0134**	0.00128**
Obj. 1 long-term elast. (p-value)	0.231	0.249	0.361	0.0396	0.0747
WT time dummies (p-value)	0.000	0.000	0.000	0.000	0.000
AR(1) (p-value)	3.19e-09	4.28e-09	9.95e-09	1.39e-07	2.15e-07
AR(2) (p-value)	0.134	0.118	0.298	0.0751	0.0233
Hansen (p-value)	0.196	0.226	0.205	0.102	0.0460
No. of instruments	122	123	120	110	97
No. of observations	1062	943	826	705	584
No. of regions	124	124	124	124	124

Notes: Standard errors are corrected using the approach by Windmeijer (2005); z-statistics are listed in parentheses; Endogenous variables are real GDP p.c., investment and Obj. 1, while all other variables are assumed to be exogenous. We instrument the endogenous variables with both its lags and its differenced lags restricting the laglimit to seven in order to prevent that the number of instruments exceeds the number of regions. Calculations are done with *xtabond2* by Roodman (2009a). * significant at 10%; ** significant at 5%; *** significant at 1%; constant and time dummies are not shown.

Table 3.14: Regression results using the Newey and West estimator (Obj. 1+2+3)

	(1)	(2)	(3)	(4)	(5)	(6)
Ln real GDP p.c. (t-1)	-0.172***	-0.171***	-0.211***	-0.266***	-0.380***	-0.609***
	(-5.900)	(-5.891)	(-5.978)	(-5.977)	(-7.803)	(-14.15)
Ln investment (t-1)	0.00258	0.00335	0.00113	0.00771	-0.0110	0.000119
	(0.521)	(0.669)	(0.199)	(1.267)	(-1.084)	(0.0105)
Ln pop. growth +0.05 (t-1)	-0.0620***	-0.0638***	-0.0735***	-0.0745***	-0.0483**	-0.0797***
	(-4.488)	(-4.536)	(-4.653)	(-4.228)	(-2.653)	(-3.937)
Ln innovation (t-1)	-0.00148	-0.00152	-0.000648	8.56e-05	0.00260	0.00321
	(-0.830)	(-0.842)	(-0.281)	(0.0234)	(0.583)	(0.707)
Ln Objective 1+2+3 p.c. (t-1)		0.00209	0.00262	0.00248	0.00385*	0.00242
		(1.520)	(1.835)	(1.581)	(2.193)	(1.394)
Ln Objective 1+2+3 p.c. (t-2)			-0.00178	-0.00212	-0.00277	0.00162
			(-1.251)	(-1.291)	(-1.702)	(0.889)
Ln Objective 1+2+3 p.c. (t-3)				-0.000680	0.000620	0.00130
				(-0.417)	(0.321)	(0.897)
Ln Objective 1+2+3 p.c. (t-4)					-0.00346*	-0.00351*
					(-2.269)	(-2.181)
Ln Objective 1+2+3 p.c. (t-5)						-0.000993
						(-0.651)
Obj. 1+2+3 joint sign. (size)			0.000838	-0.000324	-0.00177	0.000842
Obj. 1+2+3 joint sign. (p-value)			0.695	0.911	0.585	0.837
Obj. 1+2+3 long-term elast. (size)		0.0123	0.00397	-0.00122	-0.00465	0.00138
Obj. 1+2+3 long-term elast. (p-value)		0.147	0.700	0.910	0.579	0.837
WT time dummies (p-value)	0.000	0.000	0.000	0.000	2.47e-06	0.000
WT region dummies (p-value)	0.000	0.000	0.000	0.000	0.000	0.000
No. of regions	126	126	126	126	126	126
No. of observations	1096	1096	979	864	745	622

Notes: Serially adjusted standard errors according to Newey and West (1987); t-statistics are reported in parentheses; * significant at 10%; ** significant at 5%; *** significant at 1%; constant, region and time dummies are not shown.

Table 3.15: Regression results using the Newey and West estimator (Obj. 1)

	(1)	(2)	(3)	(4)	(5)
Ln real GDP p.c. (t-1)	-0.175***	-0.217***	-0.275***	-0.385***	-0.619***
	(-6.035)	(-6.256)	(-6.528)	(-8.327)	(-14.19)
Ln investment (t-1)	0.00316	0.00141	0.00806	-0.00935	0.00239
	(0.632)	(0.251)	(1.368)	(-0.948)	(0.213)
Ln pop. growth +0.05 (t-1)	-0.0586***	-0.0726***	-0.0760***	-0.0563**	-0.0877***
	(-4.294)	(-4.791)	(-4.569)	(-3.187)	(-4.430)
Ln innovation (t-1)	-0.00162	-0.000825	0.000367	0.00320	0.00351
	(-0.894)	(-0.356)	(0.102)	(0.749)	(0.813)
Ln Objective 1 p.c. (t-1)	0.00344	0.00239	0.00183	0.00220	-0.000953
	(1.923)	(1.411)	(1.001)	(1.239)	(-0.626)
Ln Objective 1 p.c. (t-2)		0.000967	-0.000995	-0.000895	0.000937
		(0.459)	(-0.493)	(-0.435)	(0.468)
Ln Objective 1 p.c. (t-3)			0.00510*	0.00363	0.00321*
			(2.001)	(1.341)	(2.071)
Ln Objective 1 p.c. (t-4)				-0.000941	-0.000533
				(-0.350)	(-0.214)
Ln Objective 1 p.c. (t-5)					0.00356
					(1.749)
Obj. 1 joint sign. (size)		0.00336	0.00593**	0.00400	0.00622**
Obj. 1 joint sign. (p-value)		0.140	0.0253	0.242	0.0945
Obj. 1 long-term elast. (size)	0.0196*	0.0155	0.0216**	0.0104	0.0101*
Obj. 1 long-term elast. (p-value)	0.0541	0.153	0.0385	0.255	0.0844
WT time dummies (p-value)	0.000	0.000	0.000	0.000	0.000
WT region dummies (p-value)	0.000	0.000	0.000	0.000	0.000
Wooldridge AR(1) (p-value)	0.000	0.000	0.000	0.000	0.000
No. of regions	126	126	126	126	126
No. of observations	1096	979	864	745	622

Notes: Serially adjusted standard errors according to Newey and West (1987); t-statistics are reported in parentheses; * significant at 10%; ** significant at 5%; *** significant at 1%; constant, region and time dummies are not shown.

Table 3.16: Regression results using the Prais-Winsten estimator (Obj. 1+2+3)

	(1)	(2)	(3)	(4)	(5)	(6)
Ln real GDP p.c. (t-1)	-0.177***	-0.175***	-0.212***	-0.256***	-0.363***	-0.643***
	(-6.149)	(-6.155)	(-6.111)	(-5.648)	(-6.243)	(-15.39)
Ln investment (t-1)	0.00252	0.00329	0.00109	0.00808	-0.00912	0.000613
	(0.503)	(0.658)	(0.193)	(1.275)	(-0.821)	(0.0570)
Ln pop. growth +0.05 (t-1)	-0.0611***	-0.0629***	-0.0734***	-0.0748***	-0.0490**	-0.0838***
	(-4.609)	(-4.680)	(-4.955)	(-4.450)	(-2.599)	(-4.255)
Ln innovation (t-1)	-0.00146	-0.00150	-0.000652	0.000177	0.00283	0.00292
	(-0.832)	(-0.844)	(-0.289)	(0.0485)	(0.636)	(0.676)
Ln Objective 1+2+3 p.c. (t-1)		0.00210	0.00262	0.00243	0.00370*	0.00233
		(1.584)	(1.755)	(1.509)	(2.082)	(1.308)
Ln Objective 1+2+3 p.c. (t-2)			-0.00178	-0.00206	-0.00250	0.00164
			(-1.262)	(-1.162)	(-1.431)	(0.849)
Ln Objective 1+2+3 p.c. (t-3)				-0.000821	0.000323	0.00134
				(-0.556)	(0.175)	(0.868)
Ln Objective 1+2+3 p.c. (t-4)					-0.00337*	-0.00351*
					(-2.089)	(-2.172)
Ln Objective 1+2+3 p.c. (t-5)						-0.000970
						(-0.634)
Obj. 1+2+3 joint sign. (size)			0.000839	-0.000449	-0.00185	0.000826
Obj. 1+2+3 joint sign. (p-value)			0.684	0.870	0.575	0.854
Obj. 1+2+3 long-term elast. (size)		0.0120	0.00396	-0.00176	-0.00510	0.00129
Obj. 1+2+3 long-term elast. (p-value)		0.121	0.687	0.870	0.567	0.853
WT time dummies (p-value)	0.000	0.000	0.000	0.000	0.000	0.000
WT region dummies (p-value)	0.000	0.000	0.000	0.000	0.000	0.000
Wooldridge AR(1) (p-value)	0.000	0.000	0.000	0.000	0.000	0.000
R-squared	0.502	0.504	0.537	0.574	0.647	0.723
Adj. R-squared	0.430	0.431	0.460	0.492	0.566	0.643
No. of regions	126	126	126	126	126	126
No. of observations	1096	1096	979	864	745	622

Notes: Serially adjusted standard errors according to the Prais-Winsten method, t-statistics are reported in parentheses; * significant at 10%; ** significant at 5%; *** significant at 1%; constant, region and time dummies are not shown.

Table 3.17: Regression results using the Prais-Winsten estimator (Obj. 1)

	(1)	(2)	(3)	(4)	(5)
Ln real GDP p.c. (t-1)	-0.179***	-0.217***	-0.265***	-0.367***	-0.652***
	(-6.224)	(-6.251)	(-6.139)	(-6.608)	(-15.68)
Ln investment (t-1)	0.00309	0.00142	0.00844	-0.00756	0.00295
	(0.620)	(0.251)	(1.377)	(-0.703)	(0.280)
Ln pop. growth +0.05 (t-1)	-0.0577***	-0.0726***	-0.0762***	-0.0564**	-0.0919***
	(-4.348)	(-5.055)	(-4.770)	(-3.115)	(-4.757)
Ln innovation (t-1)	-0.00161	-0.000825	0.000465	0.00354	0.00313
	(-0.897)	(-0.362)	(0.129)	(0.827)	(0.763)
Ln Objective 1 p.c. (t-1)	0.00344	0.00239	0.00180	0.00190	-0.000919
	(1.939)	(1.285)	(0.950)	(1.036)	(-0.580)
Ln Objective 1 p.c. (t-2)		0.000968	-0.00107	-0.000895	0.000982
		(0.451)	(-0.471)	(-0.414)	(0.487)
Ln Objective 1 p.c. (t-3)			0.00502*	0.00331	0.00316*
			(2.258)	(1.315)	(2.001)
Ln Objective 1 p.c. (t-4)				-0.000521	-0.000358
				(-0.181)	(-0.152)
Ln Objective 1 p.c. (t-5)					0.00345
					(1.606)
Obj. 1 joint sign. (size)		0.00336	0.00576**	0.00380	0.00631
Obj. 1 joint sign. (p-value)		0.139	0.0268	0.262	0.119
Obj. 1 long-term elast. (size)	0.0192**	0.0155	0.0217**	0.0104	0.00967
Obj. 1 long-term elast. (p-value)	0.0450	0.137	0.0352	0.281	0.108
WT time dummies (p-value)	0.000	0.000	0.000	0.000	0.000
WT region dummies (p-value)	0.000	0.000	0.000	0.000	0.000
Wooldridge AR(1) (p-value)	0.000	0.000	0.000	0.000	0.000
R-squared	0.506	0.537	0.576	0.643	0.723
Adj. R-squared	0.435	0.460	0.495	0.561	0.643
No. of regions	126	126	126	126	126
No. of observations	1096	979	864	745	622

Notes: Serially adjusted standard errors according to the Prais-Winsten method, t-statistics are reported in parentheses; * significant at 10%; ** significant at 5%; *** significant at 1%; constant, region and time dummies are not shown.

Table 3.18: Regression results using the Driscoll and Kraay estimator (Obj. 1+2+3), alternative specification

	(1)	(2)	(3)	(4)	(5)	(6)
Ln real GDP p.c. (t-1)	-0.145*	-0.144*	-0.177*	-0.229*	-0.318**	-0.536***
	(-2.492)	(-2.493)	(-2.366)	(-2.359)	(-2.972)	(-8.650)
Ln pop. growth +0.05 (t-1)	-0.0630*	-0.0632*	-0.0716**	-0.0680**	-0.0417*	-0.0490**
	(-2.539)	(-2.504)	(-2.711)	(-2.925)	(-2.518)	(-2.695)
Ln innovation (t-1)	0.000661	0.000728	0.00141	0.00250	0.00308	0.00246
	(0.326)	(0.357)	(0.692)	(1.014)	(0.881)	(0.709)
Ln Objective 1+2+3 p.c. (t-1)		0.000846	0.00166	0.00104	0.00272*	0.00118
		(0.781)	(1.496)	(0.868)	(2.517)	(0.914)
Ln Objective 1+2+3 p.c. (t-2)			-0.00211	-0.00241	-0.00319	-0.000117
			(-1.186)	(-1.312)	(-1.477)	(-0.140)
Ln Objective 1+2+3 p.c. (t-3)				-0.00130	0.000782	0.00200*
				(-0.809)	(1.468)	(2.321)
Ln Objective 1+2+3 p.c. (t-4)					-0.00338***	-0.00312*
					(-3.971)	(-2.474)
Ln Objective 1+2+3 p.c. (t-5)						-0.00169
						(-1.077)
Obj. 1+2+3 joint sign. (size)			-0.000451	-0.00267	-0.00307	-0.00175
Obj. 1+2+3 joint sign. (p-value)			0.801	0.258	0.127	0.614
Obj. 1+2+3 long-term elast. (size)		0.00585	-0.00254	-0.0117	-0.00965	-0.00327
Obj. 1+2+3 long-term elast. (p-value)		0.399	0.794	0.404	0.240	0.604
WT time dummies (p-value)	0.000	0.000	0.000	0.000	0.000	0.000
No. of observations	1194	1194	1073	951	828	702
No. of regions	127	127	127	127	127	127

Notes: Standard errors are adjusted according to Driscoll and Kraay (1998), t-statistics are reported in parentheses; * significant at 10%; ** significant at 5%; *** significant at 1%; constant and time dummies are not shown.

Table 3.19: Regression results using the two-step system GMM estimator (Obj. 1+2+3), alternative specification

	(1)	(2)	(3)	(4)	(5)	(6)
Ln real GDP p.c. (t-1)	-0.0225	-0.0310	-0.0342*	-0.0397*	-0.0753***	-0.0698**
	(-1.266)	(-1.725)	(-2.031)	(-2.475)	(-3.655)	(-2.789)
Ln pop. growth + 0.05 (t-1)	0.0114	0.0114	0.0145	0.0202	0.0333	0.0193
	(0.665)	(0.608)	(0.884)	(1.443)	(1.870)	(1.135)
Ln innovation (t-1)	0.00599*	0.00497	0.00613**	0.00756***	0.00882**	0.00769*
	(2.575)	(1.953)	(2.735)	(3.547)	(3.072)	(2.482)
Ln Objectives 1+2+3 p.c. (t-1)		-0.00308	0.00166	0.00403	0.00747*	0.00993**
		(-1.257)	(0.732)	(1.695)	(2.200)	(2.660)
Ln Objectives 1+2+3 p.c. (t-2)			-0.00326*	-0.00454**	-0.00717***	-0.00718***
			(-2.288)	(-2.786)	(-3.973)	(-3.477)
Ln Objectives 1+2+3 p.c. (t-3)				-0.00109	-0.00107	-0.000660
				(-0.743)	(-0.669)	(-0.327)
Ln Objectives 1+2+3 p.c. (t-4)					-0.00546**	-0.00815***
					(-2.817)	(-3.358)
Ln Objectives 1+2+3 p.c. (t-5)						-0.00243
						(-1.130)
Obj. 1+2+3 joint sign. (size)			-0.00160	-0.00159	-0.00622*	-0.00849**
Obj. 1+2+3 joint sign. (p-value)			0.497	0.547	0.0825	0.0398
Obj. 1+2+3 long-term elast. (size)		-0.0995*	-0.0468**	-0.0401**	-0.0827***	-0.122***
Obj. 1+2+3 long-term elast. (p-value)		0.0845	0.0422	0.0133	0.000257	0.00529
WT time dummies (p-value)	0.000	0.000	0.000	0.000	0.000	0.000
AR(1) (p-value)	0.000	0.000	0.000	0.000	0.000	0.000
AR(2) (p-value)	0.653	0.671	0.781	0.633	0.703	0.390
Hansen (p-value)	0.0189	0.221	0.394	0.532	0.346	0.111
No. of instruments	97	126	135	138	131	118
No. of observations	1194	1194	1073	951	828	702
No. of regions	127	127	127	127	127	127

Notes: Standard errors are corrected using the approach by Windmeijer (2005); z-statistics are listed in parentheses. All variables are assumed to be endogenous. We instrument the endogenous variables with both its lags and its differenced lags restricting the laglimit to four. Calculations are done with *xtabond2* by Roodman (2009a). * significant at 10%; ** significant at 5%; *** significant at 1%; constant and time dummies are not shown.

Table 3.20: Regression results using the Driscoll and Kraay estimator (Obj. 1), alternative specification

	(1)	(2)	(3)	(4)	(5)
Ln real GDP p.c. (t-1)	-0.148*	-0.182*	-0.236*	-0.324**	-0.545***
	(-2.561)	(-2.436)	(-2.467)	(-2.976)	(-7.916)
Ln pop. growth +0.05 (t-1)	-0.0606*	-0.0719**	-0.0738**	-0.0516**	-0.0546**
	(-2.350)	(-2.844)	(-3.334)	(-3.312)	(-3.079)
Ln innovation (t-1)	0.000626	0.00127	0.00261	0.00371	0.00312
	(0.313)	(0.619)	(1.099)	(1.101)	(0.845)
Ln Objective 1 p.c. (t-1)	0.00303***	0.00223**	0.00154*	0.00196	-0.000279
	(4.199)	(2.694)	(2.127)	(1.585)	(-0.384)
Ln Objective 1 p.c. (t-2)		0.000744	-0.000442	-0.000322	0.000652
		(0.398)	(-0.233)	(-0.151)	(0.459)
Ln Objective 1 p.c. (t-3)			0.00426**	0.00277**	0.00265*
			(3.078)	(2.761)	(2.219)
Ln Objective 1 p.c. (t-4)				-1.69e-05	0.000185
				(-0.0141)	(0.167)
Ln Objective 1 p.c. (t-5)					0.00219
					(1.192)
Obj. 1 joint sign. (size)		0.00298**	0.00536***	0.00439***	0.00540*
Obj. 1 joint sign. (p-value)		0.0345	3.79e-05	0.000199	0.0596
Obj. 1 long-term elast. (size)	0.0205**	0.0164	0.0227*	0.0136**	0.00991*
Obj. 1 long-term elast. (p-value)	0.0408	0.185	0.0731	0.0365	0.0793
WT Time dummies (p-value)	0.000	0.000	0.000	0.000	0.000
No. of observations	1194	1073	951	828	702
No. of regions	127	127	127	127	127

Notes: Standard errors are adjusted according to Driscoll and Kraay (1998), t-statistics are reported in parentheses; * significant at 10%; ** significant at 5%; *** significant at 1%; constant and time dummies are not shown.

Table 3.21: Regression results using the two-step system GMM estimator (Obj. 1), alternative specification

	(1)	(2)	(3)	(4)	(5)
Ln real GDP p.c. (t-1)	-0.0226	-0.0174	-0.0382*	-0.0542**	-0.0461*
	(-1.532)	(-1.169)	(-2.099)	(-2.986)	(-2.353)
Ln pop. growth + 0.05 (t-1)	0.0138	0.0131	0.0363*	0.0516**	0.0287
	(0.928)	(0.857)	(2.158)	(2.851)	(1.690)
Ln innovation (t-1)	0.00718**	0.00730***	0.0113***	0.0139***	0.0118***
	(3.055)	(3.553)	(4.996)	(5.146)	(4.548)
Ln Objective 1 p.c. (t-1)	0.00226	0.00521**	0.00520*	0.00794**	0.00848**
	(1.794)	(2.748)	(2.275)	(3.066)	(2.899)
Ln Objective 1 p.c. (t-2)		-0.00287	-0.00298	-0.00225	-0.00207
		(-1.725)	(-1.649)	(-0.992)	(-0.850)
Ln Objective 1 p.c. (t-3)			0.00173	0.00208	0.00282
			(0.887)	(0.829)	(0.899)
Ln Objective 1 p.c. (t-4)				-0.00407	-0.00437
				(-1.529)	(-1.640)
Ln Objective 1 p.c. (t-5)					-0.00233
					(-1.030)
Obj. 1 joint sign. (size)		0.00234*	0.00395***	0.00371*	0.00252
Obj. 1 joint sign. (p-value)		0.0671	0.00306	0.0541	0.200
Obj. 1 long-term elast. (size)	0.0998	0.134	0.104**	0.0684***	0.0547**
Obj. 1 long-term elast. (p-value)	0.126	0.242	0.0359	0.00283	0.0186
WT time dummies (p-value)	0.000	0.000	0.000	0.000	0.000
AR(1) (p-value)	0.000	0.000	0.000	0.000	0.000
AR(2) (p-value)	0.588	0.865	0.828	0.547	0.394
Hansen (p-value)	0.217	0.437	0.531	0.416	0.169
No. of instruments	126	135	138	131	118
No. of observations	1194	1073	951	828	702
No. of regions	127	127	127	127	127

Notes: Standard errors are corrected using the approach by Windmeijer (2005); z-statistics are listed in parentheses. All variables are assumed to be endogenous. We instrument the endogenous variables with both its lags and its differenced lags restricting the laglimit to four. Calculations are done with *xtabond2* by Roodman (2009a). * significant at 10%; ** significant at 5%; *** significant at 1%; constant and time dummies are not shown.

Table 3.22: Regression results using the Driscoll and Kraay estimator (Obj. 2)

	(1)	(2)	(3)	(4)	(5)
Ln real GDP p.c. (t-1)	-0.172**	-0.213**	-0.267*	-0.386**	-0.618***
	(-2.850)	(-2.686)	(-2.535)	(-3.315)	(-10.22)
Ln investment (t-1)	0.00252	0.000558	0.00714	-0.0115*	-0.00107
	(0.532)	(0.0893)	(1.173)	(-2.079)	(-0.132)
Ln pop. growth + 0.05 (t-1)	-0.0620*	-0.0742**	-0.0778**	-0.0528*	-0.0734***
	(-2.290)	(-2.819)	(-3.073)	(-2.452)	(-4.972)
Ln innovation (t-1)	-0.00148	-0.000653	0.000453	0.00334	0.00356
	(-0.594)	(-0.244)	(0.183)	(1.113)	(1.112)
Ln Objective 2 p.c. (t-1)	-0.000345	0.000263	-0.000137	0.00112	0.000468
	(-0.271)	(0.205)	(-0.100)	(0.857)	(0.295)
Ln Objective 2 p.c. (t-2)		-0.00169	-0.00155	-0.00143	0.000958
		(-0.992)	(-0.855)	(-0.679)	(0.620)
Ln Objective 2 p.c. (t-3)			-0.00334	-0.00161	7.93e-05
			(-1.750)	(-1.227)	(0.111)
Ln Objective 2 p.c. (t-4)				-0.00233*	-0.00226
				(-2.193)	(-0.994)
Ln Objective 2 p.c. (t-5)					-0.00299
					(-1.746)
Obj. 2 joint sign. (size)		-0.00142	-0.00503	-0.00425	-0.00374
Obj. 2 joint sign. (p-value)		0.529	0.163	0.192	0.218
Obj. 2 long-term elast. (size)	-0.00200	-0.00668	-0.0188	-0.0110	-0.00606
Obj. 2 long-term elast. (p-value)	0.794	0.535	0.321	0.298	0.203
WT time dummies (p-value)	0.000	0.000	0.000	0.000	0.000
No. of observations	1096	979	864	745	622
No. of regions	126	126	126	126	126

Notes: Standard errors are adjusted according to Driscoll and Kraay (1998), t-statistics are reported in parentheses; * significant at 10%; ** significant at 5%; *** significant at 1%; constant and time dummies are not shown.

Table 3.23: Regression results using the two-step system GMM estimator (Obj. 2)

	(1)	(2)	(3)	(4)	(5)
Ln real GDP p.c. (t-1)	-0.00687	-0.00763	-0.0128	-0.0229	-0.0284
	(-0.501)	(-0.624)	(-1.027)	(-1.844)	(-1.815)
Ln investment (t-1)	-0.00738	-0.00815	0.000258	-0.0145	-0.0242
	(-1.652)	(-1.939)	(0.0433)	(-1.236)	(-1.688)
Ln pop. growth + 0.05 (t-1)	-0.00644	-0.00652	0.000988	0.0119	0.00394
	(-0.398)	(-0.423)	(0.0658)	(0.889)	(0.271)
Ln innovation (t-1)	0.00301	0.00253	0.00485*	0.00598**	0.00486
	(1.716)	(1.389)	(2.370)	(2.738)	(1.783)
Ln Objective 2 p.c. (t-1)	-0.000128	0.00208	0.00335	0.00183	0.00233
	(-0.0841)	(1.191)	(1.726)	(0.871)	(0.978)
Ln Objective 2 p.c. (t-2)		-0.00264*	-0.00238	-0.00289*	-0.00197
		(-2.212)	(-1.902)	(-2.151)	(-1.079)
Ln Objective 2 p.c. (t-3)			-0.00254*	-0.00220	-0.00142
			(-2.385)	(-1.753)	(-0.963)
Ln Objective 2 p.c. (t-4)				-0.000654	-0.00206
				(-0.450)	(-1.088)
Ln Objective 2 p.c. (t-5)					-0.000155
					(-0.0931)
Obj. 2 joint sign. (size)		-0.000556	-0.00157	-0.00391	-0.00328
Obj. 2 joint sign. (p-value)		0.731	0.307	0.0154	0.0426
Obj. 2 long-term elast. (size)	-0.0187	-0.0729	-0.122	-0.171	-0.115
Obj. 2 long-term elast. (p-value)	0.616	0.533	0.304	0.0651	0.0695
WT time dummies (p-value)	0.000	0.000	0.000	0.000	0.000
AR(1) (p-value)	2.01e-09	1.55e-09	1.18e-08	2.97e-07	1.84e-09
AR(2) (p-value)	0.900	0.547	0.957	0.528	0.219
Hansen (p-value)	0.871	0.947	0.966	0.914	0.593
No. of instruments	155	165	168	159	142
No. of observations	1096	979	864	745	622
No. of regions	126	126	126	126	126

Notes: Standard errors are corrected using the approach by Windmeijer (2005); z-statistics are listed in parentheses. All variables are assumed to be endogenous. We instrument the endogenous variables with both its lags and its differenced lags restricting the laglimit to four. Calculations are done with *xtabond2* by Roodman (2009a).
significant at 10%; ** significant at 5%; *** significant at 1%; constant and time dummies are not shown.

Table 3.24: Regression results using the Driscoll and Kraay estimator (Obj. 3)

	(1)	(2)	(3)	(4)	(5)
Ln real GDP p.c. (t-1)	-0.185**	-0.232**	-0.292**	-0.405***	-0.632***
	(-3.093)	(-3.025)	(-2.884)	(-3.606)	(-13.32)
Ln investment (t-1)	0.00382	0.00254	0.00988	-0.00564	0.00725
	(0.785)	(0.401)	(1.702)	(-0.812)	(0.722)
Ln pop. growth +0.05 (t-1)	-0.0429	-0.0481*	-0.0483*	-0.0310	-0.0519***
	(-1.586)	(-2.218)	(-2.441)	(-1.663)	(-4.557)
Ln innovation (t-1)	-0.00162	-0.000975	0.000935	0.00356	0.00383
	(-0.638)	(-0.377)	(0.394)	(1.148)	(1.184)
Ln Objective 3 p.c. (t-1)	-0.00775***	-0.00360	-0.00299	-0.00235	-0.00469**
	(-4.658)	(-1.887)	(-1.782)	(-1.428)	(-3.257)
Ln Objective 3 p.c. (t-2)		-0.00986***	-0.00843***	-0.00706***	-0.00353
		(-3.584)	(-4.168)	(-3.544)	(-1.106)
Ln Objective 3 p.c. (t-3)			-0.00724**	-0.00293	-0.00669*
			(-2.804)	(-1.216)	(-2.393)
Ln Objective 3 p.c. (t-4)				-0.00641*	-0.00536**
				(-2.551)	(-3.074)
Ln Objective 3 p.c. (t-5)					-0.00729***
					(-7.567)
Obj. 3 joint sign. (size)		-0.0135	-0.0187	-0.0188	-0.0276
Obj. 3 joint sign. (p-value)		1.29e-06	5.53e-09	1.60e-08	0.000
Obj. 3 long-term elast. (size)	-0.0418	-0.0580	-0.0640	-0.0463	-0.0436
Obj. 3 long-term elast. (p-value)	4.78e-09	2.49e-06	0.000614	1.96e-08	0.000
WT Time dummies (p-value)	0.000	0.000	0.000	0.000	0.000
Wooldridge AR(1) (p-value)	0.000	0.000	0.000	0.000	0.000
No. of observations	1096	979	864	745	622
No. of regions	126	126	126	126	126

Notes: Standard errors are adjusted according to Driscoll and Kraay (1998), t-statistics are reported in parentheses; * significant at 10%; ** significant at 5%; *** significant at 1%; constant and time dummies are not shown.

Table 3.25: Regression results using the two-step system GMM estimator (Obj. 3)

	(1)	(2)	(3)	(4)	(5)
Ln real GDP p.c. (t-1)	0.0148	0.0273*	0.0305**	0.0248	0.0211
	(1.346)	(2.457)	(2.860)	(1.911)	(1.429)
Ln investment (t-1)	-0.00642	-0.00747	0.00565	-0.00139	-0.00530
	(-1.547)	(-1.864)	(1.080)	(-0.110)	(-0.340)
Ln pop. growth +0.05 (t-1)	0.0116	-0.00222	-0.00383	-0.00618	-0.00924
	(0.755)	(-0.184)	(-0.302)	(-0.485)	(-0.646)
Ln innovation (t-1)	0.00234	0.00111	0.00269	0.00315	0.00284
	(1.596)	(0.747)	(1.456)	(1.480)	(1.221)
Ln Objective 3 p.c. (t-1)	-0.0117***	0.00390	0.00730	0.00456	0.00818
	(-8.073)	(1.060)	(1.612)	(1.072)	(1.542)
Ln Objective 3 p.c. (t-2)		-0.0162***	-0.0172***	-0.0157***	-0.0209***
		(-4.763)	(-4.172)	(-4.520)	(-3.696)
Ln Objective 3 p.c. (t-3)			-0.00341	-0.00424	-0.00251
			(-1.122)	(-1.241)	(-0.819)
Ln Objective 3 p.c. (t-4)				0.00331	0.00157
				(1.331)	(0.421)
Ln Objective 3 p.c. (t-5)					0.00245
					(0.810)
Obj. 3 joint sign. (size)		-0.0123	-0.0133	-0.0120	-0.0112
Obj. 3 joint sign. (p-value)		0.000	0.000	9.02e-10	8.01e-07
Obj. 3 long-term elast. (size)	0.796	0.449	0.437	0.486	0.533
Obj. 3 long-term elast. (p-value)	0.178	0.0140	0.00423	0.0560	0.153
WT Time dummies (p-value)	0.000	0.000	0.000	0.000	0.000
AR(1) (p-value)	2.33e-09	2.35e-09	1.16e-08	3.30e-07	1.39e-09
AR(2) (p-value)	0.850	0.405	0.736	0.441	0.258
Hansen (p-value)	0.836	0.940	0.953	0.851	0.504
No. of instruments	155	164	166	156	139
No. of observations	1096	979	864	745	622
No. of regions	126	126	126	126	126

Notes: Standard errors are corrected using the approach by Windmeijer (2005); z-statistics are listed in parentheses. All variables are assumed to be endogenous. We instrument the endogenous variables with both its lags and its differenced lags restricting the laglimit to four. Calculations are done with *xtabond2* by Roodman (2009a).
significant at 10%; ** significant at 5%; *** significant at 1%; constant and time dummies are not shown.

Table 3.26: Latitudes and longitudes of the centroids of NUTS regions

NUTS code	latitude	longitude	NUTS code	latitude	longitude
be1	50° 50' 9.60"	4° 22' 13.78"	fr63	45° 46' 26.40"	1° 42' 50.76"
be2	51° 2' 16.80"	4° 14' 20.04"	fr71	45° 25' 55.20"	5° 20' 4.56"
be3	50° 18' 54.00"	5° 0' 30.96"	fr72	45° 39' 21.60"	3° 10' 37.20"
dk	55° 57' 36.00"	10° 2' 24.00"	fr81	43° 35' 38.40"	3° 13' 32.16"
de1	48° 32' 45.60"	9° 2' 48.12"	fr82	43° 57' 32.40"	6° 3' 37.80"
de2	48° 57' 3.60"	11° 25' 8.40"	fr83	42° 9' 7.20"	9° 6' 21.96"
de3	52° 30' 7.20"	13° 24' 0.00"	ie	53° 10' 30.00"	-8° 9' 12.24"
de4	52° 28' 22.80"	13° 23' 52.80"	itc1	45° 3' 25.20"	7° 55' 10.92"
de5	53° 11' 49.20"	8° 44' 45.24"	itc2	45° 43' 51.60"	7° 23' 9.96"
de6	53° 32' 42.00"	10° 1' 26.40"	itc3	44° 15' 57.60"	8° 42' 16.92"
de7	50° 36' 10.80"	9° 1' 52.68"	itc4	45° 37' 1.20"	9° 46' 9.84"
de8	53° 45' 7.20"	12° 32' 2.40"	itd1	46° 41' 49.20"	11° 24' 57.60"
de9	52° 46' 4.80"	9° 9' 40.68"	itd2	46° 8' 6.00"	11° 7' 15.60"
dea	51° 28' 48.00"	7° 33' 44.64"	itd3	45° 39' 7.20"	11° 52' 8.40"
deb	49° 54' 50.40"	7° 26' 55.68"	itd4	46° 9' 3.60"	13° 3' 21.60"
ded	51° 3' 7.20"	13° 20' 52.80"	itd5	44° 32' 9.60"	11° 1' 12.00"
dee	52° 0' 46.80"	11° 42' 3.60"	ite1	43° 27' 3.60"	11° 7' 33.60"
def	54° 10' 58.80"	9° 48' 57.60"	ite2	42° 57' 57.60"	12° 29' 24"
deg	50° 54' 14.40"	11° 1' 33.60"	ite3	43° 21' 54.00"	13° 6' 28.80"
gr11	41° 9' 46.80"	25° 8' 20.40"	ite4	41° 58' 30.00"	12° 46' 30"
gr12	40° 44' 34.80"	22° 57' 25.20"	itf1	42° 13' 40.80"	13° 51' 18"
gr13	40° 21' 43.20"	21° 29' 2.40"	itf2	41° 41' 2.40"	14° 35' 42"
gr14	39° 31' 58.80"	22° 12' 57.60"	itf3	40° 51' 36.00"	14° 50' 24.00"
gr21	39° 36' 3.60"	20° 47' 2.40"	itf4	40° 59' 2.40"	16.° 37' 12.00"
gr23	38° 16' 55.20"	21° 34' 26.40"	itf5	40° 30' 0.00"	16° 4' 51.60"
gr24	38° 39' 18.00"	22° 50' 9.60"	itf6	39° 4' 4.80"	16° 20' 49.20"
gr25	37° 20' 34.80"	22° 27' 28.80"	itg1	37° 35' 20.40"	14° 8' 45.60"
gr31	37° 50' 27.60"	23° 36' 3.60"	itg2	40° 5' 16.80"	9° 1' 51.24"
gr42	36° 44' 45.60"	26° 18' 21.60"	nl1	53° 3' 46.80"	6° 20' 7.08"
gr43	35° 13' 44.40"	24° 50' 45.60"	nl2	52° 15' 46.80"	6° 3' 25.56"
es11	42° 45' 21.60"	-7° 54' 36.72"	nl3	52° 4' 22.80"	4° 35' 33.72"
es12	43° 17' 31.20"	-5° 59' 37.32"	nl4	51° 27' 14.40"	5° 24' 51.48"
es13	43° 11' 52.80"	-4° 1' 49.08"	at1	48° 8' 60.00"	15° 53' 31.20"
es21	43° 2' 38.40"	-2° 36' 59.76"	at2	47° 5' 16.80"	14° 36' 46.80"
es22	42° 40' 1.20"	-1° 38' 45.96"	at3	47° 34' 15.60"	12° 34' 51.60"
es23	42° 16' 30.00"	-2° 31' 2.28"	pt11	41° 27' 25.20"	-7° 40' 43.68"
es24	41° 31' 12"	0° 39' 35.39"	pt15	37° 14' 38.40"	-8° 7' 54.48"
es30	40° 29' 42.00"	-3° 43' 1.92"	pt16	40° 7' 19.20"	-8° 0' 23.04"
es41	41° 45' 14.40"	-4° 46' 54.84"	pt17	38° 42' 36.00"	-9° 0' 37.08"
es42	39° 34' 51.60"	-3° 0' 16.20"	pt18	38° 29' 27.60"	-8° 0' 57.24"
es43	39° 11' 27.60"	-6° 9' 2.88"	fi1	64° 31' 19.20"	26° 12' 18.00"
es51	41° 47' 56.40"	-1° 31' 43.68"	fi2	60° 12' 50.40"	20° 6' 57.60"
es52	39° 24' 7.20"	0° 33' 17.68"	se11	59° 28' 37.20"	18° 10' 58.80"
es53	39° 34' 30.00"	2° 54' 51.479"	se12	59° 14' 31.20"	16° 8' 52.80"
es61	37° 27' 46.80"	-4° 34' 32.16"	se21	57° 13' 12.00"	15° 23' 13.20"
es62	38° 0' 7.20"	-1° 29' 8.52"	se22	56° 1' 15.60"	13° 56' 9.60"
fr10	48° 42' 32.40"	2° 30' 9.36"	se23	58° 1' 33.60"	12° 46' 19.20"
fr21	48° 44' 9.60"	4° 32' 28.32"	se31	60° 48' 14.40"	14° 34' 37.20"
fr22	49° 38' 34.80"	2° 48' 30.24"	se32	63° 12' 36.00"	15° 11' 24.00"
fr23	49° 23' 31.20"	1° 0' 43.92"	se33	66° 14' 34.80"	19° 19' 8.40"
fr24	47° 29' 6.00"	1° 41' 3.12"	ukc	55° 1' 12.00"	-1.° 54' 21.24"
fr25	48° 55' 44.40"	0° 31' 17.83"	ukd	54° 3' 25.20"	-2° 43' 23.16"
fr26	47° 14' 52.80"	4° 8' 57.48"	uke	53° 57' 54.00"	-1° 13' 44.76"
fr30	50° 28' 19.20"	2° 42' 54.36"	ukf	52° 55' 37.20"	0° 48' 24.77"
fr41	48° 45' 43.20"	6° 8' 31.92"	ukg	52° 28' 48.00"	-2° 16' 14.88"
fr42	48° 19' 48.00"	7° 26' 7.08"	ukh	52° 15' 3.60"	0° 32' 23.35"
fr43	47° 12' 28.80"	6° 5' 16.80"	uki	51° 30' 3.60"	0° 6' 42.73"
fr51	47° 28' 40.80"	0° 48' 55.98"	ukj	51° 16' 51.60"	0° 32' 4.81"
fr52	48° 10' 40.80"	-2° 50' 27.24"	ukk	51° 0' 3.60"	-3° 7' 49.80"
fr53	46° 9' 46.80"	0° 4' 52.11"	ukl	52° 20' 9.60"	-3° 45' 46.44"
fr61	44° 21' 18.00"	0° 13' 34.00"	ukm	56° 51' 0.00"	-4° 10' 42.24"
fr62	43° 46' 8.40"	1° 29' 15.00"	ukn	54° 36' 36.00"	-6° 42' 6.84"

Notes: The abbreviations of the NUTS code follow the official codes used by the European Commission (2007b). The centroids of the NUTS regions expressed in decimal degrees are calculated using the Matlab toolbox "Arc_Mat" (LeSage and Pace, 2004). Subsequently, they are converted to lattitude and longitude coordinates. Note that negative longitude values imply that the centroid of the region is located West of the Meridian (Greenwich) Line.

Table 3.27: Regression results using a spatial panel error model (Obj. 1+2+3)

	(1)	(2)	(3)	(4)	(5)	(6)
Ln real GDP p.c. (t-1)	-0.1707***	-0.1695***	-0.2113***	-0.2523***	-0.3492***	-0.5276***
	(-11.3051)	(-11.2201)	(-12.7152)	(-13.55)	(-16.944)	(-23.2889)
Ln investment (t-1)	0.0031	0.0035	0.0045	0.0082*	-0.0064	0.0007
	(0.8355)	(0.9388)	(1.0754)	(1.7084)	(-1.0195)	(0.1077)
Ln pop. growth + 0.05 (t-1)	-0.0456***	-0.0463***	-0.049***	-0.047***	-0.0298*	-0.0304*
	(-3.1057)	(-3.1495)	(-3.1362)	(-2.8402)	(-1.7274)	(-1.7031)
Ln innovation (t-1)	-0.0017	-0.0017	-0.0014	-0.0021	0.0001	0.0015
	(-1.246)	(-1.2739)	(-0.8733)	(-1.0907)	(0.0535)	(0.7575)
Ln Objectives 1+2+3 p.c. (t-1)		0.0017*	0.0017*	0.0006	0.0017	0.0012
		(1.9211)	(1.7909)	(0.5989)	(1.5148)	(1.1176)
Ln Objectives 1+2+3 p.c. (t-2)			0.0003	-0.0002	-0.0014	-0.0001
			(0.3079)	(-0.2066)	(-1.3445)	(-0.1081)
Ln Objectives 1+2+3 p.c. (t-3)				0.0004	0.0011	-0.0005
				(0.4413)	(1.0711)	(-0.4254)
Ln Objectives 1+2+3 p.c. (t-4)					-0.0026***	-0.0039***
					(-2.6205)	(-3.7355)
Ln Objectives 1+2+3 p.c. (t-5)						-0.0005
						(-0.5473)
λ	0.627***	0.64***	0.653***	0.648***	0.663***	0.694***
	(18.015)	(18.8529)	(18.7292)	(17.3448)	(17.119)	(17.7695)
Obj. 1+2+3 joint sign. (size)			0.0020	0.0009	-0.0013	-0.0038
Obj. 1+2+3 joint sign. (p-value)			0.1047	0.6039	0.5268	0.1265
Obj. 1+2+3 long-term elast. (size)		0.0098*	0.0094**	0.0034	-0.0037	-0.0072***
Obj. 1+2+3 long-term elast. (p-value)		0.0603	0.0409	0.4206	0.2309	0.0005
LR-test spatial effects (size)	435.86***	439.58***	468.17***	458.76***	531.72***	665.50***
LR-test spatial effects (p-value)	0.000	0.000	0.000	0.000	0.000	0.000
R-squared	0.5029	0.5028	0.527	0.5509	0.6129	0.687
No. of regions	126	126	126	126	126	126
No. of observations	1260	1260	1134	1008	882	756

Notes: Calculations are done with the Matlab routine *sem_panel_FE* by Elhorst (2010); t-statistics are reported parentheses; * significant at 10%; ** significant at 5%; *** significant at 1%; constant and time dummies are not shown.

Table 3.28: Regression results using a spatial panel error model (Obj. 1)

	(1)	(2)	(3)	(4)	(5)
Ln real GDP p.c. (t-1)	-0.1708***	-0.2135***	-0.2561***	-0.3467***	-0.5275***
	(-11.3567)	(-12.857)	(-13.834)	(-16.7317)	(-23.1738)
Ln investment (t-1)	0.0042	0.0050	0.0099**	-0.0043	0.0014
	(1.1271)	(1.2053)	(2.0606)	(-0.68)	(0.2183)
Ln pop. growth + 0.05 (t-1)	-0.0447***	-0.0485***	-0.0518***	-0.0357**	-0.036**
	(-3.0534)	(-3.1138)	(-3.1473)	(-2.0653)	(-2.003)
Ln innovation (t-1)	-0.0018	-0.0014	-0.0018	0.0001	0.0012
	(-1.3461)	(-0.9139)	(-0.9494)	(0.0704)	(0.5981)
Ln Objective 1 p.c. (t-1)	0.0031***	0.0017	0.0000	0.0009	0.0000
	(3.2491)	(1.5534)	(-0.0336)	(0.7564)	(-0.0261)
Ln Objective 1 p.c. (t-2)		0.0015	0.0001	-0.0005	0.0002
		(1.3908)	(0.0609)	(-0.4507)	(0.1831)
Ln Objective 1 p.c. (t-3)			0.0044***	0.0029**	0.0005
			(3.6049)	(2.3649)	(0.4422)
Ln Objective 1 p.c. (t-4)				-0.0019	-0.0037***
				(-1.4618)	(-2.9619)
Ln Objective 1 p.c. (t-5)					0.002*
					(1.6693)
λ	0.628***	0.658***	0.647***	0.668***	0.714***
	(18.0755)	(19.0676)	(17.2835)	(17.4347)	(19.1861)
Obj. 1 joint sign. (size)		0.0032***	0.0045***	0.0013	-0.0009
Obj. 1 joint sign. (p-value)		0.0090	0.0040	0.4884	0.6697
Obj. 1 long-term elast. (size)	0.0183***	0.0151***	0.0175***	0.0039	-0.0018
Obj. 1 long-term elast. (p-value)	0.0018	0.0038	0.0002	0.2630	0.4324
LR-test spatial effects (size)	438.74***	467.47***	469.70***	521.05***	660.26***
LR-test spatial effects (p-value)	0.000	0.000	0.000	0.000	0.000
R-squared	0.5068	0.5296	0.5562	0.6077	0.6795
No. of regions	126	126	126	126	126
No. of observations	1260	1134	1008	882	756

Notes: Calculations are done with the Matlab routine *sem_panel_FE* by Elhorst (2010); t-statistics are reported parentheses; * significant at 10%; ** significant at 5%; *** significant at 1%; constant and time dummies are not shown.

Chapter 4

Impact on Regional Economic Growth II: A Dose-Response Approach[1]

4.1 Introduction

One drawback of the current literature is that it relies on functional form assumptions. Although growth theory provides well-established suggestions for the estimation of growth relationships (see, among others Durlauf and Quah, 1999; Islam, 2003), it is ex ante not clear which functional form is appropriate for the relationship between SF payments and economic growth. In particular, there may be interactions with covariates and non-linearities, resulting in biased estimates if they are ignored.

Against this background, we try to avoid simple functional form assumptions by interpreting SF payments as a continuous treatment and by using the method of generalised propensity score (GPS), as proposed by Hirano and Imbens (2004) and further developed by Moodie and Stephens (2007). This method is applied using our new panel dataset of 122 NUTS-1 / NUTS-2 regions for the time period 1995–2005 in order to explain the effect of SF payments on the growth rate of average three-year real GDP. The results indicate that SF payments have a positive, but not statistically significant, impact on the regions' average three-year growth rates.

This paper is structured as follows: Section 4.2 focuses on the implementation of the method of GPS. Section 4.3 describes the data used. This is followed by a presentation of the main results in Sections 4.4 and 4.5, and a conclusion in Section 4.6.

---

[1] This paper is joint work with Tobias Hagen. An earlier version appeared as *Which is the right dose of EU Cohesion Policy for economic growth?*, *ZEW Discussion Paper* No. 08-104.

4.2 Implementation of the Method of Generalised Propensity Score

In the following, we interpret SF payments as a continuous treatment and make use of the method of GPS. So far, only few applied studies in economics using the GPS exist (see, for example Bia and Mattei, 2007; Flores-Lagunes, Gonzalez and Neuman, 2007; Kluve, Schneider, Uhlendorff and Zhao, 2007; Fryges and Wagner, 2008) and, to the best of our knowledge, there are no such studies in the field of regional economics. The aim of the method at hand is to estimate a dose-response function, representing the response (GDP growth rate) which is associated with different values of the continuous dose (SF payments). The terms "continuous treatment" and "dose" can be used synonymously.

A basic requirement of this model is the so-called "Stable Unit Treatment Value Assumption" (SUTVA; see Rubin, 1980) which claims that the distribution of the outcome for one unit (European region) is assumed to be independent of the potential treatment status of another unit, given the observed covariates (see Imai and van Dijk, 2004). Hence, interference between units, that is, spatial correlation, is ruled out. Obviously, this assumption seems to be rather strong when the unit is a region. This implies that, for example, given the covariates, SF payments in favor of Berlin do not affect growth in the region of Brandenburg, or that subsidies for the region of East of England do not affect growth in London. Moreover, recent econometric research (Dall'erba and Le Gallo, 2008; Mohl and Hagen, 2010) finds empirical evidence that cross-regional spillovers do matter. However, we are not able to control for spatial spillovers within our methodological approach. Instead, by applying a new method and by comparing the results to those in other papers using different techniques, we hope to obtain a general idea about the methodological problems and the range of the true effect of SF payments on growth.

The following brief explanation of the GPS method closely follows Hirano and Imbens (2004).[2] Their key assumption is what they call the "weak unconfoundedness assumption". Let the treatment variable S take on values in the interval $\mathbb{S} = [s_0, s_1]$. The assignment to treatment (S) is weakly unconfounded, conditional on the pre-treatment covariates X, if

$$Y(s) \perp S|X, \qquad \text{for all } s \in \mathbb{S} \tag{4.1}$$

with $Y(s)$ denoting the outcome (response) associated with the treatment level (dose) s. Equation (1) states that, conditional on the covariates X, the level of treatment received by a region is independent of the potential outcome $Y(s)$. This is also called exogeneity, unconfoundedness, or selection on observables (Imbens, 2004).

[2] Further descriptions can be found in Flores-Lagunes, Gonzalez and Neuman (2007), Kluve, Schneider, Uhlendorff and Zhao (2007) as well as in Moodie and Stephens (2007).

The GPS is defined as follows: If $r(s,x)$ is the conditional density of the treatment given the covariates $f_{S|X}(s|x)$, then the GPS is defined as $R = r(S,X)$. If the assignment to treatment is weakly unconfounded, Hirano and Imbens (2004) show that adjusting for the GPS eliminates the bias associated with differences in X. Hence, it is not necessary to condition directly on X when estimating $Y(s)$. An important feature of the GPS is the so-called balancing property: The GPS "balances" the covariates, such that the probability that $S = s$ does not depend on the value of X. Finally, using the estimated GPS, a dose-response function representing the average potential outcome $E[Y(s)]$ over the whole range of the dose can be estimated.

In concrete terms, the method is implemented as described by Hirano and Imbens (2004) with the following three step procedure:

1. We estimate the GPS by OLS: Let i denote one of N regions. We use a normal distribution for the treatment conditional on the covariates $S_i|X_i \sim N(\beta_0 + \beta_1' X_i, \sigma^2)$. The estimated GPS is calculated as:
$$\hat{R}_i = \frac{1}{\sqrt{2\pi\hat{\sigma}^2}} exp\left(-\frac{1}{2\hat{\sigma}^2}(S_i - \hat{\beta}_0 + \hat{\beta}_1' X_i)^2\right) \tag{4.2}$$

2. The conditional expectation of Y_i given S_i and R_i is modeled as a flexible function and the parameters $(\alpha_0, ..., \alpha_5)$ are estimated by OLS:
$$\begin{aligned} E[Y_i|S_i, R_i] = &\alpha_0 + \alpha_1 \cdot S_i + \alpha_2 \cdot S_i^2 \\ &+ \alpha_3 \cdot \hat{R}_i + \alpha_4 \cdot \hat{R}_i^2 + \alpha_5 \cdot S_i \cdot \hat{R}_i \end{aligned} \tag{4.3}$$

3. Finally, the average potential outcome at treatment level s is estimated as:
$$\begin{aligned} \widehat{E[Y(s)]} = &\frac{1}{N}\sum_{i=1}^{N}\Big(\hat{\alpha}_0 + \hat{\alpha}_1 \cdot s + \hat{\alpha}_2 \cdot s^2 + \hat{\alpha}_3 \cdot \hat{r}(s, X_i) \\ &+ \hat{\alpha}_4 \cdot \hat{r}(s, X_i)^2 + \hat{\alpha}_5 \cdot s \cdot \hat{r}(s, X_i)\Big) \end{aligned} \tag{4.4}$$

   The entire dose-response function is obtained by calculating this equation at each level of the treatment. The dose-response function shows how average responses vary along the interval of treatment doses. In our application, the treatment (or the dose) is defined as SF payments to a region in per cent of the region's GDP. After having dropped seven observations with zero SF payments, we have 578 observations with non-missing information on X in 122 regions, implying $\mathbb{S} = [0.001\%, 25.8\%]$. Even though we estimate the propensity score on this sample, we restrict the calculation of the dose-response function on the range up to 3.4% (corresponding to the 75% quantile) in steps of 0.1 per centage points. The reason for doing this is the small number of observations (200) in the upper tail of the distribution of $\mathbb{S}$, which may lead to unreliable estimates.

From the estimated dose-response function it is also possible to calculate pairwise treatment effects of the following form (Flores, 2004):

$$E(\Delta^{s_1,s_2}) = E[Y(s_1) - Y(s_2)], \qquad \text{for } s_1, s_2 \in \mathbb{S} \tag{4.5}$$

which, in case of small differences between s_1 and s_2, can be interpreted as derivatives indicating the growth effect of a marginal increase in SF payments per GDP.

Moodie and Stephens (2007) extend the GPS method to longitudinal data. Fryges and Wagner (2008) apply the GPS method to a panel of firms and evaluate the effect of export intensity on productivity growth simply by including time dummies into the conditioning set X of the GPS. We follow this approach. To be more precise, we explain the response of real GDP growth from $t-1$ to $t+2$ by the ratio of SF payments and GDP in t, with $t = 1999, ..., 2003$.[3] In accordance with Hirano and Imbens (2004), the associated standard errors are bootstrapped in order to account for the "generated regressor" problem. The bootstrap procedure includes all three steps described above.

4.3 Data

We use the SF data described in detail in chapter 3. As the European Commission has only published regional SF payments for the period 1995-1999 (European Commission, 1996a,b, 1997, 1998, 1999, 2000), it additionally comprises the SF payments of the last Financial Perspective 2000-2006. The latter were recalled at the European Commission in Brussels and have, to the best of our knowledge, only been analyzed by Mohl and Hagen (2010) as yet. It has to be taken into account that the remaining payments from the previous Financial Perspective 1994-1999 are excluded, as this dataset is limited to the SF payments of the period 2000-2006. In order to avoid an underestimation of the total amount of European SF, we allocate those commitments from the Financial Perspective 1994-1999 that have not been paid out by 1999 to the years 2000 and 2001. In doing so, we calculate the residual amount of SF by subtracting the aggregated payments 1994-1999 from the aggregated commitments 1994-1999. Assuming that all commitments finally lead to payments and taking into account the N+2 rule, we allocate the remaining amount at a rate of 2:1 to the years 2000 and 2001, respectively.

In our analysis, we concentrate on the total regional SF payments. These can be split up into three different Objectives, representing the key priorities of Cohesion Policy as

3 Alternatively, we use a cross-sectional approach where the impact of the total structural funds payments between 2000 and 2004 (relative to GDP) on the growth rates between 1999 and 2005 is estimated. The results are similar.

Figure 4.1: Quantile map: structural funds payments per GDP, 1995–2005

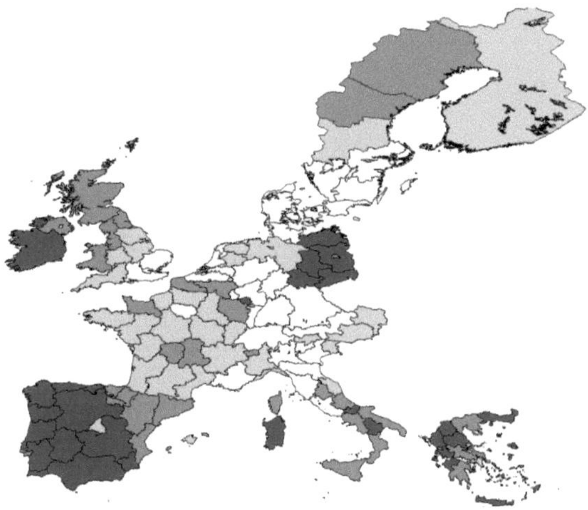

Source: Own illustration. The darker the area the wealthier is the region compared to the EU-15 average.

defined by the European Commission in the Financial Perspective 2000-2006. Almost two-thirds of the structural funds are spent for Objective 1 payments, which are to promote development in less prosperous regions. The remaining part is spent fairly equally on regions in structural decline (Objective 2) and on support for education and employment polices.[4] Note that there is a clear-cut definition concerning which regions qualify as an Objective 1 receiver (regional GDP has to be lower than 75% of the EU average), while a strict definition is missing in the case of the latter two Objectives. Multi-regional programs located at the national level (for example, SF payments for national education systems) are not taken into consideration. In order to give an overview of the distribution of SF payments, Figure 4.1 displays the quantile map of SF payments within Europe. The darker the area, the higher the relative share of SF for the respective region. Figure 4.1 shows that the highest relative transfers go to Portugal, Spain, Greece, Eastern Germany and Ireland, while the benefits of Denmark, the southern parts of Sweden and of Germany and the northern part of Italy are rather small.

Figure 4.2 shows a scatter plot of our outcome variable and the treatment variable for $\mathbb{S} = [0.001\%, 3.4\%]$. The relationship is highlighted by a nonparametric (bivariate locally

[4] Note that these Objectives in 2000-2006 consisted of two Objectives in the Financial Perspective 1994-1999. Objective 6 (1994-1999) became part of Objective 1 (2000-2006), Objective 5b (1994-1999) became part of Objective 2 (2000-2006) and Objective 4 (1994-1999) became part of Objective 3 (2000-2006).

Figure 4.2: Growth of real GDP per capita (PPS) and structural funds payments per GDP

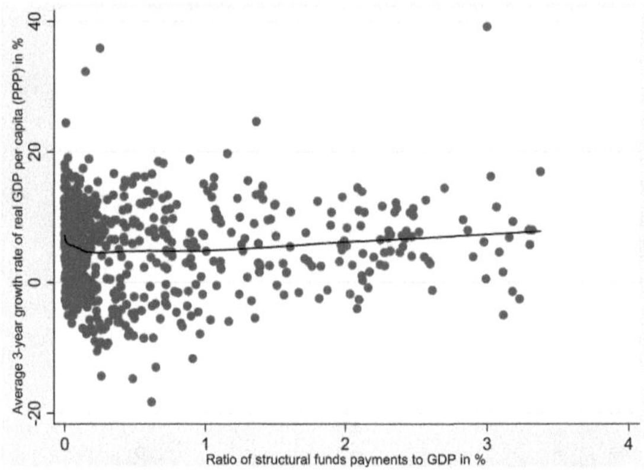

Source: Own illustration. Regions' GDP growth rate from $t-1$ to $t+3$ given the SF payments in t.

weighted) regression line, suggesting a slightly positive correlation between GDP growth and SF payments. Furthermore, it seems of particular interest that most regions receive SF payments that amount to less than 1% of GDP.

Apart from the SF variable, all other variables are from the Regio database by Eurostat. Due to recent modifications in the accounting standards (from the European System of Accounting (ESA) 1979 to ESA 1995), we only use variables available in ESA 1995. The complete list of regions and NUTS codes used in the following analysis are listed in the appendix.

4.4 Specification and Estimation of the GPS

In order to justify the weak unconfoundedness assumption, the vector X should consist of all variables simultaneously affecting the treatment variable (dose) and the outcome variable (response). Hence, it is crucial to include both the criteria for the allocation of funds and the mechanisms affecting the regions ability to call up and to co-finance the payments into the GPS specification.

In our application, the conditioning set X is limited by data availability at the NUTS level. We condition on the levels of the outcome variable (real GDP per capita in PPP) prior to the treatment ($t-1$ up to $t-3$) in order to balance pre-treatment differences in the regions' initial position. Furthermore, the variable "ratio of GDP per capita (PPP) to EU average" is included, as it is the central criterion for qualifying as a so-called "Objective 1"-region and receiving the highest transfers. Since areas with very low population densities, such as Sweden and Finland, also qualify for "Objective 1"-funding, the population density is included in the estimation of the GPS.[5]

Moreover, industrial areas can qualify for "Objective 2"-status if unemployment is above EU average, if the employment share in the industrial sectors is above EU aver-age, or if industrial employment is declining. For this reason, we include variables describing the employment structure (for example, the ratio of industrial employment to total employment), as well as the unemployment rate. In order to capture the differences in the regional labor markets and in order to take the ultimate SF funding aim of reducing long-term unemployment into account, the ratio of long-term unemployment to total unemployment is included in the specification. Note that the unemployment rate is included both lagged ($t-2$ and $t-3$) and squared, since this setup leads to a better fit in terms of adjusted R^2, Akaike's information criterion (AIC) and Schwarz Information Criterion (SIC). Finally, country dummies are considered, to account for country-specific particularities in the allocation and the use of the funding. The descriptive statistics of our variables can be found in Table 4.1.

Table 4.1: Descriptive statistics of the estimation sample

	Mean	Std. Dev.	Min.	Max.
Ratio of SF to nominal GDP (in %)	1.18	2.54	0.00	25.77
Real GDP per capita (PPP) in Euro (t-1)	22,180.3	6,131.2	11,622.2	5,3929.5
Ratio of GDP per capita (PPP) to EU average (t-3)	107.56	29.14	58.70	248.30
Unemployment rate (t-2)	0.08	0.05	0.01	0.27
Ratio of industry employment to total employment (t-2)	0.28	0.07	0.12	0.48
Ratio of agriculture employment to total employment (t-2)	0.08	0.08	0.00	0.43
Ratio of long-term unemployed to total unemployment (t-2)	0.45	0.13	0.07	0.79
Population density (t-3)	230.89	567.09	1.00	5,927.90

The final specification in Table 4.2 is found after testing how the best fit (adjusted R^2, AIC, SIC) and the best balancing results (see below) can be achieved. An adjusted R^2 of 0.57 may indicate that many important variables are accounted for. Note that the estimated coefficients of single variables cannot be interpreted, due to multicollinearity. For this reason, the bottom of Table 4.1 reports the results of joint tests.

[5] Note that variables only affecting the outcome variable but not the treatment level are irrelevant for propensity score approaches. Furthermore, variables only affecting the treatment level but not the outcome variable could be instrumental variables. If instrumental variables were available, it would be possible to take endogeneity (also called "selection on unobservables") into account.

A fundamental question is whether conditional on these X variables, exogeneity of the treatment can be assumed. Important variables summarising differences between regions, such as human capital, are missing. Hence, we have to assume that by conditioning on the available observed variables, unobserved variables are also captured, as they are correlated with the observed variables.[6]

A last safeguard against an endogeneity bias may be the fact that our dependent variable is first-differenced over time (growth of GDP instead of level of GDP) which eliminates time-constant heterogeneity in initial positions between regions.

As noted by Flores-Lagunes, Gonzalez and Neuman (2007) as well as by Imai and van Dijk (2004), one approach to check the balancing property of the GPS (the balance of the pre-treatment covariates X) is to run regressions of each covariate on the treatment variable S and the estimated GPS $\hat{R}$. If a certain covariate is balanced, the treatment variable should have no predictive power for the particular covariate conditional on the estimated GPS. By comparing the estimated t-statistics of the coefficients ("adjusted t-stat.") to the corresponding t-statistic of the coefficient of a regression that does not include the estimated GPS ("unadjusted t-stat."), one can obtain an idea about the degree of balancing generated by the GPS. For each continuous covariate we use OLS; for each binary variable we apply a logit model.

The results of this exercise are shown in Table 4.3. In almost all cases the t-statistics are significantly reduced when switching from "unadjusted" to "adjusted". Only in the case of the unemployment rate and the ratio of industry employment do the t-statistics continue to indicate statistically significant coefficients. For the ratio of long-term unemployed in total unemployment, the figures even show an increase of the t-statistics. Most importantly, however, the outcome variable "real GDP per capita (in PPP)" seems to be perfectly balanced prior to the treatment, which can be interpreted as a kind of "pre-program test" in the sense of Heckman and Hotz (1989). Since our approach turns out to be suitable for balancing pre-treatment differences in real GDP per capita, we can be optimistic that the unconfoundedness assumption may be fulfilled.

As discussed above, the outcome variable Y is the average three-year GDP growth rate (real GDP per capita (in PPP)) in per cent which is explained by the ratio of SF payments to GDP (in per cent). The estimation results of the second step (equation 3) are shown in Table 4.4. Note that the estimated coefficients do not have any causal interpretation. According to Hirano and Imbens (2004), a test on whether all coefficients involving the GPS are equal to zero in this regression can be interpreted as a test on whether the covariates introduce any bias. Joint tests can be found at the bottom of Table 4.4. They indicate a rejection of the hypothesis that the coefficients are jointly

6 Unless plausible instrumental variables are available, there is no way to test the weak unconfoundedness assumption directly.

Table 4.2: Parameter estimates of the generalised propensity score

	Coef.	t-stat.
Real GDP per capita (PPP) (t-1) / 1,000	-0.625	-5.42
Real GDP per capita (PPP) (t-2) / 1,000	0.427	2.73
Real GDP per capita (PPP) (t-3) / 1,000	-0.302	-1.13
Ratio of GDP per capita (PPP) to EU average (t-3)	0.120	1.98
Ratio of GDP per capita (PPP) to EU average (t-4)	-0.030	-1.14
ln unemployment rate (t-2)	8.708	2.78
ln unemployment rate (t-3)	-9.556	-2.99
ln unemployment rate (t-2) squared	2.215	2.14
ln unemployment rate (t-3) squared	-2.383	-2.20
Ratio of long-term unemployed (t-3)	-0.457	-0.48
ln population density (t-3)	-0.019	-0.24
ln proportion of industry employment (t-2)	-0.282	-0.22
ln proportion of agriculture employment (t-2)	0.162	0.36
ln proportion of industry employment (t-3)	-0.866	-0.67
ln proportion of agriculture employment (t-3)	-0.040	-0.09
Country dummies (Base: Belgium):		
Denmark	-0.421	0.66
Germany	-0.133	0.82
Greece	3.836	0.00
Spain	2.005	0.01
France	-0.429	0.46
Ireland	1.829	0.18
Italy	0.060	0.92
Luxembourg	1.504	0.18
Netherlands	0.035	0.96
Austria	-0.392	0.59
Portugal	0.940	0.23
Finland	-0.046	0.97
Sweden	-0.406	0.55
UK	-0.146	0.81
Time dummies (Base: 1999):		
2000	1.764	6.23
2001	2.622	6.36
2002	1.909	3.32
2003	2.199	2.69
Constant	-1.575	-0.80
Joint tests:		
F-stat. p-value (GDP variables)		0.0000
F-stat. p-value (unemployment and population variables)		0.0000
F-stat. p-value (employment variables)		0.0218
F-stat. p-value (country dummies)		0.0000
F-stat. p-value (time dummies)		0.0000
Number of regions		122
Number of observations		578
Adjusted R-squared		0.57

zero. Hence conditioning on the covariates (via the GPS) is necessary.

4.5 Estimation of the Dose-Response Function

In order to reveal the causal relationship of interest, a dose-response function is estimated via equation (4) and is displayed in Figure 4.3. The point estimates, as well as the corresponding simulated 95% confidence interval are shown. The shape of the confidence intervals can be explained by the fact that the number of observations is reduced with an increasing dose. Furthermore, a "covariate-adjusted non-participants" mean growth rate (3.8%) is shown as a horizontal line ("response at a dose of 0%").[7] This can be interpreted as an estimate of the average growth rate of the treated regions if they did not receive any SF payments.

The point estimates indicate a positive relationship: At least up to a dose of approximately 2.1%, the growth rate rises with an increasing dose. However, as documented by the confidence intervals, the relationship is far from being statistically significantly different from zero (at the 5%, as well as the 10%[8] level). Furthermore, it is not statistically significantly different from the growth rate at a dose of zero (3.8%).

Table 4.3: Tests of the balancing property: t-statistics for the coefficients of the treatment variable

Variable	Unadjusted t-stat.	Adjusted t-stat.
Real GDP per capita (PPP) (t-1) / 1,000	6.25	0.83
Real GDP per capita (PPP) (t-2) / 1,000	6.44	0.95
Real GDP per capita (PPP) (t-3) / 1,000	6.40	1.02
Ratio of GDP per capita (PPP) to EU average (t-3)	6.45	0.97
Ratio of GDP per capita (PPP) to EU average (t-4)	6.44	0.97
ln unemployment rate (t-2)	6.92	2.96
Ratio of long-term unemployed (t-3)	6.78	12.40
ln ratio of industry employment (t-2)	-12.84	-7.34
ln ratio of agriculture employment (t-2)	-5.94	1.50
ln population density (t-3)	7.52	0.37
Time dummies (Base: 1999):		
2000	-2.55	0.16
2001	-1.94	1.16
2002	-4.38	-3.01
2003	-4.75	-3.03

7 Following Flores-Lagunes, Gonzalez and Neuman (2007), we estimate the "covariate-adjusted non-participants" mean growth rate as follows. First, we estimate a linear model for the growth rate as a function of all conditioning variables in X based on regions receiving or not receiving SF payments. Second, we predict the growth rate for the sample of the regions receiving SF payments, assuming $S = 0$. The mean of this prediction is the "covariate-adjusted non-participants" mean growth rate. Since the results of the dose-response function are very clearly statistically insignificant, we do not show the confidence interval of this estimate, in order to ensure clarity of the figure.

8 The 90% confidence interval is not shown.

Table 4.4: Estimated parameters of the conditional distribution of GDP growth given SF payments (in % GDP) and the estimated GPS

	Coef.	t-stat.
S / 1,000	6.387	1.68
S^2 / 1,000	-0.145	-0.78
$\hat{R}$	1.184	1.82
$\hat{R}^2$	-6.455	-2.15
$\hat{R} \cdot S$ / 1,000	-2.283	-0.68
Constant	0.004	0.12
Joint tests:		
F-stat. p-value ($\hat{R}$,$\hat{R}^2$)		0.0342
F-stat. p-value ($\hat{R}$,$\hat{R}^2$,$\hat{R} \cdot S$)		0.0672
Number of observations		578

Figure 4.3: Estimated dose-response function: Growth rate of real GDP per capita and 95% confidence interval

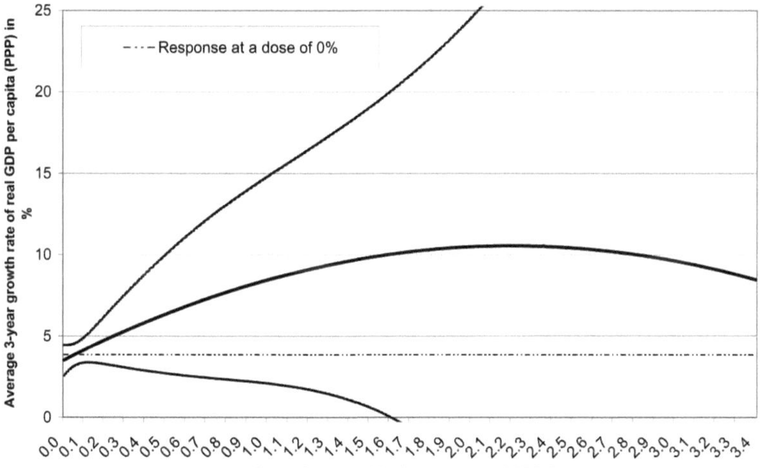

Notes:
Solid line: Estimated conditional expectation of regions' GDP growth rate from $t-1$ to $t+3$ given the SF payments in t and the estimated generalised propensity score.
Dotted lines: Simulated 95% confidence interval, using the 5th and 95th per centiles of the bootstrap distribution (5,000 replications).
Source: Own illustration.

Figure 4.4 shows the derivatives of the dose-response function, which indicate the increase in the growth rate in percentage points resulting from a marginal increase in the dose. We see diminishing returns which are, however, once again not statistically

Figure 4.4: Estimated derivatives and 95% confidence interval

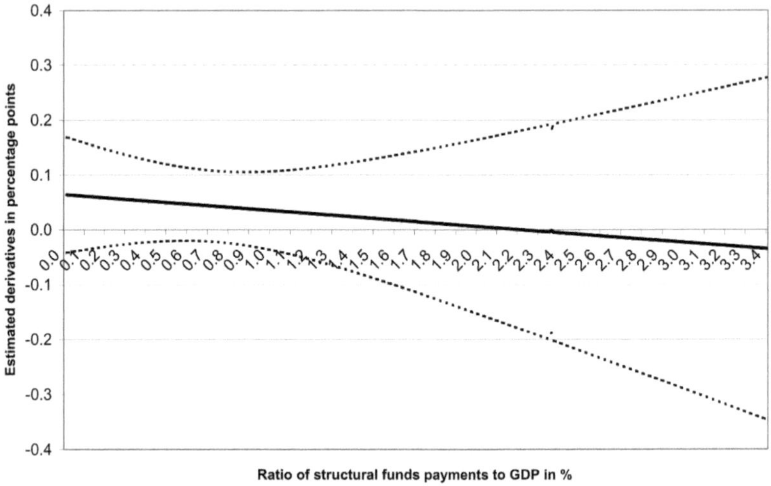

Notes:
Solid line: Estimated conditional expectation of regions' GDP growth rate from $t-1$ to $t+3$ given the SF payments in t and the estimated generalised propensity score.
Dotted lines: Simulated 95% confidence interval, using the 5th and 95th per centiles of the bootstrap distribution (5,000 replications).
Source: Own illustration.

significantly different from zero. In other words, with regard to economic growth, it does not matter which "dose" of SF payments a region receives.

4.6 Conclusions

The aim of this paper is to evaluate the growth effects of SF payments at the regional level. In contrast to the existing literature, the focus lies on avoiding functional form assumptions to a large extent. As a consequence, we apply a continuous treatment effects model to estimate a dose-response function. In doing so, we employ the dataset by Mohl and Hagen (2010) consisting of a sample of 122 NUTS-1 and NUTS-2 regions, which comprises, for the first time, structural funds payments of the Financial Perspective 2000-2006. The statistical tests suggest that the approach is suitable for balancing pre-treatment differences between regions to a large extent, implying that we may be able to yield an unbiased estimate of the regional growth effect of structural funds payments.

Our results indicate that structural funds payments have a positive, but not statistically significant, impact on the European regions' growth rates. This implies that it does not matter which "dose" of SF payments a region receives. This result is well in line with previous studies using parametric approaches that indicate rather mixed effects of the Cohesion Policy. In order to raise the plausibility of the so-called SUTVA, which rules out regional spillovers, a combination of the methodology of the generalised propensity score and spatial econometric techniques may be fruitful. However, this methodological innovation is left for future research.

4.7 Appendix

Construction of the Dataset

We follow Mohl and Hagen (2010) in the construction of the structural funds payments dataset. As structural funds payments are not available for all EU regions at the NUTS-2 level, our dataset consists of 122 NUTS-1 and NUTS-2 regions[9] (see Mohl and Hagen (2010) for a detailed description of the dataset). Here we do not consider the overseas regions of France (Départments d'outre-mer (fr9) consisting of Guadeloupe (fr91), Martinique (fr92), Guyane (fr93) and Réunion (fr94)), Portugal (Região Autónoma dos Açores (pt2, pt20), Região Autónoma da Madeira (pt3, pt30)), and Spain (Canarias (es7, es70)).

As a consequence, our dataset consists of 122 NUTS-1 and NUTS-2 regions with positive SF payments, which are listed in the following, including the abbreviations of the NUTS codes in brackets, in accordance with the classifications of the European Commission (2007).

Austria (3 NUTS-1 regions): Ostösterreich (at1), Südösterreich (at2), Westösterreich (at3);

Belgium (3 NUTS-1 regions): Région de Bruxelles-capitale (be1), Vlaams Gewest (be2), Région Wallonne (be3);

Denmark (1 NUTS-2 region): Denmark (dk);

Finland (2 NUTS-1 regions): Manner-Suomi (fi1), Åland (fi2);

France (22 NUTS-2 regions): Île de France (fr10), Champagne-Ardenne (fr21), Picardie (fr22), Haute-Normandie (fr23), Centre (fr24), Basse-Normandie (fr25), Bourgogne (fr26), Nord-Pas-de-Calais (fr30), Lorraine (fr41), Alsace (fr42), Franche-Comté (fr43), Pays-de-la-Loire (fr51), Bretagne (fr52), Poitou-Charentes (fr53), Aquitaine (fr61), Midi-Pyrénées (fr62), Limousin (fr63), Rhône-Alpes (fr71), Auvergne (fr72), Languedoc-Roussillon (fr81), Provence-Alpes-Côte d'Azur (fr82), Corse (fr83);

[9] The European Commission (2007b) classifies the EU regions according to the "Nomenclature des unités territoriales statistiques" (NUTS) which refers to the country level (NUTS-0) and to three lower subdivisions (NUTS-1, NUTS-2 and NUTS-2) which are mainly classified according to the population size.

Germany (15 NUTS-1 regions): Baden-Württemberg (de1), Bayern (de2), Berlin (de3), Brandenburg (de4), Bremen (de5), Hamburg (de6), Hessen (de7), Mecklenburg-Vorpommern (de8), Niedersachsen (de9), Nordrhein-Westfalen (dea), Rheinland-Pfalz (deb), Sachsen (ded), Sachsen-Anhalt (dee), Schleswig-Holstein (def), Thüringen (deg);

Greece (13 NUTS-2 regions): Anatoliki Makedonia, Thraki (gr11), Kentriki Makedonia (gr12), Dytiki Makedonia (gr13), Thessalia (gr14), Ipeiros (gr21), Ionia Nisia (gr22), Dytiki Ellada (gr23), Sterea Ellada (gr24), Peloponnisos (gr25), Attiki (gr30), Voreio Aigaio (gr41), Notio Aigaio (gr42), Kriti (gr43);

Ireland (1 NUTS-1 region): Irland (ie);

Italy (19 NUTS-2 regions): Piemonte (itc1), Valle d'Aosta/Vallée d'Aoste (itc2), Liguria (itc3), Lombardia (itc4), Veneto (itd3), Friuli-Venezia Giulia (itd4), Emilia-Romagna (itd5), Toscana (ite1), Umbria (ite2), Marche (ite3), Lazio (ite4), Abruzzo (itf1), Molise (itf2), Campania (itf3), Puglia (itf4), Basilicata (itf5), Calabria (itf6), Sicilia (itg1), Sardegna (itg2);

Luxembourg (1 NUTS-2 region): Luxembourg (ie);

The Netherlands (4 NUTS-1 regions): Noord-Nederland (nl1), Oost-Nederland (nl2), West-Nederland (nl3), Zuid-Nederland (nl4);

Portugal (2 NUTS-2 regions): Norte (pt11), Algarve (pt15);

Spain (16 NUTS-2 regions): Galicia (es11), Principado de Asturias (es12), Cantabria (es13), País Vasco (es21), Comunidad Foral de Navarra (es22), La Rioja (es23), Aragón (es24), Comunidad de Madrid (es30), Castilla y León (es41), Castilla-La Mancha (es42), Extremadura (es43), Cataluña (es51), Comunidad de Valenciana (es52), Illes Balears (es53), Andalucía (es61), Región de Murcia (es62);

Sweden (8 NUTS-2 regions): Stockholm (se11), Östra Mellansverige (se12), Småland med öarna (se021), Sydsverige (se22), Västsverige (se23), Norra Mellansverige (se31), Mellersta Norrland (se32), Övre Norrland (se33);

UK (12 NUTS-1 regions): North East (ukc), North West (ukd), Yorkshire and the Humber (uke), East Midlands (ukf), West Midlands (ukg), East of England (ukh), London (uki), South East (ukj), South West (ukk), Wales (ukl), Scotland (ukm), N. Ireland (ukn).

Chapter 5

Impact on Regional Employment[1]

5.1 Introduction

The current literature on the effectiveness of EU funding has mainly focused on the question whether EU aid has promoted economic growth and convergence (for a survey see Esposti and Bussoletti, 2008; Hagen and Mohl, 2011). However, the employment effects are key to understanding regional income disparities (measured, e.g. as GDP per capita), since income differences are, per definition, based on differences in the labour productivity and/or employment level, among other factors. In addition, parts of the EU expenditures (in particular Objective 2 payments) are directly aimed at reducing disparities in the employment sector. Nevertheless, only a few papers have analysed the employment effects of this policy field. While earlier contributions find positive employment effects from the European Regional Development Fund for EU regions in the 1988-1993 period (Busch, Lichtblau and Schnabel, 1998) and for firms in northern and central Italy (Bondonio and Greenbaum, 2006), the recent evidence is rather disillusioning; suggesting that there are no positive employment effects for EU countries (Heinemann, Mohl and Osterloh, 2009) or regions (Dall'erba and Le Gallo, 2007; Becker, Egger and von Ehrlich, 2010). By contrast, Bouvet (2005) finds a positive effect of EU aid on employment growth in a sample of eight EU Member States between 1975 and 1999.[2] One drawback in the literature is the poor data availability of EU funding. The annual reports on structural funds published by the European Commission (1995, 1996a,b, 1997, 1998, 1999, 2000) only comprise regional commitments / payments for the 1994–1999 period. Unfortunately, since 2000, these

---

1 This chapter is based on the following joint article with Tobias Hagen: Mohl and Hagen (2011): The employment impacts of EU structural funds. Evidence from dynamic panel data, ECB Working Paper 1403, December.

2 Apart from the studies cited, there is a growing literature which analyses more general labour market effects at the regional level in Europe, e.g. studies on the determinants of unemployment (Basile and de Benedictis, 2008) or labour force participation rates (Elhorst and Zeilstra, 2007).

reports have only consisted of aggregate data at the country level. As a consequence, no paper has analysed the employment effects using regional structural funds payments post 1999.

There are at least four theoretical arguments why EU funding is not unambiguously associated with positive total employment effects. First, structural funds payments increase the employment level if they lead to human capital investment (for example, from the European Social Fund); however, if they are used as capital subsidies (for example, investment grants for firms or business start-ups), the employment effects will be inconclusive. On the one hand, structural funds payments reduce capital costs, which leads to more output and employment (scale effect). On the other hand, reduced capital costs increase relative costs of labour, which may cause (low-skilled) labour to be substituted by capital (substitution effect). According to the "capital-skill-complementary hypothesis" (Griliches, 1969), the demand for skilled labour increases with decreasing capital costs, while the demand for unskilled labour decreases with diminishing capital costs. Second, the employment effects are inconclusive if structural funds payments have a positive effect on technological progress. According to the "skill-based technological change hypothesis" (Berman, Bound and Griliches, 1994), technological progress may lead to an increase of the relative demand for high-skilled labour, and thus to a decrease in demand for low-skilled labour. Third, in order to induce a positive employment effect, the regional labor supply must match with the additional demand for high-skilled labour. Fourth, short-term business cycle effects might impede employment growth. If Cohesion Policy was associated with a positive aggregate demand stimulus and if the economy was characterised by a positive output gap and a tight labour market situation, Cohesion Policy would not promote employment growth but would lead to an overheating of the economy, implying an acceleration of price and wage inflation. As indicated by Kamps, Leiner-Killinger and Martin (2009) this could be in particular the case for the eastern European Member States, which joined the EU in 2007 and exhibited high growth rates.

All in all, the net effect on total employment is theoretically unclear ex ante and, hence, an empirical question which is addressed in this paper. We evaluate the impact of EU structural funds on employment with a panel dataset of 130 European NUTS regions over the time period of 1999-2007. Compared with previous studies we explicitly take into account the unambiguous theoretical propositions by investigating the conditional impact of structural funds on the educational attainment. Moreover, we are, to the best of our knowledge, the first who analyse this research question with more precise measures of EU funding by distinguishing between Objective 1, 2 and 3 payments and for an extended time period using data from the Multiannual Financial Framework 2000-2006. Finally, we examine the robustness of our results by comparing different dynamic panel econometric approaches, highlighting specific methodological problems, controlling for heteroscedasticity, serial and spatial correlation, as well as for endogeneity.

Our results indicate that structural funds in total have no significant positive impact on the regional employment level. However, we find some evidence that structural funds are conditionally effective and may be interpreted as capital subsidies. They have a significant positive impact on the employment level in regions with a low share of low-skilled population, whereas they have a negative effect on the employment level in the case of a high share of low-skilled population. This implies that the high-skilled population in particular benefits from EU structural funds payments.

The outline of this paper is as follows. We start in Section 5.2 with a discussion of the econometric specification. This is followed by a presentation of the empirical results in the light of the methodological challenges in Section 5.3. Finally, Section 5.4 concludes.

5.2 Econometric Specification

5.2.1 Baseline Panel Approach

Our estimation of the employment effects of structural funds payments is based on a reduced-form approach including the implications of both a labour demand model as well as a labour supply model. We define employment (*emp*) as the regions' total employment per population aged 15 to 65 in order to account for the substantial differences in the size of the regional labour markets in Europe.

From a theoretical point of view, structural funds payments may affect employment through the channel of labour demand by increasing the endowment of private and public capital in the region. This raises the marginal product of labour, the output level, and thus, ceteris paribus, labour demand. A second transmission channel is an increase in the technological progress which may affect total labour demand positively or negatively, as discussed in the introduction.

Our baseline specification is defined as follows:[3]

$$\begin{aligned} emp_{i,t} =& \beta_0 + \beta_1\, emp_{i,t-1} + \beta_2\, comp.emp_{i,t-1} + \beta_3\, pop.young_{i,t-1} + \\ &+ \beta_4\, low\, skilled_{i,t-1} + \beta_5\, market\, potential_{i,t-1} + \beta_6\, grr_{i,t-1} + \\ &+ \beta_7\, union\, density_{i,t-1} + \beta_8\, sf_{i,t-1} + \mu_i + \lambda_t + u_{i,t} \end{aligned} \tag{5.1}$$

where the subscript $i = 1, ..., 130$ denotes the region and t indicates the time index of our sample for the time period of 1999–2007. Note that all independent variables are

3 Note that we also tested for a non-linear relationship between structural funds and employment. Our findings, which are available upon request, show that there is no evidence for a non-linear relation.

lagged and expressed in log terms. We estimate a dynamic panel data model by including the lagged employment variable in order to deal with the sluggish adjustment process (Nickell, 1987). Table 5.1 gives an overview of the precise definitions and data sources of the variables used. The correlation matrix and the summary statistics are displayed in Tables 5.2 and 5.3.

Table 5.1: Description of the variables and data sources

Variable	Definition	Source
Emp	Employment (*reg_lfe2enace*) over total population between 15 and 64 years (*reg_d2avg*)	Eurostat Regio statistics (the official Eurostat codes are listed in parentheses)
Comp. emp	Compensation of employees in the manufacturing sector in million of Euro (*reg_e2rem*)	
Pop. young	Share of population aged 15 and below (*reg_d2jan*) over total population	
Low-skilled	Share of population aged 15 and over whose highest level of education is pre-primary, primary and lower secondary education – levels 0-2 according to the International Standard Classification of Education (ISCED) 1997 (*reg_lfsd2pedu*)	
High-skilled	Share of population aged 15 and over whose highest level of education is tertiary education – levels 5-6 according to ISCED (1997) (*reg_lfsd2pedu*)	
Market potential	Sum of GDP (*reg_e2gdp*) of region i and GDP of all other regions k, weighted by the square of the Euclidean distance from region i to region k $market\,potential_{i,t} = GDP_{i,t} + \sum_k(GDP_k/d_{ik}^2)$.	
Market potential 2	GDP of all other regions k, weighted by the square of the Euclidean distance from region i to region k $market\,potential2_{i,t} = \sum_k(GDP_k/d_{ik}^2)$.	
grr	Gross replacement rate, which measures the average of the gross unemployment benefit replacement rates for two earnings levels, three family situations and three durations of unemployment divided by 100. The original data are for every second year and have been linearly interpolated.	OECD, database on unemployment benefit entitlements and replacement rates
Union density	Trade union density	OECD
SF pc Obj. 1	Objective 1 payments per capita in Euro	Data for 1999 are from the European Commission (2000); Data for the period 2000–2006 were accessed at the European Commission in Brussels on 24/25 November 2007
SF pc Obj. 2	Objective 2 payments per capita in Euro	
SF pc Obj. 3	Objective 3 payments per capita in Euro	
SF pc Obj. 1+2+3	Objectives 1+2+3 payments per capita in Euro	

Moreover, we consider a number of region-specific control variables. We have to proxy the regional wage level by the compensation of employees in the manufacturing sector (*comp.emp*) due to data availability. Note that the regional wage level is endogenous with respect to the regional employment level which has to be taken into account in the estimation strategy (Topel, 1986).

The percentage share of the population aged under 15 (*pop.young*) is added as a proxy for two unobserved variables which are relevant for the quantity and quality of regional labour supply, namely (i) the amount of experience in the labour market (human capital) and (ii) the effect of having young children (Elhorst, 2003a). We control for the share of population with low levels of education (*low skilled*), since the demand for low-skilled workers decreases according to the hypothesis of skill-based technological change cited above. Hence, an increase in (high-skilled) labour demand may not raise employment in regions with a high share of low-skilled people, due to mismatch problems. Moreover, we follow Basile and de Benedictis (2008) for our definition of *market potential*. This measure accounts for both the size of the regional market and its position relative to other regional markets. It is calculated as the sum of GDP of region i and the weighted GDP of the neighbouring regions, while the latter is weighted with its squared geographical distance between the centroids of the countries (the coordinates of the regional centroids are available upon request).

Furthermore, the scope of the regions in promoting employment is constrained by national labour market institutions. As a consequence, we take into account the level of benefits (Holmlund, 1998) by including the gross replacement rate (grr). In addition, we control for *union density* since higher union density could strengthen the bargaining position of the union, resulting in higher wage demands and/or a more compressed wage structure (Scarpetta, 1996; Nickell and Layard, 1999; Blau and Kahn, 1999; Nickell, Nunziata and Ochel, 2005).

Moreover, we included the employment protection indicator of the OECD to account for employment protection laws following the literature by Lazear (1990). We also considered indicators measuring the structure of the econo- mies, such as the share of regional employment in the agricultural/industrial sector. However, the latter variables–the employment protection indicator and the share of industry structure in regional employment–are not statistically significant, so we excluded them from our final specifications.

The main variable of interest is the structural funds variable (sf). Table 2.1 clarifies that total structural funds can be classified into three different objectives. Around two-thirds of total structural funds payments are allocated to regions with a GDP lower than 75% of the EU average. This Objective 1 funding has the primary goal to promote development in less prosperous regions. The remaining part is spent without a clear

Table 5.2: Correlation matrix

	Emp.	Comp. emp.	Pop. young	Low-skilled	Grr	Union density
Emp.	1					
Comp. emp.	0.4411	1				
Pop. young	0.1267	0.3352	1			
Low-skilled	-0.3511	-0.7035	-0.2066	1		
Grr	0.3549	0.6781	0.2533	-0.4792	1	
Union density	0.3767	0.6633	0.3282	-0.5468	0.6657	1
Market potential	0.0298	0.0821	0.097	0.2428	-0.0713	-0.0632
Market potential 2	0.3388	0.1172	0.0789	-0.3231	-0.0269	-0.0304
SF pc Obj. 1	-0.403	-0.452	-0.2357	0.2999	-0.3702	-0.3348
SF pc Obj. 2	0.0757	0.1218	0.0103	-0.088	-0.0196	0.1219
SF pc Obj. 3	0.0663	-0.1118	-0.2965	0.1362	-0.0372	-0.0018
SF pc Obj. 1+2+3	-0.4062	-0.4644	-0.2778	0.3121	-0.406	-0.3284
	Market potential	**Market potential 2**	**SF pc Obj. 1**	**SF pc Obj. 2**	**SF pc Obj. 3**	**SF pc Obj. 1+2+3**
Market potential	1					
Market potential 2	-0.0431	1				
SF pc Obj. 1	-0.144	-0.0851	1			
SF pc Obj. 2	0.1441	-0.0935	-0.3468	1		
SF pc Obj. 3	0.0923	0.1068	-0.2243	0.2284	1	
SF pc Obj. 1+2+3	-0.1092	-0.1047	0.9637	-0.0989	-0.088	1

Table 5.3: Summary statistics

Variable		Mean	Std. dev.	Minimum	Maximum	Observations
Emp.	overall	0.6334	0.0833	0.2456	0.8398	N = 1142
	between		0.0803	0.3669	0.8253	n = 130
	within		0.0244	0.5121	0.7119	T = 8.7846
Comp. emp.	overall	24,377.8	8,389.6	5,899.5	47,353.4	N = 961
	between		8,585.8	7,504.2	47,080.6	n = 130
	within		1,490.1	15,193.8	30,414.2	T = 7.3923
Pop. young	overall	0.1608	0.0261	0.1000	0.2340	N = 1163
	between		0.0257	0.1034	0.2249	n = 130
	within		0.0054	0.1408	0.1888	T = 8.9462
Low-skilled	overall	0.4443	0.1789	0.0911	0.8746	N = 1163
	between		0.1669	0.1557	0.8352	n = 130
	within		0.0671	0.0133	0.6447	T = 8.9462
Grr	overall	0.3127	0.1012	0.1207	0.6107	N = 1168
	between		0.0986	0.1329	0.5166	n = 130
	within		0.0238	0.1954	0.4068	T = 8.9846
Union density	overall	0.2779	0.1813	0.0782	0.8063	N = 1106
	between		0.1775	0.0813	0.7705	n = 130
	within		0.0124	0.2151	0.3193	T = 8.5077
Market potential	overall	155,565.6	109,534.1	22,697.7	606,570.4	N = 1032
	between		109,565.2	24,062.4	595,974.7	n = 129
	within		8,641.8	78,995.9	207,308.0	T = 8
Market potential 2	overall	78,719.1	37,566.6	16,052.9	282,920.6	N = 1032
	between		37,495.7	16,687.0	257,092.1	n = 129
	within		3,855.2	43,116.4	104,547.6	T = 8
SF pc Obj. 1	overall	44.2765	71.8250	0.0000	408.1175	N = 1169
	between		63.0015	0.0000	272.1494	n = 130
	within		34.9174	0.0000	280.3748	T = 8.9923
SF pc Obj. 2	overall	10.2749	16.8297	0.0000	300.6687	N = 1170
	between		11.9288	0.0000	67.8109	n = 130
	within		11.9129	0.0000	243.1328	T = 9
SF pc Obj. 3	overall	2.5094	6.3707	0.0000	51.3384	N = 1170
	between		5.6338	0.0000	33.4844	n = 130
	within		3.0106	0.0000	23.9043	T = 9
SF pc Obj. 1+2+3	overall	57.0718	66.9904	0.0000	408.1175	N = 1169
	between		56.0263	0.0000	272.1494	n = 130
	within		37.0368	0.0000	298.6794	T = 8.9923

allocation scheme on regions in structural decline (Objective 2) and to support education, training and employment policies (Objective 3). For our empirical analysis we draw on a dataset, which has, to the best of our knowledge, only been used by Mohl and Hagen (2010) in the context of the evaluation of economic growth effects of EU funding. This dataset includes precise measures of EU structural funds by distinguishing between Objective 1, 2 and 3 payments over the time period of 1999-2007.

To present an overview of the regional distribution of the structural funds, Figure 5.1 shows the quantile maps displaying the distribution of the funds over nine intervals by assigning the same number of values to each of the nine categories in the map. The payments are expressed as a share of population and are displayed as averages over the entire time period of observation. The darker the area, the higher the share of that region's payments of structural funds per capita. The figures show that Ireland, Eastern Germany, Greece, Southern Italy and Spain benefit most from Objective 1 payments, whereas France, the UK, Northern Spain and Sweden show particularly high gains from Objective 2 and Objective 3 payments, respectively.

We are not only interested in analysing the employment impact of total regional structural funds payments, we are also keen on distinguishing between Objective 1, 2 and 3 payments. For this reason we start with specifications including the total sum of Objective 1+2+3 payments and then continue by investigating the impact of each single Objective.

Figure 5.1: Quantile maps of structural funds per capita, averages 1999–2006

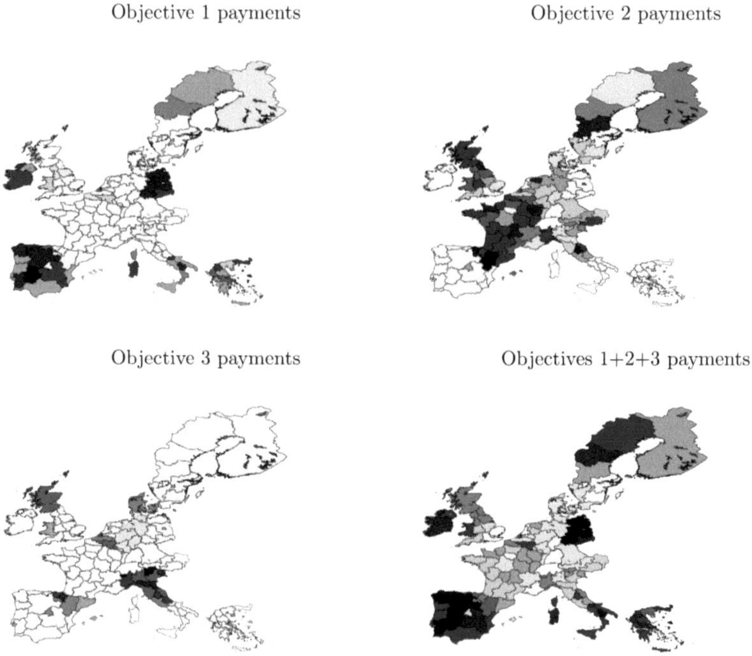

Notes: Own illustration. The payments of structural funds do not include multiregional funding programmes. The darker the area, the higher the relative share of regions' payments of structural funds per capita.

It could be argued that structural funds projects, such as infrastructure investment, only become effective after some time lag. Thus, we follow Mohl and Hagen (2010) and analyse the impact of time lags in greater detail: We start our empirical analysis by excluding any structural funds variable before gradually adding the lagged structural funds variables; beginning with a lag of one year and ending up with a specification comprising structural funds with lag of up to four-years ($sf_{i,t-j}$ with j = 1, ..., 4).

Due to multicollinearity the coefficients and standard errors of the structural funds variable cannot be interpreted if the variable is included into the regression with several lags. As a consequence, we calculate the sum of structural funds coefficients ($\sum_{j=1}^{J} sf_{i,t-j}$) corresponding to the short-run elasticity (Obj. short-term elast. (size)) and then use a simple Wald test to determine whether the short-run elasticity is statistically different from zero (Obj. short-term elast. (p-value)). As our estimation specification displayed in equation (5.1) equals a dynamic approach, it is more convincing to interpret the long-term impact of the structural funds. We do so and list its size (Obj. long-term elast. (size)) and significance level (Obj. long-term elast. (p-value)) in the regression output tables. The estimated long-term elasticity could be used to show that a one per cent increase of structural funds (per capita) leads to a rise of the regional employment level by $X\%$.

Moreover, we provide a more parsimonious specification and control for both country- and region-fixed effects by subtracting the annual country mean from each of the variables instead of including dummy variables (Bond, Hoeffler and Temple, 2001). For variables (union density, gross replacement rate) or countries (Denmark, Ireland and Luxembourg) where region-specific variables are not available, we subtract the annual EU mean. For illustrative purposes, the transformed employment level for Bavaria in year t is computed by subtracting the German employment level in year t, whereas in the case of Ireland, which only consists of one NUTS region, we subtract the EU mean of year t.

Furthermore, in order to avoid losing observations, we replace missing entries of the compensation per employee variable with zero and include a dummy variable which is equal to 1 if the variable contains a missing entry (for a similar approach see Fitzenberger, Kohn and Wang, 2011). The dummy variable is never statistically significant and thus not displayed in the regression output tables. Finally, $u_{i,t}$ is the i.i.d. error term of the specification.

5.2.2 Spatial Panel Approach

The results of our baseline panel regression approach might be influenced by regional spillover effects, which have been neglected so far, resulting in biased estimates. In our sample of 130 European regions, the regions which are located next to each other might disclose a stronger spatial dependence than regions at a greater distance to one another.

In order to take these considerations into account, we apply spatial econometric techniques, using a $N \times N$ weight matrix (W) containing information about the connectivity between regions. Its diagonal consists of zeros, while each w_{ij} specifies the way region i is spatially connected to region j. To standardise the external influence upon each region, the weight matrix is normalised so that the elements amount to one. We follow the approach by Le Gallo and Ertur (2003) and Ertur and Koch (2006) and use a weight matrix consisting of the k-nearest neighbours computed from the distance between the centroids of the NUTS regions.[4] This weight matrix is based purely on geographical distance, which has the big advantage that exogeneity of geographical distance is unambiguous. It

[4] We use the Matlab toolbox "Arc_Mat" (LeSage and Pace, 2004) to determine the centroids of the polygons (regions) expressed in decimal degrees. These are converted to latitude and longitude coordinates and are available upon request. The x nearest neighbours of each region are then calculated with the help of the Spatial Statistics Toolbox 2.0 (Pace, 2003).

is defined as follows:

$$W(k) = \begin{cases} w^*_{ij}(k) = 0 \text{ if } i = j \\ w^*_{ij}(k) = 1 \text{ if } d_{ij} \leq d_i(k) \text{ and } w_{ij}(k) = w^*_{ij}(k)/\sum_j w^*_{ij}(k) \\ w^*_{ij}(k) = 0 \text{ if } d_{ij} > d_i(k) \end{cases}$$

where w^*_{ij} is an element of the unstandardised weight matrix W and w_{ij} is an element of the standardised weight matrix, $d_i(k)$ is the smallest distance of the kth order between regions i and j so that each region i has exactly k neighbours.[5]

Generally, the inclusion of a spatially lagged dependent variable into a panel fixed effects model generates an endogeneity problem because the spatially weighted dependent variable is correlated with the disturbance term (Elhorst, 2010). In order to control for this simultaneity, the following results are based on a quasi-maximum likelihood estimator for spatial dynamic panel models as proposed by Yu, de Jong and Lee (2008). This model foresees spatially-weighted coefficients for both the lagged and the contemporaneous employment level. Apart from the inclusion of the spatial weight variables, the selection of variables remains the same as in equation (1), so we estimate the following model:

$$\begin{aligned} emp_{i,t} = & \beta_0 + \lambda W\, emp_{i,t} + \rho W\, emp_{i,t-1} + \gamma\, emp_{i,t-1} + \beta_2\, comp.emp_{i,t-1} + \\ & + \beta_3\, pop.young_{i,t-1} + \beta_4\, low\, skilled_{i,t-1} + \beta_5\, market\, potential_{i,t-1} + \\ & + \beta_6\, grr_{i,t-1} + \beta_7\, union\, density_{i,t-1} + \beta_8\, sf_{i,t-j} + \mu_i + \lambda_t + u_{i,t} \end{aligned} \tag{5.2}$$

Unfortunately, it is currently not feasible to estimate a spatial lag model and to control simultaneously for endogeneity of the other independent variables, for example with a (system) GMM approach. The reason for this is that introducing a spatial weight matrix creates a non-zero log-Jacobian transformation from the disturbances of the model to the dependent variable, while the system GMM procedure by Blundell and Bond (1998) is based on the assumption of no Jacobian term involved.[6]

5.2.3 Panel Approach with Interaction Term

As indicated in the introduction, it is not clear from a theoretical perspective whether EU funding is indeed associated with higher employment levels. According to the capital-skill-complementary hypothesis (Griliches, 1969) and the skill-based technological change hypothesis (Berman, Bound and Griliches, 1994) the demand for skilled labour increases with decreasing capital costs, while the demand for unskilled labour decreases with dimin-

[5] For example, for $k = 10$ the elements of the row / column vector of the weight matrix (W) for the region "Region de Bruxelles-capitale" (be) are all zeros with the exception of the ten nearest neighbours (be2, be3, fr10, fr21, fr22, fr30, fr41, nl2, nl3 and nl4) whose elements are 0.1.

[6] We thank James LeSage for his helpful advice.

ishing capital costs. Hence, it might be argued that structural funds are only conditionally effective depending on the regional education level. In order to test this conditionality, we include an interaction term in the model of equation (1) and estimate the following specification:

$$\begin{aligned} emp_{i,t} = & \beta_0 + \beta_1\, emp_{i,t-1} + \beta_2\, comp.emp_{i,t-1} + \beta_3\, pop.young_{i,t-1} + \\ & + \beta_4\, low\, skilled_{i,t-1} + \beta_5\, market\, potential_{i,t-1} + \beta_6\, grr_{i,t-1} + \\ & + \beta_7\, union\, density_{i,t-1} + \beta_8\, sf_{i,t-1} + \beta_9\, sf_{i,t-1} \times low\, skilled_{i,t-1} + \\ & + \beta_{10} high\, skilled_{i,t-1} + \mu_i + \lambda_t + u_{i,t} \end{aligned} \tag{5.3}$$

To interpret this model, we calculate the marginal effects of structural funds on the employment level, which consists of the first derivative of the above regression model (for a general overview on interaction models see Braumoeller, 2004; Brambor, Clark and Golder, 2006). This implies that we have to evaluate the marginal effects at different values of *low skilled*. In doing so, we take into account that the low-skilled variable is only defined over a certain interval, and we calculate the marginal effects for a set of percentiles ($5^{th}, 10^{th} ..., 95^{th}$) between the minimum and the maximum of the variable *low skilled*. In contrast to plotting the marginal effects over evenly spaced values between the minimum and maximum of the *low skilled* variable, the use of percentiles has the advantage that it illustrates the frequency distribution of the variable and thus enables a more meaningful interpretation of the marginal effects. In addition, we indicate the level of uncertainty regarding the marginal effects by plotting the lower and upper bound of the 95% confidence intervals. The details of the calculations are described in the appendix in Section B.

5.3 Econometric Results

From an econometric point of view, the investigation of employment effects of EU funding poses several methodological challenges. First, the empirical results might be biased due to simultaneity: the allocation criteria of the structural funds are likely to be correlated with the dependent variable employment since its allocation depends, *inter alia*, on the regional unemployment rate and the employment structure. Second, regional employment variables might be influenced by regional spillover effects, as structural funds payments may increase one region's employment which, in turn, may affect neighbouring regions' employment positively or negatively. Finally, the estimation results might strongly depend on the choice of the econometric approach.

5.3.1 Baseline Panel Approach

We start with checking all specifications for autocorrelation using the test proposed by Wooldridge (2002) (Table 5.4). As the Wooldridge test clearly rejects the null hypothesis of no first-order autocorrelation, standard errors are specified to be robust not only to heteroskedasticity but also to serial correlation as proposed by Newey and West (1987).[7] We find a positive and strongly significant impact of the lagged dependent variable. The size and significance level of the coefficient hardly change, irrespective of how many lags of the structural funds variable are included. As expected, our wage variable (*comp.emp*) shows a negative coefficient, which is, however, not significant. A high share of young population and of low level education leads to a statistically significant reduction of the employment level. Moreover, the regional market potential has a positive and significant impact on the employment level. Both variables measuring labour market regulations at the national level–the gross replacement rate and the union density–are not statistically significant.

The main variable of interest is the structural funds variable. Table 5.4 reveals that the total Objective 1+2+3 payments are not statistically significant. One reason for this might be that the estimation results are biased due to endogeneity of the structural funds variable, since the employment structure is one criterion for the allocation of structural funds. In order to deal with this issue, the literature has suggested two kinds of external instrument variables. Dall'erba and Le Gallo (2008) instrument structural funds payments by the regions' distance to Brussels, arguing that the spatial distribution of structural funds payments follows a centre-periphery pattern. Bouvet (2005) uses partisan affinity as an instrument for structural funds. However, while the first set of instruments shows no variation over time at all, the time variation of variables related to political affinity is low and in some regions even zero. Thus, their effect on structural funds payments is absorbed once regional fixed effects are controlled for, rendering them unsuitable for a panel fixed effects approach.

As a consequence, we address the problem of endogeneity by basing the identification on internal instruments via a system GMM estimator (Blundell and Bond, 1998). We assume that lagged employment, compensation per employee, education, market potential and structural funds payments are endogenous. The standard errors are finite-sample adjusted following Windmeijer (2005). When using the system GMM estimator the number of instruments grows quadratically with T. Too many instruments can overfit the instrumented variables (Roodman, 2009b), reduce the power properties of the Hansen test (Bowsher, 2002) and lead to a downward-bias in two-step standard errors (Windmeijer,

7 As a robustness check, we used the estimation procedure proposed by Prais-Winsten and Driscoll and Kraay (1998). The results hardly change and they are available upon request.

2005). In order to guarantee a parsimonious use of instruments, we follow Mehrhoff (2009) and limit the number of instruments by using the 'collapse' option Roodman (2009b). As a robustness check we also increased the number of instruments in the system GMM regressions; however, the results hardly differ.

Given this parsimonious specification, the estimation results show that the Hansen test of overidentifying restrictions is not statistically significant, i.e. the null hypothesis which states that the instruments are not correlated with the residual cannot be rejected (Table 5.4). We also report the p-values for the tests of serial correlation. These tests are based on first-differenced residuals and we expect the disturbances $u_{i,t}$ not to be serially-correlated in order to yield valid estimation results. The regression output in Table 5.4 shows no second-order serial correlation (AR(2) (p-value)). For most variables, the size and significance level are comparable to the results of the previous regressions. The use of the system GMM estimator slightly increases the size of the coefficients of the lagged dependent variable, while the market potential variable is no longer statistically significant. Above all, the Objective 1+2+3 variable is still not statistically significant.

Even though the total payments of structural funds have no significant impact, it cannot be ruled out that sub-parts of the EU funding significantly affect the employment level. As a consequence, we re-run our regression model using more precise measures of structural funds, distinguishing between Objective 1, 2 and 3 payments. The results show that the size of the coefficients of the Newey and West specifications are in line with the results of the more aggregated analysis (Table 5.5). In particular, the coefficients of the disaggregated structural funds variable are not statistically significant. Switching to the system GMM estimator again slightly increases the size of the coefficients of the lagged dependent variable (Table 5.5). Moreover, the short- and long-term elasticities of Objective 1 payments now show jointly statistically significant negative coefficients when the structural funds variable is included with more than one lag, while Objective 3 payments have a significantly positive coefficient when more than two lags are included.

As mentioned above, the most likely channel through which structural funds affect employment is an increase in the regional capital endowment, which leads to an increase of the marginal product of labour, the output level, and, ceteris paribus, the labour demand, given a matching labour supply. When estimating the effect of EU funding on employment, some part of the causal effect might be, at least in an indirect way, absorbed by the inclusion of the market potential. For this reason we replace our proxy for the output level and define *market potential 2* for region i as the weighted GDP of the neighbouring regions, thereby excluding the GDP of region i. The reduced-form approach including the regions' output level may be interpreted as being based on a 'conditional labour demand model', the estimation strategy without the regions' output level as being based on an 'unconditional labour demand model'.

In line with the results of described above, the size and significance level of the independent variables hardly change.[8] In particular, our indicator measuring market potential is still positive and the total structural funds variable is not significant. We also estimated the model using the disaggregated structural funds variables. The size and significance levels remain broadly unchanged except that the Objective 3 variable is no longer statistically significant.

The use of the *market potential 2* variable is still associated with the potential problem of regional spillover effects. As a consequence, we drop the market potential variable and re-run the regressions. Table 5.6 reveals that the results of the independent variables broadly remain unchanged and that the structural funds variable is still not statistically significant. Switching to the disaggregated analyses shows that Objective 1 payments partly show a negative and significant coefficient, while Objective 3 funding has a jointly significant positive impact if the structural funds variable is included with more than one lag.

5.3.2 Spatial Panel Approach

The estimation of a spatial panel model requires the definition of a spatial weight matrix. We start our regression analysis with a very low value for the indicator measuring the closeness; assuming that the spillover effects are limited to the four closest regions ($k = 4$). Table 5.7 reveals that the contemporaneous spatial weight matrix (γ) has a positive and strongly significant coefficient, while the lagged spatial weight matrix (ρ) has a negative and statistically significant coefficient. This implies that spillover effects seem to have an immediate positive cross-regional effect, boosting the employment level before they turn negative. This negative impact may be explained by migration and commuting, i.e. people tend to move or commute to the neighbouring regions if economic differences of the regional labour market persist, resulting in negative employment effects in the origin region.

Apart from the spillover effect, the results show that the significance levels of the coefficients are broadly comparable with the non-spatial regressions. The size of most coefficients is slightly reduced as some of the causal relationship can be explained by regional spillover effects. The lagged dependent variable still has a strong positive impact on the employment level. A high share of young population and low levels of education have a significantly negative effect. Market potential promotes the regional employment, and the coefficients of union density and the gross replacement rate are not statistically significant.

[8] The detailed regression results are available upon request.

As regards the structural funds variable, Table 5.7 reveals that total structural funds now seem to have a jointly negative impact if more than two lags are included. Using more disaggregated structural funds data, we find a small negative impact of Objective 3 payments (Table 5.8). The results do not change when switching to the model excluding the market potential variable (Tables 5.7, 5.8).

As some papers claim that the regression results are very sensitive to the choice of the weight matrix (LeSage and Fischer, 2008; LeSage and Pace, 2010), we also estimate our regression model for various spatial weight matrices, i.e. we use different parameters of k, an inverse euklidean ($W.dist$) and an inverse squared euklidean ($W.dist2$) distance weight matrix. Table 5.9 shows that with a larger coefficient of the weight matrix the coefficients of the contemporaneous and lagged weight matrices rise. However, the increases are limited to a certain range, and the size and significance levels of the other independent variables are not substantially affected. Irrespective of the choice of the matrix, the weight coefficients are statistically significant at the 1% level. Furthermore, the size and significance levels of the other independent variables hardly change with a different weight matrix.

5.3.3 Panel Approach with Interaction Term

Finally, we investigate whether structural funds are conditionally effective depending on the education levels of the working age population, i.e. the skill-level of labour supply. For this purpose, we estimate an interaction model using the structural funds and the low-skill variable in an interaction framework. Unlike the remaining independent variables, the low-skilled variable is only available from the year 1999 onwards, so we restrict our estimation to three lags only.

The results displayed in Table 5.10 show that the lagged dependent variable is still strongly significant, while the statistical significance of the remaining coefficients is reduced. The coefficient of the interaction term tells us how the marginal effect varies according to values of low education, while its significance level tests whether low education (linearly) conditions the effect of structural funds on employment (and vice versa). However, as indicated above, it is more convincing to base the interpretation on the calculation of the marginal effects.

We graph the marginal effects of the short- and long-term elasticities for varying values of the education variable, starting with the total structural funds (top left panel) and followed by Objective 1 (top right panel), Objective 2 (bottom left panel) and Objective 3 (bottom right panel) payments (Figure 5.2). The straight line displayed in the graphs represent the marginal effect of structural funds surrounded by 95% confidence intervals. The marginal effects of structural funds are a linear function of *low skilled*. Moreover, the coefficients displayed in Table 5.10 indicate the impact of structural funds when *low skilled* is zero, while the interaction coefficient gives our estimate of the slope of the marginal effect line.

Figure 5.2 shows that the marginal effects of structural funds and our confidence regarding the marginal effects vary with values of *low skilled*. Moreover, the marginal effects of total structural funds payments clearly show a negative slope. The total structural funds payments have a positive impact on the employment level in regions with a low share of low-skilled population, while they have a negative impact in regions with a high share of low-skilled population. These insights are particularly valid for the marginal effects of the long-term elasticities of Objective 1+2+3 and of Objective 1 payments. As regards Objective 2 payments, the slope of the marginal effects depends on the number of lags and the confidence intervals point to no significant impact. Finally, the marginal effects of the Objective 3 payments have a slight negative slope but do not turn negative.

These results are still valid when switching to the model excluding market potential and when including the high-skilled variable as an additional independent variable. Moreover, the results hardly change when estimating a dynamic spatial panel interaction model in the model including or excluding market potential.[9] Finally, we estimate our interaction model by replacing the variable measuring educational attainment. We interact the structural funds variable with an indicator measuring the share of high-skilled population. Figure 5.7 illustrates that this leads to a positive linear effect, implying that structural funds have a positive impact on the employment level in regions with a high share of high-skilled population, whereas they negatively affect the employment level in regions with a low share of high-skilled population.

5.4 Conclusions

While the current literature on the effectiveness of EU funding has primarily concentrated on the investigation of the economic growth effects, the aim of this paper is to evaluate their employment impact. From a theoretical perspective higher expenditures on EU funding do not necessarily lead to higher total employment levels. Instead, its effectiveness depends, in particular, on whether structural funds payments are used as capital subsidies or as human capital investment and it is subject to the educational attainment of the population as well as to the labour market tightness. The paper contributes to the

[9] The estimation results are not displayed in their entirety due to space constraints but are available upon request. We also estimated the regression model with various spatial weight matrices in order to check the robustness of the results. The empirical evidence, which is available upon request, shows that the spatial panel interaction model does not depend on the choice of the spatial weight matrix.

literature by (i) investigating the relevance of the inconclusive theoretical prediction via the estimation of interaction effects, (ii) analysing more precise measures of EU aid over an extended time period and (iii) applying dynamic (spatial) panel techniques, controlling for heteroscedasticity, serial and spatial correlation, as well as for endogeneity. In particular, using a spatial dynamic panel approach, we find that regional spillovers do have a significant impact on the regional employment level irrespective of which Objective and time lag is analysed.

In line with the theoretical predictions, we find no clear evidence that EU funding promotes employment. Instead, structural funds payments seem to be used as capital subsidies: they have a statistically positive impact on employment in regions with a low share of low-skilled population, and they have a negative impact on the employment level in regions with a high share of low-skilled population. Broadly summarising, we find that a one per cent increase of total structural funds payments leads to a positive (negative) impact on the regional employment by approximately 0.05% in regions with a high (low) share of skilled population. These results seem to be mainly driven by Objective 1 funding, which corresponds to the largest part of total structural funds payments.

Apart from the theoretically-founded explanation, a statistically insignificant, or even negative, impact of structural funds payments can be explained by at least four factors: First, in contrast to Objective 1 payments, Objective 2 and 3 payments are not solely based on clear criteria. Hence, there is room for political bargaining and/or side payments so that politically motivated projects are financed rather than economically efficient and growth-increasing projects. Second, de jure the structural funds payments have to be co-financed. However, recent panel studies using country data provide evidence that some crowding out of national public investment may take place (Hagen and Mohl, 2009b; Mohl, 2012). This, in turn, might have a negative impact on the regional GDP. Third, Cohesion policy could be ineffective with regard to human capital investment. Finally, a positive employment effect due to additional labour demand driven by a short-term aggregate demand stimulus is only possible if the quality and quantity of labour supply suffices. This may not be the case in periods of positive output gaps, for example, in the new East-European member states.

The results have policy implications for the setup of future Multiannual Financial Frameworks. It becomes evident that EU funding lacks a clear concept on how to promote employment in the medium- to long-run. Our results indicate that the high-skilled population in particular benefits from EU structural funds payments. As a consequence, a strategy should define objectives which are clearly measurable and allow for an ex-post assessment of this policy field. This, in turn, would contribute to a more effective policy.

Acknowledgements

We thank Theodor Martens, Gabriel Glöckler, Stefan Huemer, Heidi Hellerich, one anonymous referee and the Editorial Board of the ECB Working Paper Series for providing fruitful comments.

5.5 Appendix

5.5.1 Description of the Dataset

The dataset is constructed as described in Chapter 1 and consists of the following 130 NUTS-1 and NUTS-2 regions, for which we have structural funds payments:

Belgium (3 NUTS-1 regions): Région de Bruxelles-capitale (be1), Vlaams Gewest (be2), Région Wallonne (be3);

Denmark (1 NUTS-2 region): Denmark (dk);

Germany (16 NUTS-1 regions): Baden-Württemberg (de1), Bayern (de2), Berlin (de3), Brandenburg (de4), Bremen (de5), Hamburg (de6), Hessen (de7), Mecklenburg-Vorpommern (de8), Niedersachsen (de9), Nordrhein-Westfalen (dea), Rheinland-Pfalz (deb), Saarland (dec), Sachsen (ded), Sachsen-Anhalt (dee), Schles- wig-Holstein (def), Thüringen (deg);

Greece (13 NUTS-2 regions): Anatoliki Makedonia, Thraki (gr11), Kentriki Makedonia (gr12), Dytiki Makedonia (gr13), Thessalia (gr14), Ipeiros (gr21), Dytiki Ellada (gr23), Ionia Nisia (gr22), Sterea Ellada (gr24), Peloponnisos (gr25), Attiki (gr30), Voreio Aigaio (gr41), Notio Aigaio (gr42), Kriti (gr43);

Spain (16 NUTS-2 regions): Galicia (es11), Principado de Asturias (es12), Cantabria (es13), País Vasco (es21), Comunidad Foral de Navarra (es22), La Rioja (es23), Aragón (es24), Comunidad de Madrid (es30), Castilla y León (es41), Castilla-La Mancha (es42), Extremadura (es43), Cataluña (es51), Comunidad de Valenciana (es52), Illes Balears (es53), Andalucía (es61), Región de Murcia (es62), Ciudad Autónoma de Ceuta (es63), Ciudad Autónoma de Melilla (es64);

France (22 NUTS-2 regions): Île de France (fr10), Champagne-Ardenne (fr21), Picardie (fr22), Haute-Normandie (fr23), Centre (fr24), Basse-Normandie (fr25), Bourgogne (fr26), Nord-Pas-de-Calais (fr30), Lorraine (fr41), Alsace (fr42), Franche-Comté (fr43), Pays-de-la-Loire (fr51), Bretagne (fr52), Poitou-Charentes (fr53), Aquitaine (fr61), Midi-Pyrénées (fr62), Limousin (fr63), Rhône-Alpes (fr71), Auvergne (fr72), Languedoc-Roussillon (fr81), Provence-Alpes-Côte d'Azur (fr82), Corse (fr83);

Ireland (1 NUTS-1 region): Irland (ie);

Italy (21 NUTS-2 regions): Piemonte (itc1), Valle d'Aosta/Vallée d'Aoste (itc2), Liguria (itc3), Lombardia (itc4), Provincia autonoma Bolzano (itd1), Provincia autonoma Trento (itd2), Veneto (itd3), Friuli-Venezia Giulia (itd4), Emilia-Romagna (itd5), Toscana (ite1), Umbria (ite2), Marche (ite3), Lazio (ite4), Abruzzo (itf1), Molise (itf2), Campania (itf3), Puglia (itf4), Basilicata (itf5), Calabria (itf6), Sicilia (itg1), Sardegna (itg2);

The Netherlands (4 NUTS-1 regions): Noord-Nederland (nl1), Oost-Nederland (nl2), West-Nederland (nl3), Zuid-Nederland (nl4);

Luxembourg (1 NUTS-1 region): Luxembourg (lu);

Austria (3 NUTS-1 regions): Ostösterreich (at1), Südösterreich (at2), Westösterreich (at3);

Portugal (5 NUTS-2 regions): Norte (pt11), Algarve (pt15), Centro (P) (pt16), Lisboa (pt17), Alentejo (pt18);

Finland (2 NUTS-1 regions): Manner-Suomi (fi1), Åland (fi2);

Sweden (8 NUTS-2 regions): Stockholm (se11), Östra Mellansverige (se12), Småland med öarna (se021), Sydsverige (se22), Västsverige (se23), Norra Mellansverige (se31), Mellersta Norrland (se32), Övre Norrland (se33);

UK (12 NUTS-1 regions): North East (ukc), North West (ukd), Yorkshire and the Humber (uke), East Midlands (ukf), West Midlands (ukg), East of England (ukh), London (uki), South East (ukj), South West (ukk), Wales (ukl), Scotland (ukm), Northern Ireland (ukn).

For the spatial econometric analysis, we additionally need data to specify the spatial weight matrix. In this context, we were given access to the Gisco Eurostat dataset containing spherical coordinates measured in latitudes and longitudes of the European Union and of the candidate countries (Eurostat, 2007). We adjust the data according to the selection of our dataset, which comprises 130 NUTS-1 and NUTS-2 regions. We use the Matlab toolbox "Arc_Mat" (LeSage and Pace, 2004) to determine the centroids of the polygons (regions) expressed in decimal degrees. These are converted to lattitude and longitude coordinates and are displayed in Table 3.26.

5.5.2 Regression Results

Table 5.4: Regression results using a reduced-form employment model including market potential (Obj. 1+2+3)

	(1)	(2)	(3)	(4)	(5)	(6)	(7)	(8)	(9)	(10)
	Newey and West (1987)					Two-step system GMM				
Emp. per wp. (t-1)	0.469***	0.469***	0.468***	0.466***	0.467***	0.593***	0.594***	0.664***	0.718***	0.737***
	(4.063)	(4.060)	(4.095)	(4.077)	(4.083)	(6.738)	(7.799)	(9.635)	(9.830)	(11.21)
Comp. emp. (t-1)	-0.00329	-0.00331	-0.00237	-0.00252	-0.00252	-0.00392	-0.00529	-0.0349	-0.0303	-0.0301
	(-0.241)	(-0.242)	(-0.175)	(-0.185)	(-0.185)	(-0.0596)	(-0.112)	(-0.779)	(-0.852)	(-0.711)
Pop. young (t-1)	-0.156***	-0.155***	-0.157***	-0.158***	-0.158***	-0.113**	-0.120**	-0.0858*	-0.0817*	-0.0812*
	(-4.381)	(-4.361)	(-4.399)	(-4.384)	(-4.383)	(-2.586)	(-3.072)	(-2.174)	(-2.157)	(-2.163)
Low-skilled (t-1)	-0.0749*	-0.0750*	-0.0725*	-0.0724*	-0.0726*	-0.0632	-0.0696*	-0.100**	-0.0701	-0.0645
	(-2.010)	(-2.012)	(-1.990)	(-1.995)	(-1.991)	(-1.762)	(-2.326)	(-2.658)	(-1.694)	(-1.745)
Grr (t-1)	0.000342	0.000346	0.000199	0.000155	0.000172	-0.000719	0.00163	0.00247	0.00173	0.000825
	(0.0362)	(0.0366)	(0.0203)	(0.0157)	(0.0175)	(-0.125)	(0.317)	(0.416)	(0.348)	(0.197)
Union density (t-1)	0.00410	0.00405	0.00542	0.00609	0.00599	-0.00230	-0.00231	-0.00119	-0.00195	-0.00195
	(0.128)	(0.126)	(0.168)	(0.187)	(0.183)	(-0.580)	(-0.571)	(-0.302)	(-0.466)	(-0.627)
Market potential (t-1)	0.122*	0.123*	0.105*	0.100	0.0999	0.0542	0.0483	0.0416	0.0309	0.0360
	(2.449)	(2.472)	(2.063)	(1.946)	(1.945)	(1.062)	(1.337)	(0.951)	(1.164)	(1.377)
SF pc Obj. 1+2+3 (t-1)		0.000177	0.000437	0.000453	0.000451		-0.00236	-0.00258	-0.00486	-0.00519
		(0.0968)	(0.240)	(0.249)	(0.248)		(-0.436)	(-0.523)	(-0.991)	(-1.074)
SF pc Obj. 1+2+3 (t-2)			-0.00347*	-0.00336*	-0.00337*			7.94e-05	0.000337	3.91e-05
			(-2.045)	(-2.040)	(-2.057)			(0.0396)	(0.124)	(0.0165)
SF pc Obj. 1+2+3 (t-3)				-0.00147	-0.00149				0.000787	0.000542
				(-0.941)	(-0.945)				(0.387)	(0.316)
SF pc Obj. 1+2+3 (t-4)					0.000237					0.00213
					(0.214)					(1.269)
Constant	-0.117**	-0.117**	-0.100	-0.0970	-0.0960	0.00213	0.00226	0.00233	0.00169	0.00139
	(-2.599)	(-2.598)	(-1.436)	(-1.358)	(-1.350)	(0.790)	(0.842)	(0.869)	(0.830)	(0.796)
Obj. 1+2+3 short-term elast. (size)			-0.00303	-0.00437	-0.00417			-0.00250	-0.00374	-0.00248
Obj. 1+2+3 short-term elast. (p-value)			0.153	0.103	0.144			0.599	0.545	0.634
Obj. 1+2+3 long-term elast. (size)		0.000334	-0.00571	-0.00819	-0.00783		-0.00582	-0.00743	-0.0133	-0.00942
Obj. 1+2+3 long-term elast. (p-value)		0.923	0.152	0.105	0.154		0.666	0.607	0.519	0.618
Wooldridge AR(1) (p-value)	0	0	0	0	0					
AR(1) (p-value)						0.00243	0.00168	0.000473	0.000342	0.000273
AR(2) (p-value)						0.248	0.246	0.265	0.278	0.300
Hansen (p-value)						0.422	0.455	0.449	0.392	0.645
No. of instruments						33	41	49	57	65
No. of observations	959	959	959	959	959	959	959	959	959	959
No. of regions	129	129	129	129	129	129	129	129	129	129

Notes: In columns (1) to (5) standard errors are calculated according to Newey and West (1987), t-statistics are reported in parentheses. In columns (6) to (10) z-statistics are listed in parentheses applying the two-step system GMM estimator as proposed by (Blundell and Bond, 1998). The lagged dependent variable, compensation per employee, low-skilled, market potential and the structural funds variables are assumed to be endogenous. We instrument the endogenous variables with both its lags and its differenced lags and use the "collapse" option. Standard errors are corrected using the approach by Windmeijer (2005). * significant at 10%; ** significant at 5%; *** significant at 1%.

Table 5.5: Regression results using a reduced-form employment model including market potential (Obj. 1, 2, 3)

	(1)	(2)	(3)	(4)	(5)	(6)	(7)	(8)	(9)
	Newey and West (1987)					Two-step system GMM			
Emp. per wp. (t-1)	0.469***	0.467***	0.468***	0.467***	0.468***	0.588***	0.629***	0.670***	0.677***
	(4.063)	(4.026)	(4.045)	(4.034)	(4.040)	(8.791)	(11.39)	(14.18)	(16.92)
Comp. emp. (t-1)	-0.00329	-0.00368	-0.00336	-0.00363	-0.00352	-0.0503	-0.0760*	-0.0587*	-0.0509
	(-0.241)	(-0.268)	(-0.244)	(-0.263)	(-0.255)	(-1.049)	(-1.973)	(-2.208)	(-1.190)
Pop. young (t-1)	-0.156***	-0.154***	-0.151***	-0.151***	-0.150***	-0.104*	-0.0658	-0.0471*	-0.0258
	(-4.381)	(-4.296)	(-4.154)	(-4.053)	(-4.003)	(-2.532)	(-1.657)	(-2.069)	(-0.960)
Low-skilled (t-1)	-0.0749*	-0.0746*	-0.0722	-0.0707	-0.0720	-0.0947**	-0.103***	-0.0746	-0.0635
	(-2.010)	(-1.988)	(-1.946)	(-1.900)	(-1.885)	(-2.688)	(-3.439)	(-1.754)	(-1.657)
Grr (t-1)	0.000342	0.000384	0.000125	0.000167	0.000228	-0.00180	-0.000712	-0.00277	-0.00155
	(0.0362)	(0.0409)	(0.0130)	(0.0172)	(0.0236)	(-0.265)	(-0.114)	(-0.547)	(-0.322)
Union density (t-1)	0.00410	0.00417	0.00542	0.00593	0.00570	-0.00237	-0.00239	-0.00218	-0.00161
	(0.128)	(0.130)	(0.166)	(0.180)	(0.173)	(-0.547)	(-0.608)	(-0.534)	(-0.335)
Market potential (t-1)	0.122*	0.125*	0.119*	0.116*	0.115*	0.0599	0.0359	0.0215	0.0196
	(2.449)	(2.502)	(2.346)	(2.255)	(2.288)	(1.272)	(1.191)	(1.055)	(1.145)
SF pc Obj. 1 (t-1)		0.000650	0.00156	0.00150	0.00143	-0.00394	-0.00416	-0.00692	-0.00632
		(0.452)	(1.082)	(1.058)	(1.018)	(-0.866)	(-1.266)	(-1.539)	(-1.784)
SF pc Obj. 1 (t-2)			-0.00363*	-0.00389*	-0.00398*		-0.00234	-0.00186	-0.00216
			(-2.140)	(-2.336)	(-2.311)		(-1.215)	(-0.682)	(-0.888)
SF pc Obj. 1 (t-3)				-0.000244	-0.000316			0.000920	0.000875
				(-0.177)	(-0.222)			(0.372)	(0.452)
SF pc Obj. 1 (t-4)					0.000579				0.000953
					(0.389)				(0.635)
SF pc Obj. 2 (t-1)		-0.00116	-0.00198	-0.00192	-0.00185	0.000992	0.00399	0.00813	0.00527
		(-0.603)	(-1.049)	(-1.000)	(-0.948)	(0.204)	(0.535)	(1.043)	(0.804)
SF pc Obj. 2 (t-2)			0.00105	0.00120	0.00114		0.000819	-0.000518	0.000460
			(0.726)	(0.833)	(0.766)		(0.266)	(-0.126)	(0.149)
SF pc Obj. 2 (t-3)				-0.00181	-0.00174			-0.00134	-0.000178
				(-1.195)	(-1.170)			(-0.542)	(-0.0922)
SF pc Obj. 2 (t-4)					0.000365				0.00164
					(0.264)				(1.132)
Constant	-0.117**	-0.122**	-0.114**	-0.113	-0.112	0.00259	0.00254	0.00171	0.000849
	(-2.599)	(-3.089)	(-2.891)	(-1.567)	(-1.561)	(0.882)	(0.767)	(0.738)	(0.368)
Obj. 1 short-term elast. (size)			-0.00207	-0.00264	-0.00228		-0.00649	-0.00786	-0.00665
Obj. 1 short-term elast. (p-value)			0.353	0.337	0.417		0.0194	0.0169	0.0594
Obj. 1 long-term elast. (size)		0.00122	-0.00390	-0.00495	-0.00429	-0.00957	-0.0175	-0.0238	-0.0206
Obj. 1 long-term elast. (p-value)		0.657	0.358	0.347	0.433	0.370	0.00929	0.0115	0.0456
Obj. 2 short-term elast. (size)			-0.000936	-0.00254	-0.00209		0.00481	0.00628	0.00719
Obj. 2 short-term elast. (p-value)			0.654	0.232	0.390		0.419	0.176	0.164
Obj. 2 long-term elast. (size)		-0.00218	-0.00176	-0.00477	-0.00393	0.00241	0.0130	0.0190	0.0222
Obj. 2 long-term elast. (p-value)		0.545	0.545	0.201	0.366	0.842	0.435	0.194	0.186
Obj. 3 short-term elast. (size)			0.00126	0.00153	0.000987		0.00628	0.0135	0.0164
Obj. 3 short-term elast. (p-value)			0.614	0.600	0.764		0.610	0.152	0.0265
Obj. 3 long-term elast. (size)		0.00246	0.00237	0.00287	0.00185	0.0133	0.0169	0.0410	0.0506
Obj. 3 long-term elast. (p-value)		0.504	0.613	0.602	0.763	0.486	0.613	0.129	0.0172
Wooldridge test AR(1) (p-value)	0	0	0	0	0				
AR(1) (p-value)						0.000676	0.000236	7.59e-05	5.49e-05
AR(2) (p-value)						0.238	0.217	0.208	0.226
Hansen (p-value)						0.858	0.466	0.255	0.340
No. of instruments						57	81	105	129
No. of observations	959	959	959	959	959	959	959	959	959
No. of regions	129	129	129	129	129	129	129	129	129

Notes: In columns (1) to (5) standard errors are calculated according to Newey and West (1987), t-statistics are reported in parentheses. In columns (6) to (9) z-statistics are listed in parentheses applying the two-step system GMM estimator as proposed by (Blundell and Bond, 1998). The lagged dependent variable, compensation per employee, low-skilled, market potential and the structural funds variables are assumed to be endogenous. We instrument the endogenous variables with both its lags and its differenced lags and use the "collapse" option. Standard errors are corrected using the approach by Windmeijer (2005). The Obj. 3 specific results are omitted due to space constraint, but are available upon request. * significant at 10%; ** significant at 5%; *** significant at 1%.

Table 5.6: Regression results using a reduced-form employment model excluding market potential

	(1)	(2)	(3)	(4)	(5)	(6)	(7)	(8)	(9)	(10)
		Obj. X = Obj. 1+2+3					Obj. X = Obj. 1			
Emp. per wp. (t-1)	0.622***	0.606***	0.692***	0.756***	0.832***	0.639***	0.613***	0.670***	0.692***	0.704***
	(5.997)	(8.186)	(10.10)	(10.31)	(14.90)	(6.133)	(9.324)	(12.25)	(14.60)	(15.67)
Comp. emp. (t-1)	0.0223	0.0347	-0.00402	-0.0313	-0.0255	0.0203	-0.00679	-0.0575	-0.0508	-0.0467
	(0.476)	(0.740)	(-0.108)	(-1.046)	(-0.861)	(0.463)	(-0.202)	(-1.623)	(-1.846)	(-1.315)
Pop. young (t-1)	-0.0569	-0.0775*	-0.0461	-0.0497	-0.0317	-0.0695	-0.0689	-0.0283	-0.0250	-0.00977
	(-1.482)	(-2.427)	(-1.479)	(-1.688)	(-1.494)	(-1.560)	(-1.941)	(-0.825)	(-1.114)	(-0.332)
Low-skilled (t-1)	-0.111*	-0.0953**	-0.130**	-0.0943*	-0.107*	-0.102*	-0.0894**	-0.117**	-0.0937*	-0.0707
	(-2.317)	(-2.767)	(-2.610)	(-2.144)	(-2.569)	(-2.228)	(-2.751)	(-2.904)	(-2.207)	(-1.738)
Grr (t-1)	0.00311	0.00269	0.00360	0.00149	0.00177	0.00228	0.00161	0.00105	-0.00261	-0.00202
	(0.552)	(0.457)	(0.566)	(0.302)	(0.462)	(0.420)	(0.250)	(0.178)	(-0.523)	(-0.401)
Union density (t-1)	-0.00139	-0.000934	0.000473	-0.000602	0.000793	-0.00183	-0.00238	-0.00185	-0.00158	-0.000769
	(-0.349)	(-0.236)	(0.121)	(-0.142)	(0.252)	(-0.445)	(-0.625)	(-0.479)	(-0.401)	(-0.150)
SF pc Obj. X (t-1)		-0.00272	-0.00142	-0.00616	-0.00565		-0.00499	-0.00306	-0.00875	-0.00722
		(-0.503)	(-0.296)	(-0.889)	(-0.873)		(-1.268)	(-0.901)	(-1.862)	(-1.686)
SF pc Obj. X (t-2)			0.000630	-0.000688	-0.00105			-0.00182	-0.00102	-0.00164
			(0.314)	(-0.207)	(-0.404)			(-1.036)	(-0.416)	(-0.759)
SF pc Obj. X (t-3)				-0.000274	-0.000463				0.00183	0.00126
				(-0.129)	(-0.262)				(0.806)	(0.558)
SF pc Obj. X (t-4)					0.00188					0.00138
					(0.985)					(0.778)
SF pc Obj. 2 (t-1)							0.00126	0.00418	0.00677	0.00601
							(0.232)	(0.541)	(0.980)	(0.980)
SF pc Obj. 2 (t-2)								0.000695	-0.000772	0.000554
								(0.207)	(-0.203)	(0.173)
SF pc Obj. 2 (t-3)									-0.00129	-0.000418
									(-0.563)	(-0.198)
SF pc Obj. 2 (t-4)										0.00148
										(0.953)
Constant	0.00293	0.00261	0.00291	0.00207	0.00189	0.00254	0.00267	0.00333	0.00167	0.00129
	(0.993)	(0.876)	(0.937)	(1.101)	(1.031)	(0.869)	(1.019)	(1.156)	(0.724)	(0.531)
Obj. X short-term elast. (size)			-0.000786	-0.00712	-0.00528			-0.00488	-0.00795	-0.00623
Obj. X short-term elast. (p-value)			0.860	0.361	0.380			0.120	0.0243	0.124
Obj. X long-term elast. (size)		-0.00690	-0.00255	-0.0292	-0.0314		-0.0129	-0.0148	-0.0258	-0.0210
Obj. X long-term elast. (p-value)		0.617	0.861	0.308	0.318		0.184	0.0778	0.0145	0.0870
Obj. 2 short-term elast. (size)								0.00488	0.00471	0.00763
Obj. 2 short-term elast. (p-value)								0.396	0.206	0.121
Obj. 2 long-term elast. (size)							0.00326	0.0148	0.0153	0.0257
Obj. 2 long-term elast. (p-value)							0.820	0.415	0.226	0.154
AR(1) (p-value)	0.00251	0.00139	0.000290	0.000288	0.000139	0.00207	0.000398	8.16e-05	6.07e-05	4.83e-05
AR(2) (p-value)	0.251	0.250	0.274	0.293	0.332	0.255	0.234	0.205	0.205	0.232
Hansen (p-value)	0.200	0.171	0.258	0.206	0.226	0.174	0.491	0.436	0.346	0.280
No. of instruments	26	34	42	50	58	26	50	74	98	122
No. of observations	964	964	964	964	964	964	964	964	964	964
No. of regions	130	130	130	130	130	130	130	130	130	130

Notes: In columns (1) to (5) standard errors are calculated according to Newey and West (1987), t-statistics are reported in parentheses. In columns (6) to (9) z-statistics are listed in parentheses applying the two-step system GMM estimator as proposed by (Blundell and Bond, 1998). The lagged dependent variable, compensation per employee, low-skilled, market potential and the structural funds variables are assumed to be endogenous. We instrument the endogenous variables with both its lags and its differenced lags and use the "collapse" option. Standard errors are corrected using the approach by Windmeijer (2005). The Obj. 3 specific results are omitted due to space constraint, but are available upon request. * significant at 10%; ** significant at 5%; *** significant at 1%.

Table 5.7: Regression results using a spatial panel model (Obj. 1+2+3)

	(1)	(2)	(3)	(4)	(5)	(6)	(7)	(8)	(9)	(10)
	Reduced-form employment model including market potential					Reduced-form employment model excluding market potential				
γ	0.34154***	0.34157***	0.34173***	0.3381***	0.33821***	0.35114***	0.35093***	0.34989***	0.34537***	0.34563***
	-11.8197	-11.8221	-11.8487	-11.7104	-11.6907	-12.2548	-12.2495	-12.2401	-12.0608	-12.0516
ρ	-0.22456***	-0.22542***	-0.2276***	-0.22404***	-0.22412***	-0.23212***	-0.23312***	-0.23459***	-0.23023***	-0.23042***
	(-5.1052)	(-5.1214)	(-5.1788)	(-5.1011)	(-5.1005)	(-5.2817)	(-5.3028)	(-5.3482)	(-5.2515)	(-5.2543)
Emp. per w.p. (t-1)	0.38197***	0.38197***	0.38197***	0.38197***	0.38197***	0.38197***	0.38197***	0.38197***	0.38197***	0.38197***
	-11.3023	-11.3033	-11.31	-11.3159	-11.316	-11.3032	-11.3049	-11.3123	-11.3185	-11.3186
Comp. emp. (t-1)	-0.01255	-0.012424	-0.011004	-0.010827	-0.010841	-0.009644	-0.009546	-0.008308	-0.008318	-0.008371
	(-0.73969)	(-0.73231)	(-0.64912)	(-0.63959)	(-0.64038)	(-0.56861)	(-0.56295)	(-0.49082)	(-0.49225)	(-0.49532)
Pop. young (t-1)	-0.18847***	-0.19002***	-0.19126***	-0.19172***	-0.19161***	-0.18125***	-0.18357***	-0.18582***	-0.18671***	-0.18643***
	(-4.3752)	(-4.4003)	(-4.4349)	(-4.4511)	(-4.4445)	(-4.206)	(-4.2476)	(-4.3069)	(-4.3342)	(-4.3244)
Low-skilled (t-1)	-0.043752**	-0.043146**	-0.040268**	-0.039195**	-0.039277**	-0.048713**	-0.04775**	-0.043891**	-0.042463**	-0.042674**
	(-2.0353)	(-2.0042)	(-1.8692)	(-1.8214)	(-1.8215)	(-2.2723)	(-2.2232)	(-2.0412)	(-1.9771)	(-1.9834)
Grr (t-1)	0.0020002	0.0020406	0.0022363	0.0023245	0.0023232	0.0031164	0.0031432	0.0032223	0.0032439	0.0032355
	-0.15657	-0.15975	-0.17536	-0.18255	-0.18245	-0.24349	-0.24564	-0.25239	-0.25452	-0.25387
Union density (t-1)	0.012178	0.01226	0.012716	0.013553	0.013549	-0.001901	0.0093358	0.010231	0.01132	0.01132
	-0.42196	-0.42486	-0.44141	-0.47111	-0.47097	(-0.43053)	-0.32308	-0.35485	-0.3932	-0.39322
Market potential (t-1)	0.15636**	0.15343**	0.13591**	0.12651**	0.12627**					
	-2.2736	-2.2232	-1.9558	-1.8181	-1.8115					
SF pc Obj. 1+2+3 (t-1)		-0.0009578	-0.00062332	-0.00056028	-0.00056063		-0.001911	-0.001944	-0.002004	-0.002008
		(-0.50043)	(-0.3249)	(-0.29243)	(-0.29261)		(-0.43281)	(-0.44125)	(-0.45575)	(-0.45651)
SF pc Obj. 1+2+3 (t-2)			-0.0034714**	-0.0032124**	-0.0032201**			-0.0039358**	-0.0036218**	-0.003641**
			(-1.9207)	(-1.7742)	(-1.7739)			(-2.1926)	(-2.0127)	(-2.0192)
SF pc Obj. 1+2+3 (t-3)				-0.0030335**	-0.0030405**				-0.0032725**	-0.0032906**
				(-1.7652)	(-1.7652)				(-1.9069)	(-1.9136)
SF pc Obj. 1+2+3 (t-4)					9.59E-05					0.0002672
					-0.059439					-0.16563
Obj. 1+2+3 short-term elast. (size)		-0.0009578	-0.0040948	-0.0068063	-0.0067253		-0.001319	-0.004829	-0.007699	-0.007469
Obj. 1+2+3 short-term elast. (p-value)		-0.50043	0.12457	0.029199	0.050505		-0.69004	0.067509	0.012494	0.02882
Obj. 1+2+3 long-term elast. (size)		-0.0014547	-0.0062204	-0.010283	-0.010162		-0.002032	-0.007428	-0.011761	-0.011414
Obj. 1+2+3 long-term elast. (p-value)		0.63715	0.045153	0.00093857	0.0010769		0.51541	0.018151	0.0001848	0.0002834
Sum $\|\gamma\|+\|\rho\|+\|p\|$	0.94807	0.94896	0.95129	0.9441	0.94429	0.96523	0.96601	0.96645	0.95756	0.95802
No. of regions	130	130	130	130	130	130	130	130	130	130

Notes: The spatial dynamic panel estimator uses a quasi-maximum likelihood estimator applying the Matlab routine *sar_panel_jihai* by Yu, de Jong and Lee (2008). t-statistics are reported parentheses; * significant at 10%; ** significant at 5%; *** significant at 1%.

Table 5.8: Regression results using a spatial panel model (Obj. 1, 2, 3)

	(1)	(2)	(3)	(4)	(5)	(6)	(7)	(8)
	Reduced-form employment model including market potential				Reduced-form employment model excluding market potential			
γ	0.337***	0.33722***	0.33746***	0.34609***	0.34714***	0.34677***	0.34689***	0.35502***
	(-11.6425)	(-11.6595)	(-11.7298)	(-12.0723)	(-12.0977)	(-12.0952)	(-12.1556)	(-12.501)
ρ	-0.23042***	-0.23468***	-0.24356***	-0.22012***	-0.23835***	-0.2417***	-0.25018***	-0.22565***
	(-5.231)	(-5.309)	(-5.5465)	(-5.0069)	(-5.4153)	(-5.4708)	(-5.6974)	(-5.1329)
Emp. per w.p. (t-1)	0.38197***	0.38197***	0.38197***	0.38197***	0.38197***	0.38197***	0.38197***	0.38197***
	(-11.3309)	(-11.3468)	(-11.4942)	(-11.5887)	(-11.3346)	(-11.351)	(-11.4966)	(-11.5918)
Comp. emp. (t-1)	-0.010529	-0.009244	-0.008821	-0.010644	-0.007605	-0.006396	-0.005928	-0.008137
	(-0.62117)	(-0.54578)	(-0.52601)	(-0.63909)	(-0.44871)	(-0.37782)	(-0.35361)	(-0.48886)
Pop. young (t-1)	-0.20562***	-0.20722***	-0.19739***	-0.19394***	-0.19823***	-0.20029***	-0.19039***	-0.18719***
	(-4.7044)	(-4.7243)	(-4.5362)	(-4.476)	(-4.5319)	(-4.5635)	(-4.3723)	(-4.3201)
Low-skilled (t-1)	-0.043395**	-0.040953**	-0.046785**	-0.042372**	-0.048301**	-0.044929**	-0.050513**	-0.045677**
	(-2.0201)	(-1.893)	(-2.1718)	(-1.9737)	(-2.2532)	(-2.0789)	(-2.3459)	(-2.1292)
Grr (t-1)	0.0025073	0.0026931	0.0019783	0.002664	0.0036454	0.0037598	0.0030686	0.0036533
	(-0.19674)	(-0.21176)	(-0.1571)	(-0.21317)	(-0.28549)	(-0.29511)	(-0.24323)	(-0.29191)
Union density (t-1)	0.010906	0.010813	0.010265	0.0067268	0.0078653	0.0081114	0.0075839	0.004229
	(-0.37865)	(-0.37606)	(-0.36049)	(-0.23796)	(-0.27263)	(-0.28167)	(-0.2659)	(-0.14943)
Market potential (t-1)	0.16151**	0.15407**	0.15611**	0.14119**				
	(-2.3461)	(-2.2311)	(-2.279)	(-2.0701)				
SF pc Obj. 1 (t-1)	0.0016257	0.0023661	0.0032246	0.0031731	0.0012348	0.0020178	0.002893	0.0028602
	(-0.82966)	(-1.1745)	(-1.601)	(-1.5836)	(-0.63082)	(-1.0022)	(-1.4366)	(-1.4286)
SF pc Obj. 1 (t-2)		-0.00349**	-0.001338	-0.001822		-0.0038228**	-0.001641	-0.002153
		(-1.8771)	(-0.69695)	(-0.93888)		(-2.0579)	(-0.85433)	(-1.111)
SF pc Obj. 1 (t-3)			-0.0037218**	-0.0049366***			-0.0039226**	-0.0051717***
			(-1.9798)	(-2.5941)			(-2.0837)	(-2.7169)
SF pc Obj. 1 (t-4)				0.002582				0.002871
				(-1.3937)				(-1.5508)
SF pc Obj. 2 (t-1)	-0.001663	-0.002241	-0.003181	-0.002844	-0.001702	-0.002253	-0.003192	-0.002835
	(-0.84348)	(-1.1037)	(-1.5575)	(-1.399)	(-0.86099)	(-1.1071)	(-1.5588)	(-1.3916)
SF pc Obj. 2 (t-2)		3.46E-05	-0.001182	-0.00076		-0.000295	-0.001527	-0.001026
		(-0.017492)	(-0.59811)	(-0.38199)		(-0.14937)	(-0.77268)	(-0.51567)
SF pc Obj. 2 (t-3)			0.0068472***	0.0075695***			0.0067059***	0.0074734***
			(-3.7631)	(-4.1526)			(-3.6786)	(-4.093)
SF pc Obj. 2 (t-4)				-0.0062745***				-0.006344***
				(-3.5706)				(-3.6034)
Obj. 1 short-term elast. (size)		-0.001124	-0.001835	-0.001004		-0.001805	-0.00267	-0.001594
Obj. 1 short-term elast. (p-value)		0.67026	0.53127	0.74863		0.49187	0.35935	0.60994
Obj. 1 long-term elast. (size)	0.002452	-0.001696	-0.00277	-0.001535	0.0018914	-0.002763	-0.004088	-0.002471
Obj. 1 long-term elast. (p-value)	0.43369	0.59932	0.39138	0.63704	0.55187	0.39879	0.21287	0.45364
Obj. 2 short-term elast. (size)		-0.002207	0.002484	-0.002309		-0.002548	0.0019875	-0.002732
Obj. 2 short-term elast. (p-value)		0.41144	0.43535	0.52557		0.34311	0.53248	0.45286
Obj. 2 long-term elast. (size)	-0.002509	-0.003329	0.0037492	-0.003532	-0.002608	-0.003901	0.0030432	-0.004235
Obj. 2 long-term elast. (p-value)	0.42563	0.30485	0.2538	0.283	0.41606	0.2371	0.36188	0.20496
Sum $\|\gamma\|+\|\rho\|+\|p\|$	0.94938	0.95387	0.96298	0.94818	0.96746	0.97044	0.97904	0.96263
No. of observations								
No. of regions	130	130	130	130	130	130	130	130

Notes: The spatial dynamic panel estimator uses a quasi-maximum likelihood estimator applying the Matlab routine *sar_panel_jihai* by Yu, de Jong and Lee (2008). The Obj. 3 specific results are omitted due to space constraint, but are available upon request. t-statistics are reported parentheses; * significant at 10%; ** significant at 5%; *** significant at 1%.

Table 5.9: Size of the estimated spatial coefficients for different weight matrices (W)

Obj. 1, 2, 3	sf not included			sf up to 1 lag			sf up to 2 lags			sf up to 3 lags			sf up to 4 lags		
W	λ	ρ	γ	λ	ρ	γ	λ	ρ	γ	λ	ρ	γ	λ	ρ	γ
W2	0.32856	-0.1865	0.38197	0.32413	-0.18943	0.38197	0.32482	-0.19205	0.38197	0.32448	-0.19767	0.38197	0.33392	-0.17771	0.38197
W3	0.34154	-0.22456	0.38197	0.337	-0.23042	0.38197	0.33722	-0.23468	0.38197	0.33746	-0.24356	0.38197	0.34609	-0.22012	0.38197
W4	0.37156	-0.34118	0.53699	0.36791	-0.34606	0.54398	0.36716	-0.34877	0.53999	0.36603	-0.35288	0.52999	0.37292	-0.32835	0.51296
W5	0.38225	-0.38921	0.56596	0.37802	-0.39406	0.57	0.37788	-0.39841	0.56397	0.37713	-0.40448	0.55296	0.38329	-0.38017	0.53499
W6	0.38957	-0.45783	0.60199	0.38465	-0.46014	0.59195	0.385	-0.46692	0.58998	0.3847	-0.47585	0.57598	0.3915	-0.448	0.56698
W7	0.38546	-0.49458	0.602	0.38096	-0.49693	0.60196	0.38001	-0.50066	0.585	0.38017	-0.51256	0.575	0.38776	-0.48332	0.567
W8	0.37296	-0.50608	0.59696	0.36857	-0.50748	0.59099	0.36812	-0.51292	0.591	0.36687	-0.52166	0.56696	0.37688	-0.49287	0.55698
W9	0.36686	-0.51819	0.59398	0.36322	-0.52285	0.60295	0.36245	-0.52942	0.59895	0.36123	-0.53723	0.57899	0.37179	-0.50432	0.576
W10	0.36616	-0.56535	0.58698	0.36247	-0.57089	0.59299	0.36141	-0.57675	0.59097	0.35926	-0.58485	0.55697	0.37104	-0.55318	0.56397
W11	0.3632	-0.5758	0.589	0.35949	-0.58131	0.59398	0.35832	-0.58506	0.589	0.35657	-0.59123	0.56996	0.36768	-0.55659	0.557
W12	0.36044	-0.58417	0.60098	0.356	-0.59104	0.60599	0.35409	-0.5927	0.587	0.35255	-0.60396	0.568	0.36373	-0.56673	0.56499
W13	0.35468	-0.57504	0.61299	0.34913	-0.58129	0.60198	0.34858	-0.58531	0.60397	0.34682	-0.59689	0.583	0.35775	-0.55863	0.57
W14	0.34763	-0.58281	0.60298	0.34214	-0.58981	0.59196	0.34156	-0.59462	0.59594	0.33854	-0.59996	0.56499	0.35126	-0.56369	0.54796
W15	0.34088	-0.56878	0.61199	0.33552	-0.57599	0.606	0.33453	-0.57942	0.59497	0.33263	-0.58849	0.585	0.34595	-0.54928	0.57199
W.dist	0.34763	-0.58281	0.60298	0.34214	-0.58981	0.59196	0.34156	-0.59462	0.59594	0.33854	-0.59996	0.56499	0.35126	-0.56369	0.54796
W.dist2	0.37963	-0.67363	0.71899	0.37576	-0.6856	0.70098	0.37627	-0.69549	0.706	0.37476	-0.70408	0.68798	0.38238	-0.66052	0.671

Obj. 1+2+3	sf not included			sf up to 1 lag			sf up to 2 lags			sf up to 3 lags			sf up to 4 lags		
W	λ	ρ	γ	λ	ρ	γ	λ	ρ	γ	λ	ρ	γ	λ	ρ	γ
W2	0.32856	-0.1865	0.38197	0.32853	-0.18699	0.38197	0.32833	-0.1879	0.38197	0.32444	-0.18469	0.38197	0.32447	-0.1847	0.38197
W3	0.34154	-0.22456	0.38197	0.34157	-0.22542	0.38197	0.34173	-0.2276	0.38197	0.3381	-0.22404	0.38197	0.33821	-0.22412	0.38197
W4	0.37156	-0.34118	0.53699	0.37175	-0.34237	0.54299	0.37158	-0.3437	0.54497	0.36842	-0.33965	0.54999	0.36809	-0.33899	0.54397
W5	0.38225	-0.38921	0.56596	0.38259	-0.3913	0.57298	0.38222	-0.39189	0.57397	0.37909	-0.38781	0.57195	0.37933	-0.38805	0.57399
W6	0.38957	-0.45783	0.60199	0.38936	-0.45883	0.59698	0.38917	-0.46041	0.59796	0.3866	-0.45642	0.60199	0.38631	-0.45616	0.60096
W7	0.38546	-0.49458	0.602	0.38511	-0.49515	0.59599	0.38539	-0.49798	0.60598	0.38233	-0.49289	0.59797	0.38259	-0.49353	0.61098
W8	0.37296	-0.50608	0.59696	0.37285	-0.50681	0.59498	0.3734	-0.51314	0.59497	0.37147	-0.51093	0.60598	0.37055	-0.51004	0.59398
W9	0.36686	-0.51819	0.59398	0.36725	-0.51999	0.60498	0.36813	-0.52801	0.61095	0.36588	-0.52541	0.611	0.36531	-0.52526	0.611
W10	0.36616	-0.56535	0.58698	0.36669	-0.56725	0.60195	0.36705	-0.57349	0.60299	0.36466	-0.5707	0.59599	0.36406	-0.57073	0.596
W11	0.3632	-0.5758	0.589	0.36329	-0.57664	0.594	0.36388	-0.58273	0.60396	0.36158	-0.58031	0.598	0.36079	-0.58046	0.59696
W12	0.36044	-0.58417	0.60098	0.36034	-0.58487	0.603	0.3603	-0.58825	0.60498	0.35834	-0.5859	0.61096	0.35717	-0.58539	0.60297
W13	0.35468	-0.57504	0.61299	0.35454	-0.57547	0.61295	0.35433	-0.57913	0.60799	0.35195	-0.57747	0.60296	0.35107	-0.57762	0.59997
W14	0.34763	-0.58281	0.60298	0.34718	-0.58234	0.59499	0.34737	-0.58815	0.598	0.34503	-0.58702	0.59497	0.3442	-0.58805	0.59497
W15	0.34088	-0.56878	0.61199	0.34054	-0.56834	0.60597	0.34082	-0.57492	0.611	0.33852	-0.57399	0.60997	0.33768	-0.57473	0.60894
W.dist	0.34763	-0.58281	0.60298	0.34718	-0.58234	0.59499	0.34737	-0.58815	0.598	0.34503	-0.58702	0.59497	0.3442	-0.58805	0.59497
W.dist2	0.37963	-0.67363	0.71899	0.37934	-0.67385	0.71098	0.37944	-0.67817	0.70899	0.37699	-0.67499	0.72197	0.37616	-0.67349	0.70497

Notes: The spatial dynamic panel estimator uses a quasi-maximum likelihood estimator applying the Matlab routine *sar_panel_jihai* by Yu, de Jong and Lee (2008). Irrespective of which weight matrix is used, all indicators are statistically significant at the 1% level. The coefficients refer to equation (2) and correspond to $W\,emp_{i,t}$ (λ), $W\,emp_{i,t-1}$ (ρ) and $emp_{i,t-1}$ (γ).

Table 5.10: Regression results using an interaction model (Obj. 1+2+3)

	(1)	(2)	(3)	(4)
Emp. per wp. (t-1)	0.611***	0.588***	0.545***	0.727***
	(6.164)	(5.010)	(7.929)	(9.349)
Comp. emp. (t-1)	0.0417	0.0722	0.0967**	0.103
	(1.083)	(1.450)	(2.880)	(1.893)
Pop. young (t-1)	-0.0626	-0.0670	-0.0912*	-0.0430
	(-1.452)	(-1.444)	(-2.526)	(-0.988)
Grr (t-1)	0.00407	0.00219	0.00608	0.00190
	(0.691)	(0.478)	(0.870)	(0.236)
Union density (t-1)	-0.00178	-0.000570	-0.00189	-0.00253
	(-0.489)	(-0.131)	(-0.500)	(-0.551)
SF pc Obj. 1+2+3 (t-1)	-0.00325	-0.00137	-0.000596	-0.00301
	(-0.687)	(-0.283)	(-0.140)	(-0.670)
SF pc Obj. 1+2+3 x Low-skilled (t-1)	-0.0684	-0.0562	-0.0213	-0.0411
	(-1.507)	(-1.342)	(-0.437)	(-0.686)
Low-skilled (t-1)	0.156	0.189	0.200	0.347
	(1.161)	(1.303)	(1.292)	(1.054)
SF pc Obj. 1+2+3 (t-2)		0.000102	-0.00113	-0.000849
		(0.0476)	(-0.462)	(-0.232)
SF pc Obj. 1+2+3 x Low-skilled (t-2)		-0.0116	-0.0219	-0.00415
		(-0.458)	(-0.640)	(-0.0726)
Low-skilled (t-2)		-0.0587	-0.108	-0.358
		(-0.621)	(-0.887)	(-1.187)
SF pc Obj. 1+2+3 (t-3)			0.000281	-0.000613
			(0.117)	(-0.235)
SF pc Obj. 1+2+3 x Low-skilled (t-3)			-0.00939	0.0205
			(-0.684)	(0.988)
Low-skilled (t-3)			0.0316	-0.0485
			(0.588)	(-0.568)
SF pc Obj. 1+2+3 (t-4)				-0.00125
				(-0.575)
SF pc Obj. 1+2+3 x Low-skilled (t-4)				0.00517
				(0.287)
Low-skilled (t-4)				-0.0269
				(-0.366)
Constant	0.0142	0.00712	0.00649	0.0221
	(0.903)	(0.475)	(0.357)	(1.207)
Obj. 1+2+3 short-term elast. (size)		-0.00127	-0.00144	-0.00572
Obj. 1+2+3 short-term elast. (p-value)		0.788	0.784	0.294
Obj. 1+2+3 long-term elast. (size)	-0.00835	-0.00308	-0.00317	-0.0209
Obj. 1+2+3 long-term elast. (p-value)	0.510	0.783	0.784	0.266
AR(1) (p-value)	0.00115	0.00961	0.0189	0.00324
AR(2) (p-value)	0.246	0.606	0.186	0.411
Hansen (p-value)	0.606	0.560	0.358	0.200
No. of instruments	40	43	46	49
No. of observations	964	834	705	576
No. of regions	130	130	129	129

Notes: z-statistics are listed in parentheses applying the two-step system GMM estimator as proposed by (Blundell and Bond, 1998). The lagged dependent variable, compensation per employee, low-skilled, market potential and the structural funds variables are assumed to be endogenous. We instrument the endogenous variables with both its lags and its differenced lags and use the "collapse" option. Standard errors are corrected using the approach by Windmeijer (2005). * significant at 10%; ** significant at 5%; *** significant at 1%.

Figure 5.2: Marginal effects of structural funds on employment conditional on the share of low-skilled population

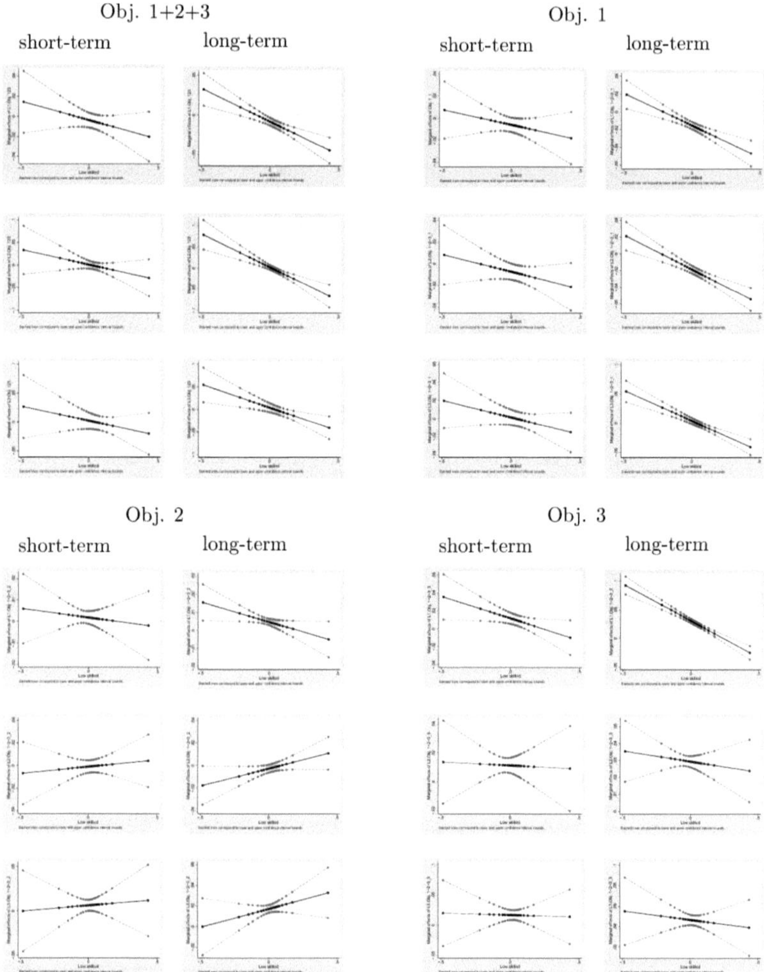

Notes: The estimation results are based on the baseline specification Reduced-form employment model including market potential displayed in equation (5.3). The regressions are estimated using the two-step system GMM estimator proposed by Blundell and Bond (1998), while standard errors are corrected using the approach by Windmeijer (2005). The lagged dependent variable, compensation per employee, low-skilled, market potential and the structural funds variables are assumed to be endogenous. We instrument the endogenous variables with both its lags and its differenced lags and use the "collapse" option. The marginal effects are calculated for short-term and long-term elasticities as well as for one to up to three lags. The marginal effects are displayed on the y-axes, the share of low-skilled population on the x-axes.

Figure 5.3: Marginal effects of structural funds on employment conditional on the share of high-skilled population

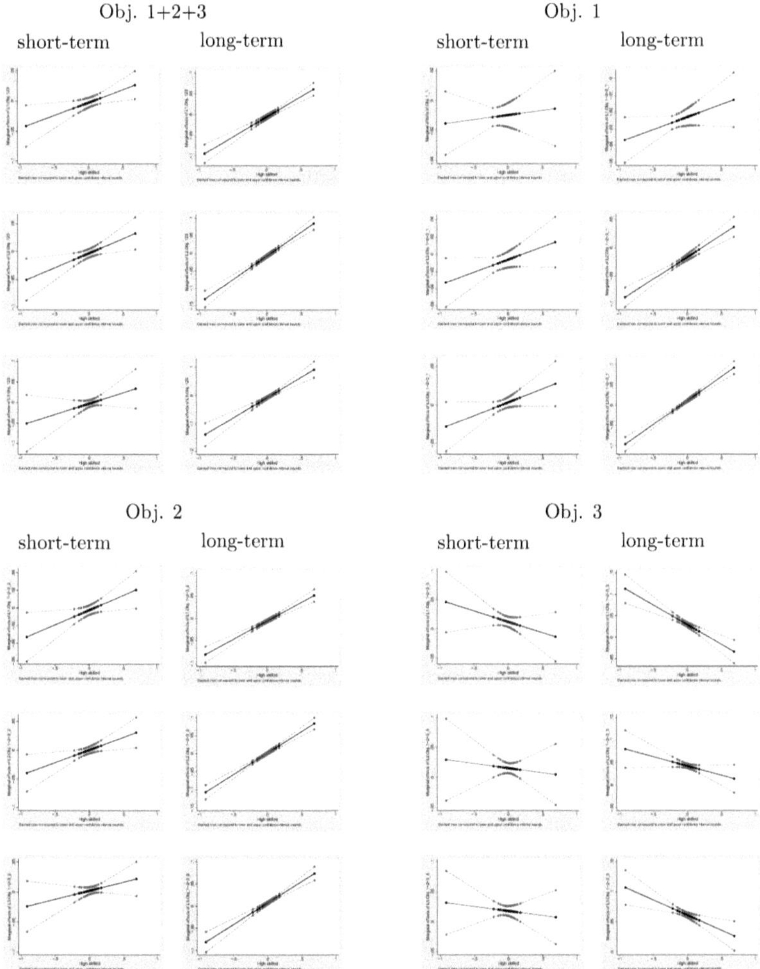

Notes: The estimation results are based on the baseline specification of the reduced-form employment model including market potential and interacting the structural funds variable with the share of high-skilled population. The regressions are estimated using the two-step system GMM estimator proposed by Blundell and Bond (1998), while standard errors are corrected using the approach by Windmeijer (2005). The lagged dependent variable, compensation per employee, high-skilled, market potential and the structural funds variables are assumed to be endogenous. We instrument the endogenous variables with both its lags and its differenced lags and use the "collapse" option. The marginal effects are calculated for short-term and long-term elasticities as well as for one to up to three lags. The marginal effects are displayed on the y-axes, the share of high-skilled population on the x-axes.

5.5.3 Calculation of the Interaction Effects

We estimate an interaction model, interacting two variables, namely structural funds (sf) and percentage share of low-skilled population (z). The marginal effects are calculated by taking the first derivative of our specification listed in equation (5.3), i.e.:

$$\frac{\partial\,\widehat{emp}}{\partial\, sf} = \widehat{\beta}_{L1.sf} + \widehat{\beta}_{L1.sf\cdot z} \cdot z$$

where $L.$ denotes the use of a lagged variable. The level of uncertainty regarding the marginal effects is indicated by the variance (Var) of the marginal effects. If the marginal effects consists of two addends (as it is the case in the equation above), the variance of the short-term elasticity can be calculated as follows:

$$\begin{aligned} Var\left(\frac{\partial\,\widehat{emp.}}{\partial\, sf}\right) &= Var(\widehat{\beta}_{L1.sf}) + z^2\, Var(\widehat{\beta}_{L1.sf\cdot z}) + \\ &+ 2\, z\, Cov(\widehat{\beta}_{L1.sf}, \widehat{\beta}_{L1.z}) \end{aligned}$$

Generally, if the marginal effects consists of more than two addends, the variance can be approximated using the following Taylor rule,

$$\begin{aligned} Var\left(g(X,Y)\right) \sim & \left(\frac{\partial g(X,Y)}{\partial X}\right)^2 \cdot Var(X) + \left(\frac{\partial g(X,Y)}{\partial Y}\right)^2 \cdot Var(Y) + \\ & + 2\left(\frac{\partial g(X,Y)}{\partial X} \cdot \frac{\partial g(X,Y)}{\partial Y} \cdot Cov(X,Y)\right) \end{aligned}$$

where $g(X,Y)$ stands for the function of the marginal effects.
This implies that the long-term elasticity is calculated as:

$$\begin{aligned} Var\left(\frac{\partial\,\widehat{emp.}}{\partial\, sf}\right) &= (Var(\widehat{\beta}_{L1.sf}) + z^2\, Var(\widehat{\beta}_{L1.sf\cdot z}) + \\ &+ 2\, z\, Cov(\widehat{\beta}_{L1.sf}, \widehat{\beta}_{L1.z})) \cdot (1 - \widehat{\beta}_{L1.emp})^{-1} \end{aligned}$$

If the estimation equation includes the structural funds variable with up to two lags, the marginal effects are computed via the following expression:

$$\frac{\partial\,\widehat{emp}}{\partial\, sf} = \widehat{\beta}_{L1.sf} + \widehat{\beta}_{L2.sf} + z\,(\widehat{\beta}_{L1.sf\cdot z} + \widehat{\beta}_{L2.sf\cdot z})$$

The variance of the short-term elasticity is then defined as:

$$
\begin{aligned}
Var\left(\frac{\partial \widehat{emp.}}{\partial sf}\right) &= Var(\widehat{\beta}_{L1.sf}) + Var(\widehat{\beta}_{L2.sf}) + z^2\, Var(\widehat{\beta}_{L1.sf\cdot z}) + \\
&+ z^2\, Var(\widehat{\beta}_{L2.sf\cdot z}) + 2\, Cov(\widehat{\beta}_{L1.sf}, \widehat{\beta}_{L2.sf}) + \\
&+ 2\, z\, Cov(\widehat{\beta}_{L1.sf}, \widehat{\beta}_{L1.sf\cdot z}) + 2\, z\, Cov(\widehat{\beta}_{L1.sf}, \widehat{\beta}_{L2.sf\cdot z}) + \\
&+ 2\, z\, Cov(\widehat{\beta}_{L2.sf}, \widehat{\beta}_{L1.sf\cdot z}) + 2\, z\, Cov(\widehat{\beta}_{L2.sf}, \widehat{\beta}_{L2.sf\cdot z}) + \\
&+ 2\, z^2\, Cov(\widehat{\beta}_{L1.sf\cdot z}, \widehat{\beta}_{L2.sf\cdot z})
\end{aligned}
$$

whereas the variance of the dynamic long-term elasticity is given by:

$$
\begin{aligned}
Var\left(\frac{\partial \widehat{emp.}}{\partial sf}\right) &= (Var(\widehat{\beta}_{L1.sf}) + Var(\widehat{\beta}_{L2.sf}) + z^2\, Var(\widehat{\beta}_{L1.sf\cdot z}) + \\
&+ z^2\, Var(\widehat{\beta}_{L2.sf\cdot z}) + 2\, Cov(\widehat{\beta}_{L1.sf}, \widehat{\beta}_{L2.sf}) + \\
&+ 2\, z\, Cov(\widehat{\beta}_{L1.sf}, \widehat{\beta}_{L1.sf\cdot z}) + 2\, z\, Cov(\widehat{\beta}_{L1.sf}, \widehat{\beta}_{L2.sf\cdot z}) + \\
&+ 2\, z\, Cov(\widehat{\beta}_{L2.sf}, \widehat{\beta}_{L1.sf\cdot z}) + 2\, z\, Cov(\widehat{\beta}_{L2.sf}, \widehat{\beta}_{L2.sf\cdot z}) + \\
&+ 2\, z^2\, Cov(\widehat{\beta}_{L1.sf\cdot z}, \widehat{\beta}_{L2.sf\cdot z}))\, \cdot (1 - \widehat{\beta}_{L1.emp})^{-1}
\end{aligned}
$$

Finally, we take account of the lower and upper bound of the 95% confidence intervals, which can be calculated as follows:

$$
\frac{\partial\, \widehat{emp}}{\partial\, sf} \pm t_{df,p} \sqrt{Var(d\, \widehat{emp}/d\, sf)},
$$

using the inverse t-distribution function to create the multiplier. $t_{df,p}$ is the critical value in a t-distribution and df stands for the degrees of freedom $(n-k)$, where n refers to the number of observations and k refers to the number or regressors, including the intercept, that produces a p-value at which hypothesis tests are to be made.

5.5.4 Additional Sensitivity Analyses

Alternative Specification Controlling for Serial Correlation

As indicated in the main text, we use an alternative approach to control for the serial correlation as indicated by the Wooldridge test of no first-order autocorrelation. We use the Prais-Winsten transformation matrix to transform the AR(1) disturbances in the error term into serially uncorrelated classical errors. This method slightly reduces the coefficients of the joint significance compared to the tables in the main text (Tables 5.11–5.12). Overall, the results and the significance levels remain very similar to those of the main specifications.

Sensitivity of the Results to the Number of Instruments Used in the Context of the System GMM Regressions

When using the system GMM estimator the number of instruments grows quadratically with T. Too many instruments can overfit instrumented variables (Roodman, 2009b), reduce the power properties of the Hansen test (Bowsher, 2002) and lead to a downward-bias in two-step standard errors (Windmeijer, 2005). In order to guarantee a parsimonious use of instruments, we follow Mehrhoff (2009) and limit the number of instruments to three and use the 'collapse' option Roodman (2009b). As indicated in the text, we also decreased the number of instruments in the system GMM regressions. The Tables 5.13, 5.14, 5.15 show that our key results are unchanged.

Testing for Non-Linear Effects

In Tables 5.16 - 5.17 we investigate whether there is a non-linear relationship between structural funds and employment by including the squared structural funds variable into the regression model. The results reveal that there is no evidence for a non-linear causal relationship between structural funds and employment.

Unconditional Labour Demand Model

As indicated in the main text, we replace our proxy for the output level and define market potential for region i as the weighted GDP of the neighbouring regions, thereby excluding the GDP of region i. The model including the regions' output level (*market potential 1*) may be interpreted as 'conditional labour demand model'; the model without the regions' output level (*market potential 2*) as 'unconditional labour demand model'.

In line with the results of the conditional labour demand model described above, the size and significance level of the independent variables hardly change (Table 5.18 - 5.19). In particular, our indicator measuring market potential is still positive and the total structural funds variable is not significant. We also estimated the model using the disaggregated structural funds variables. The size and significance levels remain broadly unchanged except that the Objective 3 variable is no longer statistically significant.

Alternative Specifications of the Interaction Model

We ran several robustness checks for our interaction model. Our main results are still valid when estimating

- an unconditional labour demand model (Figure 5.4)
- a conditional labour demand model including the high-skilled variable as an independent variable. The high-skilled variable is defined as the share of population aged 15 and over whose highest level of education is tertiary education, according to the International Standard Classification of Education (ISCED) 1997 levels 5-6 (Figure 5.5)
- an unconditional labour demand model including the high-skilled variable as an independent variable (Figure 5.6)

Moreover, we estimated the model, interacting the structural funds variable with the high-skilled variable share. According to the "capital-skill-complementary hypothesis" (Griliches, 1969), the demand for skilled labour increases with decreasing capital costs, while the demand for unskilled labour decreases with diminishing capital costs. In addition, the employment effects are inconclusive if structural funds payments have a positive effect on technological progress. According to the "skill-based technological change hypothesis" (see Berman, Bound and Griliches, 1994) technological progress may lead to an increase in the relative demand for high-skilled labour and thus, a decrease in demand for low-skilled labour. Our results reveal a positive relationship, i.e. structural funds have a significantly positive impact in regions with a high share of high-skilled population, and a negative impact in regions with a low share of high-skilled population. This result holds for the

- conditional labour demand model (Figure 5.7)
- conditional labour demand model including the low-skilled variable as an independent variable (Figure 5.8)
- unconditional labour demand model (Figure 5.9)

Spatial Interaction Model

Furthermore, we estimated the interaction model applying spatial econometric techniques. The results displayed in Figures 5.10 and 5.11 do not point to substantial differences compared with the classic panel regression results displayed in the main text.

Tables and Figures of the Additional Sensitivity Analyses

Table 5.11: Regression results using a conditional labour demand model, Prais-Winsten (Obj. 1+2+3)

	(1)	(2)	(3)	(4)	(5)
Emp. per wp. (t-1)	0.347*	0.345*	0.348*	0.345*	0.345*
	(2.338)	(2.330)	(2.364)	(2.342)	(2.344)
Comp. emp. (t-1)	-0.00153	-0.00154	-0.000543	-0.000819	-0.000826
	(-0.109)	(-0.109)	(-0.0385)	(-0.0579)	(-0.0584)
Pop. young (t-1)	-0.162***	-0.159***	-0.162***	-0.163***	-0.163***
	(-4.301)	(-4.254)	(-4.290)	(-4.295)	(-4.310)
Low skilled (t-1)	-0.0556	-0.0558	-0.0534	-0.0534	-0.0535
	(-1.500)	(-1.511)	(-1.474)	(-1.478)	(-1.470)
grr (t-1)	0.00118	0.00121	0.00106	0.000999	0.00101
	(0.113)	(0.116)	(0.0993)	(0.0929)	(0.0939)
Union density (t-1)	0.000802	0.000448	0.00182	0.00278	0.00272
	(0.0252)	(0.0141)	(0.0571)	(0.0865)	(0.0846)
Market potential (t-1)	0.132*	0.137*	0.121*	0.114*	0.114*
	(2.377)	(2.437)	(2.145)	(2.014)	(2.015)
SF pc Obj. 1+2+3 (t-1)		0.00121	0.000802	0.000794	0.000791
		(0.672)	(0.454)	(0.451)	(0.449)
SF pc Obj. 1+2+3 (t-2)			-0.00303*	-0.00328*	-0.00329*
			(-2.022)	(-2.096)	(-2.092)
SF pc Obj. 1+2+3 (t-3)				-0.00176	-0.00175
				(-1.220)	(-1.220)
SF pc Obj. 1+2+3 (t-4)					0.000133
					(0.116)
Constant	0.0807	0.0829	0.0763	0.0742	0.0740
	(1.570)	(1.601)	(1.495)	(1.456)	(1.453)
Obj. 1+2+3 short-term elast. (size)			-0.00223	-0.00425	-0.00411
Obj. 1+2+3 short-term elast. (p-value)			0.330	0.141	0.171
Obj. 1+2+3 long-term elast. (size)		0.00185	-0.00342	-0.00648	-0.00627
Obj. 1+2+3 long-term elast. (p-value)		0.508	0.311	0.118	0.156
Wald test region dummies (p-value)	0.280	0.362	0.363	0.337	0.333
Wooldridge AR(1) (p-value)	0	0	0	0	0
R-squared	0.925	0.924	0.925	0.925	0.925
Adj. R-squared	0.912	0.912	0.913	0.912	0.912
No. of observations	959	959	959	959	959

Notes: Serially adjusted standard errors according to the Prais-Winsten method, t-statistics are reported in parentheses; * significant at 10%; ** significant at 5%; *** significant at 1%; constant, region and time dummies are not shown.

Table 5.12: Regression results using a conditional labour demand model, Prais-Winsten (Obj. 1, 2, 3)

	(1)	(2)	(3)	(4)
Emp. per wp. (t-1)	0.340*	0.345*	0.342*	0.343*
	(2.288)	(2.327)	(2.310)	(2.310)
Comp. emp. (t-1)	-0.00163	-0.00141	-0.00164	-0.00165
	(-0.116)	(-0.0994)	(-0.116)	(-0.116)
Pop. young (t-1)	-0.160***	-0.157***	-0.157***	-0.156***
	(-4.255)	(-4.101)	(-4.038)	(-4.023)
Low skilled (t-1)	-0.0544	-0.0524	-0.0506	-0.0507
	(-1.463)	(-1.428)	(-1.384)	(-1.359)
grr (t-1)	0.00130	0.00107	0.00103	0.00108
	(0.126)	(0.102)	(0.0978)	(0.102)
Union density (t-1)	0.000458	0.00159	0.00272	0.00244
	(0.0143)	(0.0494)	(0.0838)	(0.0750)
Market potential (t-1)	0.141*	0.136*	0.131*	0.129*
	(2.526)	(2.421)	(2.308)	(2.325)
SF pc Obj. 1 (t-1)	0.00189	0.00195	0.00187	0.00181
	(1.356)	(1.297)	(1.243)	(1.185)
SF pc Obj. 1 (t-2)		-0.00312*	-0.00344*	-0.00354*
		(-2.355)	(-2.418)	(-2.351)
SF pc Obj. 1 (t-3)			-0.000597	-0.000604
			(-0.495)	(-0.489)
SF pc Obj. 1 (t-4)				0.000523
				(0.385)
SF pc Obj. 2 (t-1)	-0.00145	-0.00189	-0.00182	-0.00176
	(-0.789)	(-1.045)	(-0.995)	(-0.943)
SF pc Obj. 2 (t-2)		0.00108	0.000858	0.000886
		(0.701)	(0.554)	(0.561)
SF pc Obj. 2 (t-3)			-0.00193	-0.00186
			(-1.266)	(-1.258)
SF pc Obj. 2 (t-4)				-5.24e-05
				(-0.0384)
SF pc Obj. 3 (t-1)	0.00100	0.00147	0.00140	0.00153
	(0.532)	(0.776)	(0.744)	(0.785)
SF pc Obj. 3 (t-2)		-0.000612	-0.000679	-0.000587
		(-0.359)	(-0.389)	(-0.341)
SF pc Obj. 3 (t-3)			0.00127	0.00130
			(0.787)	(0.783)
SF pc Obj. 3 (t-4)				-0.000344
				(-0.235)
Constant	-0.131	-0.123	-0.121	-0.00142
	(-1.867)	(-1.714)	(-1.641)	(-0.0330)
Obj. 1 short-term elast. (size)		-0.00117	-0.00216	-0.00181
Obj. 1 short-term elast. (p-value)		0.588	0.415	0.494
Obj. 1 long-term elast. (size)	0.00287	-0.00179	-0.00329	-0.00275
Obj. 1 long-term elast. (p-value)	0.227	0.579	0.404	0.494
Obj. 2 short-term elast. (size)		-0.000803	-0.00290	-0.00279
Obj. 2 short-term elast. (p-value)		0.710	0.220	0.300
Obj. 2 long-term elast. (size)	-0.00219	-0.00123	-0.00441	-0.00425
Obj. 2 long-term elast. (p-value)	0.453	0.707	0.191	0.271
Obj. 3 short-term elast. (size)		0.00100	0.00199	0.00189
Obj. 3 short-term elast. (p-value)		0.745	0.534	0.597
Obj. 3 long-term elast. (size)	0.00152	0.00131	0.00303	0.00288
Obj. 3 long-term elast. (p-value)	0.593	0.745	0.540	0.599
WT region dummies (p-value)	0.270	0.352	0.262	0.153
Wooldridge test AR(1) (p-value)	0	0	0	0
R-squared	0.924	0.925	0.925	0.925
Adj. R-squared	0.911	0.912	0.911	0.911
No. of observations	959	959	959	959
No. of regions	129	129	129	129

Notes: Serially adjusted standard errors according to the Prais-Winsten method, t-statistics are reported in parentheses; * significant at 10%; ** significant at 5%; *** significant at 1%; constant, region and time dummies are not shown.

Table 5.13: Regression results using an unconditional labour demand model, two-step system GMM (Obj. 1+2+3)

	(1)	(2)	(3)	(4)	(5)
Emp. per wp. (t-1)	0.635***	0.580***	0.580***	0.725***	0.765***
	(5.470)	(6.843)	(7.020)	(13.03)	(14.81)
Comp. emp. (t-1)	0.0223	0.0144	0.0157	-0.00909	-0.0133
	(0.534)	(0.346)	(0.479)	(-0.218)	(-0.250)
Pop. young (t-1)	-0.0707	-0.0779*	-0.0897**	-0.0616*	-0.0483*
	(-1.431)	(-2.022)	(-2.656)	(-2.476)	(-2.145)
Low skilled (t-1)	-0.0869	-0.0559	-0.0742	0.0103	-0.0129
	(-1.787)	(-1.569)	(-1.893)	(0.301)	(-0.307)
grr (t-1)	0.00304	0.00439	0.00511	0.00296	0.00138
	(0.591)	(0.800)	(0.959)	(0.609)	(0.305)
SF pc Obj. 1 (t-1)		-0.00986*	-0.00595	-0.0155	-0.0124
		(-2.082)	(-1.265)	(-1.434)	(-1.768)
SF pc Obj. 1 (t-2)			0.00142	0.00244	0.00172
			(0.627)	(0.510)	(0.537)
SF pc Obj. 1 (t-3)				0.00358	0.00195
				(0.897)	(0.735)
SF pc Obj. 1 (t-4)					3.69e-05
					(0.0206)
Constant	0.00287	0.00141	0.00167	-0.000686	-0.000248
	(0.930)	(0.588)	(0.593)	(-0.325)	(-0.130)
Obj. 1 short-term elast. (size)			-0.00453	-0.00944	-0.00875
Obj. 1 short-term elast. (p-value)			0.242	0.101	0.101
Obj. 1 long-term elast. (size)		-0.0235	-0.0108	-0.0344	-0.0373
Obj. 1 long-term elast. (p-value)		0.0559	0.283	0.0558	0.0562
AR(1) (p-value)	0.00234	0.000767	0.000689	1.70e-05	1.05e-05
AR(2) (p-value)	0.284	0.301	0.289	0.295	0.342
Hansen (p-value)	0.113	0.458	0.490	0.0553	0.108
No. of instruments	25	33	41	49	57
No. of observations	988	988	988	988	988
No. of regions	130	130	130	130	130

Notes: Standard errors are corrected using the approach by Windmeijer (2005); z-statistics are listed in parentheses. The lagged dependent variable, compensation per employee, low skilled, market potential and the structural funds variables are assumed to be endogenous. We instrument the endogenous variables with both its lags and its differenced lags restricting the lag limit to three and use the "collapse" option. significant at 10%; ** significant at 5%; *** significant at 1%.

Table 5.14: Regression results using a conditional labour demand model, two-step system GMM (Obj. 1, 2, 3)

	(1)	(2)	(3)	(4)
Emp. per wp. (t-1)	0.579***	0.654***	0.706***	0.712***
	(10.26)	(13.64)	(13.32)	(17.61)
Comp. emp. (t-1)	-0.0157	-0.0491	-0.0375	-0.0272
	(-0.350)	(-1.180)	(-1.300)	(-0.955)
Pop. young (t-1)	-0.0986**	-0.0576	-0.0429	-0.0383
	(-2.640)	(-1.772)	(-1.599)	(-1.400)
Low skilled (t-1)	-0.0831*	-0.113**	-0.0816**	-0.0839*
	(-2.265)	(-2.592)	(-2.840)	(-2.041)
grr (t-1)	-0.00121	0.00300	-3.18e-05	0.00147
	(-0.144)	(0.550)	(-0.00528)	(0.273)
Market potential (t-1)	0.368	0.258	0.277	0.238*
	(1.572)	(1.845)	(1.852)	(2.321)
SF pc Obj. 1 (t-1)	-0.00540	-0.00459	-0.00636	-0.00699
	(-1.293)	(-1.619)	(-1.306)	(-1.450)
SF pc Obj. 1 (t-2)		-0.000457	-0.000129	0.000105
		(-0.246)	(-0.0404)	(0.0457)
SF pc Obj. 1 (t-3)			0.00278	0.00281
			(0.952)	(1.344)
SF pc Obj. 1 (t-4)				0.00128
				(0.860)
SF pc Obj. 2 (t-1)	0.00114	0.00271	0.00599	0.00495
	(0.250)	(0.586)	(0.832)	(0.999)
SF pc Obj. 2 (t-2)		-0.000891	-0.00222	-0.00141
		(-0.426)	(-0.448)	(-0.347)
SF pc Obj. 2 (t-3)			-0.00225	-0.000422
			(-0.928)	(-0.210)
SF pc Obj. 2 (t-4)				0.000811
				(0.618)
SF pc Obj. 3 (t-1)	-0.00642	0.00191	0.00366	0.0107*
	(-0.457)	(0.301)	(0.414)	(2.455)
SF pc Obj. 3 (t-2)		-0.00251	-0.000241	-0.00323
		(-0.479)	(-0.0526)	(-0.576)
SF pc Obj. 3 (t-3)			0.00389	0.00251
			(1.787)	(0.757)
SF pc Obj. 3 (t-4)				-0.00662
				(-1.950)
Constant	0.00120	0.00280	0.000350	7.02e-06
	(0.312)	(1.144)	(0.138)	(0.00294)
Obj. 1 short-term elast. (size)		-0.00505	-0.00371	-0.00280
Obj. 1 short-term elast. (p-value)		0.0143	0.191	0.307
Obj. 1 long-term elast. (size)	-0.0128	-0.0146	-0.0126	-0.00973
Obj. 1 long-term elast. (p-value)	0.210	0.0186	0.163	0.310
Obj. 2 joint sign. (size)		0.00181	0.00152	0.00392
Obj. 2 joint sign. (p-value)		0.678	0.683	0.254
Obj. 2 long-term elast. (size)	0.00270	0.00525	0.00515	0.0136
Obj. 2 long-term elast. (p-value)	0.805	0.674	0.685	0.253
Obj. 3 joint sign. (size)		-0.000597	0.00730	0.00338
Obj. 3 joint sign. (p-value)		0.952	0.519	0.738
Obj. 3 long-term elast. (size)	-0.0152	-0.00173	0.0248	0.0117
Obj. 3 long-term elast. (p-value)	0.657	0.952	0.498	0.736
AR(1) (p-value)	0.000409	0.000196	5.33e-05	1.54e-05
AR(2) (p-value)	0.276	0.269	0.235	0.272
Hansen (p-value)	0.533	0.742	0.538	0.457
No. of instruments	56	80	104	128
No. of observations	982	982	982	982
No. of regions	129	129	129	129

Notes: Standard errors are corrected using the approach by Windmeijer (2005); z-statistics are listed in parentheses. The lagged dependent variable, compensation per employee, low skilled, market potential and the structural funds variables are assumed to be endogenous. We instrument the endogenous variables with both its lags and its differenced lags restricting the lag limit to three and use the "collapse" option. significant at 10%; ** significant at 5%; *** significant at 1%.

Table 5.15: Regression results using an unconditional labour demand model, two-step system GMM (Obj. 1, 2, 3)

	(1)	(2)	(3)	(4)	(5)
Emp. per wp. (t-1)	0.635***	0.621***	0.670***	0.704***	0.704***
	(5.470)	(8.855)	(12.66)	(16.44)	(18.21)
Comp. emp. (t-1)	0.0223	-0.0191	-0.0578	-0.0400	-0.0425
	(0.534)	(-0.497)	(-1.603)	(-1.596)	(-1.367)
Pop. young (t-1)	-0.0707	-0.0621	-0.0340	-0.0199	-0.00869
	(-1.431)	(-1.581)	(-1.076)	(-0.935)	(-0.302)
Low skilled (t-1)	-0.0869	-0.0924**	-0.111**	-0.0726*	-0.0604
	(-1.787)	(-2.692)	(-2.855)	(-1.971)	(-1.806)
grr (t-1)	0.00304	0.00182	0.00222	-0.000531	0.00145
	(0.591)	(0.315)	(0.406)	(-0.132)	(0.284)
SF pc Obj. 1 (t-1)		-0.00558	-0.00349	-0.00687	-0.00584
		(-1.564)	(-1.078)	(-1.352)	(-1.498)
SF pc Obj. 1 (t-2)			-0.00196	-0.00139	-0.00215
			(-1.232)	(-0.486)	(-0.939)
SF pc Obj. 1 (t-3)				0.00214	0.00190
				(1.021)	(0.822)
SF pc Obj. 1 (t-4)					0.00144
					(0.927)
SF pc Obj. 2 (t-1)		0.00414	0.00528	0.00754	0.00610
		(0.636)	(0.671)	(1.227)	(0.930)
SF pc Obj. 2 (t-2)			0.000632	-0.00114	0.00102
			(0.192)	(-0.322)	(0.287)
SF pc Obj. 2 (t-3)				-0.00154	4.76e-06
				(-0.722)	(0.00200)
SF pc Obj. 2 (t-4)					0.00170
					(1.060)
SF pc Obj. 3 (t-1)		0.00762	0.0150*	0.0135*	0.0199*
		(0.919)	(1.964)	(2.322)	(2.326)
SF pc Obj. 3 (t-2)			-0.00359	0.000954	-0.00207
			(-0.892)	(0.242)	(-0.423)
SF pc Obj. 3 (t-3)				0.00572	0.00488
				(1.838)	(1.471)
SF pc Obj. 3 (t-4)					-0.00493
					(-1.208)
Constant	0.00287	0.00289	0.00313	0.00121	0.000390
	(0.930)	(1.024)	(1.106)	(0.525)	(0.162)
Obj. 1 short-term elast. (size)			-0.00545	-0.00613	-0.00464
Obj. 1 short-term elast. (p-value)			0.0545	0.0431	0.171
Obj. 1 long-term elast. (size)		-0.0147	-0.0165	-0.0207	-0.0157
Obj. 1 long-term elast. (p-value)		0.105	0.0298	0.0310	0.139
Obj. 2 joint sign. (size)			0.00591	0.00486	0.00883
Obj. 2 joint sign. (p-value)			0.316	0.166	0.0707
Obj. 2 long-term elast. (size)		0.0109	0.0179	0.0164	0.0299
Obj. 2 long-term elast. (p-value)		0.551	0.327	0.171	0.0918
Obj. 3 joint sign. (size)			0.0114	0.0202	0.0178
Obj. 3 joint sign. (p-value)			0.160	0.00203	0.00198
Obj. 3 long-term elast. (size)		0.0201	0.0345	0.0683	0.0603
Obj. 3 long-term elast. (p-value)		0.349	0.167	0.00217	0.000394
AR(1) (p-value)	0.00234	0.000300	4.47e-05	2.10e-05	2.27e-05
AR(2) (p-value)	0.284	0.253	0.212	0.214	0.255
Hansen (p-value)	0.113	0.527	0.403	0.429	0.268
No. of instruments	25	49	73	97	121
No. of observations	988	988	988	988	988
No. of regions	130	130	130	130	130

Notes: Standard errors are corrected using the approach by Windmeijer (2005); z-statistics are listed in parentheses. The lagged dependent variable, compensation per employee, low skilled, market potential and the structural funds variables are assumed to be endogenous. We instrument the endogenous variables with both its lags and its differenced lags restricting the lag limit to three and use the "collapse" option. significant at 10%; ** significant at 5%; *** significant at 1%.

Table 5.16: Regression results using a conditional labour demand model, two-step system GMM, non-linear effects (Obj. 1+2+3)

	(1)	(2)	(3)	(4)	(5)
Emp. per wp. (t-1)	0.593***	0.589***	0.639***	0.732***	0.762***
	(6.738)	(8.675)	(11.34)	(9.626)	(11.95)
Comp. emp. (t-1)	-0.00392	-0.0203	-0.0377	-0.0555	-0.0495
	(-0.0596)	(-0.400)	(-0.972)	(-1.008)	(-1.017)
Pop. young (t-1)	-0.113**	-0.120**	-0.110*	-0.0931	-0.0874*
	(-2.586)	(-2.856)	(-2.573)	(-1.790)	(-2.045)
Low skilled (t-1)	-0.0632	-0.0898**	-0.0852*	-0.0584	-0.0241
	(-1.762)	(-2.742)	(-2.352)	(-0.930)	(-0.494)
grr (t-1)	-0.000719	-0.000604	0.00123	0.00175	0.00134
	(-0.125)	(-0.0968)	(0.224)	(0.355)	(0.301)
Union density (t-1)	-0.00230	-0.00303	-0.000916	-0.00186	0.000472
	(-0.580)	(-0.690)	(-0.242)	(-0.406)	(0.0855)
Market potential (t-1)	0.0542	0.0529	0.0467	0.0253	0.0302
	(1.062)	(1.328)	(1.318)	(0.788)	(1.075)
SF pc Obj. 1 (t-1)		-0.000238	-0.00619	-0.00853	-0.00484
		(-0.0294)	(-1.490)	(-1.401)	(-0.976)
SF pc Obj. 1 sq- (t-1)		-0.00112	0.000826	0.000922	0.00151
		(-0.449)	(0.408)	(0.333)	(0.375)
SF pc Obj. 1 (t-2)			-0.00142	-0.00342	-0.00328
			(-0.642)	(-1.002)	(-0.846)
SF pc Obj. 1 sq. (t-2)			-0.00360*	-0.00331	-0.00339
			(-2.277)	(-1.192)	(-1.054)
SF pc Obj. 1 (t-3)				-0.00214	-0.000974
				(-0.668)	(-0.338)
SF pc Obj. 1 sq. (t-3)				-0.000647	-0.000528
				(-0.538)	(-0.476)
SF pc Obj. 1 (t-4)					-0.000668
					(-0.250)
SF pc Obj. 1 sq. (t-4)					0.000272
					(0.347)
Constant	0.00213	0.00283	0.00620*	0.00447	0.00395
	(0.790)	(0.799)	(2.037)	(1.379)	(1.265)
Obj. 1+2+3 joint sign. (size)			-0.0104	-0.0171	-0.0119
Obj. 1+2+3 joint sign. (p-value)			0.0597	0.161	0.173
Obj. 1+2+3 long-term elast. (size)		-0.00332	-0.0288	-0.0639	-0.0500
Obj. 1+2+3 long-term elast. (p-value)		0.895	0.0576	0.0826	0.119
AR(1) (p-value)	0.00243	0.00145	0.000336	0.000374	9.74e-05
AR(2) (p-value)	0.248	0.241	0.269	0.320	0.309
Hansen (p-value)	0.422	0.525	0.674	0.418	0.353
No. of instruments	33	49	65	81	97
No. of observations	959	959	959	959	959
No. of regions	129	129	129	129	129

Notes: Standard errors are corrected using the approach by Windmeijer (2005); z-statistics are listed in parentheses. The lagged dependent variable, compensation per employee, low skilled, market potential and the structural funds variables are assumed to be endogenous. We instrument the endogenous variables with both its lags and its differenced lags restricting the lag limit to three and use the "collapse" option. significant at 10%; ** significant at 5%; *** significant at 1%.

Table 5.17: Regression results using a conditional labour demand model, two-step system GMM, non-linear effects (Obj. 1, 2, 3)

	(1)	(2)	(3)	(4)	(5)
Emp. per wp. (t-1)	0.639***	0.622***	0.687***	0.754***	0.805***
	(6.133)	(8.104)	(11.25)	(11.30)	(16.58)
Comp. emp. (t-1)	0.0203	0.0175	-0.0121	-0.0422	-0.0335
	(0.463)	(0.491)	(-0.429)	(-1.211)	(-0.950)
Pop. young (t-1)	-0.0695	-0.0836*	-0.0592	-0.0576	-0.0450
	(-1.560)	(-2.000)	(-1.611)	(-1.868)	(-1.852)
Low skilled (t-1)	-0.102*	-0.120**	-0.112**	-0.0946	-0.0873
	(-2.228)	(-2.725)	(-2.760)	(-1.724)	(-1.843)
grr (t-1)	0.00228	0.00140	0.00442	0.00317	0.00224
	(0.420)	(0.235)	(0.841)	(0.677)	(0.604)
Union density (t-1)	-0.00183	-0.00342	0.000656	-0.000697	0.000575
	(-0.445)	(-0.793)	(0.167)	(-0.191)	(0.165)
SF pc Obj. 1+2+3 (t-1)		0.00315	-0.00309	-0.00642	-0.00309
		(0.358)	(-0.541)	(-1.125)	(-0.643)
SF pc Obj. 1+2+3 sq- (t-1)		0.000775	0.00137	0.00102	0.000408
		(0.303)	(0.474)	(0.285)	(0.111)
SF pc Obj. 1+2+3 (t-2)			-0.00282	-0.00340	-0.00355
			(-1.231)	(-1.093)	(-0.937)
SF pc Obj. 1+2+3 sq. (t-2)			-0.00314	-0.00278	-0.00211
			(-1.349)	(-0.954)	(-0.725)
SF pc Obj. 1+2+3 (t-3)				-0.00183	-0.000858
				(-0.546)	(-0.268)
SF pc Obj. 1+2+3 sq. (t-3)				-0.000473	-0.000329
				(-0.404)	(-0.278)
SF pc Obj. 1+2+3 (t-4)					0.000113
					(0.0476)
SF pc Obj. 1+2+3 sq. (t-4)					0.000329
					(0.559)
Constant	0.00254	2.81e-05	0.00507	0.00364	0.00322
	(0.869)	(0.00755)	(1.583)	(1.691)	(1.578)
Obj. 1+2+3 joint sign. (size)			-0.00768	-0.0139	-0.00909
Obj. 1+2+3 joint sign. (p-value)			0.224	0.166	0.309
Obj. 1+2+3 long-term elast. (size)		0.0104	-0.0246	-0.0565	-0.0465
Obj. 1+2+3 long-term elast. (p-value)		0.728	0.226	0.0940	0.273
AR(1) (p-value)	0.00207	0.000836	0.000137	0.000270	9.68e-05
AR(2) (p-value)	0.255	0.239	0.284	0.329	0.315
Hansen (p-value)	0.174	0.353	0.485	0.435	0.476
No. of instruments	26	42	58	74	90
No. of observations	964	964	964	964	964
No. of regions	130	130	130	130	130

Notes: Standard errors are corrected using the approach by Windmeijer (2005); z-statistics are listed in parentheses. The lagged dependent variable, compensation per employee, low skilled, market potential and the structural funds variables are assumed to be endogenous. We instrument the endogenous variables with both its lags and its differenced lags restricting the lag limit to three and use the "collapse" option. significant at 10%; ** significant at 5%; *** significant at 1%.

Table 5.18: Regression results using an unconditional labour demand model, two-step system GMM (Obj. 1+2+3)

	(1)	(2)	(3)	(4)	(5)
Emp. per wp. (t-1)	0.560***	0.579***	0.661***	0.681***	0.693***
	(5.807)	(6.962)	(8.606)	(8.861)	(10.65)
Comp. emp. (t-1)	0.0254	0.00257	-0.0347	-0.0499	-0.0528
	(0.430)	(0.0516)	(-0.676)	(-0.902)	(-0.916)
Pop. young (t-1)	-0.105*	-0.112*	-0.0880	-0.0806	-0.0840*
	(-2.571)	(-2.277)	(-1.608)	(-1.759)	(-2.254)
Low skilled (t-1)	-0.0601	-0.0806	-0.124**	-0.110*	-0.105**
	(-1.643)	(-1.831)	(-2.592)	(-2.495)	(-2.682)
grr (t-1)	0.00112	0.00163	0.000504	0.00650	0.00455
	(0.151)	(0.145)	(0.0462)	(0.567)	(0.510)
Union density (t-1)	-0.00189	0.00124	0.00183	1.58e-05	0.000208
	(-0.335)	(0.190)	(0.251)	(0.00221)	(0.0340)
Market potential 2 (t-1)	0.353	0.402	0.427	0.651*	0.598*
	(1.614)	(1.728)	(1.691)	(2.110)	(2.564)
SF pc Obj. 1+2+3 (t-1)		-0.00764	-0.00618	-0.00777	-0.00891
		(-0.861)	(-0.866)	(-1.105)	(-1.472)
SF pc Obj. 1+2+3 (t-2)			0.000553	-0.000708	-0.000443
			(0.275)	(-0.284)	(-0.185)
SF pc Obj. 1+2+3 (t-3)				-0.000583	-0.000295
				(-0.289)	(-0.153)
SF pc Obj. 1+2+3 (t-4)					0.00173
					(1.017)
Constant		0.00125	0.00126	-0.000655	-0.000570
		(0.306)	(0.303)	(-0.157)	(-0.161)
Obj. 1+2+3 short-term elast. (size)			-0.00563	-0.00906	-0.00792
Obj. 1+2+3 short-term elast. (p-value)			0.445	0.236	0.266
Obj. 1+2+3 long-term elast. (size)		-0.0181	-0.0166	-0.0284	-0.0258
Obj. 1+2+3 long-term elast. (p-value)		0.383	0.427	0.183	0.234
AR(1) (p-value)	0.00520	0.00205	0.000754	0.000426	0.000269
AR(2) (p-value)	0.238	0.227	0.248	0.253	0.268
Hansen (p-value)	0.138	0.429	0.612	0.434	0.549
No. of instruments	33	41	49	57	65
No. of observations	959	959	959	959	959
No. of regions	129	129	129	129	129

Notes: Standard errors are corrected using the approach by Windmeijer (2005); z-statistics are listed in parentheses. The lagged dependent variable, compensation per employee, low skilled, market potential and the structural funds variables are assumed to be endogenous. We instrument the endogenous variables with both its lags and its differenced lags restricting the lag limit to three and use the "collapse" option. * significant at 10%; ** significant at 5%; *** significant at 1%.

Table 5.19: Regression results using an unconditional labour demand model, two-step system GMM (Obj. 1, 2, 3)

	(1)	(2)	(3)	(4)	(5)
Emp. per wp. (t-1)	0.584***	0.574***	0.655***	0.681***	0.702***
	(6.335)	(10.19)	(14.03)	(12.80)	(14.78)
Comp. emp. (t-1)	0.0227	-0.00702	-0.0407	-0.0481	-0.0359
	(0.403)	(-0.166)	(-1.066)	(-1.459)	(-1.189)
Pop. young (t-1)	-0.109*	-0.102**	-0.0492	-0.0435	-0.0301
	(-2.478)	(-2.707)	(-1.472)	(-1.643)	(-1.143)
Low skilled (t-1)	-0.0559	-0.0829*	-0.118**	-0.0875**	-0.0878
	(-1.480)	(-2.085)	(-2.787)	(-3.153)	(-1.934)
grr (t-1)	0.00142	0.000224	0.00144	-0.00115	0.00254
	(0.194)	(0.0240)	(0.234)	(-0.186)	(0.366)
Union density (t-1)	-0.00193	7.64e-05	-0.00195	-0.000892	0.000216
	(-0.338)	(0.0112)	(-0.475)	(-0.189)	(0.0401)
Market potential 2 (t-1)	0.331	0.392	0.253*	0.278*	0.230*
	(1.571)	(1.612)	(2.107)	(1.974)	(2.502)
SF pc Obj. 1 (t-1)		-0.00551	-0.00488	-0.00653	-0.00843
		(-1.178)	(-1.422)	(-1.488)	(-1.711)
SF pc Obj. 1 (t-2)			-0.000395	-0.000851	0.000229
			(-0.181)	(-0.303)	(0.107)
SF pc Obj. 1 (t-3)				0.00185	0.00306
				(0.736)	(1.323)
SF pc Obj. 1 (t-4)					0.00136
					(0.943)
SF pc Obj. 2 (t-1)		-6.59e-05	0.00285	0.00537	0.00429
		(-0.0164)	(0.706)	(0.835)	(0.958)
SF pc Obj. 2 (t-2)			-0.00155	-0.00191	-0.000612
			(-0.671)	(-0.415)	(-0.172)
SF pc Obj. 2 (t-3)				-0.00270	-0.000639
				(-1.195)	(-0.356)
SF pc Obj. 2 (t-4)					0.000936
					(0.741)
SF pc Obj. 3 (t-1)		-0.00842	0.00184	0.00536	0.0123*
		(-0.564)	(0.262)	(0.626)	(2.465)
SF pc Obj. 3 (t-2)			-0.00215	-0.000725	-0.00369
			(-0.453)	(-0.154)	(-0.607)
SF pc Obj. 3 (t-3)				0.00383	0.00318
				(1.523)	(0.911)
SF pc Obj. 3 (t-4)					-0.00712
					(-1.791)
Constant	0.00225	0.000799	0.00246	0.000151	7.54e-05
	(0.823)	(0.181)	(1.007)	(0.0567)	(0.0310)
Obj. 1 short-term elast. (size)			-0.00528	-0.00553	-0.00377
Obj. 1 short-term elast. (p-value)			0.0347	0.0296	0.208
Obj. 1 long-term elast. (size)		-0.0129	-0.0153	-0.0173	-0.0127
Obj. 1 long-term elast. (p-value)		0.253	0.0407	0.0234	0.215
Obj. 2 short-term elast. (size)			0.00130	0.000760	0.00397
Obj. 2 short-term elast. (p-value)			0.751	0.824	0.272
Obj. 2 long-term elast. (size)		-0.000155	0.00377	0.00238	0.0133
Obj. 2 long-term elast. (p-value)		0.987	0.749	0.825	0.283
Obj. 3 short-term elast. (size)			-0.000307	0.00846	0.00469
Obj. 3 short-term elast. (p-value)			0.974	0.449	0.676
Obj. 3 long-term elast. (size)		-0.0198	-0.000888	0.0265	0.0157
Obj. 3 long-term elast. (p-value)		0.586	0.974	0.426	0.666
AR(1) (p-value)	0.00337	0.000607	0.000234	0.000127	3.86e-05
AR(2) (p-value)	0.244	0.253	0.252	0.211	0.240
Hansen (p-value)	0.133	0.533	0.619	0.393	0.472
No. of instruments	33	57	81	105	129
No. of observations	959	959	959	959	959
No. of regions	129	129	129	129	129

Notes: Standard errors are corrected using the approach by Windmeijer (2005); z-statistics are listed in parentheses. The lagged dependent variable, compensation per employee, low skilled, market potential and the structural funds variables are assumed to be endogenous. We instrument the endogenous variables with both its lags and its differenced lags restricting the lag limit to three and use the "collapse" option. * significant at 10%; ** significant at 5%; *** significant at 1%.

Figure 5.4: Marginal effects of structural funds on employment conditional on the share of low-skilled population (unconditional labour demand model)

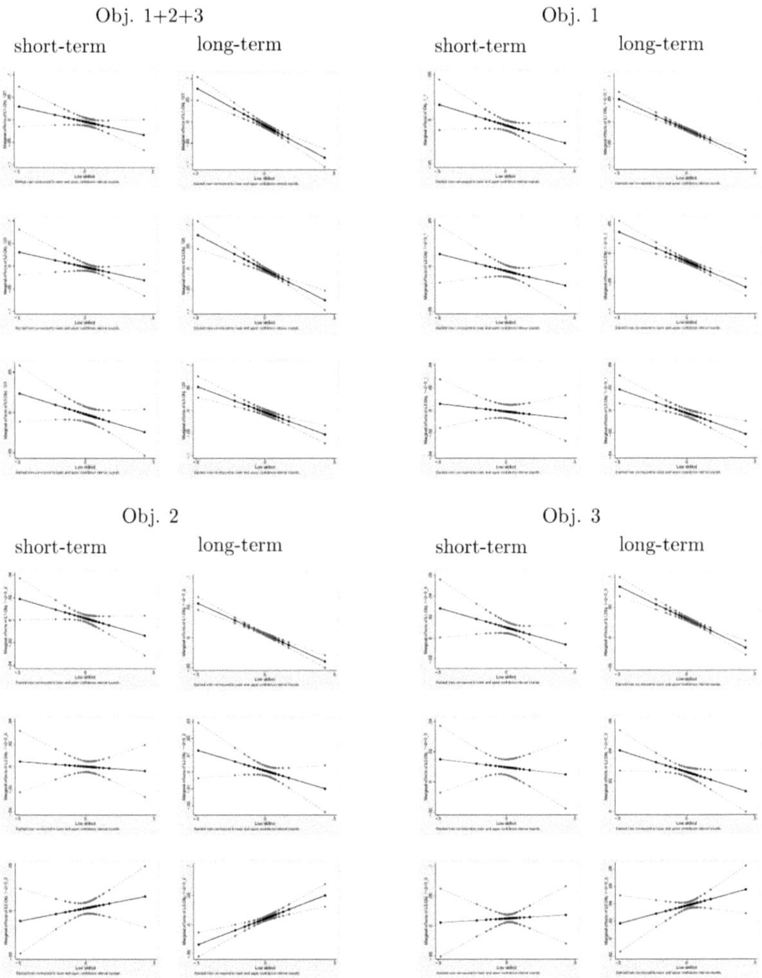

Notes: The estimation results are based on the baseline specification of the *un*conditional labour market demand model displayed in equation 5.1, i.e. excluding the market potential variable. The regressions are estimated using the two-step system GMM estimator proposed by Blundell and Bond (1998), while standard errors are corrected using the approach by Windmeijer (2005). The lagged dependent variable, compensation per employee, low skilled, market potential and the structural funds variables are assumed to be endogenous. We instrument the endogenous variables with both its lags and its differenced lags restricting the lag limit to three and use the "collapse" option. The marginal effects are displayed on the y-axes, the share of low-skilled population on the x-axes.

Figure 5.5: Marginal effects of structural funds on employment conditional on the share of low-skilled population (conditional labour demand model)

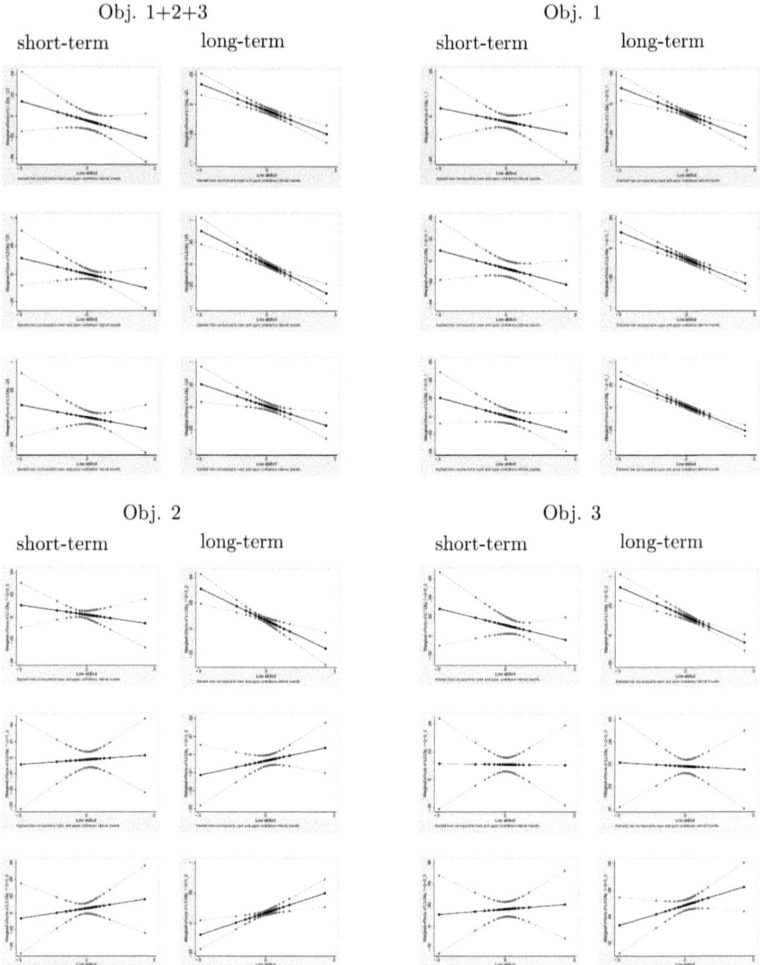

Notes: The estimation results are based on the baseline specification of the conditional labour market demand model displayed in equation 5.1 including a variable measuring the share of population with high education (high skilled). The regressions are estimated using the two-step system GMM estimator proposed by Blundell and Bond (1998), while standard errors are corrected using the approach by Windmeijer (2005). The lagged dependent variable, compensation per employee, low skilled, market potential and the structural funds variables are assumed to be endogenous. We instrument the endogenous variables with both its lags and its differenced lags restricting the lag limit to three and use the "collapse" option. The marginal effects are displayed on the y-axes, the share of low-skilled population on the x-axes.

Figure 5.6: Marginal effects of structural funds on employment conditional on the share of low-skilled population (unconditional labour demand model, including the share of high-skilled population as a control variable)

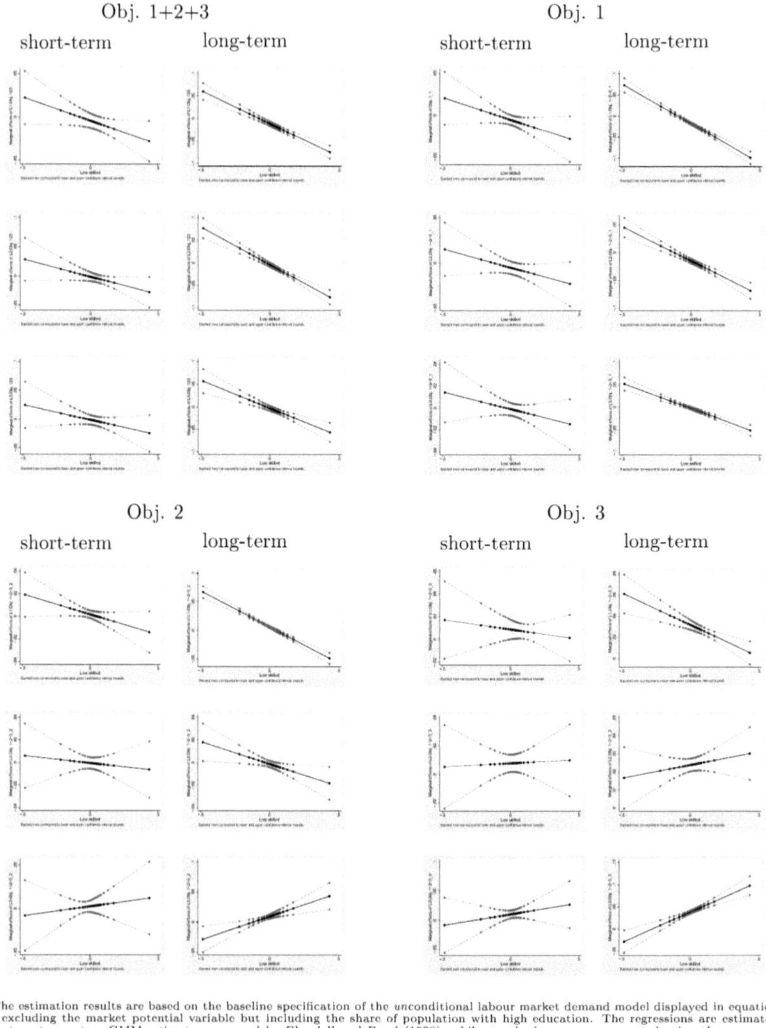

Notes: The estimation results are based on the baseline specification of the *un*conditional labour market demand model displayed in equation 5.1, i.e. excluding the market potential variable but including the share of population with high education. The regressions are estimated using the two-step system GMM estimator proposed by Blundell and Bond (1998), while standard errors are corrected using the approach by Windmeijer (2005). The lagged dependent variable, compensation per employee, low skilled, market potential and the structural funds variables are assumed to be endogenous. We instrument the endogenous variables with both its lags and its differenced lags restricting the lag limit to three and use the "collapse" option. The marginal effects are displayed on the y-axes, the share of low-skilled population on the x-axes.

Figure 5.7: Marginal effects of structural funds on employment conditional on the share of high-skilled population (conditional labour demand model)

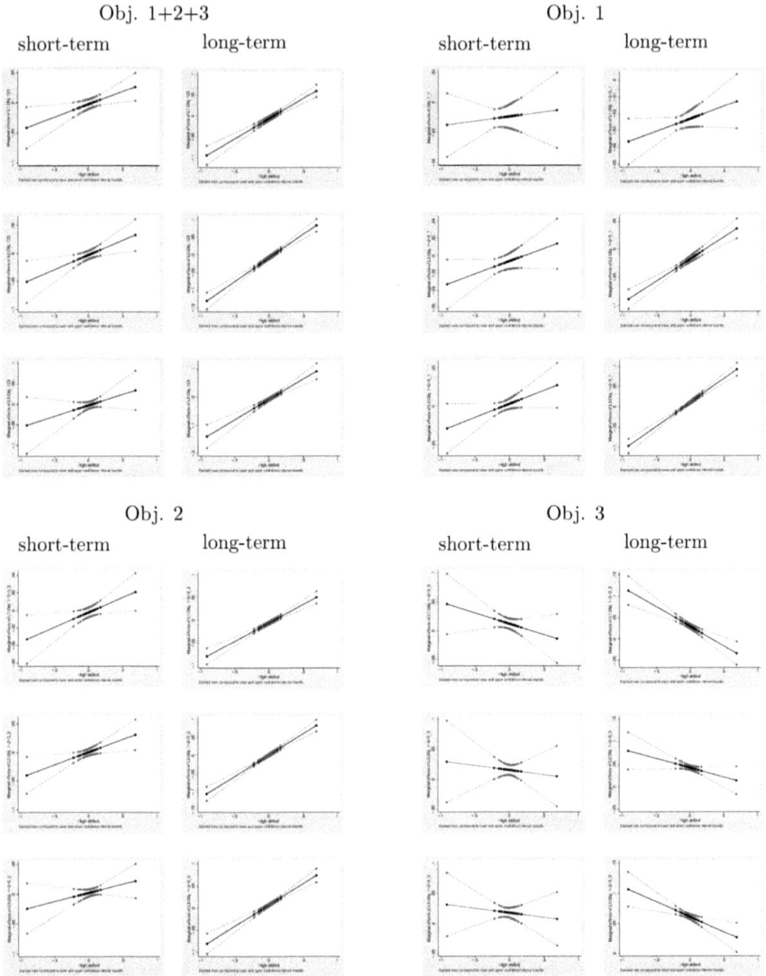

Figure 5.8: Marginal effects of structural funds on employment conditional on the share of high-skilled population (conditional labour demand model, including the share of low-skilled population as a control variable)

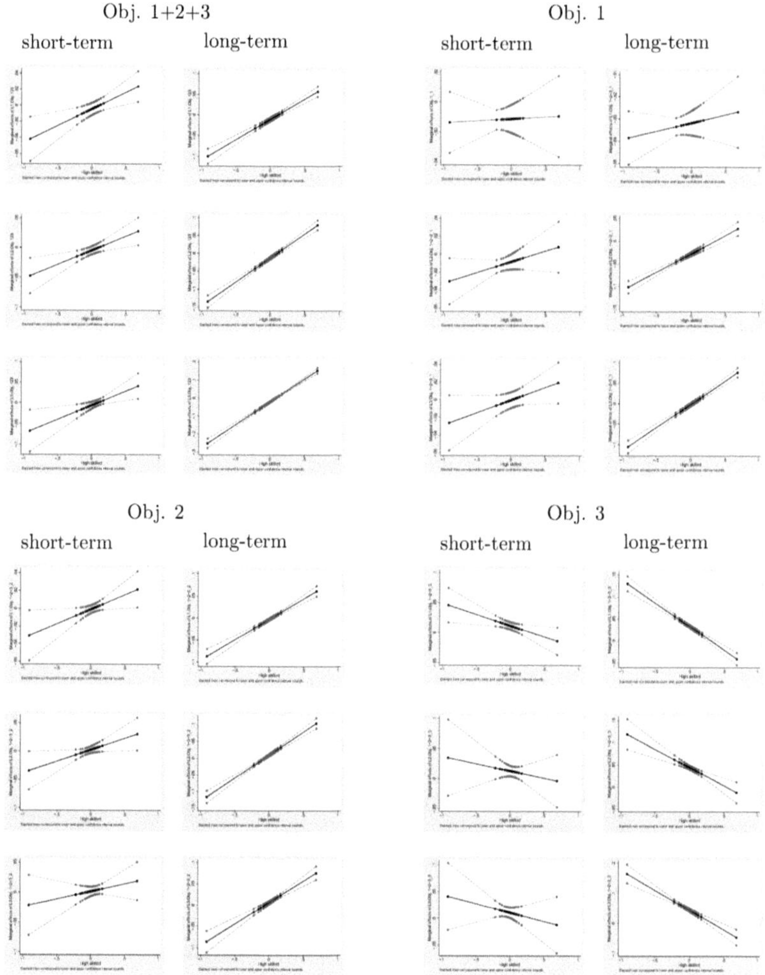

Figure 5.9: Marginal effects of structural funds on employment conditional on the share of high-skilled population (unconditional labour demand model)

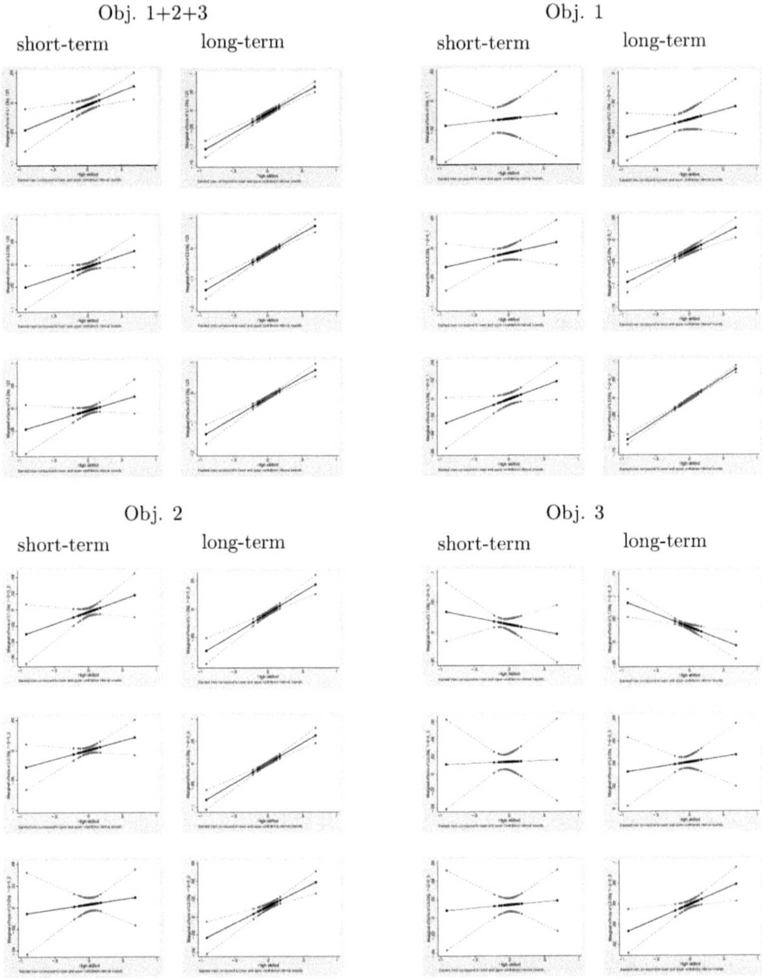

Figure 5.10: Marginal effects of structural funds on employment conditional on the share of low-skilled population (including spatial weight matrix, conditional labour demand model)

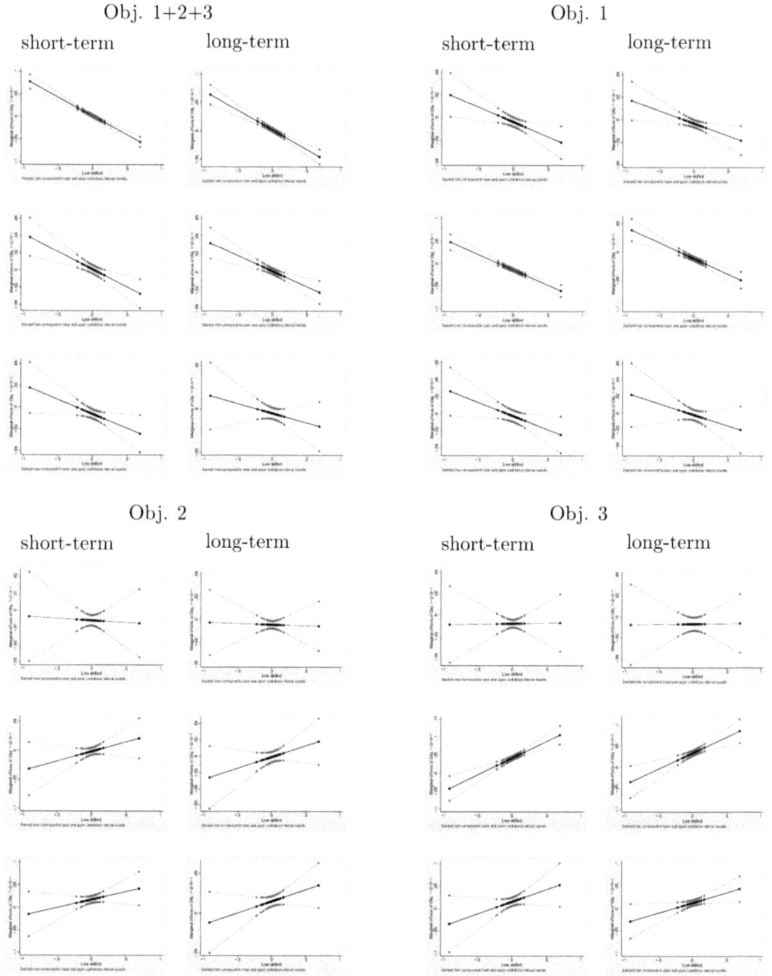

Notes: The estimation results are based on the baseline specification of the *unconditional* labour market demand model displayed in equation 5.9. The regressions are estimated using the dynamic spatial panel data estimator proposed by Yu, de Jong and Lee (2008).

Figure 5.11: Marginal effects of structural funds on employment conditional on the share of low-skilled population (including spatial weight matrix, unconditional labour demand model)

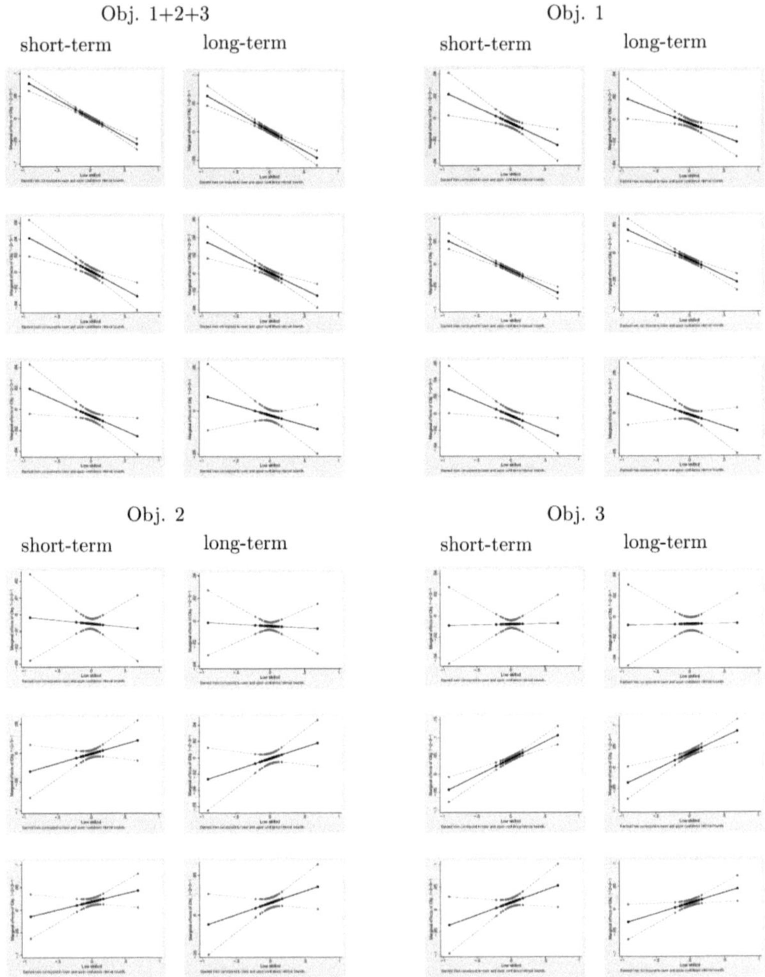

Notes: The estimation results are based on the baseline specification of the *un*conditional labour market demand model displayed in equation 5.9. The regressions are estimated using the dynamic spatial panel data estimator proposed by Yu, de Jong and Lee (2008).

Chapter 6

Does EU Cohesion Policy Really Increase Public Investment?[1]

6.1 Introduction

The strong focus of the evaluation literature of EU Cohesion Policy on economic growth raises the question of whether EU funding has an impact on public investment, to which a major part of total EU aid is allocated (European Commission, 2004a). According to the principle of additionality, EU-funded projects must not crowd out investment spending elsewhere (European Commission, 2007a). Thus, the EU Commission aims to ensure that Cohesion Policy payments do not replace domestically-financed public or structural expenditure.

Nevertheless, there are several reasons why EU Cohesion Policy could replace at least some part of the domestic public investment. First, studies in the field of development economics show that aid flows may be "fungible", i.e. recipient governments use aid according to their own national preferences, regardless of the givers' intentions (for example Pack and Pack, 1993; Feyzioglu, Swaroop and Zhu, 1998). Although the empirical evidence is not clear-cut (for example, Mishra and Newhouse (2007) conclude that aid earmarked for health does significantly increase total health care spending and Dreher, Nunnenkamp and Thiele (2008) find that higher per-capita aid given for education significantly increases primary school enrolment), it may well be that aid is at least partly "fungible". For Cohesion Policy, this implies that recipient countries use EU aid not only on spending targets approved by Cohesion Policy, but also on other, unrelated, projects.

[1] A similar version of this chapter is under review at the ECB Working Paper Series and is being published in the Journal of European Economics. A related version appeared as: Hagen and Mohl (2009b): *How does EU Cohesion Policy work? Evaluating its effects on fiscal outcome variables*, ZEW Discussion Paper No. 09-051, Mannheim.

The second reason is related to the so-called 'common pool problem' (Shepsle and Weingast, 1981). This problem results from politicians attempting to increase their popularity with policy projects which are visible within their constituency. This is of particular relevance in the case of the EU budget, where the financing costs are spread over the EU and the benefits are country-specific (Heinemann, 2006; Osterloh, Heinemann and Mohl, 2009). Given that national preferences are expected to be unchanged, this could explain why governments have an incentive to use EU funds for spending projects which they would have undertaken anyway. Finally, additionality is hard to control, and, more importantly, it has not been sanctioned in the past. This poses the risk that policymakers may try to finance previously planned domestic investment projects via EU funds.

The impact of Cohesion Policy payments on national public investment in the EU has not yet been evaluated. One paper analyses the principle of additionality based on an intra-national approach. Using a cross-section of European regions, Ederveen, Gorter, de Mooij and Nahuis (2002) investigate the impact of being an Objective 1 region (that is, being eligible for the highest transfers) on national regional support. They find that, on average, one euro of cohesion support crowds out 17 cents of national regional policy.

Against this background, we aim to investigate whether, and to which extent, EU Cohesion Policy payments have an impact on national public investment. Put differently, we evaluate if cohesion payments are 'additional', or if they only lead to a displacement of national public investment. To address this research question, we use a new comprehensive dataset comprising total EU Cohesion Policy payments for the EU-27 sample covering the period 1982-2006. Our results show no significantly positive effects on national public investment, indicating a crowding out of national investment.

The paper is structured as follows. Section 6.2 describes the data, followed by an outline of the empirical model in Section 6.3. Section 6.4 presents the econometric specification, before Section 6.5 discusses the empirical results. Finally, Section 6.6 concludes.

6.2 Data

We investigate our research question using an EU-27 annual country dataset consisting of total EU Cohesion Policy payments for the period 1982-2006 (European Commission, 2008). The dataset contains measures from the various structural funds[2] as well as the Cohesion Fund and the Instrument for Structural Policies for Pre-accession (ISPA).[3]

[2] These are the European Regional Development Fund (ERDF), the European Social Fund (ECP), the European Agricultural Guidance and Guarantee Fund (EAGGF), and the Financial Instrument for Fisheries Guidance (FIFG).

[3] A detailed description of the institutional setup can be found, among others, in European Commission (2007a).

Figure 2.1 shows the historical development displaying the total EU Cohesion Policy payments (vertical bars) and their shares relative to the EU-GNI (solid line) and to the public national spending (dotted line). It becomes clear that there is a long-term upward trend in payments when measured in absolute terms, which can be explained, *inter alia*, by the enlargement steps of the EU (Heinemann, Hagen, Mohl, Osterloh and Sellenthin, 2010). By contrast, the level of payments measured in per cent of EU GNI and public national spending has remained rather unchanged since 1993. Furthermore, Figure 2.1 in Chapter 2 shows that–on average–Cohesion payments do not seem to be very large compared to total public spending totalling approximately 0.65 per cent in 2007.

Table 6.1 compares the expenditures for the EU Cohesion Policy with the national public investment. It becomes clear that Cohesion payments per GDP are quite important compared to total public investment in the so-called "old" (Spain, Greece, Ireland, and Portugal) and "new" (Eastern European member states) cohesion countries. This indicates that it may indeed be difficult for some countries to absorb the transfers and to co-finance additional European projects.

Table 6.1: EU Cohesion Policy payments and national public investment

	EU CP payments (as % of GDP)	**Public investment** (as % of GDP)	**Time period from ... until 2007**
	(1)	(2)	(3)
Austria	0.13	1.59	1995
Belgium	0.10	2.12	1982
Bulgaria	1.00	3.62	2000
Czech Republic	0.07	3.26	2000
Cyprus	0.34	4.39	2002
Denmark	0.08	1.84	1982
Estonia	0.93	4.13	2000
Finland	0.21	2.71	1995
France	0.13	3.21	1982
Germany	0.12	2.16	1982
Greece	1.53	3.00	1982
Hungary	0.54	3.85	2000
Ireland	1.34	3.12	1982
Italy	0.24	2.69	1982
Latvia	1.69	2.87	2000
Lithuania	1.09	3.34	2000
Luxembourg	0.09	4.17	1990
Malta	0.25	4.31	2002
Netherlands	0.06	3.28	1982
Poland	0.58	3.41	2000
Portugal	2.19	3.45	1986
Romania	0.59	3.52	2000
Slovak Republic	0.59	2.53	2000
Slovenia	0.27	3.37	2000
Spain	0.84	3.76	1986
Sweden	0.10	3.13	1995
UK	0.15	1.83	1982

Notes: Own calculations based on European Commission (2008). We restrict the statistics to the years in which positive CP payments are observable; the earliest year is 1982.

The EU co-finances on average around 50 per cent of the projects, while the remaining part must be paid by the member states. However, the share of co-financing is not equal across projects, but may reach up to 85 per cent for poor regions and drop to only 20 per cent for wealthier regions (Nam and Wamser, 2010).

6.3 Empirical Model

Our econometric analysis of the impact of EU Cohesion Policy on national public investment (*pinv*) is based on a similar specification as that of Mehrotra and Välilä (2006). We estimate the following model:

$$\begin{aligned} pinv_{i,t} = & \beta_0 + \alpha\, pinv_{i,t-1} + \beta_1\, d_{i,t-1} + \beta_2\, g_{i,t-1} + \beta_3\, gdppc_{i,t-1} + \beta_4\, EU_{i,t} \\ & + \beta_5\, cp_{i,t} + \beta_6\, contrib_{i,t} + \beta_7\, li_{i,t} + \beta_8\, open_{i,t-1} + \beta_9\, elect_{i,t} \\ & + \beta_{10}\, left_{i,t} + \gamma_i t_i + \mu_i + \lambda_t + \varepsilon_{i,t} \end{aligned} \tag{6.1}$$

where i corresponds to the country and t to the time period. The lagged dependent variable (*pinv*) controls for serial correlation of the specification. Since public debt (d) indicates the need for consolidating public finances, it should have a negative impact on public investment. The growth rate of real GDP per capita (g) serves as a business cycle indicator. On the one hand, it has a positive effect on public investment if the amount of public investment depends on tax revenues. On the other hand, the government may conduct an anti-cyclical policy, which leads to a negative effect. The level of real GDP per capita (*gdppc*) controls for the hypothesis that demand for public investment may depend on the income level. Moreover, real GDP per capita is the most important allocation criteria for CP.

Generally, we are keen on the estimation of "policy reaction" functions. Since the level of CP commitments is decided for several years in advance within so-called "financial frameworks", national governments can anticipate, and react instantaneously to the forthcoming EU support. As a consequence, we include the contemporaneous CP variable, i.e. not lagged, in the regression model. *cp* measures total CP payments to country i in per cent of GDP. Moreover, *contrib* are total contributions from the member states to the EU (total revenues of the EU from so-called own resources) in percentage of GDP. This variable controls for the fact that payments to the EU may limit the fiscal scope of national governments. Furthermore, the national claims for payments from the EU may simply be determined by the member states' considerations with regard to their net contribution to the EU budget (the difference between what the countries pay into the

EU budget and what they receive from EU policies).[4]

The long-term interest rate (*li*) serves a proxy for the opportunity costs of public investment, while *open* (export plus imports per GDP) controls for the possibility that the demand for public investment may depend on the openness of the economy. *EU* controls for possible membership effects. In addition, there is evidence that political economic variables might have an impact on the dependent variable (Persson and Tabellini, 2000; Tabellini and Alesina, 1990). Thus, we include two further control variables as a proxy for political effects: *elect* measures the share of pre-election months in each year and *left* stands for the share of left parties in per cent of total cabinet posts.

An obvious problem may arise from the fact that we do not observe all possibly relevant variables that determine the scale and timing of national public investment. For example, not only macroeconomic variables are relevant, but also unobserved variables such as government programmes and country specific peculiarities (for example natural constraints). Since these variables may simultaneously affect CP payments, their omission may lead to biased estimates. In order to deal with this problem, we follow, *inter alia*, Nunziata (2005) by using a very flexible specification, where not only fixed country effects (μ_i) and fixed (annual) time effects (λ_t) are included, but also country-specific linear time trends (t_i). In this manner, we intend to control for unobserved fixed and time varying heterogeneity that affect all outcome variables apart from CP payments. Note that country-specific time trends are not possible for the SYS-GMM estimator since this would inflate the IV matrix. A description of the variables and the descriptive statistics for the estimation sample can be found in Table 6.2 and 6.3.

6.4 Estimation Approach

In order to render the empirical results as robust as possible, we use different samples and methodological approaches. Regarding the choice of countries, we use two different samples. First, the regressions are estimated for the whole period for which data is available ("all time periods"). Thus, countries are included even before their accession. For example, Austria and Finland are included even before 1994 and the Eastern European countries before 2004. Since the latter countries also received EU support before their accession, it is (potentially) possible to distinguish between the "EU effect" and the "CP payments effect". Second, we only include the time periods in which the countries are members of the EU ("only EU members"). By definition, the second strategy reduces the number of observations significantly.

[4] *contrib* and *cp* are weakly positively correlated with a correlation coefficient of 0.14 (p-value 0.008) in our sample.

Table 6.2: Definition of the variables

Variable	Definition	Source
cp	Total EU Cohesion Policy payments as per cent of nominal GDP	European Commission (2008) and WDI
contrib	National payments to the EU (revenues of the EU from so-called own resources) as per cent of nominal GDP	European Commission (2008) and WDI
pinv	Gross fixed capital formation of the general government as per cent of GDP	AMECO
d	General government gross financial liability as per cent of GDP	WEO
g	Growth of real GDP per capita	WDI
gdppc	Level of real GDP per capita in US Dollar in PPP	WDI
li	Real long-term interest rate in per cent	AMECO
open	Openness of the economy (imports plus exports as per cent of GDP)	WEO
elect	Per cent of election months in year	Armingeon et al.
left	Cabinet composition: Social-Democratic and other left parties as per cent of total cabinet posts, weighted by days	Armingeon et al.
EU	Dummy for membership in the EU	

Notes: WDI = World Development Indicators (Worldbank); WEO = World Economic Outlook (IMF); AMECO = Annual Macro-Economic Database of the European Commission, DG ECFIN; OECD = OECD Economic Outlook Database, Armingeon et al. = Armingeon, Gerber, Leimgruber and Beyeler (2008).

Table 6.3: Descriptive statistics for the estimation sample

Variable	Number of obs.	Mean	Std. dev.	Min.	Max.
cp	439	0.47	0.69	0.00	3.50
contrib	439	7.36	4.19	0.00	15.12
pinv	439	2.99	0.88	0.67	5.13
d	439	56.54	28.55	4.06	134.16
g	439	2.60	2.50	-6.75	12.31
gdppc/1,000	439	23.70	10.86	0.43	112.81
li	439	7.82	3.84	3.30	27.53
open	439	91.34	52.24	35.89	347.18
elect	439	0.15	0.28	0.00	1.00
left	439	39.87	37.00	0.00	100.00
EU	439	0.79	0.41	0.00	1.00

Concerning the econometric approaches, we start the estimation using a simple fixed effects estimator. We report standard errors to be robust to serial and spatial correlation, following Driscoll and Kraay (1998) and Hoechle (2007). The error structure is then assumed to be heteroskedastic, autocorrelated, and possibly correlated between the countries (panels). Since Driscoll and Kraay (1998) standard errors have not been very common in applied work yet, we also report–as a kind of robustness check–the White-Huber robust standard errors (White, 1980).

Due to the structure of our dataset (depending on the specification, N varies between 25 and 27, T varies between 2 and 27 with an average of 17.1), simply applying a fixed effects estimator in a dynamic setup leads to the well-known Nickell bias (Nickell, 1981).

One way to control for this is to use the first-differenced GMM estimator proposed by Arellano and Bond (1991). Since this estimator has been found to have a large finite sample bias and poor precision when the time series are persistent, we use, whenever possible, the two-step system GMM (SYS-GMM) estimator by Blundell and Bond (1998). In addition, using the SYS-GMM estimator has the advantage of taking into account potential endogeneity of further explanatory variables, i.e., there may be unobserved variables simultaneously affecting the independent and the dependent variables. The consistency of the SYS-GMM estimator is based on large N, which is obviously not given in our application. However, recent Monte Carlo simulations show that, given the pre-determined variables in X, the SYS-GMM estimator has a lower bias and higher efficiency than the first-differenced GMM or the fixed effects estimator (Soto, 2010).

The small sample size leads to a further problem: it is not possible to use the full set of instrumental variables since Windmeijer (2005) or Roodman (2009b,a) show that using too many instruments leads to biased results. For this reason, only recent values up to three lags are used. For a small N, Soto (2010) shows that not using all potentially available instruments does not decrease the reliability of the SYS-GMM estimator. Furthermore, in order to mitigate the problem of too many instruments in the case of the SYS-GMM specification, we transform all our variables into deviations from time means, which is equivalent to the inclusion of time dummies. This decreases the total number of instruments and increases the degrees of freedom (Bond, Hoeffler and Temple, 2001). Instead of using all possible instruments for each available time period, we "collapse" the matrix of instruments and only use the lags up to $t-2$ which leads to a smaller set of instruments. In addition, regarding the two-step SYS-GMM estimations, the standard errors are corrected following Windmeijer (2005).

Another estimation strategy to deal with the Nickell bias is to apply the bias-corrected least square dummy variable (LSDVc) estimator proposed by Kiviet (1995) and extended by Bruno (2005a,b) to unbalanced panel data, which turns out to have better properties in the case of small N (Bruno, 2005a; Judson and Owen, 1999). An obvious drawback of this estimator is the assumption of strict exogeneity of all explanatory variables (except for the lagged dependent variable). The standard errors of the LSDVc are bootstrapped (500 replications), while the SYS-GMM estimator (Blundell and Bond, 1998) is used to initialise the bias correction.

Due to our long time series, which comprises more than 20 years, our results might be affected by the problem of non-stationarity. Hence, we run Fisher type unit root tests for panel data following Maddala and Wu (1999). The results, which are available upon request, reject the null hypothesis that the main variables of interest (CP payments per GDP, public investment per GDP and primary surplus per GDP) are non-stationary for all countries.

6.5 Results and Discussion

The estimation results can be found in Table 6.4. As mentioned above, we differentiate between two samples ("all time periods" and "only EU members"). Furthermore, various estimators are applied. Columns (1) and (5) contain static fixed effects estimators restricting α to zero, where the displayed standard errors are either White-Huber robust or specified following Driscoll and Kraay (1998). Column (2) shows the results of fixed effects estimators applied to a dynamic specification. Since the latter strategy leads to the Nickell bias,[5] we also present the results of the bias-corrected dummy variable estimator (LSDVc) in columns (3) and (6). Finally, in columns (4) and (7) the results of the SYS-GMM specifications are shown, which allow for endogeneity of d, $gdppc$, $contrib$, and cp (besides $pinv$). As mentioned above, the SYS-GMM specification should be interpreted with caution, since N may be too small.

It can be seen that many of the estimated coefficients of the covariates have the expected signs. An increasing stock of public debt (d) leads to less public investment, which corresponds to the findings of Mehrotra and Välilä (2006). By contrast, the effect of a rise in the opportunity costs (real interest rates li) is less clear, suggesting that cost considerations seem to play only a minor role in government investment decisions. While GDP growth (g) affects public investment positively, indicating a pro-cyclical behaviour, the GDP level ($gdppc$) has (with one exception) a negative effect.[6] Moreover, we find significant robust results in all specifications for the lagged dependent variable. The political variables also have the expected sign and the coefficient of $left$ is statistically significant, whereas the indicator measuring the influence of an election year ($elect$) do not have a significant impact. Contributions to the EU ($contrib$) do not seem to reduce public investment.

Generally, the results do not change substantially when standard errors are specified according to Driscoll and Kraay (1998). The disregard of the Nickell bias in column (2) leads, as expected, to an underestimation of the lagged dependent variable. Moreover, the restriction of the sample to EU members only does not alter the conclusions. Instead, the signs and the significance levels remain stable regardless of the choice of the specification.

The focus of our investigation lies on the Cohesion Policy variable. As Table 6.4

[5] Since T varies between 3 and 31 with an average of 16.3, the bias may still be substantial (Judson and Owen, 1999).

[6] This result is in contrast to the one by Mehrotra and Välilä (2006). They interpret their result of a positive effect of the output level as evidence in favour of the hypothesis that public investment have characteristics of a luxury good.

shows, all coefficients of *cp* are far from being significant. This is true for all econometric techniques and both samples. The resulting long-term effects of $\widehat{cp}$ $(\widehat{\beta}_5/(1-\widehat{\alpha}))$ are not shown since they are far from being significantly different from zero.

In order to validate our results we run further sensitivity analyses. First, one may argue that using country-specific time trends may lead to an "over-specification" in the sense of multicollinearity with other explanatory variables or the possibility that the variance of the dependent variable is "absorbed" to a large extent. For this reason, Table 6.5 shows the results when country-specific time trends are omitted. Note that the SYS-GMM models in the paper already omit the country-specific time trends so that this sensitivity analysis is limited to the FE and LSDVc models. It can be seen that the basic results do not change.

Second, we exclude the political variables (*elect*, $left$) as well as the contributions to EU (*contrib*) variable in order to receive a more parsimonious estimation. The regression output displayed in Table 6.6 reveals that this leaves our main finding untouched: *cp* is still not significant.

Third, the governments might not have complete knowledge on the future CP payments, for example due to problems in absorbing total structural funds. Thus, we re-run the regressions using lagged CP variables (*cp*), which does not change our key message (Table 6.7).

Fourth, in the SYS-GMM specifications we assume that apart from the lagged dependent variable, only Cohesion Policy and the contributions to the EU are endogenous, which allows for a very parsimonious use of instruments. Nevertheless, the *cp* variable is still far from being significant.[7]

Fifth, some empirical applications question the superiority of the SYS-GMM estimator mainly because the additional instruments might not be valid (Lucchetti, Papi and Zazzaro, 2001). As a consequence, we use the first-differenced GMM approach as an alternative estimator and again instrument *d*, *gdppc*, *contrib* and *cp* (besides *pinv*), using a lag-limit and the collapse option. Again, the effect of *cp* is not statistically significant (Table 6.8).

Finally, one may argue that the planning, monitoring and control framework for EU-financed projects may be comparatively demanding for countries with low administrative capacity. For this reason, those countries may only be able to implement a limited amount of projects. In order to test whether the results are driven by this aspect, we define a sample including only the 11 EU countries which have received support from the EU Cohesion Fund.[8] The results based on our baseline specification can be found in Table 6.9.

7 These results are not shown, but are available upon request.

8 The sample now includes Austria, Belgium, Denmark, Finland, France, Germany, Italy, Luxembourg, Sweden, the Netherlands and the United Kingdom.

The estimated coefficient of $cp_{i,t}$ is now positive, however, still statistically insignificant at the 10 per cent level.

Summarising the results, no statistically significant positive effect of EU CP on national public investment can be detected, irrespective of which sample and which method is used. As a consequence, it cannot be ruled out that CP simply serves as a substitute for domestically-financed investment projects.

6.6 Conclusions

The existing literature has mainly focused on the impact of EU Cohesion Policy on economic growth, whereas the effects on its major spending target; public investment, have not been evaluated. Both policy fields are linked through the principle of additionality, which implies that EU funds can only be paid in addition to the member states' investment and not instead of it. In practice, however, policymakers have an incentive to spend EU funding for (visible) projects they had previously planned to undertake anyway, and additionality has so far not been sanctioned. These arguments suggest that cohesion payments could displace at least some part of the domestic public investment.

Against this background, we analyse whether EU Cohesion Policy payments really increase domestic public investment using a new comprehensive dataset and applying a panel data setup for 27 EU countries. Our results show that EU Cohesion Policy payments do not significantly increase public investment in the EU countries, which points to a crowding out of national investment. Our approach has some drawbacks. First, EU funding also comprises, to a lesser extent, spending items which are classified outside the public investment category according to ESA 95 definitions, such as expenditure on human capital. Second, EU aid is not subject to the principle of additionality in its entirety. Despite these limitations, one would still expect that EU funding leads to an–at least marginally statistically significant–increase of public investment.

Our findings have at least two implications. First, the policy conclusions are that in future, the principle of additionality should be monitored and sanctioned more carefully in order to ensure that Cohesion Policy payments are effective and lead to higher public investment. Second, our findings might explain the weak growth effects that are the subject of the previous literature on Cohesion Policy. These studies are almost exclusively based on the assumption that Cohesion Policy raises investment, leading to a higher steady-state capital per capita, which, in turn, increases the GDP growth rates (for example Esposti and Bussoletti, 2008). Our results indicate that, at least at national level, this transmission channel does not seem to work.

Acknowledgements

Particular thanks go to Tobias Hagen for many fruitful discussions and valuable suggestions. In addition, I would like to thank Friedrich Heinemann, Steffen Osterloh and Gabriel Glöckler for helpful comments.

6.7 Appendix

Table 6.4: Determinants of national public investment (baseline regression model)

	All time periods				Only EU members		
	FE	**FE dyn.**	**LSDVc**	**SYS-GMM**	**FE**	**LSDVc**	**SYS-GMM**
	(1)	(2)	(3)	(4)	(5)	(6)	(7)
$pinv_{i,t-1}$		0.461	0.622	0.639		0.639	0.630
		(7.11)	(13.86)	(4.49)		(10.54)	(4.06)
		[4.86]					
$d_{i,t-1}$	-0.038	-0.02	-0.015	-0.012	-0.041	-0.017	-0.016
	(-10.24)	(-5.95)	(-4.67)	(-2.25)	(-10.90)	(-3.90)	(-1.97)
	[-11.77]	[-5.86]			[-11.18]		
$li_{i,t}$	-0.02	-0.019	-0.021	0.025	-0.01	-0.011	0.029
	(-1.42)	(-1.63)	(-0.97)	(-1.28)	(-0.57)	(-0.37)	(-1.46)
	[-0.98]	[-1.34]			[-0.38]		
$open_{i,t-1}$	0.005	0.002	0.002	0.002	0.004	0.001	0.001
	(1.19)	(0.57)	(0.64)	(0.75)	(0.89)	(0.25)	(0.34)
	[1.18]	[0.76]			[0.83]		
$g_{i,t-1}$	0.017	0.02	0.021	0.004	0.002	0.012	0.011
	(1.40)	(1.76)	(1.52)	(0.31)	(0.14)	(0.53)	(0.58)
	[1.78]	[2.11]			[0.15]		
$gdppc_{i,t-1}/1,000$	-0.019	-0.011	-0.009	0.005	-0.016	-0.004	-0.003
	(-2.64)	(-1.78)	(-0.50)	(0.53)	(-1.97)	(-0.18)	(-0.58)
	[-2.62]	[-1.90]					
$cp_{i,t}$	**-0.133**	**-0.035**	**-0.029**	**0.026**	**-0.063**	**0.032**	**-0.003**
	(-1.49)	**(-0.52)**	**(-0.38)**	**(0.14)**	**(-0.63)**	**(0.34)**	**(-0.01)**
	[-1.60]	**[-0.68]**					
$contrib_{i,t}$	0.013	0.014	0.017	0.005	0.042	0.034	0.071
	(0.69)	(0.87)	(0.86)	(1.02)	(1.98)	(1.60)	(1.61)
	[0.43]	[0.66]					
$elect_{i,t}$	0.029	0.062	0.073	0.069	-0.011	0.027	0.032
	(0.45)	(1.24)	(1.27)	(1.33)	(-0.16)	(0.34)	(0.74)
	[0.50]	[1.35]					
$left_{i,t}$	0.002	0.001	0.001	0.002	0.003	0.001	0.002
	(3.05)	(2.35)	(1.27)	(1.23)	(3.48)	(1.78)	(1.25)
	[3.04]	[2.48]					
$EU_{i,t}$	0.234	-0.069	-0.135	-0.313			
	(-0.69)	(-0.37)	(-0.68)	(-0.60)			
	[0.90]	[-0.43]					
Time dummies	yes	yes	yes	yes	yes	yes	yes
(p-value)	0.000	0.000	0.000	time demean	0.000	0.000	time demean
Time trend	specific	specific	specific	no	specific	specific	no
(p-value)	0.000	0.000	0.000		0.000	0.000	
No. instrum.				40			39
Hansen (p-value)				0.988			0.946
AR(2) test (p-value)				0.296			0.430
R^2 (within)	0.692	0.761			0.678		
No. of countries	27	27	27	27	25	25	25
No. of obs.	439	436	436	408	347	347	320

Notes: t-values in parentheses if not stated otherwise: FE: (White-Huber robust s.e.) / [Driscoll-Kraay s.e.]; LSDVc: 500 bootstrap replications, while the SYS-GMM estimator (Blundell and Bond, 1998) is used to initialise the bias correction.

Table 6.5: Determinants of national public investment (without country-specific time trend)

	All time periods			Only EU members	
	FE	**FE dyn.**	**LSDVc**	**FE**	**LSDVc**
	(1)	(2)	(3)	(4)	(5)
$pinv_{i,t-1}$		0.685 (16.4) [14.38]	0.782 (21.27)		0.757 (16.16)
$d_{i,t-1}$	-0.017 (-6.88) [-5.63]	-0.008 (-4.24) [-4.92]	-0.007 (-3.55)	-0.018 (-7.17) [-5.49]	-0.008 (-3.40)
$li_{i,t}$	-0.046 (-3.62) [-3.20]	-0.019 (-2.20) [-2.45]	-0.018 (-1.39)	-0.014 (-0.88) [-0.55]	-0.005 (-0.30)
$open_{i,t-1}$	0.007 (2.66) [2.09]	0.002 (1.01) [1.30]	0.002 (1.25)	0.005 (2.02) [1.45]	0.001 (0.79)
$g_{i,t-1}$	0.014 (0.94) [1.23]	0.024 (2.14) [2.94]	0.026 (2.03)	0.001 (0.04) [0.05]	0.022 (1.36)
$gdppc_{i,t-1}/1,000$	-0.029 (-7.86) [-7.56]	-0.007 (-2.06) [-2.16]	0.022 (0.30)	-0.031 (-8.62) [-8.42]	-0.006 (-0.98)
$cp_{i,t}$	**-0.007** **(-0.08)** **[-0.07]**	**0.042** **(0.73)** **[1.48]**	**0.021** **(0.30)**	**-0.202** **(-1.90)** **[-1.64]**	**-0.024** **(-0.29)**
$contrib_{i,t}$	0.062 (2.6) [1.93]	0.033 (1.97) [1.85]	0.032 (1.84)	0.094 (4.2) [2.68]	0.043 (1.48)
$elect_{i,t}$	0.103 (1.04) [1.40]	0.111 (2.02) [2.19]	0.113 (1.98)	0.069 (0.73) [0.92]	0.051 (0.59)
$left_{i,t}$	0.002 (2.26) [1.91]	0.001 (1.89) [1.65]	0.001 (1.19)	0.001 (0.19) [0.12]	0.001 (0.59)
$EU_{i,t}$	-0.471 (-2.11)	-0.329 (-2.17) [-2.64]	-0.315 (-1.88)		
Time dummies	yes	yes	yes	yes	yes
(p-value)	0.000	0.000	0.000	0.000	0.000
Time trend	no	no	no	no	no
R^2 (within)	0.372	0.703		0.416	
No. of countries	27	27	27	25	25
No. of obs.	439	436	436	347	331

Notes: t-values in parentheses if not stated otherwise: FE: (White-Huber robust s.e.) / [Driscoll-Kraay s.e.]; LSDVc: 500 bootstrap replications, while the SYS-GMM estimator (Blundell and Bond, 1998) is used to initialise the bias correction.

Table 6.6: Determinants of national public investment (without contributions to the EU and political variables)

	All time periods				**Only EU members**		
	FE	**FE dyn.**	**LSDVc**	**SYS-GMM**	**FE**	**LSDVc**	**SYS-GMM**
	(1)	(2)	(3)	(4)	(5)	(6)	(7)
$pinv_{i,t-1}$		0.512	0.678	0.77		0.691	0.723
		(5.69)	(15.54)	(8.42)		(11.68)	(6.62)
		[6.02]					
$d_{i,t-1}$	-0.034	-0.016	-0.011	-0.010	-0.038	-0.012	-0.012
	(-4.09)	(-4.57)	(-3.50)	(-2.89)	(-4.72)	(-3.14)	(-2.49)
	[-10.57]	[-5.26]			[-11.27]		
$li_{i,t}$	-0.02	-0.017	-0.018	0.007	-0.023	-0.016	0.017
	(-0.73)	(-1.30)	(-3.50)	(0.68)	(-0.54)	(-0.52)	(0.98)
	[-0.87]	[-1.25]			[-0.80]		
$open_{i,t-1}$	-0.001	-0.002	-0.002	-0.001	-0.002	-0.003	-0.001
	(-0.23)	(-0.65)	(-0.73)	(-0.18)	(-0.49)	(-0.88)	(-0.11)
	[-0.16]	[-0.49]			[-0.37]		
$g_{i,t-1}$	0.022	0.024	0.026	0.017	0.008	0.016	0.014
	(1.26)	(2.58)	(1.96)	(1.79)	(0.28)	(0.93)	(0.92)
	[2.32]	[2.71]			[0.49]		
$gdppc_{i,t-1}/1,000$	-0.022	-0.012	-0.009	0.007	-0.023	-0.006	0.009
	(-2.19)	(-2.65)	(-0.58)	(0.97)	(-1.56)	(-0.32)	(1.19)
	[-2.73]	[-2.05]			[-2.22]		
$cp_{i,t}$	**-0.134**	**-0.047**	**-0.037**	**0.010**	**-0.079**	**0.022**	**-0.074**
	(-0.59)	**(-0.38)**	**(-0.48)**	**(0.08)**	**(-0.30)**	**(0.26)**	**(-0.48)**
	[-1.36]	**[-0.84]**			**[-0.67]**		
$EU_{i,t}$	0.367	0.063	0.015	0.029			
	(1.18)	(0.44)	(0.12)	(0.52)			
	[1.93]	[0.67]					
Time dummies	yes	yes	yes	yes	yes	yes	yes
(p-value)	0.000	0.000	0.000	time demean	0.000	0.798	time demean
Time trend	specific	specific	specific	no	specific	specific	no
(p-value)	0.000	0.000	0.000		0.000	0.955	
No. instrum.				33			32
Hansen (p-value)				0.777			0.923
AR(2) test (p-value)				0.270			0.999
R^2 (within)	0.689	0.779			0.647		
No. of countries	27	27	27	27	27	25	27
No. of obs.	466	463	463	435	374	356	362

Notes: t-values in parentheses if not stated otherwise: FE: (White-Huber robust s.e.) / [Driscoll-Kraay s.e.]; LSDVc: 500 bootstrap replications, while the SYS-GMM estimator (Blundell and Bond, 1998) is used to initialise the bias correction.

Table 6.7: Determinants of national public investment (lagged CP variable)

	All time periods				Only EU members		
	FE	**FE dyn.**	**LSDVc**	**SYS-GMM**	**FE**	**LSDVc**	**SYS-GMM**
	(1)	(2)	(3)	(4)	(5)	(6)	(7)
$pinv_{i,t-1}$		0.462	0.624	0.792		0.636	0.518
		(7.11)	(13.85)	(5.13)		(10.49)	(3.48)
		[4.91]					
$d_{i,t-1}$	-0.038	-0.02	-0.015	-0.005	-0.041	-0.017	-0.015
	(-10.42)	(-5.92)	(-4.59)	(-0.53)	(-11.01)	(.3.91)	(-3.34)
	[-11.54]	[-5.83]			[-11.11]		
$li_{i,t}$	-0.022	-0.019	-0.02	0.011	-0.013	-0.012	0.031
	(-1.53)	(-1.66)	(-0.96)	(0.46)	(0.729	(-0.38)	(1.01)
	[-1.05]	[-1.33]			[-0.47]		
$open_{i,t-1}$	0.005	0.002	0.002	0.002	0.005	0.001	0.001
	(1.29)	(0.6)	(0.64)	(0.39)	(0.98)	(0.23)	(0.37)
	[1.26]	[0.77]			[0.90]		
$g_{i,t-1}$	0.016	0.020	0.021	-0.01	0.002	0.011	0.001
	(1.28)	(1.72)	(1.52)	(-0.40)	(0.1)	(0.6)	(0.05)
	[1.77]	[2.07]			[0.12]		
$gdppc_{i,t-1}/1,000$	-0.018	-0.011	-0.009	0.036	-0.017	-0.005	0.003
	(-2.59)	(-1.68)	(-0.47)	(1.15)	(-2.08)	(-0.23)	(0.25)
	[-2.59]	[-1.92]			[-1.71]		
$cp_{i,t-1}$	**-0.122**	**-0.026**	**-0.019**	**-0.281**	**-0.087**	**0.112**	**-0.252**
	(-1.36)	**(-0.38)**	**(-0.22)**	**(-0.94)**	**(-0.90)**	**(0.12)**	**(-0.94)**
	[-1.30]	**[-0.45]**			**[-0.85]**		
$contrib_{i,t}$	0.015	0.015	0.017	0.087	0.046	0.035	0.116
	(0.83)	(0.88)	(0.87)	(1.48)	(2.14)	(1.68)	(2.2)
	[0.56]	[0.70]			[1.51]		
$elect_{i,t}$	0.03	0.062	0.074	0.122	-0.013	0.028	0.026
	(0.48)	(1.24)	(1.26)	(2.32)	(-0.20)	(0.36)	(0.49)
	[0.52]	[1.34]			[-0.21]		
$left_{i,t}$	0.002	0.001	0.001	0.001	0.003	0.001	0.002
	(3.32)	(2.45)	(1.43)	(0.67)	(3.70)	(1.75)	(2.34)
	[3.18]	[2.62]			[3.11]		
$EU_{i,t}$	0.194	-0.077	-0.141	-0.555			
	(0.93)	(-0.42)	(-0.70)	(-1.48)			
	[0.79]						
Time dummies	yes	yes	yes	yes	yes	yes	yes
(p-value)	0.000	0.000	0.000	time demean	0.000	0.000	time demean
Time trend	specific	specific	specific	no	specific	specific	no
(p-value)	0.000	0.000	0.000		0.000	0.000	
No. instrum.				34			33
Hansen (p-value)				0.919			0.550
AR(2) test (p-value)				0.382			0.619
R^2 (within)	0.691	0.762			0.679		
No. of countries	27	27	27	26	25	25	25
No. of obs.	439	436	436	408	347	331	294

Notes: t-values in parentheses if not stated otherwise: FE: (White-Huber robust s.e.) / [Driscoll-Kraay s.e.]; LSDVc: 500 bootstrap replications, while the SYS-GMM estimator (Blundell and Bond, 1998) is used to initialise the bias correction.

Table 6.8: Determinants of national public investment (one-step first-differenced GMM instead of SYS-GMM)

	All time periods	**Only EU members**
	(1)	(2)
$pinv_{i,t}$	0.778	0.490
	(5.26)	(3.21)
$d_{i,t}$	-0.004	-0.014
	(-0.52)	(-3.32)
$li_{i,t}$	0.019	0.032
	(0.87)	(1.10)
$open_{i,t}$	0.002	0.001
	(0.32)	(0.21)
$g_{i,t}$	-0.010	-0.002
	(-0.40)	(-0.07)
$gdppc_{i,t}/1,000$	0.037	0.001
	(1.07)	(0.06)
$cp_{i,t}$	**-0.473**	**-0.321**
	(-1.29)	**(-0.90)**
$contrib_{i,t}$	0.098	0.104
	(2.02)	(2.07)
$elect_{i,t}$	0.109	0.024
	(2.20)	(0.47)
$left_{i,t}$	0.000	0.002
	(0.31)	(2.33)
$EU_{i,t}$	-0.571	
	(-1.89)	
Time dummies	yes	yes
(p-value)	time demean	time demean
Time trend	no	no
No. instrum.	34	33
Hansen (p-value)	0.998	0.576
AR(2) test (p-value)	0.399	0.509
No. of countries	26	25
No. of obs.	381	294

Notes: t-values in parentheses if not stated otherwise.

Table 6.9: Determinants of national public investment (without Cohesion countries)

	FE dyn.	LSDVc
	(1)	(2)
$pinv_{i,t-1}$	-0.023	0.498
	(-3.77)	(7.42)
	[-8.95]	
$d_{i,t-1}$	-0.023	-0.012
	(-3.77)	(-3.02)
	[-8.95]	
$li_{i,t}$	-0.026	-0.026
	(-1.07)	(-1.00)
	[-1.33]	
$open_{i,t-1}$	-0.003	-0.003
	(-0.69)	(-0.74)
	[-0.91]	
$g_{i,t-1}$	0.020	0.019
	(1.22)	(1.09)
	[1.73]	
$gdppc_{i,t-1}/1,000$	0.014	0.009
	(0.50)	(0.47)
	[0.82]	
$cp_{i,t}$	**0.411**	**0.737**
	(1.09)	**(1.46)**
	[0.79]	
$contrib_{i,t}$	-0.016	-0.001
	(-0.78)	(-0.05)
	[-0.86]	
$elect_{i,t}$	-0.011	-0.007)
	(-0.18)	(-0.10)
	[-0.24]	
$left_{i,t}$	0.000	0.000
	(-0.20)	(-0.27)
	[-0.33]	
$EU_{i,t}$	0.242	-0.069
	(1.04)	(-0.22)
	[0.87]	
Time dummies	yes	yes
(p-value)	0.000	0.000
Time trend	specific	specific
(p-value)	0.000	0.000
R^2 (within)	0.803	
No. of countries	11	11
No. of obs.	267	266

Notes: t-values in parentheses if not stated otherwise: FE: (White-Huber robust s.e.) / [Driscoll-Kraay s.e.]; LSDVc: 500 bootstrap replications, while the SYS-GMM estimator (Blundell and Bond, 1998) is used to initialise the bias correction.

Chapter 7

Summary and Conclusions

More than one third of the total EU budget is spent on Cohesion Policy in the Multiannual Financial Framework ranging from 2007 - 2013. Its main goal as laid down in the Treaty is to promote the "overall harmonious development" of the EU, to reduce disparities between the levels of development of the various regions, and to strengthen its "economic, social and territorial cohesion". The empirical literature has in particular investigated its economic growth impact and has revealed mixed, if not contradictory, findings: the results range from positive growth effects (Beugelsdijk and Eijffinger, 2005), to no statistically significant (Dall'erba and Le Gallo, 2007) or even negative effects (Eggert, von Ehrlich, Fenge and König, 2007). However, there are at least two aspects which have been insufficiently analysed in this research area. First, several methodological issues need to be addressed. For example, the evaluation literature has hardly taken into account that regional growth rates are also influenced by spatial spillover effects. Second, the existing literature has mainly focused on the analysis of the economic growth effects of EU aid and has disregarded that EU Cohesion Policy might also affect other policy areas such as employment and public investment. Against this background, this thesis addresses the open research questions analysing the empirical evidence on the macroeconomic effects of EU Cohesion Policy.

Chapter 2 reviews the empirical studies on the effectiveness of EU funding to find explanations for the diverging results. It becomes clear that there are several methodological issues which impede the evaluation of this policy field. They can be summarised under the keywords: measurement error resulting from poor data quality of EU Cohesion Policy payments, endogeneity problems, omitted spatial spillover effects and underlying strict functional form assumptions. As the current state of the art does not allow to account for all methodological issues simultaneously, a comparison of different approaches seems to be advisable to derive robust conclusions.

Based on the methodological issues presented above, Chapter 2 discusses the related literature. In general, using regional level data is the preferable option, since, firstly, the greater part of EU aid focuses on the development of regions and, secondly, a higher number of observations increases the robustness of the empirical estimation results. However, one drawback is that data availability at the regional level has remained limited. Summing up, one could conclude from the empirical studies that EU funding is only conditionally effective. The Cohesion Policy does, in fact, have a positively significant impact on economic growth if the quality of the institutional setup is high (Ederveen, de Groot and Nahuis, 2006), the governmental structures are decentralised (Bähr, 2008), or if it is spent for less-developed regions (Ramajo, Márquez, Hewings and Salinas, 2008).

Chapter 3 analyses the economic growth effects of EU structural funds. It expands on the current literature with regard to at least three aspects: First, the time period of investigation is extended by compiling a new dataset comprising structural funds payments of the Financial Perspective 2000 - 2006 that have not been analysed before. Second, more precise measures of structural funds are used by distinguishing between Objective 1, 2 and 3 payments and by investigating the impact of time lags more carefully. Third, the robustness of the results is examined by comparing different econometric approaches highlighting specific methodological problems. Apart from "classical" panel data methods (such as system GMM), we apply spatial panel econometric techniques.

The empirical findings confirm the relevance of regional spatial spillover effects, which implies that the regional growth rates also depend on the economic developments of the neighbouring regions. Furthermore, the results indicate that Objective 1 payments in particular have a positive and significant impact on growth, whereas both Objective 2 and 3 payments negatively affect the regions' growth rates. One reason for the weak effects of Objective 2 and 3 payments is that their allocation is at least partly determined by politico-economic aspects, so that their allocation is affected by political bargaining which possibly results in the support of politically feasible, and less economically efficient, projects. Moreover, the results show that the time lag plays a key role in affecting the results. As a consequence, rather than appearing immediately, the growth impact occurs with a time lag of approximately two to three years.

Chapter 4 builds on the fact that the current empirical literature on the impact of EU Cohesion Policy on growth mainly relies on (strict) functional form assumptions. However, it is ex ante not clear which functional form is appropriate with regard to the relationship between structural funds payments and regional economic growth. In order to avoid such assumptions, this article uses the method of generalised propensity score, which leads to the estimation of a dose-response function (Hirano and Imbens, 2004). The method is applied to our new dataset of total structural funds payments of 122 NUTS-1 and NUTS-2 regions in the EU-15 for the time period 1995 - 2005. The results indicate that it does not matter which "dose" of structural funds payments a region receives, implying that total structural funds payments have no statistically significant impact on the regions' growth rates.

The literature overview provided in Chapter 2 reveals that the previous studies analysing the impact of EU aid have mainly concentrated on its growth effects. EU Cohesion Policy, however, is likely to have an impact on other policy fields as well. There are at least two reasons why the investigation of the employment effects are of relevance. First, EU Cohesion Policy partly aims at reducing disparities in the employment sector. Second, employment effects contribute to building up regional income disparities, which are based on differences in the employment level and labour productivity, respectively. Nevertheless, the employment effects have hardly been evaluated. Furthermore, theoretical considerations show that increasing EU aid does not necessarily result in more employment. Instead, EU aid can be spent as capital subsidy or human capital investment, resulting in different employment effects depending on the educational attainment of the population.

The net effect of EU funding on total employment is an empirical question which is raised in *Chapter 5* with a panel dataset of 130 European NUTS regions over the time period 1999 - 2007. The empirical results confirm the theoretical predictions since total structural funds have no significant positive impact on the regional employment level. However, we find evidence that structural funds may be interpreted as capital subsidies and that they are conditionally effective. The funds have a significant positive impact on the total employment level in regions with a low share of low-skilled population, and have a negative effect in the case of a high share of low-skilled population. From a policy perspective our findings show that EU funding currently lacks a clear concept with clearly measurable goals on how to promote employment within the EU. Clearly measurable goals would allow for a better ex-post assessment of this policy field.

Apart from the employment effects, EU Cohesion Policy should have an impact on another policy field, namely that of public investment. Due to the principle of additionality, EU funds have to be paid out in addition to the national public investment and must not displace it. However, there are at least two arguments which suggest that EU Cohesion Policy might crowd out some part of national public investment. First, a political economic reasoning suggests that politicians prefer to spend EU money for (visible) projects which they had intended to undertake anyway. Second, the principle of additionality has so far not been monitored carefully and, more importantly, has not yet been sanctioned, which reduces the incentive to comply with it.

Against this background, *Chapter 6* analyses the impact of EU funding on national public investment in order to find out whether EU Cohesion payments are indeed "additional" or whether they crowd out national projects. The investigation is based on a panel dataset of 27 EU member states for the period 1982 - 2006 using a new comprehensive dataset of total EU Cohesion Policy payments. Our findings reveal that EU aid has no positive and significant impact on national public investment, which implies that the payments crowd out national public investment. As a consequence, the principle of additionality should in future be monitored and sanctioned more carefully.

In conclusion, the thesis shows that

- the existing empirical evidence on the growth effects of EU Cohesion Policy is mixed and that several methodological issues hamper its evaluation (Chapter 2),
- EU Cohesion Policy seems to be only conditionally effective, since only Objective 1 payments do, in fact, promote economic growth (Chapter 3),
- total structural funds payments have no positive and significant effects on economic growth even when softening the strict functional form assumptions of the underlying growth model (Chapter 4),
- EU aid only has a positive and statistically significant employment effect for the high-skilled, but not for the low-skilled part of the population (Chapter 5),
- despite the principle of additionality EU Cohesion Policy payments seem to crowd out national public investment (Chapter 6).

Overall, the thesis contributes to a greatly improved understanding of the empirical macroeconomic effects of EU Cohesion Policy. In order to facilitate a precise evaluation of EU aid in the future, two things are essential. First, the thesis shows that the evaluation of this policy field is impeded by data availability of EU Cohesion payments. The thesis addresses this gap by compiling a new dataset of Cohesion Policy payments for the time period 1999 -2007. However, this database should be extended to include payments for the period pre-1999 and post-2007 to allow for a better ex-post assessment of this policy field in the future. Moreover, the EU Commission should make the entire dataset for EU Cohesion Policy payments available, including total EU funding categorised by objective, structural fund and region. Second, the focus of EU Cohesion Policy has broadened over the last years and new policy objectives and initiatives have been introduced. However, EU Cohesion Policy should focus on clearly measurable goals in order to allow for a comprehensive ex-post evaluation of this policy field.

The thesis also serves as an excellent starting point for further evaluation studies on EU Cohesion Policy. Chapter 6 shows that EU funding crowds out national public investment. In this context, very little is known about the detailed transmission channels through which EU Cohesion Policy works. With this in mind, one task for future studies will be to more thoroughly investigate the channels through which EU Cohesion Policy affects the national budgets. For example, it could be analysed whether EU funding affects the national tax policy or whether EU aid has had an impact on the quality of public finances by changing the composition of fiscal policy spending.

Bibliography

ABREU, M., H. DE GROOT AND R. FLORAX (2005): "Space and growth: A survey of empirical evidence and methods," *Région et Développement*, 2005-21, 12–43.

ALLEN, D. (2005): "Cohesion and structural funds," in *Policy-making in the European Union*, ed. by H. Wallace, W. Wallace and M. Pollack, pp. 213–242. Oxford University Press, Oxford.

ANGRIST, J. AND J. PISCHKE (2009): *Mostly harmless econometrics: An empiricist's companion.* Princeton University Press, Princeton.

ANSELIN, L. (1988): *Spatial econometrics: Methods and models.* Kluwer, Dordrecht.

——— (2006): "Spatial econometrics," in *Palgrave handbook of econometrics*, ed. by T. Mills and K. Patterson, vol. 1, pp. 901–969. Palgrave Macmillan, Basingstoke.

ANSELIN, L. AND A. BERA (1998): "Spatial dependence in linear regression models with an introduction to spatial econometrics," in *Handbook of applied economic statistic*, ed. by A. Ullah and D. Giles, pp. 237–289. Marce Dekker, New York.

ANSELIN, L., R. FLORAX AND S. REY (2004): *Advances in spatial econometrics.* Springer, Berlin, Heidelberg, New York.

ANSELIN, L. AND S. HUDAK (1992): "Spatial econometrics in practice: A review of software options," *Regional Science and Urban Economics*, 22, 509–536.

ARBIA, G., J. LE GALLO AND G. PIRAS (2008): "Does evidence on regional economic convergence depend on the estimation strategy? Outcomes from analysis of a set of NUTS2 EU regions," *Spatial Economic Analysis*, 3(2), 209–224.

ARELLANO, M. AND S. BOND (1991): "Some tests of specification for panel data: Monte Carlo evidence and an application to employment equations," *The Review of Economic Studies*, 58, 277–297.

ARMINGEON, K., M. GERBER, P. LEIMGRUBER AND M. BEYELER (2008): "Comparative political data set 1960-2006," *Institute of Political Science, University of Berne.*

AUSTIN, N. (2007): "Causal inference with observational data," *The Stata Journal*, 7(4), 507–541.

BADINGER, H., W. MÜLLER AND G. TONDL (2004): "Regional convergence in the European Union 1985-1999: A spatial dynamic panel analysis," *Regional Studies*, 38(3), 241–253.

BÄHR, C. (2008): "How does sub-national autonomy affect the effectiveness of structural funds?," *Kyklos*, 61(1), 3–18.

BALDWIN, R. AND C. WYPLOSZ (2009): *The economics of European integration.* Mcgraw-Hill Higher Education, London.

BALTAGI, B. H. (2008): *Econometric analysis of panel data.* John Wiley & Sons, Chichester.

BARRO, R. (1990): "Government spending in a simple model of endogenous growth," *Journal of Political Economy*, 98, 103–125.

BARRO, R. AND J.-W. LEE (2001): "International comparisons of educational attainment," *Journal of Monetary Economics*, 32(3), 363–394.

BARRO, R. AND X. SALA-I-MARTIN (1991): "Convergence across states and regions," *Brookings Papers on Economic Activity*, 1, 107–182.

——— (1992): "Convergence," *Journal of Political Economy*, 100(2), 223–251.

BARRO, R. AND X. SALA-I MARTIN (2004): *Economic growth.* The MIT Press, Cambridge, Massachusetts.

BASILE, R. AND L. DE BENEDICTIS (2008): "Regional unemployment and productivity in Europe," *Papers in Regional Science*, 87(2), 182.

BECKER, S., P. EGGER AND M. VON EHRLICH (2010): "Going NUTS: The effect of EU Structural Funds on regional performance," *Journal of Public Economics*, 94(9-10), 578–590.

BECKER, S., P. EGGER, M. VON EHRLICH AND R. FENGE (2008): "Going NUTS: The effect of EU structural funds on regional performance," *CESifo Working Paper*, 2495.

BELL, K. AND N. BOCKSTAEL (2000): "Applying the generalized moments-estimation approach to spatial problems involving microlevel data," *Review of Economics and Statistics*, 82, 72–82.

BERMAN, E., L. BOUND AND Z. GRILICHES (1994): "Changes in the demand for skilled labor within U.S. manufacturing: Evidence from the annual survey of manufactures," *The Quarterly Journal of Economics*, 109(2), 367–397.

BEUGELSDIJK, M. AND S. EIJFFINGER (2005): "The effectiveness of structural policy in the European Union: An empirical analysis for the EU-15 in 1995-2001," *Journal of Common Market Studies*, 40, 37–51.

BIA, M. AND A. MATTEI (2007): "Application of the Generalized Propensity Score. Evaluation of public contributions to Piedmont enterprises," *Working Paper of the Department of Public Policy and Public Choice (POLIS)*, No. 89.

BLANKART, C. B. AND C. KIRCHNER (2003): "The deadlock of the EU budget: An economic analysis of ways in and ways out," *CESifo Working Paper*, 989.

BLAU, F. AND L. KAHN (1999): "Institutions and laws in the labor market," in *Handbook of Labor Economics*, ed. by O. Ashenfelter and D. Card, vol. 3A, pp. 1399–1461. North-Holland, Amsterdam.

BLUNDELL, R. AND S. BOND (1998): "Initial conditions and moment restrictions in dynamic panel data models," *Journal of Econometrics*, 87, 115–143.

BODENSTEIN, T. AND A. KEMMERLING (2008): "Ripples in a Rising Tide: Why Some EU Regions Receive More Structural Funds than Otherss," *CES Working Paper*, 157.

BOND, S., A. HOEFFLER AND J. TEMPLE (2001): "GMM estimation of empirical growth models," *Nuffield College Economics Working Paper*, 2001-W21.

BONDONIO, D. AND R. GREENBAUM (2006): "Do business investment incentives promote employment in declining areas? Evidence from EU Objective-2 regions," *European Urban and Regional Studies*, 13, 225–244.

BOUVET, F. (2005): "European Union regional policy: allocation determinants and effects on regional economic growth," *Working Paper*, Department of Economics, University of California, Davis.

BOUVET, F. AND S. DALL'ERBA (2010): "European regional structural funds: How large is the influence of politicas on the allocation process?," *Journal of Common Market Studies*, 48(3), 501–528.

BOWSHER, C. (2002): "On testing overidentifying restrictions in dynamic panel data models," *Economic Letters*, 77, 211–220.

BRADLEY, J. AND G. UNTIEDT (2007): "Do economic models tell us anything useful about Cohesion Policy impacts? A comparison of HERMIN, QUEST and ECOMOD," *GEFRA Working Paper*, July.

——— (2008): "EU Cohesion Policy and "conditional" effectiveness: What do cross-section regression tell us?," *GEFRA Working Paper*, May 2008(4).

BRAMBOR, T., W. CLARK AND M. GOLDER (2006): "Understanding interaction models: Improving empirical analyses," *Political Analysis*, 14, 63–82.

BRAUMOELLER, B. (2004): "Hypothesis testing and multiplicative interaction terms," *International Organization*, 58, 807–820.

BRONZINI, R. AND P. PISELLI (2009): "Determinants of long-run regional productivity with geographical spillovers: The role of R&D, human capital and public infrastructure," *Regional Science and Urban Economics*, 39, 187–199.

BRUNO, G. (2005a): "Approximating the bias of the LSDV estimator for dynamic unbalanced panel data models," *Economic Letters*, 87, 361–366.

——— (2005b): "Estimation and inference in dynamic unbalanced panel data models with a small number of individuals," *Stata Journal*, 5(4), 473–500.

BUSCH, B., K. LICHTBLAU AND C. SCHNABEL (1998): "Kohäsionspolitik, Konvergenz und Arbeitslosigkeit in der Europäischen Union: Eine empirische Analyse mit Regionaldaten," *Jahrbuch für Wirtschaftswissenschaften*, 49, 1–25.

CAPPELEN, A., F. CASTELLACCI, J. FAGERBERG AND B. VERSPAGEN (2003): "The impact of EU regional support on growth and convergence in the European Union," *Journal of Common Market Studies*, 41(4), 621–644.

CHECHERITA, C., C. NICKEL AND P. ROTHER (2009): "The role of fiscal transfers for regional economic convergence in Europe," *ECB Working Paper*, No 1029(March).

COHEN, D. AND M. SOTO (2007): "Growth and human capital: good data, good results," *Journal of Economic Growth*, 12, 51–76.

CUARESMA, J., D. RITZBERGER-GRÜNWALD AND M. SILGONER (2008): "Growth, convergence and EU membership," *Applied Economics*, 40(5), 643–656.

DALL'ERBA, S. (2005): "Distribution of regional income and regional funds in Europe 1989-1999: An exploratory spatial data analysis," *The Annals of Regional Science*, 39, 121–148.

DALL'ERBA, S. AND J. LE GALLO (2007): "The impact of EU regional support on growth and employment," *Czech Journal of Economics and Finance*, 57(7), 325–340.

——— (2008): "Regional convergence and the impact of European structural funds 1989-1999: A spatial econometric analysis," *Papers in Regional Science*, 82(2), 219–244.

DAVIES, S., J. BACHTLER, F. GROSS, R. MICHIE, H. VIRONEN AND D. YUILL (2007): "The impact of structural funds programmes in Scotland 1994-2006," *European Policy Research Paper*, 60(University of Strathclyde, Glasgow).

DE FREITAS, M., F. PEREIRA AND F. TORRES (2003): "Convergence among EU regions, 1990-2001. Quality of national institutions and "Objective 1" status," *Intereconomics*, September/October(2003), 270–275.

DE LA FUENTE, A. AND R. DOMÉNECH (2006): "Human capital in growth regressions: How much difference does data quality make?," *Journal of the European Economic Association*, 4(1), 1–36.

DREHER, A., P. NUNNENKAMP AND R. THIELE (2008): "Does aid for education educate children: evidence from panel data," *World Bank Economic Review*, 22(2), 291–314.

DRISCOLL, J. AND A. KRAAY (1998): "Consistent covariance matrix estimation with spatially dependent panel data," *The Review of Economics and Statistics*, 80(4), 549–560.

DURLAUF, S., P. JOHNSON AND J. TEMPLE (2005): "Growth econometrics," in *Handbook of economic growth*, ed. by P. Aghion and S. Durlauf, vol. 1 A, pp. 555–677. Elsevier.

DURLAUF, S., A. KOURTELLOS AND C. TAN (2008): "Are any growth theories robust?," *The Economic Journal*, 118(March), 329–346.

DURLAUF, S. N. AND D. QUAH (1999): "The new empirics of economic growth," in *Handbook of Macroeconomics*, ed. by J. Taylor and M. Woodford, vol. 1. North Holland, Amsterdam.

EDERVEEN, S., H. DE GROOT AND R. NAHUIS (2006): "Fertile soil for structural funds? A panel data analysis of the conditional effectiveness of European cohesion policy," *Kyklos*, 59, 17–42.

Ederveen, S., J. Gorter, R. de Mooij and R. Nahuis (2002): *Funds and games. The economics of European Cohesion Policy.* CPB Bureau for Economic Policy Analysis, The Hague.

Eggert, W., M. von Ehrlich, R. Fenge and G. König (2007): "Konvergenz- und Wachstumseffekte der europäischen Regionalpolitik in Deutschland," *Perspektiven der Wirtschaftspolitik*, 8(2), 130–146.

Elhorst, P. (2003a): "The mystery of regional unemployment differentials: A survey of theoretical and empirical explanations," *Journal of Economic Surveys*, 17, 709–748.

Elhorst, P., G. Piras and G. Arbia (2006): "Growth and convergence in a multiregional model with space-time dynamics," *Paper presented at the Spatial Econometric Workshop, May 25-27, 2006, Rome.*

Elhorst, P. and A. Zeilstra (2007): "Labour force participation rates at the regional and national levels of the European Union: An integrated analysis," *Papers in Regional Science*, 86(4), 525–549.

Elhorst, P. J. (2003b): "Specification and estimation of spatial panel data models," *International Regional Science Review*, 26, 244–268.

——— (2010): "Spatial panel data models," in *Handbook of applied spatial analysis*, ed. by M. Fischer and A. Getis, pp. 377–407. Springer, Berlin.

Ertur, C. and W. Koch (2006): "Regional disparities in the European Union and the enlargement process: An exploratory spatial data analysis, 1995-2000," *Journal of Regional Science*, 40, 723–765.

——— (2007): "Growth, technological interdependence and spatial externalities: Theory and evidence," *Journal of Applied Econometrics*, 22(6), 1033–1062.

Esposti, R. and S. Bussoletti (2008): "Impact of Objective 1 funds on regional growth convergence in the European Union: A panel-data approach," *Regional Studies*, 42(2), 159–173.

European Commission (1995): *The implementation of the reform of the structural funds 1993: Fifth annual report.* European Commission, Brussels.

——— (1996a): *Seventh annual report on the structural funds 1995.* European Commission, Brussels.

——— (1996b): *Sixth annual report on the structural funds 1994*. European Commission, Brussels.

——— (1997): *Eighth annual report on the structural funds 1996*. European Commission, Brussels.

——— (1998): *Ninth annual report on the structural funds 1997*. European Commission, Brussels.

——— (1999): *Tenth annual report on the structural funds 1998*. European Commission, Brussels.

——— (2000): *Report from the Commission. 11th annual report on the structural funds 1999*. European Commission, Brussels.

——— (2004a): "Capping of ressources," *Working Document of the Commission Services, Multiannual Financial Framework 2007-2013, Fiche no. 27.*

——— (2004b): *Third report on economic and social cohesion: A new partnership for cohesion*. Bruxelles.

——— (2007a): *Cohesion policy 2007–13. Commentaries and official texts*. European Commission, Luxembourg.

——— (2007b): "Commission regulation (EC) No. 105/2007," *Official Journal of the European Union*, L 39.

——— (2007c): *Growing regions, growing Europe: fourth report on economic and social cohesion*. European Commission, Brussels.

——— (2008): *EU budget 2007. Financial report*. Office for Official Publications of the European Communities, Luxembourg.

EUROSTAT (2007): *Geographic information system of the European Commission (GISCO): NUTS 2003*. European Commission, Luxembourg.

FALK, M. AND F. SINABELL (2008): "The effectiveness of Objective 1 structural funds in the EU15: New empirical evidence from NUTS 3 regions," *WIFO Working Papers*, 310(February).

FELD, L. (2005): "European public finances: Much ado about nothing?," in *Handbook of public administration and policy in the European Union*, ed. by M. van der Hoek, vol. 13, pp. 257–310. CRC Press, Taylor and Francis Group, Boca Raton.

FELD, L. AND J. SCHNELLENBACH (2007): "Das Finanzierungssystem der Europäischen Union und die Nettozahlerdebatte," *Wirtschaftsdienst*, 87(2), 114–120.

FEYZIOGLU, T., V. SWAROOP AND M. ZHU (1998): "A panel data analysis of the fungibility of foreign aid," *The World Bank Economic Review*, 12(1), 29–58.

FITZENBERGER, B., K. KOHN AND Q. WANG (2011): "The erosion of union membership in Germany: determinants, densities, decompositions," *Journal of Population Economics*, 24(1), 141–165.

FLORES, C. (2004): "Estimation of dose-response functions and optimal doses with a continuous treatment," *Job Market Paper, University of California, Berkeley.*

FLORES-LAGUNES, A., A. GONZALEZ AND T. NEUMAN (2007): "Estimating the effects of length of exposure to a training program: The case of job corps," *IZA Discussion Paper*, 2846.

FRYGES, H. AND J. WAGNER (2008): "Exports and productivity growth – first evidence from a continuous treatment approach," *Review of World Economics*, 144(4), 694–721.

GARCIA-MILÁ, T. AND T. MCGUIRE (2001): "Do interregional transfers improve the economic performance of poor regions? The case of Spain," *International Tax and Public Finance*, 8, 281–295.

GRILICHES, Z. (1969): "Capital-skill complementarity," *The review of Economics and Statistics*, 51(4), 465–468.

HAGEN, T. AND P. MOHL (2008): "Which is the right dose of EU Cohesion Policy for economic growth?," *ZEW Discussion Paper*, 08-104.

——— (2009a): "Econometric evaluation of EU Cohesion Policy: A survey," *ZEW Discussion Paper*, 09-052.

——— (2009b): "How does EU Cohesion Policy work? Evaluating its effects on fiscal outcome variables," *ZEW Discussion Paper*, 09-50.

——— (2011): "Econometric evaluation of EU Cohesion Policy: A survey," in *International Handbook of Economic Integration*, ed. by M. Jovanovic, vol. 3, pp. 343–370. Edward Elgar, Cheltenham (UK) and Northampton (USA).

HECKMAN, J. J. AND V. J. HOTZ (1989): "Choosing among nonexperimental methods for estimating the impact of social programs: The case of manpower training," *Journal of the American Statistical Association*, 84, 862–874.

HEINEMANN, F. (2006): "Das Common Pool-Problem in der EU Finanzverfassung," *Journal for Comparative Government and European Policy*, 4(2), 188–213.

HEINEMANN, F., T. HAGEN, P. MOHL, S. OSTERLOH AND M. SELLENTHIN (2010): *Die Zukunft der EU-Strukturpolitik*, ZEW Wirtschaftsanalysen 94. Nomos, Baden-Baden.

HEINEMANN, F., P. MOHL AND S. OSTERLOH (2008): *Reform options for the EU own resource system*, vol. 40. ZEW Economic Studies, Heidelberg.

——— (2009): "Who's afraid of an EU tax and why? Revenue system preferences in the European Parliament," *The Review of International Organizations*, 4(1), 73–99.

——— (2010): "Reforming the EU budget: Reconciling needs with political-economic constraints," *Journal of European Integration*, 32(1), 59–76.

HIRANO, K. AND G. W. IMBENS (2004): "The propensity score with continuous treatments," in *Applied bayesian modeling and causal inference from incomplete-data perspectives*, ed. by A. Gelman and X.-L. Meng, pp. 73–84. John Wiley and Sons, West Sussex.

HOECHLE, D. (2007): "Robust standard errors for panel regressions with cross-sectional dependence," *Stata Journal*, 7(3), 281–312.

HOLMLUND, B. (1998): "Unemployment insurance in theory and practice," *Scandinavian Journal of Economics*, 100(1), 113–141.

IMAI, K. AND D. A. VAN DIJK (2004): "Causal inference with general treatment regimes: Generalizing the propensity score," *Journal of the American Statistical Association*, 99, 854–866.

IMBENS, G. (2004): "Nonparametric estimation of average treatment effects under exogeneity: A review," *Review of Economics and Statistics*, 86, 4–29.

IMBENS, G. AND T. LEMIEUX (2008): "Regression dicontinuity design: A guide to practice," *Journal of Econometrics*, 142, 615–635.

ISLAM, N. (1995): "Growth empirics: A panel data approach," *Quarterly Journal of Economics*, 110, 1127–1170.

——— (2003): "What have we learnt from the convergence debate?," *Journal of Economic Surveys*, 17, 309–362.

JOVANOVIC, M. (2009): *Evolutionary economic geography: Location of production and the European Union*. Routledge, London and New York.

JUDSON, R. AND L. OWEN (1999): "Estimating dynamic panel data models: A guide for macroeconomics," *Economics Letters*, 65(9-15).

KAMPS, C., N. LEINER-KILLINGER AND R. MARTIN (2009): "The cyclical impact of EU Cohesion policy in fast growing countries," *Intereconomics*, January/February, 23–29.

KELEJIAN, H. AND I. PRUCHA (1998): "A generalized spatial two-stage least squares procedure for estimating a spatial autoregressive models with autoregressive disturbance," *Journal of Real Estate Finance and Economics*, 17(1), 99–121.

——— (1999): "A generalized moments estimator for the autoregressive parameter in a spatial model," *International Economic Review*, 40, 509–533.

KIVIET, J. F. (1995): "On bias, inconsistency, and efficiency of various estimators in dynamic panel data models," *Journal of Econometrics*, 68, 53–78.

KLUVE, J., H. SCHNEIDER, A. UHLENDORFF AND Z. ZHAO (2007): "Evaluating continuous training programs using the generalized propensity score," *Ruhr Economic Papers*, 35.

KRUGMAN, P. (1991): "Increasing returns and economic geography," *Journal of Political Economy*, 99(3), 483–499.

KRUGMAN, P. AND A. VENABLES (1995): "Globalization and the inequality of nations," *Quarterly Journal of Economics*, 110, 857–880.

LAZEAR, E. (1990): "Job security provisions and employment," *Quarterly Journal of Economics*, 105, 699–726.

LE GALLO, J. AND C. ERTUR (2003): "Exploratory spatial data analysis of the distribution of regional per capita GDP in Europe, 1980-1995," *Papers in Regional Science*, 82, 175–201.

LEE, K., M. PESARAN AND R. SMITH (1998): "Growth and convergence in a multi-country empirical stochastic Solow model," *Journal of Applied Econometrics*, 12(4), 357–392.

LEE, L.-F. (2003): "Best spatial two-stage least squares estimators for a spatial autoregressive model with autoregressive disturbances," *Econometric Reviews*, 22(4), 307–335.

LESAGE, J. AND M. FISCHER (2008): "Spatial growth regressions: Model specification, estimation and interpretation," *Spatial Economic Analysis*, 3(3), 275–304.

LeSage, J. and K. R. Pace (2010): "The biggest myth in spatial econometrics," *mimeo*, (version from 1 December 2010).

LeSage, J. P. and K. R. Pace (2004): *Arc_Mat, a toolbox for using ArcView shape files for spatial econometrics and statistics*, vol. 3234/2004 of *Lecture Notes in Computer Science*. Springer, Berlin, Heidelberg.

——— (2009): *Introduction to spatial econometrics*. CRC Press/Taylor and Francis Group, London.

López-Bazo, E., E. Vayá, A. Mora and J. Suriñach (1999): "Regional economic dynamics and convergence in the European Union," *Annals of Regional Science*, 33, 343–370.

Lucchetti, R., L. Papi and A. Zazzaro (2001): "Banks' inefficiency and economic growth: a micro-macro approach," *Scottish Journal of Political Economy*, 48, 400–424.

Maddala, G. and S. Wu (1999): "A comparative study of unit root tests with panel data and a new simple test," *Oxford Bulletin of Economics and Statistics*, 61, 631–652.

Magrini, S. (2004): "Regional (di)convergence," in *Handbook of regional and urban economics*, ed. by V. Henderson and J.-F. Thisse, vol. 4.

Mankiw, N., P. Romer and D. Weill (1992): "A contribution to the empirics of economic growth," *Quarterly Journal of Economics*, 107, 407–437.

Martin, P. (1998): "Can regional policies affect growth and geography in Europe?," *World Economy*, 21(6), 757–774.

Mehrhoff, J. (2009): "A solution to the problem of too many instruments in dynamic panel data GMM," *Deutsche Bundesbank Discussion Paper*, 31/2009.

Mehrotra, A. and T. Välilä (2006): "Public investment in Europe: Evolution and determinants in perspective," *Fiscal Studies*, 27(4), 443–471.

Milio, S. (2007): "Can administrative capacity explain differences in regional performances? Evidence from structural funds implementation in southern Italy," *Regional Studies*, 41(4), 429–442.

Mishra, P. and D. Newhouse (2007): "Health aid and infant mortality," *IMF Working Papers*, 07/100.

Mohl, P. (2012): "Does EU Cohesion policy really increase public investment?," *ECB Working Paper (forthcoming)*.

MOHL, P. AND T. HAGEN (2008): "Does EU Cohesion Policy promote growth? Evidence from regional data and alternative econometric approaches," *ZEW Discussion Paper*, 08-086.

——— (2010): "Do EU structural funds promote regional growth? New evidence from various panel data approaches," *Regional Science and Urban Economics*, 40, 353–365.

——— (2011): "The employment impacts of EU structural funds. Evidence from dynamic panel data," *ECB Working Paper Series*, 1403(December).

MOODIE, E. E. M. AND D. A. STEPHENS (2007): "Estimation of dose-Response functions for longitudinal data," *COBRA Preprint Series*, 32.

NAM, C. AND G. WAMSER (2010): "Application of regionally varying additionality degrees in the practice of EU Cohesion policy," *CESifo Working Paper*, 2971.

NEWEY, W. AND K. WEST (1987): "A simple, positive semi-definite, heteroskedasticity and autocorrelation consistent covariance matrix," *Econometrica*, 55(3), 703–708.

NICKELL, S. (1981): "Biases in dynamic models with fixed effects," *Econometrica*, 49, 1417–1426.

NICKELL, S. (1987): "Dynamic models of labour demand, handbook of labor economics," in *Handbook of Labor Economics*, ed. by O. Ashenfelter and R. Layard, pp. 473–522. Elsevier, Amsterdam.

NICKELL, S. AND R. LAYARD (1999): "Labor market institutions and economic performance," in *Handbook of labor economics*, ed. by O. Ashenfelter and D. Card, vol. 3, pp. 3029–3084. North Holland, Amsterdam.

NICKELL, S., L. NUNZIATA AND W. OCHEL (2005): "Unemployment in the OECD since the 1960s. What do we know?," *The Economic Journal*, 115(January), 1–27.

NUNZIATA, L. (2005): "Institutions and wage determination: A multi-country approach," *Oxford Bulletin of Economics and Statistics*, 67(4), 435–466.

OAXACA, R. AND M. RANSOM (1994): "On discrimination and the decomposition of wage differentials," *Journal of Econometrics*, 61, 5–21.

OSTERLOH, S. (2011): "Can regional transfers buy public support? Evidence from EU structural policy," *ZEW Discussion Paper*, 11-011.

OSTERLOH, S., F. HEINEMANN AND P. MOHL (2008): "The EU tax revisited: Should there be one? And will there be one?," *Zeitschrift für Staats- und Europawissenschaften (ZSE) / Journal for Comparative Government and European Policy*, 6(6), 444–475.

——— (2009): "EU budget reform options and the common pool problem," *Public Finance and Management*, 9(4), 644–685.

PACE, K. R. (2003): "Spatial Statistics Toolbox 2.0," *mimeo.*

PACK, H. AND J. PACK (1993): "Foreign aid and the question of fungibility," *The Review of Economics and Statistics*, 75(2), 258–265.

PERCOCO, M. (2005): "The impact of structural funds on the Italian Mezzogiorno, 1994-1999," *Région et Développement*, 21, 141–152.

PERSSON, T. AND G. TABELLINI (2000): *Political economics: Explaining economic policy.* MIT Press, Cambridge (MA) and London.

PUIGCERVER-PEÑALVER, M. (2007): "The impact of structural funds policy on European regions' growth. A theoretical and empirical approach," *The European Journal of Comparative Economics*, 4(2), 179–208.

QUAH, D. (1996): "Empirics for economic growth and convergence," *European Economic Review*, 40, 1353–1375.

RAMAJO, J., M. MÁRQUEZ, G. HEWINGS AND M. SALINAS (2008): "Spatial heterogeneity and interregional spillovers in the European Union: Do cohesion policies encourage convergence across regions?," *European Economic Review*, 52, 551–567.

RODRÍGUEZ-POSE, A. AND U. FRATESI (2004): "Between development and social policies: The impact of European structural funds in Objective 1 regions," *Regional Studies*, 38(1), 97–113.

RODRIK, D. (2005): "Why we learn nothing from regressing economic growth on policies," *Harvard University Working Paper*, March.

ROMER, P. (1986): "Increasing returns and long run growth," *Journal of Political Economy*, 95(5), 1002–1037.

——— (1990): "Endogenous technological change," *Journal of Political Economy*, 98(5), 71–102.

ROODMAN, D. (2009a): "How to do xtabond2: An introduction to difference and system GMM in Stata," *The Stata Journal*, 9(1), 86–136.

——— (2009b): "A note on the theme of too many instruments," *Oxford Bulletin of Economics and Statistics*, 71(1), 135–158.

RUBIN, D. (1980): "Discussion of "Randomization analysis of experimental data: The Fisher randomization test" (by D. Basu)," *Journal of American Statistical Association*, 75, 591–93.

SALA-I-MARTIN, X. (1996): "Region cohesion: Evidence and theories of regional growth and convergence," *European Economic Review*, 40, 1325–1352.

SCARPETTA, S. (1996): "Assessing the role of labour market policies and institutional settings on unemployment: a cross country study," *OECD Economic Studies*, 26, 43–98.

SHEPSLE, K. A. AND B. R. WEINGAST (1981): "Political preferences for the pork barrel: a generalisation," *American Journal of Political Sciences*, 25, 96–111.

SOLOW, R. (1956): "A contribution to the theory of economic growth," *Quarterly Journal of Economics*, 70(1), 65–94.

SOTO, M. (2006): "System GMM estimation with a small number of individuals," *Institute for Economic Analysis, Barcelona.*

——— (2010): "System GMM estimation with a small number of individuals," *Institute for Economic Analysis Barcelona Working Paper*, 780.

SOUKIAZIS, E. AND M. ANTUNES (2006): "Two speed regional convergence in Portugal and the importance of structural funds on growth," *Ekonomia*, 9(2), 222–241.

SWAN, T. (1956): "Economic growth and capital accumulation," *Economic Record*, 32(334-361).

TABELLINI, G. AND A. ALESINA (1990): "Voting on the budget deficit," *American Economic Review*, 80(1), 37–49.

TOPEL, R. (1986): "Local labor markets," *Journal of Political Economy*, 94(3), 111–143.

VAN DER BEEK, G. AND L. NEAL (2004): "The dilemma of enlargement for the European Union's regional policy," *The World Economy*, April, 587–607.

WHITE, H. (1980): "A heteroskedastic-consistent covariance matrix estimator and a direct test for heteroskedasticity," *Econometrica*, 48, 817–838.

WINDMEIJER, F. (2005): "A finite sample correction for the variance of linear efficient two-step GMM estimators," *Journal of Econometrics*, 126(1), 25–51.

WOOLDRIDGE, J. M. (2002): *Econometric analysis of cross section and panel data.* The MIT Press, Cambridge, MA.

YOUNG, A., M. HIGGINS AND L. DANIEL (2008): "Sigma convergence versus beta convergence: Evidence from U.S. county-level data," *Journal of Money, Credit and Banking*, 50(5), 1083–1093.

YU, J., R. DE JONG AND L.-F. LEE (2008): "Quasi-maximum likelihood estimators for spatial dynamic panel data with fixed effects when both n and T are large," *Journal of Econometrics*, 146, 118–134.

MIX
Papier aus verantwortungsvollen Quellen
Paper from responsible sources
FSC® C105338

If you have any concerns about our products,
you can contact us on
ProductSafety@springernature.com

In case Publisher is established outside the EU,
the EU authorized representative is:
Springer Nature Customer Service Center GmbH
Europaplatz 3, 69115 Heidelberg, Germany

Printed by Libri Plureos GmbH
in Hamburg, Germany